REINSURANCE AND THE LA

In excess of loss reinsurance, the reinsurer covers the amount of *a loss* exceeding the policy's deductible but not piercing its cover limit. Accordingly, a policy's quantitative scope of cover is significantly affected by the parties' agreement of a deductible and a cover limit. Yet, the examination of whether *a loss* has exceeded deductible or cover limit necessitates an educated understanding of what constitutes *one loss*. In so-called aggregation clauses, the parties to (re-)insurance contracts regularly provide that multiple individual losses are to be added together for presenting *one loss* to the reinsurer when they arise from the same event, occurrence, catastrophe, cause or accident. Aggregation mechanisms are one of the core instruments for structuring reinsurance contracts.

This book systematically examines each element of an aggregation mechanism, tracing the inconsistent usage of aggregation language in the markets and scrutinizing the tests developed by courts and arbitral tribunals. In doing so, it seeks to support insurers, reinsurers, brokers and lawyers in drafting aggregation clauses and in settling claims.

Focusing on an analysis of primary sources, particularly judicial decisions, the book interprets each judicial decision to describe a system of inter-related rules, collating, organising and describing the English law of aggregation as applied by the courts and arbitral tribunals. It further draws a comparison between the English position and the corresponding rules in the Principles of Reinsurance Contract Law (PRICL).

Oliver D. William is a senior lecturer and researcher at the University of Bern, an of-counsel at mbh ATTORNEYS AT LAW, Zurich, and a vice chair of the Dispute Resolution Working Party of the Association Internationale de Droit des Assurances (AIDA).

Contemporary Commercial Law

For more information about this series, please visit: www.routledge.com/Contemporary-Commercial-Law/book-series/CCL

REINSURANCE AND THE LAW OF AGGREGATION

EVENT, OCCURRENCE, CAUSE

OLIVER D. WILLIAM

Routledge
Taylor & Francis Group
LONDON AND NEW YORK

First published 2021
by Routledge
2 Park Square, Milton Park, Abingdon, Oxon OX14 4RN

and by Routledge
52 Vanderbilt Avenue, New York, NY 10017

Routledge is an imprint of the Taylor & Francis Group, an informa business

Published with the support of the Swiss National Science Foundation.

British Library Cataloguing-in-Publication Data
A catalogue record for this book is available from the British Library

Library of Congress Cataloging-in-Publication Data
A catalog record has been requested for this book

ISBN: 978-0-367-50285-0 (hbk)
ISBN: 978-0-367-68868-4 (pbk)
ISBN: 978-1-003-08048-0 (ebk)

DOI: 10.4324/9781003080480

Typeset in Times New Roman by
MPS Limited, Dehradun

To Evi

CONTENTS

CONTENTS

viii

CONTENTS

CONTENTS

CONTENTS

FOREWORD

Carlos Estebenet and Christian Felderer

Through 'Reinsurance and the Law of Aggregation', Oliver D William treats all the matters that we consider critical in the area of expertise. Besides approaching the main subject, he presents a deep analysis of many terms, concepts and practices that turn the work into a comprehensive piece.

Reinsurance is a specialized business, very much driven by its international custom and practice. Over time it has seen a steady development of the legal principles, mainly in the form of court decisions reflecting legal practice in the key jurisdictions. Much of this development is based upon English case law, which is the legal basis for one of the centres of traditional insurance and reinsurance, the London Market.

The question 'how' risks are reinsured in a non-proportional reinsurance contract, particularly in relation to the occurrence of multiple losses arising from a common cause or event, is essential and of vital importance for the structuring of the reinsurance contract. From a business perspective, it is perhaps the core element for the contracting parties, next to the definition of the subject matter of the reinsurance, and a key determinant for the price, the reinsurance premium.

Given the inherent complexity of aggregation issues and the interests involved in case of disputes, court or arbitration cases dealing with aggregation issues are frequently time consuming, expensive and their resolution is paired with a considerable degree of uncertainty. Large past reinsurance disputes have demonstrated this, for instance the disputes around the reinsurance of World Trade Center risks. Similar questions may, perhaps, be emerging from the consequences of Covid-19, and the occurrence of multiple pandemic-related losses.

Oliver embraces and tests the full landscape of the key aggregation cases in a comprehensive and interesting way for the reader. His research is a highly valuable contribution with practical relevance to both, the academia and the reinsurance practice. It provides an excellent overview and discussion of case law on 'aggregation' and related subjects. Moreover, the research which has gone into this treatise is also an important contribution in the process of creating a uniform framework of reinsurance principles, including the ones of how aggregation should be applied to reinsurance. An initiative, which is targeted by an international project group offering a comprehensive framework of reinsurance contract law by way of the 'Principles of Reinsurance Contract Law' (PRICL), in which he participates.

Congratulations to Oliver for tackling a very demanding subject in a highly competent manner in this treatise. We would like to thank him for his contribution

FOREWORD

to the legal practice, which, no doubt, sheds more light onto the long-standing debate on the concept of aggregation and its related areas.

This is particularly of interest to organizations like AIDA with its Reinsurance Working Party and to AIDA Europe, which are dedicated to the furtherance and development of (re-)insurance and related law.

Carlos Estebenet – Chairman AIDA Reinsurance Working Party
and Member of the AIDA Presidential Council
Christian Felderer – Chairman ADIA Europe and Member of the ADIA
Presidential Council

PREFACE

In 2016, *Prof Dr Helmut Heiss* (University of Zurich), *Prof Dr Manfred Wandt* (Goethe University Frankfurt) and *Prof Dr Martin Schauer* (University of Vienna) initiated a research project whose aim is to develop a set of uniform reinsurance contract law rules, the Principles of Reinsurance Contract Law, and to offer reinsurance markets a neutral choice of law that provides enhanced legal certainty. Academics from a variety of countries as well as experts from leading (re-)insurance companies joined the project.

The project group identified the law of the aggregation of losses as one topic to be dealt with in the principles. It is beyond doubt that this area of the law presents substantial legal uncertainty which, particularly in England, triggered a considerable number of disputes. I had the privilege of becoming a research fellow in the project entrusted with the research into the English law of the aggregation of losses and to write my doctoral thesis on the subject. This book is an updated version of my doctoral thesis '(Re-)insurance and the Law of Aggregation', which was submitted to the University of Zurich, Faculty of Law, in 2019 and awarded the distinction *summa cum laude*.

I am grateful to *Prof Dr Helmut Heiss* for involving me in the project, supervising my PhD study and for opening many doors for me; for this, I will always be deeply indebted to him. My thanks also go to *Prof Dr Leander D Loacker* who has kindly reviewed my thesis as a second examiner and who has provided invaluable remarks on the subject.

Participation in this project not only afforded an insight into the practice of reinsurance but also a fruitful exchange with participating academics and practitioners. Special thanks go to *Christian Lang*, *Peter Wedge*, *Marcus Vergi* (Swiss Re) and *Pirmin Stalder* (LGT ILS Partners) for numerous discussions about the aggregation of losses in practice and to my colleagues *Dr Kevin Bork* and *Adam Horvath*, LLM for being open to exchanging views and sources. I am further indebted to *Mandeep Lakhan*, LLB, MA, LLM for proofreading my manuscript and her helpful comments.

I am further deeply indebted to my parents *Esther* and *Dean William* who have provided every imaginable kind of support during my life journey and who have taught me to always reach for the stars. Finally and most importantly, I would like to express my sincerest gratitude to *Evi Kapoudis*, who has stood by my side for more than half of my life and without whom I would not have been able to write this book.

TABLE OF CASES

American cases

Australian Cases

English cases

TABLE OF CASES

TABLE OF CASES

TABLE OF CASES

New Zealand Case
Moore v IAG New Zealand Ltd [2019] NZHC 1549, [2020] Lloyd's Rep IR 167

Singaporean Case
Hanwha Non-Life Insurance Co Ltd v Alba Pte Ltd [2011] SGHC 271, [2012] Lloyd's Rep IR 505

Swiss Cases
Judgment of the Swiss Federal Supreme Court of 10 June 1981, BGE 107 II 196
Judgment of the Swiss Federal Supreme Court of 17 January 2014, BGE 140 III 115

TABLE OF LEGISLATION AND MATERIALS

Legislation

Directive 2009/138/EC of the European Parliament and of the Council of 25 November 2009 on the taking-up and pursuit of the business of Insurance and Reinsurance (Solvency II) [2009] OJ L335/1

Financial Services Act 1986

Insurance Act 2015

Marine Insurance Act 1906

Life Assurance and Unit Trust Regulatory Organisation Rules (LAUTRO Rules)

Principles of Reinsurance Contract Law 2019

Services and Markets Act 2000

Unidroit Principles of International Commercial Contracts 2016

Materials

Explanatory Notes to the UK Insurance Act 2015

'Hiscox War, Terrorism and Political Violence Insurance' <https://www.awris.com/Clauses/S&T%20andor%20PV%20business/Hiscox%20WTPV%20180507.pdf> accessed 4 March 2019

'IUA 01-018 Hours Clause (NP61)' <http://www.iuaclauses.co.uk/site/cms/contentDocumentLibraryView.asp?chapter=9&category=59> accessed 1 March 2019

'IUA 01-019 Loss Occurrence (NP64)' <http://www.iuaclauses.co.uk/site/cms/contentDocumentLibraryView.asp?chapter=9&category=59> accessed 1 March 2019

'IUA 01-023 United Kingdom Hours Clause (NP65)' <http://www.iuaclauses.co.uk/site/cms/contentDocumentLibraryView.asp?chapter=9&category=59> accessed 1 March 2019

'IUA 01-033 Definition of Loss Occurrence (Hours Clause) - Commentary' <http://www.iuaclauses.co.uk/site/cms/contentDocumentLibraryView.asp?chapter=5> accessed 1 March 2019

'IUA 01-034 Definition of Loss Occurrence (Hours Clause)' <http://www.iuaclauses.co.uk/site/cms/contentDocumentLibraryView.asp?chapter=5> accessed 1 March 2019

'IUA 01-034 Definition of Loss Occurrence (Hours Clause) - Technical Document' <http://www.iuaclauses.co.uk/site/cms/contentDocumentLibraryView.asp?chapter=5> accessed 1 March 2019

'LMA3030 - Terrorism Insurance - Physical Loss or Physical Damage Wording' <https://www.lmalloyds.com/LMA/Wordings/lma3030.aspx> accessed 4 March 2019

'LMA3092 - Physical Loss or Physical Damage - Riots, Strikes, Civil Commotion, Malicious Damage, Terrorism and Sabotage Insurance' <https://www.lmalloyds.com/LMA/Wordings/lma3092.aspx> accessed 4 March 2019

'LMA5223 Definition of Loss Occurrence (with Freeze Aggregate Extension)' (London Market Association 2015) <http://www.lmalloyds.com/LMA/Underwriting/Non-Marine/Property_Reinsurance/LMA/Underwriting/Non-Marine/PRBP/Property_Reinsurance.aspx?hkey=c34153bf-b969-4e53-a433-012644640a4a> accessed 1 March 2019

'LMA5224 Definition of Loss Occurrence (Risk)' (London Market Association 2015) <http://www.lmalloyds.com/LMA/Underwriting/Non-Marine/Property_Reinsurance/LMA/Underwriting/Non-Marine/PRBP/Property_Reinsurance.aspx?hkey=c34153bf-b969-4e53-a433-012644640a4a> accessed 1 March 2019

ABBREVIATIONS

AC	Law Reports, Appeal Cases
AD2d	New York's Appellate Division Reports
AJA	Acting Justice of Appeal
ANZ	Australian and New Zealand
BGE	Bundesgerichtsentscheid (decision of the Swiss Federal Supreme Court)
BLR	Building Law Reports
CA	Court of Appeal
Cf	compare (confer)
Ch	Law Reports, Chancery Division
CLC	Commercial Law Cases
CLR	Commonwealth Law Reports, Australia
Co	Company
Conn	Connecticut
Corp	Corporation
D&O	Directors and Officers
EC	European Community
edn	edition
ed(s)	editor(s)
eg	for example (exempli gratia)
eV	eingetragener Verein (registered association)
EWCA Civ	England and Wales Court of Appeal (Civil Division)
EWHC	England and Wales High Court
f/ff	next/following
F	Federal Reporter
F2d	Federal Reporter, Second Series
F3d	Federal Reporter, Third Series
FedAppx	Federal Appendix
GmbH	Gesellschaft mit beschränkter Haftung (limited liability company)
HCA	High Court of Australia
HL	House of Lords
ie	this is (id est)
IMC	Insurance Market Conference
In re	in the matter of
Inc	Incorporated
Insur	Insurance

ABBREVIATIONS

IPR	Internationales Privatrecht (private international law)
IUA	International Underwriting Association
J	Justice
JA	Judge of Appeal
KB	Law Reports, King's Bench Division
L	Loi
LJ	Lord Justice
LLC	Limited Liability Company
LLID	Lloyd's List Insurance Day
Lloyd's Rep IR	Lloyd's Law Reports, Insurance and Reinsurance
LLP	Limited Liability Partnership
LMA	London Market Association
LQR	Law Quarterly Review
LRLR	Lloyd's Reinsurance Law Reports
Ltd	Limited
MR	Master of the Rolls
n	footnote
no	number
NP	Non-Proportional
Nr.	number
NSWCA	New South Wales Court of Appeal
NSWSC	New South Wales Supreme Court
NY2d	New York Reports, Second Series
NZHC	New Zealand High Court
para(s)	paragraph(s)
PC	Privy Council
Plc	Public Limited Company
PRICL	Principles of Reinsurance Contract Law
Pty Ltd	Proprietary Limited Company
Pub	Publisher
QB	Law Reports, Queen's Bench Division
QC	Queen's Counsel
RE	In the matter
Rt Hon	The Right Honourable
s(s)	section(s)
SA	Sociedade Anonima (stock company)
SC	Supreme Court
SGHC	High Court of Singapore
SpA	Società per azioni (stock company)
TCC	Technology and Construction Court
TLR	Times Law Reports
UK	United Kingdom
US	United States of America
UKHL	United Kingdom House of Lords
UKSC	United Kingdom Supreme Court
v	against (versus)

ABBREVIATIONS

vol	volume
VSCA	Supreme Court of Victoria, Court of Appeal
VVW	Verlag Versicherungswirtschaft
WLR	Weekly Law Reports
WLR (D)	Weekly Law Reports – Daily Case Summaries
WTPV	War, Terrorism and Political Violence
£	Pound sterling
$	US dollar

Introduction

I Subject matter, scope and aim of the analysis

Under excess of loss reinsurance agreements, a reinsurer is liable for the sum of the reinsured's ultimate net loss exceeding the latter's retention up to the policy cover limit.[1] Establishing a schedule of retentions and cover limits for any particular loss allows any participant in the reinsurance market to (re-)insure a greater number of risks and to thereby diversify its risk portfolio so that no disproportionate amount of risk is borne by any one participant.[2]

Yet, the ability of the (re-)insurance markets to absorb large losses will crucially depend on the mechanism used to calculate the monetary value of a loss to be tested against the reinsureds' retention and the reinsurers' cover limit.[3] In their contracts of insurance and reinsurance,[4] the parties often provide for so-called aggregation clauses, which specify that the relevant loss is to be determined on the basis of any one event or cause.[5]

In excess of loss reinsurance, aggregation clauses are, therefore, of cardinal importance.[6] In fact, the construction of aggregation clauses contained in excess of loss reinsurances

---

1 Klaus Gerathewohl, *Rückversicherung, Grundlagen und Praxis*, vol 1 (Verlag Versicherungswirtschaft eV 1976) 143; Özlem Gürses, *Reinsuring Clauses* (Informa Law from Routledge 2010) paras 1.07, 6.182; cf Colin Edelman and Andrew Burns, *The Law of Reinsurance* (2nd edn, OUP 2013) para 1.61; Sieglinde Cannawurf and Andreas Schwepcke, '§ 8 Das Vertragsrecht der Rückversicherung' in Dieter W Lüer and Andreas Schwepcke (eds), *Rückversicherungsrecht* (C.H. Beck 2013) paras 368 f; Andreas Schwepcke and Alexandra Vetter (eds), *Praxishandbuch: Rückversicherung* (VVW 2017) para 661.

2 Barlow Lyde and Gilbert LLP, *Reinsurance Practice and the Law* (Informa Law from Routledge 2009) para 1.15.

3 Barlow Lyde and Gilbert LLP (n 2) para 4.54.

4 *Axa Reinsurance (UK) Ltd v Field* (1996) 1 WLR 1026 (HL); Robert Viney and William M Sneed, 'Aggregation of Reinsurance Claims in the UK and the US: Court Decisions' (2000) 4 Andrews International Reinsurance Dispute Reporter.

5 Barlow Lyde and Gilbert LLP (n 2) paras 28.7 ff, 28.37 ff; Rob Merkin, 'The Christchurch Earthquakes Insurance and Reinsurance Issues' (2012) 18 Canterbury Law Review 119, 145; Edelman and Burns (n 1) paras 4.55 ff, 4.59 ff.

6 Cf *Axa Reinsurance (UK) Ltd v Field* (n 4) 1035 (Lord Mustill); Viney and Sneed (n 4).

DOI: 10.4324/9781003080480-101

often represents a multi-billion-dollar issue.[7] As a consequence, in calculating reinsurance premiums, aggregation mechanisms must be taken into consideration.[8]

The courts have stated that '[t]he choice of language by which the parties designated the unifying factor in an aggregation clause is (...) of critical importance and can be expected to be the subject of careful negotiation'.[9] Moreover, Lord Hobhouse opined in one case that the points of aggregation under the House of Lord's consideration were all points of construction 'which could easily have been avoided by the exercise of care in the preparation and drafting of the insurance contract'.[10]

O'Neill and Woloniecki claim that Lord Hobhouse was too sanguine in thinking that uncertainties as to the correct construction of aggregation clauses could always be avoided.[11] Early on, they argued that

> the richness of the English language, having so many words with different shades of meaning–loss, claim, accident, event, occurrence, cause, incident, peril–with the added ingredients of proximity and causation suggest that there may be more disputes over aggregation.[12]

Their prognosis turned out to be true. In fact, since 1995, when the first major case on the subject matter was tried in *Caudle v Sharp*,[13] disputes concerning aggregation were heard before English courts practically every year.[14] O'Neill and Woloniecki note that there is now an 'embarrassment of jurisprudential riches' on the subject matter.[15] In light of the fact that gigantic sums of money are often involved, they pose the question: '[h]ow are the underwriters to write their contracts in the future and achieve their objectives, when faced with unpredictable decisions of the courts?'[16] Tompkinson adds that

---

7 Darlene K Alt, Nathan Hull and James Killelea, 'A Reinsurance Perspective: The Aggregation of Losses Following the Tohoku Earthquake and Tsunami' (2011) 22 Mealey's Litigation Report 1, 2; Kristin Suga Heres and Patricia St. Peter, 'The "Number of Occurrences" Dispute of the Century' (2016) 46 Fall Brief 15.

8 Cf *Lloyd's TSB General Insurance Holdings Ltd v Lloyd's Bank Group Insurance Co Ltd* [2003] UKHL 48, [2003] 4 All ER 43 [51] (Lord Hobhouse); Ken Louw and Deborah Tompkinson, 'Curiouser and Curiouser: The Meaning of "Event"' (1996) 4 International Insurance Law Review 6, 11; Barlow Lyde and Gilbert LLP (n 2) para 4.53.

9 *Lloyd's TSB General Insurance Holdings Ltd v Lloyd's Bank Group Insurance Co Ltd* (n 8) [17] (Lord Hoffmann). See also *Axa Reinsurance (UK) Ltd v Field* (n 4) 1035 (Lord Mustill).

10 *Kuwait Airways Corp v Kuwait Insurance Co SAK* [1999] CLC 934, [1999] 1 Lloyd's Rep 803 (HL).

11 PT O'Neill, JW Woloniecki and F Arnold-Dwyer, *The Law of Reinsurance in England and Bermuda* (5th edn, Sweet & Maxwell/Thomson Reuters 2019) para 7–015.

12 O'Neill, Woloniecki and Arnold-Dwyer (n 11) para 7–015. This point was first made in the first edition of their treatise.

13 *Caudle v Sharp* [1995] CLC 642 (CA). For cases dealing with the subject matter before 1995, see for instance *The South Staffordshire Tramways Co Ltd v The Sickness and Accident Assurance Association Ltd* (1891) 1 QB 402 (CA); *Allen v London Guarantee and Accident Co Ltd* (1912) 28 TLR 254 (Comm); *Forney v Dominion Insurance Co Ltd* [1969] 1 WLR 928 (Comm).

14 Some of the more recent ones are *MIC Simmonds v Gammell* [2016] EWHC 2515 (Comm), [2016] Lloyd's Rep IR 693; *AIG Europe Ltd v Woodman* [2017] UKSC 18, [2018] 1 All ER 936; *Spire Healthcare Ltd v Royal and Sun Alliance Insurance Plc* [2018] EWCA Civ 317, [2018] Lloyd's Rep IR 425.

15 O'Neill, Woloniecki and Arnold-Dwyer (n 11) para 7–013.

16 O'Neill, Woloniecki and Arnold-Dwyer (n 11) para 7–015.

[t]he history of reinsurance litigation in [England] is littered with the corpses of underwriters and brokers who found out too late, and to their disadvantage, that a word in common use and thought to be understood by everybody was not so understood by the Commercial Court. The spectre of carnage has once again raised its head over the definition of 'event' and 'occurrence'.[17]

Barlow Lyde and Gilbert LLP consider questions relating to the aggregation of losses as '[o]ne of the most vexing issues facing the reinsurance market in recent years'.[18]

The goal of this book is to provide a systematic analysis of the subject matter of aggregation under English law. It shall discuss terms that are adopted in aggregation clauses and identify words that are used inconsistently in the reinsurance market. The aim of this treatise is to clarify the concepts that are behind these words as well as to examine questions of causation and proximity that are linked to aggregation mechanisms. In this regard, tests that were developed by English courts to deal with questions of aggregation shall be scrutinised. In pursuing these goals, sources concerning the subject matter of aggregation in direct insurance, reinsurance and retrocession shall be analysed. It should be noted that contracts of reinsurance and retrocession are treated as contracts of insurance at common law.[19] Further, judicial authorities dealing with aggregation in the context of reinsurance and retrocession refer to judicial decisions that were rendered in the context of primary insurance and *vice versa*.[20]

Entire books could be dedicated to the analysis of aggregation mechanisms in different classes of insurance and reinsurance. Certainly, it would be interesting and worthwhile examining issues of aggregation in the fields of employer's liability, product liability, errors and omissions, natural catastrophe, cyber risk reinsurance as well as the current Covid-19 pandemic. This would, however, exceed this treatise's scope. Using examples and illustrations from different classes of insurance and reinsurance, the following analysis shall be limited to the English general law of aggregation as applied by the courts of England and Wales. Moreover, the analysis is limited to aggregation mechanisms that are based on a unifying concept of causation, ie to the aggregation of 'related losses' as the Court of Appeal terms it.[21] By contrast, aggregation concepts that are simply based on the losses that occurred during one policy period but are otherwise unrelated, so-called policies on an aggregate basis, will not be discussed.

---

17 Deborah Tompkinson, 'Jabberwocky: Recent Decisions on the Meaning of "Event" and "Occurrence" in the English Courts' (1995) 3 International Insurance Law Review 82, 82.

18 Barlow Lyde and Gilbert LLP (n 2) para 28.1.

19 Explanatory Notes to the Insurance Act 2015, para 36; *Delver, Assignee of Bunn v Barnes* (1807) 1 Taunt 48.

20 See *Countrywide Assured Group Plc v Marshall* [2002] EWHC 2082 (Comm), [2003] 1 All ER 237 [8] (Morison J); *Midland Mainline Ltd v Eagle Star Insurance Co Ltd* [2003] EWHC 1771 (Comm), [2004] Lloyd's Rep IR 22 [75] (Steel J); *Lloyd's TSB General Insurance Holdings Ltd v Lloyd's Bank Group Insurance Co Ltd* (n 8) [16] (Lord Hoffmann); *Aioi Nissay Dowa Insurance Co Ltd v Heraldglen Ltd and Advent Capital Ltd* [2013] EWHC 154 (Comm), [2013] 2 All ER 231 [30] (Field J); *AIG Europe Ltd v Woodman* (n 14) [22] (Lord Toulson SCJ).

21 *Denby v English and Scottish Maritime Insurance Co Ltd; Yasuda Fire and Marine Co of Europe Ltd v Lloyd's Underwriting Syndicates no 209, 356* [1998] Lloyd's Rep IR 343 (CA), [1998] CLC 870, 880 (Hobhouse LJ). Cf also Jacques Bourthoumieux, 'La notion d'événement dans les traités de réassurance en excédent de sinistres' (1969) 40 Revue générale des assurances terrestres 457, 461.

It may be noted that the English law of reinsurance contracts has significance internationally. For example, in 2014, the Swiss Federal Supreme Court stated that the English law of reinsurance contracts was of great importance in characterising reinsurance practice.[22] Thus, even where a contract of reinsurance is not governed by English law, courts around the world may consult the English position for guidance.

A number of states in the US have developed their own laws of aggregation which deviate from the English position.[23] Yet, a detailed analysis of the tests developed by American courts is beyond the scope of this book.

It is the author's hypothesis that there is substantial legal uncertainty in the English law of aggregation. This can be briefly illustrated by way of a comparison of two[24] cases following the terror attacks on the Twin Towers of the World Trade Center on 11 September 2001:

The question before the courts was whether the terror attacks, which involved two aircraft, amounted to one single or multiple separate events. If the former was the case, all the individual losses that arose from the devastating attacks could be added together to form one big loss that would then be tested against the reinsured's retention and the reinsurer's cover limit. The reinsurer would be required to pay the amount of the aggregated loss that exceeded the reinsured's retention up to its cover limit. By contrast, if the attacks were to be considered as more than one event, then only losses resulting from the same event could be added together, so that there would be one aggregated loss per event. Accordingly, the reinsurer would be liable for one loss per event.

In *Aioi Nissay Dowa Insurance Co Ltd v Heraldglen Ltd and Advent Capital Ltd*, the dispute concerned the wording of a whole account catastrophe excess of loss reinsurance. The Commercial Court was required to assess an arbitral tribunal's award on the question of whether a plurality of losses arising under liability policies taken out by American Airlines as operator of the hijacked aircraft resulted from one single or two events for the purposes of applying policy limits and deductibles under four contracts of reinsurance.[25] It was held by the Commercial Court that the arbitral tribunal made no error of law finding that 'the insured losses caused by the attacks on the World Trade Center arose out of two events and not one'.[26]

---

22 Judgment of the Swiss Federal Supreme Court of 17 January 2014, *BGE 140 III 115* consideration 6.3.

23 Viney and Sneed (n 4).

24 There is a third case that is notable. See *If P and C Insurance Ltd v Silversea Cruises Ltd* [2003] EWHC 473 (Comm), [2004] Lloyd's Rep IR 217, where an insurance policy covering loss of income resulting from government warnings regarding terrorism per any one occurrence was disputed before the Commercial Court. Following 11 September 2001, the US Department of State had repeatedly warned US citizens that they were at risk of terrorist attacks. After these warnings, many people had cancelled their travel plans. The court was required to determine the relevant occurrence(s) that caused the substantial loss of income sustained by the assured cruise ship service provider. The court decided that an occurrence was the same thing as an event and that all the income loss that was caused by the happenings in New York and the warnings issued by the US government resulted from one single event, ie the attack on the World Trade Center on 11 September 2001.

25 *Aioi Nissay Dowa Insurance Co Ltd v Heraldglen Ltd and Advent Capital Ltd* (n 20) [2] (Field J).

26 *Aioi Nissay Dowa Insurance Co Ltd v Heraldglen Ltd and Advent Capital Ltd* (n 20) [40] (Field J).

MIC Simmonds v AJ Gammell was another case following the terror attacks on the World Trade Center. In this case, multiple claims had been filed against the owner of the land where the Twin Towers had stood. The claims fell into two categories: First, there were claims by employees (or their estates) of the landowner that were at the site at the time of the attacks and 'were either struck by or became trapped under the debris'.[27] Secondly, there were claims by 'firemen, policemen, clean-up and construction workers and volunteers engaged in the rescue and recovery operations'.[28] The question before the Commercial Court was whether the arbitral tribunal was right to decide that the terror attacks on the Twin Towers constituted one sole event and that all the individual losses arising from this event–no matter whether suffered by the landowner's employees who were at the site at the time of the attacks or by the people involved in the clean-up operations following the attacks–were to be aggregated. In this instance, the Commercial Court held that there was a clear and obvious causal connection between the attacks and the claims and that the attacks constituted one single event.[29]

The reinsurance contracts in these two cases could undeniably be distinguished in a variety of aspects. Therefore, it might be argued that it is due to these variations that the arbitral tribunals and courts reached different conclusions when determining the number of events. This may partly be so. Yet, it is submitted that the differences in the arbitral tribunals' and the Commercial Court's conclusions are mainly due to the legal uncertainty inherent in the English law of aggregation.[30]

In an unrelated case, the Court of Appeal noted that legal certainty and predictability was of paramount importance to the efficient conduct of business in the reinsurance market.[31] Hence, if the hypothesis that there is substantial legal uncertainty in the English law of aggregation were confirmed, this would represent a severe inefficiency affecting the excess of loss reinsurance market. In this regard, a solution may be provided by chapter 5 of the Principles of Reinsurance Contract Law (PRICL 2019) as drafted by the PRICL Project Group, for which the present author acted as rapporteur in respect of the rules on the aggregation of related losses. Due to their potential to eliminate uncertainty in this regard, the rules contained in the PRICL will be laid out and discussed briefly. However, there shall be no focus on these Principles.

---

27 *MIC Simmonds v Gammell* (n 14) [8] (Sir Jeremy Cooke).

28 *MIC Simmonds v Gammell* (n 14) [8] (Sir Jeremy Cooke).

29 *MIC Simmonds v Gammell* (n 14) [30] (Sir Jeremy Cooke).

30 See paras 4.8 ff, 4.80 ff, 5.6 ff.

31 *Equitas Insurance Ltd v Municipal Mutual Insurance Ltd* [2019] EWCA Civ 718, [2020] 1 All ER 16 [91] (Males LJ).

II Plan and structure of the treatise

This book will be divided into two parts. In the first part, the reader will be led through the subject matter of the aggregation of losses. In chapter 1, different types and methods of reinsurance will be discussed. It is to be examined for which re-insurance products the aggregation of losses is relevant. In chapter 2, the concepts of 'individual loss', 'cover limit' and 'retention' will be outlined. The different elements and concepts contained in an aggregation mechanism will be dealt with in chapter 3. It shall be demonstrated that the concept of causation lies at the heart of the aggregation mechanisms discussed in this book. In chapters 4 and 5, the focus will be placed on event-based and cause-based aggregation mechanisms, respectively.

The relation between the concept of aggregation and other reinsurance-specific concepts will be addressed in the second part of the book. More specifically, the concepts of aggregation and the allocation of losses and their interplay will be compared and discussed, respectively, in chapter 6, followed by an examination of the relation between the concepts of aggregation and back-to-back coverage in chapter 7. Subsequently, in chapter 8, the interaction between the concepts of aggregation and follow the settlements will be addressed.

PART I

AGGREGATION OF RELATED CLAIMS

Relevance of aggregation in various reinsurance products

1.1 The aim of chapter 1 is to offer an overview of the reinsurance products in which the aggregation of losses based on causation may be an issue. It appears sensible to first concisely outline the idea of reinsurance. The basic distinctions of different types and forms of reinsurance shall then be discussed. Finally, the findings of the chapter will be presented in a summary.

1.2 Hereafter, the distinction between different 'forms' of reinsurance will be used to differentiate between facultative and treaty reinsurance.[1] Further, reinsurance contracts are divided into the 'types and methods' of proportional and non-proportional contracts.[2] However, the terminology of 'forms' and 'types and methods' of reinsurance is not used consistently in legal literature.[3]

1.3 Both distinctions are essential for the analysis of the subject matter of the aggregation of losses. The workings of the different forms and types of reinsurance contracts allow for a better understanding of the circumstances under which the aggregation of losses may become relevant.

I Basic idea of reinsurance

1.4 Just as individuals and businesses have an interest in protecting themselves against certain risks, insurance companies have a need to protect themselves against risks they accept under primary insurance contracts.[4] Similarly, a reinsurer may need

---

1 Andreas Schwepcke, *Rückversicherung, Produktorientierte Qualifikationen* (2nd edn, VVW 2004) 111; Sieglinde Cannawurf and Andreas Schwepcke, '§ 8 Das Vertragsrecht der Rückversicherung' in Dieter W Lüer and Andreas Schwepcke (eds), *Rückversicherungsrecht* (C.H. Beck 2013) paras 264 ff; Andreas Schwepcke and Alexandra Vetter, *Praxishandbuch: Rückversicherung* (VVW 2017) paras 632 ff; Peter Liebwein, *Klassische und moderne Formen der Rückversicherung* (3rd edn, VVW 2018) paras 59 ff.

2 Colin Edelman and Andrew Burns, *The Law of Reinsurance* (2nd edn, OUP 2013) paras 1.33 ff; Cannawurf and Schwepcke (n 1) paras 270 ff. See also Schwepcke (n 1) para 111; Schwepcke and Vetter (n 1) paras 655 ff.

3 Barlow Lyde & Gilbert LLP, *Reinsurance Practice and the Law* (Informa Law from Routledge 2009) paras 4.1 ff, distinguish between the different types of facultative and treaty reinsurance and use the term 'form' for a multitude of different distinctions within the broad types of reinsurance; Özlem Gürses, *Reinsuring Clauses* (Informa Law from Routledge 2010) paras 1.04 ff, refers to different 'forms' of reinsurance when distinguishing between all four different categories, ie facultative, treaty, proportional, non-proportional reinsurance. See also Cannawurf and Schwepcke (n 1) n 456; Stefan Pohl and Joseph Iranya, *The ABC of Reinsurance* (VVW 2018) 8, differentiate between the different types of facultative and treaty reinsurance.

4 Barlow Lyde & Gilbert LLP (n 3) para 1.4; Gürses (n 3) para 1.01.

DOI: 10.4324/9781003080480-1

to take out insurance for the risk it accepts under the reinsurance contract. A contract reinsuring a reinsurer is termed a retrocession agreement.[5]

1.5 By taking out reinsurance, a reinsured[6] or retrocedent passes a share of the underlying risk onto a reinsurer or retrocessionaire.[7] The reinsured party thereby safeguards its solvency and at the same time increases the volume or size of risk it can accept.[8]

1.6 According to Kiln, 'reinsurance' is simply the insurance of an insurance company.[9] In most national jurisdictions, there is no statutory definition of what constitutes a reinsurance contract.[10] On a European level, however, 'reinsurance' is defined in point 7(a) of Article 13 of Directive 2009/138/EC as 'the activity consisting in accepting risks ceded by an insurance undertaking (...), or by another reinsurance undertaking (...)'.[11] In Article 1.2.1 paragraph (1) PRICL,[12] a contract of reinsurance is defined as 'a contract under which one party, the reinsurer, in consideration of a premium, promises another party, the reinsured, cover against the risk of exposure to insurance or reinsurance claims'.[13] As early as in 1807, Lord Mansfield provided a similar definition for contracts of reinsurance under English law. In *Delver v Barnes*, he suggested that reinsurance 'consist of a new assurance, effected by a new policy, on the same risk which was before insured in order to indemnify the underwriters from their previous subscription (...)'.[14]

1.7 These definitions suggest that a primary insurance contract must be in place before a reinsurance contract can be taken out.[15] In practice, however, reinsurance contracts are often concluded with the prospect that a primary insurance contract to be reinsured will be concluded later in the process.[16] This may be the case if a risk is of the quality that a primary insurer will only accept it after having ensured that reinsurance cover for this risk is in place.[17] This is, however, not to say that a

---

5 Barlow Lyde & Gilbert LLP (n 3) para 1.5; Edelman and Burns (n 2) para 1.18; Cannawurf and Schwepcke (n 1) para 202.

6 Also referred to as 'reassured', 'cedent', 'ceding company', 'direct insurer', 'original insurer' or 'primary insurer'.

7 Edelman and Burns (n 2) para 1.09. Hereinafter, unless specifically indicated otherwise, any references to a reinsured or a reinsurer includes retrocedents or retrocessionaires, respectively.

8 Gürses (n 3) para 1.01; Edelman and Burns (n 2) paras 1.10 f.

9 Robert Kiln, *Reinsurance in Practice* (4th edn, Witherby 1991) 1. See also Barlow Lyde & Gilbert LLP (n 3) para 1.4; Gürses (n 3) para 1.01.

10 Barlow Lyde & Gilbert LLP (n 3) para 1.6, highlighting an exemption in section 620 of the Californian Civil Code which defines a reinsurance contract as a contract 'by which an insurer procures a third person to insure him against loss or liability by reason of such original insurance'.

11 Parliament and Council Directive 2009/138/EC of 25 November 2009 on the taking-up and pursuit of the business of Insurance and Reinsurance (Solvency II) [2009] OJ L 335.

12 For more details as to the PRICL 2019, see paras 4.123 ff.

13 Article 1.2.1 PRICL.

14 *Delver, Assignee of Bunn v Barnes* [1807] 1 Taunton 48, 51.

15 Cf Barlow Lyde & Gilbert LLP (n 3) para 1.7; Edelman and Burns (n 2) para 1.22.

16 See, for instance, *Forsikringsaktieselskapet Vesta v Butcher* [1989] AC 852 (HL) 893 (Lord Griffith).

17 Edelman and Burns (n 2) para 1.22.

reinsurance contract would be effective if subsequently no primary insurance contract were concluded.[18]

1.8 On a more functional level, a 'reinsurance contract' is a contract whereby a primary insurer takes out insurance with a reinsurer against the costs it may incur if it has to indemnify its primary insured for claims under a primary insurance policy issued by it.[19] Under such a contract, the reinsurer agrees to indemnify 'the original insurer against the whole or against a specified amount or proportion (...) of the risk which the latter has himself insured'.[20] In return, the reinsured promises the payment of a premium.[21]

1.9 The reinsured's insurable interest is to be identified by reference to the original insurance policy.[22] Consequently, unless there is a primary insurance contract to be reinsured, there cannot be said to be a contract of reinsurance. In German legal literature, the term 'accessoriness' (*Akzessorietät*) is used to describe the dependence of a reinsurance contract on the primary insurance contract.[23] Similarly, English legal commentary suggests that '[t]he indemnity afforded by reinsurance is (...) against the discharge of liability by the reinsured' so that the reinsured could not make a profit out of the reinsurance.[24]

II Different forms of reinsurance

1.10 Reinsurance contracts are generally divided into two forms: treaty and facultative reinsurance.[25] At the core of the distinction between the two categories lie the questions of whether the reinsured is bound to offer a specific risk and whether the reinsurer is bound to accept such a risk.[26] The answers to these questions essentially determine the design and, hence, the form of the reinsurance contract. However, many hybrid forms of reinsurance contracts exist so that it may be too simplistic to regard there to be a dichotomy between facultative and treaty reinsurance.[27]

---

18 Cannawurf and Schwepcke (n 1) paras 4 f.

19 Cf Barlow Lyde & Gilbert LLP (n 3) para 1.4; Cannawurf and Schwepcke (n 1) para 3; Pohl and Iranya (n 3) 7.

20 *Forsikringsaktieselskapet Vesta v Butcher* (n 16) 852, 908 (Lord Lowry).

21 Edelman and Burns (n 2) para 1.29.

22 *Eagle Star Insurance Co Ltd v Toomey* [1994] 3 Lloyd's Rep IR 1 (CA) 7 (Hobhouse LJ); Edelman and Burns (n 2) para 1.29.

23 Cannawurf and Schwepcke (n 1) para 4.

24 Edelman and Burns (n 2) para 1.29.

25 William Hoffman, 'Facultative Reinsurance Contract Formation, Documentation, and Integration' (2003) 38 Tort Trial & Insurance Practice Law Journal 763, 768; Pohl and Iranya (n 3) 8.

26 Hoffman (n 25) 769.

27 Hoffman (n 25) 769.

1 Treaty reinsurance

1.11 A reinsurance treaty is a contract *for* reinsurance rather than a contract *of* reinsurance.[28] More specifically, a reinsurance treaty is not used to transfer a portion of the reinsured's risk to the reinsurer by itself. Rather, the parties to a reinsurance treaty agree that the reinsured cedes and the reinsurer accepts specified primary insurance risks to the extent that they are underwritten by the reinsured.[29] Consequently, a reinsurance treaty can be considered obligatory.[30]

1.12 The reinsured is generally free to decide whether to accept primary insurance business. Where it chooses so, it is obliged to cede a certain amount or proportion of the risks to the reinsurer and the reinsurer is bound to accept such amount or proportion of the risk if it is within the scope of the reinsurance treaty.[31] Commonly, a reinsurance treaty encompasses all or a substantial part of the primary insurance policies of a specified kind, ie potentially a whole book of business.[32]

1.13 The transfer of risks from the reinsured to the reinsurer generally occurs automatically.[33] In line with this, the High Court of Singapore in *Hanwha Non-Life Insurance Co Ltd v Alba Pte Ltd* held that a risk attaches to a reinsurance treaty as soon as the reinsured accepts it under the underlying insurance policy.[34]

1.14 Treaty reinsurance is efficient because the reinsured does not have to apply for reinsurance cover in respect of each primary insurance policy underwritten by it. The reinsured has certainty that it will obtain appropriate reinsurance cover for a primary insurance risk that it wishes to accept.[35] Moreover, the reinsured does not have to provide the reinsurer with detailed information regarding each and every ceded risk[36] and the reinsurer does not assess each and every ceded risk.[37] By doing away with these steps, the parties reduce their administrative costs of business.[38]

---

28 Edelman and Burns (n 2) para 1.50; Graydon Shaw Staring and Dean Hansell, *Law of Reinsurance* (Thomson Reuters Westlaw 2020) s 1:1.

29 Schwepcke and Vetter (n 1) para 642; Staring and Hansell (n 28) s 2:4.

30 However, reinsurance treaties are not necessarily obligatory for both parties. In facultative obligatory treaty reinsurance, the reinsured is free to choose the risks it wishes to cede to the treaty, whereas the reinsurer is bound to accept any such risk. In obligatory facultative treaty reinsurance, the reinsured is bound to offer specified business, whereas the reinsurer is free to accept or decline it.

31 Klaus Gerathewohl, *Rückversicherung, Grundlagen und Praxis*, vol 1 (Verlag Versicherungswirtschaft eV 1976) 70; Klaus Gerathewohl, *Rückversicherung, Grundlagen und Praxis*, vol 2 (Verlag Versicherungswirtschaft eV 1979) 1; Schwepcke and Vetter (n 1) para 642.

32 Gerathewohl, *Rückversicherung, Grundlagen und Praxis*, vol 2 (n 31) 2; Schwepcke and Vetter (n 1) para 641.

33 Cannawurf and Schwepcke (n 1) para 267; Schwepcke and Vetter (n 1) para 641.

34 *Hanwha Non-Life Insurance Co Ltd v Alba Pte Ltd* [2011] SGHC 271, [2012] Lloyd's Rep IR 505 [48] (Tan J); Edelman and Burns (n 2) para 1.51.

35 Edelman and Burns (n 2) para 1.50; Cannawurf and Schwepcke (n 1) para 268.

36 Schwepcke and Vetter (n 1) para 643; Liebwein (n 1) 62.

37 With regard to the latter point, Edelman and Burns (n 2) para 1.50.

38 Edelman and Burns (n 2) para 1.50.

Another aspect is that treaty reinsurance can be effected proportionally or non-proportionally.[39]

1.15 As reinsurance treaties often contain aggregation clauses, the subject matter of aggregation may be relevant in the context of treaty reinsurance.[40] In fact, it is even possible that losses covered under different primary insurance policies within the portfolio may be aggregated under a reinsurance treaty if they result from the same event or cause.[41]

2 Facultative reinsurance

1.16 In the case of facultative reinsurance, a primary insurer, ie a reinsured, decides whether it wishes to reinsure a specific risk.[42] It is up to the reinsured to choose the right reinsurer for the deal.[43] Yet, the reinsurer is equally free to accept the risk or to decline it.[44]

1.17 Facultative reinsurance contracts generally cover individual primary insurance policies.[45] However, this is not necessarily so. In fact, it is possible to reinsure multiple primary insurance policies under one facultative contract.[46] In either case, it is to be emphasised that facultative reinsurance entails a separate underwriting for each risk transferred from the reinsured to the reinsurer.[47]

1.18 The advantage of facultative reinsurance lies in the fact that the reinsurer is free to accept or decline any risk. The terms of a facultative reinsurance contract can, therefore, be negotiated with respect to a specific risk and, thus, be tailored to it.[48] Consequently, a prospective reinsurer will carefully evaluate the risk insured under the underlying primary insurance contract before deciding.[49] This generally requires

---

39 See paras 1.26 ff, 1.40 ff.

40 See, for instance, *Axa Reinsurance (UK) Ltd v Field* (1996) 1 WLR 1026 (HL); *IRB Brasil Resseguros SA v CX Reinsurance Co Ltd* [2010] EWHC 974 (Comm), [2010] Lloyd's Rep IR 560; *Aioi Nissay Dowa Insurance Co Ltd v Heraldglen Ltd and Advent Capital Ltd* [2013] EWHC 154 (Comm), [2013] 2 All ER 231.

41 Gerathewohl, *Rückversicherung, Grundlagen und Praxis*, vol 1 (n 31) 229; Schwepcke and Vetter (n 1) para 887; Liebwein (n 1) 190. See also Rob Merkin, 'The Christchurch Earthquakes Insurance and Reinsurance Issues' (2012) 18 Canterbury Law Review 119, 144 ff.

42 Hoffman (n 25) 769; Liebwein (n 1) 62 f; Pohl and Iranya (n 3) 8.

43 Gerathewohl, *Rückversicherung, Grundlagen und Praxis*, vol. 2 (n 31) 1; Barlow Lyde & Gilbert LLP (n 3) para 4.8; Edelman and Burns (n 2) para 1.41; Pohl and Iranya (n 3) 8.

44 Gerathewohl, *Rückversicherung, Grundlagen und Praxis*, vol. 2 (n 31) 1; Hoffman (n 25) 769; Cannawurf and Schwepcke (n 1) para 265; Edelman and Burns (n 2) para 1.41; Schwepcke and Vetter (n 1) para 704; Pohl and Iranya (n 3) 8; Liebwein (n 1) 62; Staring and Hansell (n 28) s 2:2.

45 Cf Gerathewohl, *Rückversicherung, Grundlagen und Praxis*, vol. 1 (n 31) 70; Gerathewohl, *Rückversicherung, Grundlagen und Praxis*, vol. 2 (n 31) 1; Barlow Lyde & Gilbert LLP (n 3) para 4.8; Gürses (n 3) para 1.08; Cannawurf and Schwepcke (n 1) para 265; Schwepcke and Vetter (n 1) para 645; Pohl and Iranya (n 3) 65.

46 Hoffman (n 25) 769. See also Edelman and Burns (n 2) para 1.40; Terry O'Neill, Jan Woloniecki and Franziska Arnold-Dwyer, *The Law of Reinsurance in England and Bermuda* (5th edn, Sweet & Maxwell/Thomson Reuters 2019) para 1–017.

47 Hoffman (n 25) 769.

48 Hoffman (n 25) 770; Liebwein (n 1) 63. Cf also Staring and Hansell (n 28) s 2:2.

49 Cf Schwepcke and Vetter (n 1) para 645.

the prospective reinsured to make reasonably clear and correct information accessible to the prospective reinsurer. More specifically, it involves a disclosure of information about any material circumstances, ie circumstances that 'would influence the judgment of a prudent reinsurer in determining whether to take the risk and, if so, on what terms'.[50] In providing such detailed information, the prospective reinsured commonly incurs high administrative costs.[51] A further disadvantage of facultative reinsurance may be seen in the fact that, when negotiating the primary insurance contract, the prospective reinsured has no certainty as to whether it will be able to obtain appropriate reinsurance cover for it.[52]

1.19 Despite the disadvantages that come with it, facultative reinsurance is a sensible option under certain circumstances. For example, a prospective reinsured may seek facultative reinsurance where a risk exceeds the available treaty capacity[53] or where it is not covered by the treaty.[54] Furthermore, facultative reinsurance may be justified if a reinsurance company wishes to specialise in reinsuring a certain unusual and complex risk.[55] Generally, it may be said that reinsureds take out facultative reinsurance for unusual or particularly large risks.[56] Another aspect is that facultative reinsurance can be effected proportionally or non-proportionally.[57]

1.20 As facultative reinsurance agreements often contain aggregation clauses, the subject matter of aggregation may be relevant in the context of facultative reinsurance.[58]

III Different types and methods of reinsurance

1.21 Reinsurance contracts are further divided into two types: proportional and non-proportional contracts.[59] In both proportional and non-proportional reinsurance, a certain part of the risk is transferred from the reinsured to the reinsurer.[60]

---

50 Insurance Act 2015, s 7(3), with regard to English law; Cannawurf and Schwepcke (n 1) para 97, with regard to German law; Comments 6 ff to Article 2.2.1 PRICL, with regard to the PRICL.

51 Barlow Lyde & Gilbert LLP (n 3) para 4.8; Edelman and Burns (n 2) para 1.42; Pohl and Iranya (n 3) 69.

52 Edelman and Burns (n 2) para 1.42. Cf also Pohl and Iranya (n 3) 65.

53 Liebwein (n 1) 62; Pohl and Iranya (n 3) 65. See also Hoffman (n 25) 770.

54 Liebwein (n 1) 62; Pohl and Iranya (n 3) 66. See also Hoffman (n 25) 770.

55 Barlow Lyde & Gilbert LLP (n 3) para 4.8.

56 Edelman and Burns (n 2) para 1.42. See also Barlow Lyde & Gilbert LLP (n 3) para 4.8; Liebwein (n 1) 62.

57 See paras 1.24 f, 1.37 ff.

58 See for instance *Municipal Mutual Insurance Ltd v Sea Insurance Co Ltd* [1998] EWCA Civ 546, [1998] CLC 957; *Tokio Marine Europe Insurance Ltd v Novae Corporate Underwriting Ltd* [2014] EWHC 2105 (Comm), [2014] Lloyd's Rep IR 638.

59 Barlow Lyde & Gilbert LLP (n 3) paras 1.11 f; Gürses (n 3) paras 1.06 f; Edelman and Burns (n 2) para 1.33; Cannawurf and Schwepcke (n 1) paras 270 ff; Schwepcke and Vetter (n 1) paras 655 ff, 661 ff; Liebwein (n 1) 69 ff; Pohl and Iranya (n 3) 13 ff, 27 ff.

60 Edelman and Burns (n 2) para 1.33; Cannawurf and Schwepcke (n 1) para 270.

The distinction between proportional and non-proportional reinsurance lies in the definition of the part of the risk to be ceded[61] as well as the way the premiums are shared.[62] However, it should be noted that proportional and non-proportional reinsurance can each be subdivided into smaller categories.[63]

1 Proportional reinsurance

1.22 In proportional reinsurance,[64] the reinsured and the reinsurer agree to proportionally share both the primary insurance risk or risks and the primary insurance premium or premiums.[65] The terms 'risk' and 'risks' in this context refer to the risk of incurring liability resulting from insurance cover under an underlying insurance policy or multiple underlying insurance policies respectively.[66]

1.23 Proportional reinsurance can be taken out either on an obligatory or a facultative basis.[67] Basically, three different types of proportional reinsurance contracts are to be distinguished: proportional facultative reinsurance contract, quota share treaty and surplus treaty.

1.1 Proportional facultative reinsurance contract

1.24 Under a proportional facultative reinsurance contract, the reinsurer reinsures a single risk, ie a single primary insurance policy on a proportional basis.[68] Whenever the reinsured is liable under the primary insurance contract, it is entitled to be reimbursed for the relevant portion of the liability by the reinsurer under the reinsurance contract.[69] In return, the reinsurer has a right to be paid the relevant portion of the primary insurance premium as a reinsurance premium.[70] It is presumed that the underlying policy and the reinsurance policy

---

61 Edelman and Burns (n 2) para 1.33; Cannawurf and Schwepcke (n 1) para 270; Schwepcke and Vetter (n 1) para 655.

62 Pohl and Iranya (n 3) 13.

63 In proportional reinsurance, a distinction is made between quota share and surplus reinsurance, whereas non-proportional reinsurance is divided into excess of loss and stop loss reinsurance.

64 Proportional reinsurance is also termed 'proportionate' or 'pro rata' reinsurance.

65 The primary insurance premium is shared proportionally after deduction of the costs the reinsured incurs in acquiring the business (so-called commissions).

66 Cf *Charter Reinsurance Co Ltd v Fagan* [1996] AC 313 (HL) 341, where Mance J's first instance decision is transcribed; Gerathewohl, *Rückversicherung, Grundlagen und Praxis*, vol. 1 (n 31) 102; Marcel Grossmann, *Rückversicherung – Eine Einführung* (2nd edn, Institut für Versicherungswirtschaft an der Hochschule St Gallen 1982) 75; Kiln (n 9) 1; Robert M Merkin, *A Guide to Reinsurance Law* (Informa Law by Routledge 2007) 8; Barlow Lyde & Gilbert LLP (n 3) para 1.11; Gürses (n 3) para 1.06; Edelman and Burns (n 2) para 1.34; Cannawurf and Schwepcke (n 1) paras 271 f; Schwepcke and Vetter (n 1) paras 656 ff; Pohl and Iranya (n 3) 13; O'Neill, Woloniecki and Arnold-Dwyer (n 46) para 1–015.

67 Edelman and Burns (n 2) paras 1.43 ff, 1.52 ff; Cannawurf and Schwepcke (n 1) para 275; Liebwein (n 63); O'Neill, Woloniecki and Arnold-Dwyer (n 46) paras 1–017, 1–019.

68 Gürses (n 3) para 1.25; Schwepcke and Vetter (n 1) para 719.

69 Gürses (n 3) para 1.25.

70 Schwepcke and Vetter (n 1) para 719.

are designed to be back-to-back, ie provide for identical or closely matching cover.[71]

1.25 Proportional facultative reinsurance contracts generally do not provide for a retention, a limit per event or a limit per cause.[72] Consequently, the issue of aggregation based on causation is irrelevant in respect of purely proportional facultative reinsurance contracts.[73]

1.2 Quota share treaty

1.26 The reinsured agrees to cede and the reinsurer agrees to accept a fixed percentage of each risk, ie of each primary insurance policy, that is within the scope of the reinsurance treaty.[74] Usually, primary insurance risks are ceded to the treaty on identical terms.[75] In any case, the reinsurer is entitled to be paid the relevant percentage of the primary insurance premium as a reinsurance premium.[76] In return, whenever a reinsured is liable for a loss under a primary insurance policy forming part of the reinsured portfolio, the reinsurer is required to pay its percentage of that loss.

1.27 The parties often agree to limit the reinsurer's liability per risk. This is to say that the parties agree to limit the reinsurer's liability to a maximum monetary amount for losses arising under one single primary insurance policy.[77] In such a case, the reinsurer is only bound to pay his percentage of a loss up until the per risk limit, ie the limit for losses under one single primary insurance policy, is exceeded.[78]

1.28 Particularly in case of a natural catastrophe, multiple primary insurance policies in the portfolio may be triggered. This may lead to a large-scale liability on the part of the reinsurer under the quota share treaty. The parties, therefore, regularly agree on a limit per event to ease the situation for the reinsurer.[79] It is only

---

71 Gürses (n 3) para 1.25; Edelman and Burns (n 2) paras 1.43 ff; regarding the presumption of back-to-back cover in proportional reinsurance, see *Axa Reinsurance (UK) Ltd v Field* (n 40) 1033 f (Lord Mustill).

72 If they do, they are not entirely proportional.

73 Cf Ken Louw and Deborah Tompkinson, 'Curiouser and Curiouser: The Meaning of "Event"' (1996) 4 International Insurance Law Review 6, 6 f.

74 Merkin, *A Guide to Reinsurance Law* (n 66) 15; Gürses (n 3) para 1.11; O'Neill, Woloniecki and Arnold-Dwyer (n 46) para 1–019. See also Gerathewohl, *Rückversicherung, Grundlagen und Praxis*, vol. 1 (n 31) 102; Kiln (n 9) 31; Cannawurf and Schwepcke (n 1) para 275.

75 Barlow Lyde & Gilbert LLP (n 3) para 4.25.

76 Gerathewohl, *Rückversicherung, Grundlagen und Praxis*, vol. 1 (n 31) 102; Merkin, *A Guide to Reinsurance Law* (n 66) 16 f; Barlow Lyde & Gilbert LLP (n 3) para 4.25; Gürses (n 3) para 1.11; Edelman and Burns (n 2) para 1.54; O'Neill, Woloniecki and Arnold-Dwyer (n 46) para 1–019.

77 Merkin, *A Guide to Reinsurance Law* (n 66) 15; Barlow Lyde & Gilbert LLP (n 3) para 4.28; Gürses (n 3) para 1.11. It may be noted that, in this context, 'one risk' does not refer to an insured asset but rather to a reinsured original policy; Edelman and Burns (n 2) para 1.54.

78 Barlow Lyde & Gilbert LLP (n 3) para 4.25; Edelman and Burns (n 2) para 1.54; Cannawurf and Schwepcke (n 1) para 271; O'Neill, Woloniecki and Arnold-Dwyer (n 46) para 1–109.

79 Liebwein (n 1) 71. This means introducing a non-proportional element into an otherwise proportional type of reinsurance.

where the quota share treaty contains a limit per event[80] that the topic of aggregation of losses based on causation may become relevant.

1.3 Surplus treaty

1.29 In a surplus treaty, the parties agree that the reinsured's retention is a fixed sum per risk rather than a percentage of all the risks in the portfolio.[81] The reinsurer accepts the surplus liability, ie the part of the risk that exceeds the reinsured's retention.[82] This means that the reinsurer agrees to cover the difference between the reinsured's retention and the cover limit of the underlying insurance policy.

1.30 The relevant loss need not exceed the reinsured's retention in order for the reinsurer's liability to be triggered. Rather, the ratio between the cover limit under the ceded primary insurance policy and the reinsured's retention under the reinsurance treaty regarding one specific risk equals the percentage according to which the parties share the risk under the reinsurance treaty. Consequently, the parties share the liability and the premiums according to that percentage from the first pound on.[83]

1.31 This is perhaps better understood by way of example. Imagine that a reinsured has a portfolio of primary insurance policies. Primary insurance policy A has a cover limit of £1million, whereas primary insurance policy B has a cover limit of £500,000. Both primary insurance policies are ceded to the surplus treaty. The parties agree that the reinsured retains liability to the amount of £200,000 with regard to policy A and £250,000 in respect of policy B. Therefore, the reinsured retains a maximum of 20% of the losses under policy A and 50% of the losses under policy B. Under primary insurance policy A, losses totalling £800,000 have occurred. The reinsured covers 20% of these losses, ie £160,000, whereas the reinsurer is liable for £640,000. Under primary insurance policy B, losses totalling £200,000 have occurred. The reinsured covers 50% of these losses, ie £100,000, whereas the reinsurer is liable for the remaining £100,000.

1.32 This example illustrates that the parties may agree on a different retention with regard to each ceded risk and the cover limit of each underlying policy may be different. Consequently, the relevant percentages of liability may differ for each risk.[84]

1.33 Particularly in case of a natural catastrophe, cover under multiple primary insurance policies in the portfolio may be triggered. This may translate into a massive liability on the part of the reinsurer under the surplus treaty. The parties, therefore, regularly agree on a limit per event to ease the situation for the reinsurer.[85]

---

80 Or per another unifying factor.

81 Edelman and Burns (n 2) para 1.56; Schwepcke and Vetter (n 1) para 823; O'Neill, Woloniecki and Arnold-Dwyer (n 46) para 1–020.

82 This is not so by definition. Rather, it is possible that the difference between the cover limit under the primary insurance policy and the reinsured's retention is not fully covered by the reinsurer, see Schwepcke and Vetter (n 1) para 827.

83 Cf Schwepcke and Vetter (n 1) para 826.

84 Schwepcke and Vetter (n 1) para 822.

85 Liebwein (n 1) 78. This means introducing a non-proportional element into an otherwise proportional type of reinsurance.

It is only where the surplus treaty contains a limit per event that the topic of aggregation of losses based on causation, as discussed henceforth, may become relevant.

2 Non-proportional reinsurance

1.34 In non-proportional reinsurance, the reinsurer provides cover for the amount of a loss exceeding the reinsured's deductible up to a maximum limit.[86] This is to say that the reinsured retains a layer of liability which is generally expressed in a monetary amount.[87] The reinsured covers any losses that do not exceed this retained layer.[88] In contrast to surplus reinsurance,[89] the reinsurer's liability is triggered only if the reinsured's liability exceeds the deductible agreed in the non-proportional reinsurance contract.

1.35 Consequently, the reinsurance premium is not calculated on a *pro rata* basis.[90] Rather, it is based on the probability that a loss or losses that attach the reinsurance contract, ie exceed the reinsured's deductible, will occur.[91]

1.36 In excess of loss reinsurance, provisions relating to deductibles and cover limits, such as aggregation clauses, are said to be of cardinal importance.[92] With respect to the calculation of the reinsured's deductible and the reinsurer's maximum cover limit under a reinsurance contract, different methods of non-proportional reinsurance are to be distinguished:[93] facultative excess of loss reinsurance contract, per risk excess of loss treaty, per event excess of loss treaty and stop loss treaty.

2.1 Facultative excess of loss reinsurance contract

1.37 In facultative excess of loss reinsurance, the reinsured is free to cede and the reinsurer is free to accept any risk.[94] As the reinsurance is non-proportional, the underlying risk and premium are not shared on a *pro rata* basis between the reinsured and the reinsurer.[95] Rather, the parties agree that the reinsured is liable for any loss that does not exceed its deductible. Once the amount of a loss exceeds the reinsured's deductible, the reinsurer's liability up to a specified cover limit will be triggered.[96] Generally, both the reinsured's deductible and the reinsurer's cover limit are expressed in a monetary amount.[97]

---

86 Gerathewohl, *Rückversicherung, Grundlagen und Praxis*, vol. 1 (n 31) 143; Gürses (n 3) paras 1.07, 6.182; Edelman and Burns (n 2) para 1.61; Cannawurf and Schwepcke (n 1) paras 368 f; Schwepcke and Vetter (n 1) para 661.

87 Cf Edelman and Burns (n 2) para 1.61.

88 Cf Edelman and Burns (n 2) para 1.61; Schwepcke and Vetter (n 1) para 663.

89 See paras 47 f.

90 Schwepcke and Vetter (n 1) para 665.

91 Cf Merkin, *A Guide to Reinsurance Law* (n 66) 42.

92 *Axa Reinsurance (UK) Ltd v Field* (n 40) 1035.

93 Schwepcke and Vetter (n 1) para 666.

94 Kiln (n 9) 17; Edelman and Burns (n 2) para 1.49.

95 Kiln (n 9) 17.

96 Edelman and Burns (n 2) para 1.49.

97 Kiln (n 9) 17. Cf also Cannawurf and Schwepcke (n 1) para 368.

1.38 A facultative reinsurance contract may provide for a per event excess of loss mechanism.[98] Where a facultative excess of loss contract provides for an aggregation mechanism using a unifying factor, such as an event or a cause, the aggregation of losses based on causation may become relevant.

1.39 This is so, because it is possible that a facultative excess of loss contract provides cover for multiple individual risks[99] or assets.[100] Accordingly, multiple individual losses may occur as the result of one event or one cause so that a corresponding aggregation mechanism would require the aggregation of any individual losses that arose from the same event or cause.

2.2 Per risk excess of loss treaty

1.40 In per risk excess of loss reinsurance, the reinsured's deductible is applied on a per risk basis. This is to say that reinsurance cover is taken out for single losses which exceed the reinsured's deductible on any one risk.[101] A risk may refer to a single primary insurance policy or to an asset that is insured under a primary insurance policy, such as a vehicle or a building.[102]

1.41 In pure per risk excess of loss treaties, multiple losses that occur under one or multiple primary insurance policies are, therefore, not aggregated. Rather, the reinsured's deductible and the reinsurer's cover limit are tested against the loss that occurs to one single risk, such as a vehicle or a building.[103]

1.42 However, multiple primary insurance policies in the portfolio may be triggered by one event. One event may, in fact, translate into a massive liability on the part of the reinsurer if the loss on each risk exceeds the per risk deductible. In such situations, the reinsurer may wish to additionally limit its liability on a per event basis.[104] In such cases, the reinsurance treaty contains both a per risk and

---

98 Cf Kiln (n 9) 24. Of course, any unifying factor other than 'event' may equally be used to aggregate a plurality of losses; see for instance the facultative excess of loss reinsurance contracts discussed in *Municipal Mutual Insurance Ltd v Sea Insurance Co Ltd* (n 58), which contained aggregation clauses using the unifying factor of 'original cause'.

99 O'Neill, Woloniecki and Arnold-Dwyer (n 46) para 1–017. In this context, 'one risk' refers to one underlying policy.

100 Robert Kiln, *Reinsurance in Practice* (Witherby 1981) 194. Cf also *Kuwait Airways Corp v Kuwait Insurance Co SAK* [1996] 1 Lloyd's Rep 664 (Comm), [1997] 2 Lloyd's Rep 687 (CA), [1999] 1 Lloyd's Rep 252 (HL) where multiple aircraft were insured under one policy.

101 Gerathewohl, *Rückversicherung, Grundlagen und Praxis*, vol. 1 (n 31) 209; Liebwein (n 1) 183; Pohl and Iranya (n 3) 32.

102 Schwepcke and Vetter (n 1) para 910. See also Kiln (n 9) 194; *Amlin Corporate Member Ltd v Oriental Assurance Corp* [2012] EWCA Civ 1341, [2013] Lloyd's Rep IR 131 [6] (Longmore LJ). This case concerned a marine cargo primary insurance liability policy under which multiple different vessels (risks) were insured. However, the limit was per risk and per event.

103 Schwepcke and Vetter (n 1) para 909.

104 Cf Kiln (n 9) 24. Of course, any unifying factor other than 'event' may equally be used to aggregate a plurality of losses. See for instance the facultative excess of loss reinsurance contracts discussed in *Municipal Mutual Insurance Ltd v Sea Insurance Co Ltd* (n 58), which contained aggregation clauses using the unifying factor of 'original cause'.

a per event limit.[105] Where the reinsurance treaty provides for such a per event element, an aggregation of individual losses may become relevant.

2.3 Per event excess of loss treaty

1.43 Per event excess of loss reinsurance protects the reinsured in cases where multiple single losses on multiple different risks or primary insurance policies in the same portfolio arise out of one single event.[106] The reinsured's deductible is applied on a per event basis.[107] The reinsured's deductible and the reinsurer's cover limit are both tested against the aggregate of any individual losses that result from any one event.[108] Hence, losses arising under different primary insurance policies within the portfolio, possibly covering multiple different risks, are to be aggregated if they are provoked by the same event.[109]

1.44 As individual losses on the basis of an event are aggregated in per event excess of loss reinsurance, it is fundamental that the parties clearly define what they mean by the term 'event'.[110] It is generally said that the term 'event' is defined by three different dimensions: a causal, a spatial as well as a temporal dimension.[111] Some commentators believe that defining the term 'event' by these three dimensions will not by itself bring clarity to the matter. Bourthomieux argues, for instance, that there is a significant need for clarification and systematisation as regards the operation of per event excess of loss reinsurance agreements.[112]

1.45 However, the parties to a reinsurance contract do not always use the unifying factor of event in order to aggregate individual losses based on causation. In practice, further terms such as 'occurrence',[113] 'disaster',[114] 'calamity',[115] 'accident'[116] or 'cause'[117] are regularly used. Irrespective of the term used, such insurance products are often classified as 'per event excess of loss' reinsurance agreements.

---

105 Gerathewohl, *Rückversicherung, Grundlagen und Praxis*, vol. 1 (n 31) 209; Cannawurf and Schwepcke (n 1) para 276; Liebwein (n 1) 185.

106 Liebwein (n 1) 190. An excess of loss treaty may certainly also use a unifying factor other than 'event'.

107 Grossmann (n 66) 121; Liebwein (n 1) 190.

108 Liebwein (n 1) 190.

109 Cf Liebwein (n 1) 190 f.

110 Grossmann (n 66) 122; Liebwein (n 1) 194.

111 Pohl and Iranya (n 3) 33.

112 Jacques Bourthoumieux, 'La notion d'événement dans les traités de réassurance en excédent de sinistres' (1969) 40 Revue générale des assurances terrestres 457, 473.

113 *Caudle v Sharp* [1995] CLC 642 (CA) 644.

114 *Caudle v Sharp* (n 113) 644.

115 *Caudle v Sharp* (n 113) 644.

116 *Hartford Accident and Indemnity Co v Edward Wesolowski* (1973) 33 NY2d 169 (Court of Appeals of New York) dealing with primary insurance; *National Liability and Fire Insurance Co v Itzkowitz* (2015) 624 FedAppx 758 (United States Court of Appeals for the Second Circuit) 759 f, dealing with primary insurance.

117 *Cox v Bankside Members Agency Ltd* [1995] CLC 671 (CA) 680 (Sir Thomas Bingham), dealing with primary insurance; *Municipal Mutual Insurance Ltd v Sea Insurance Co Ltd* (n 58) 966 (Hobhouse LJ).

1.46 Per event excess of loss reinsurance is the most important type of reinsurance with regard to the aggregation of losses based on causation. In fact, it is even possible that losses covered under different primary insurance policies within the portfolio may be aggregated under a reinsurance treaty if they result from the same event or cause.[118]

2.4 Stop loss treaty

1.47 Stop loss policies are used to protect the reinsured's solvency. However, the reinsured cannot increase the volume or size of primary insurance risks it is able to accept by entering into a stop loss treaty.[119] In *Eagle Star Insurance Co Ltd v Toomey*,[120] Hobhouse LJ, therefore, found that under English law stop loss policies cannot be considered contracts of reinsurance; a view that was later upheld by Lord Mance in *Wasa International Insurance Co Ltd v Lexington Insurance Co.*[121] By contrast, Lord Steyn stated in *Society of Lloyd's v Robinson* that 'stop loss insurance cover is a form of reinsurance'.[122] Moreover, a number of English commentators are sceptical about denying stop loss policies the quality of reinsurance.[123] Equally, commentators from other jurisdictions generally regard stop loss policies as a type of reinsurance.[124]

1.48 Irrespective of these uncertainties, it is clear that stop loss reinsurance comes in two different types:[125] excess of loss ratio and aggregate excess of loss. The difference between the two lies in the way the reinsured's deductible and the reinsurer's cover limit are defined.

a Excess of loss ratio

1.49 Where an excess of loss ratio applies, this means that the parties to the reinsurance treaty agree on a certain percentage as the reinsured's deductible and the reinsurer's cover limit, say 50% excess of 100%. Subsequently, the ratio between the annual losses under the primary insurance policies in the portfolio and the net retained premium income is determined and expressed in a percentage. This ratio is then tested against the percentages agreed upon as the reinsured's deductible and the reinsurer's cover limit.

---

118 Gerathewohl, *Rückversicherung, Grundlagen und Praxis*, vol. 1 (n 31) 229; Schwepcke and Vetter (n 1) para 887; Liebwein (n 1) 190. Cf also Merkin, 'The Christchurch Earthquakes Insurance and Reinsurance Issues' (n 41) 144 ff.

119 Gürses (n 3) para 1.13.

120 *Eagle Star Insurance Co Ltd v Toomey* (n 22) 8 (Hobhouse LJ).

121 *Wasa International Insurance Co Ltd v Lexington Insurance Co* [2009] UKHL 40, [2009] 4 All ER 909 [33] (Lord Mance).

122 *Society of Lloyd's v Robinson* [1999] 1 WLR 756 (HL) 763 (Lord Steyn).

123 Merkin, *A Guide to Reinsurance Law* (n 66) 63; Gürses (n 3) para 1.13; Edelman and Burns (n 2) paras 1.66 ff; O'Neill, Woloniecki and Arnold-Dwyer (n 46) para 1–023.

124 Gerathewohl, *Rückversicherung, Grundlagen und Praxis*, vol. 1 (n 31) 107 ff; Cannawurf and Schwepcke (n 1) para 276; Liebwein (n 1) 201 ff; Pohl and Iranya (n 3) 35 f.

125 Sometimes, aggregate excess of loss is not regarded as a subset of stop loss reinsurance. However, aggregate excess of loss policies operate very similarly to excess of loss ratio policies.

1.50 This is perhaps better understood by way of example: Imagine that the parties in their stop loss treaty agree that the reinsurer covers 50% excess of 100%. 50% applies to the reinsurer's cover limit, whereas the 100% applies to the reinsured's deductible. The reinsured's net premium income in the relevant year was £800,000. It covered losses in the amount of £2,000,000. Hence, the loss/income ratio equals 250% (£2,000,000/£800,000). The reinsured's loss/income ratio is then tested against the deductible and the cover limit. In this case, 250% exceeds the deductible of 100% by 150%, so that the reinsurance is triggered. However, the latter 150% also exceeds the cover limit of 50%. Hence, the reinsurer covers 50% of the reinsured's net premium income, ie £400,000 (50% of the net premium income). The reinsured bears its deductible of 100% as well as the amount of the loss exceeding the cover limit, ie further 100% (150% of the loss exceeding the retention – 50% cover limit). This amounts to £1,600,000 (200% of the net premium income).[126]

1.51 Consequently, in the case of stop loss treaties that apply an excess of loss ratio, multiple individual losses are aggregated on the basis of a specific period of time. By contrast, they are not aggregated based on causal links between each of them and a unifying factor of some kind. Therefore, this type of reinsurance treaty is irrelevant where the aggregation of losses based on causation is concerned.

b Aggregate excess of loss

1.52 Under an aggregate excess of loss treaty, the reinsured is covered for the aggregate of any losses that occur within a defined period of time, usually one year.[127] Where an aggregate excess of loss applies, the parties agree on the reinsured's deductible and the reinsurer's cover limit and express both in a monetary amount, say £500,000 in excess of £100,000. The aggregate of the annual losses under the reinsured primary insurance portfolio is then tested against these figures. If the aggregate exceeds £100,000, the reinsurance treaty is triggered; if it also exceeds £600,000, the reinsurer's liability is capped.[128]

1.53 Accordingly, in the case of stop loss treaties that apply an aggregate excess of loss method, multiple individual losses that occur under the primary insurance policies in the portfolio are aggregated. This is done, however, on the basis of a specific period of time, not on a causal basis. Therefore, this type of reinsurance treaties is irrelevant where the aggregation of losses based on causation is concerned. The exception is where the treaty additionally provides for an aggregation clause on the basis of any one event or cause, in which case the subject matter of aggregation may become relevant.

IV Summary of the chapter

1.54 Insurance companies regularly have a need to protect themselves against the risks that they accept in the course of their insurance business. Taking out

---

126 For an example, see Pohl and Iranya (n 3) 35.

127 Pohl and Iranya (n 3) 36.

128 For an example, see Pohl and Iranya (n 3) 36.

reinsurance safeguards their compliance with solvency requirements and correspondingly increases the volume or size of risk that they can accept.

1.55 Reinsurance can be taken out in different forms. In treaty reinsurance, the reinsured cedes multiple insurance policies, the portfolio, to the reinsurance treaty and the reinsurer accepts all the risks ceded under one sole reinsurance contract. In facultative reinsurance, the reinsured generally cedes a single risk or policy to the reinsurer so that the terms and conditions of reinsurance can be tailored to each cession.

1.56 Moreover, different types and methods of reinsurance can be distinguished. In proportional reinsurance, the parties agree to share both the underlying risk and the underlying premium on a proportional basis. Three kinds of proportional reinsurance can be taken out. In proportional facultative reinsurance contracts, the aggregation of losses based on causation is generally not an issue. The same is true for quota share and surplus treaties. However, the parties may provide for a per event or per catastrophe limit in quota share and surplus policies, particularly when it comes to reinsuring natural hazards. Where this is the case, the aggregation of losses based on causation may become an issue.

1.57 In non-proportional reinsurance, the parties do not share the underlying risk on a proportional basis. Rather, the reinsurer provides cover for the amount of a loss exceeding the reinsured's deductible. Non-proportional reinsurance can be divided into facultative excess of loss, per risk excess of loss, per event excess of loss and stop loss reinsurance. In stop loss reinsurance, individual losses occurring within a specified period of time are aggregated. Hence, the aggregating factor is a period of time rather than causation. Thus, aggregation based on causation is irrelevant in stop loss reinsurance. Similarly, in per risk excess of loss reinsurance, individual losses resulting from the same risk may be aggregated based on the unifying factor of risk rather than on a causal basis. Generally, the aggregation of losses based on causation is irrelevant in such policies. However, the parties to a per risk excess of loss treaty sometimes additionally agree on a per event element. In such cases, the aggregation of losses based on causation may become relevant.

1.58 Further, the aggregation of losses based on causation is most important in per event or per cause excess of loss reinsurance, whether in the form of a treaty or a facultative arrangement. Policies of this kind provide that any losses resulting from any one event or a single cause may be considered as one single loss for the purposes of the reinsured's deductible and the reinsurer's cover limit.

CHAPTER 2

Context in which the aggregation of losses takes place

2.1 In *Lloyd's TSB General Insurance Holding Ltd v Lloyd's Bank Group Insurance Co Ltd*, it was stated that the purpose of an aggregation clause was 'to enable two or more separate losses covered by the policy to be treated as a single loss for deductible or other purposes when they are linked by a unifying factor of some kind'.[1] In *Scott v Copenhagen Reinsurance Co (UK) Ltd*, it was noted that the function of an aggregation clause was 'to police the imposition of a limit by treating a plurality of linked losses as if they were one loss'.[2]

2.2 In line with this, the significance of aggregation clauses is twofold. First, where the policy of reinsurance provides that a deductible applies to the aggregate of all individual losses, which arise from a unifying factor of some kind, the aggregation clause will determine the number of deductibles to be borne by the reinsured.[3] Secondly, as the reinsurance cover limit or sublimit may apply to any one loss, a mechanism of adding together multiple individual losses to form one single aggregate loss is essential in determining whether the policy's financial ceiling has been exceeded.[4]

2.3 This chapter shall not be dedicated to the question how different aggregation mechanisms operate. Rather, the concepts of 'aggregated loss' and 'individual losses to be aggregated' shall be discussed. Furthermore, as the aggregated loss is to be tested against a deductible and a cover limit, the concepts of 'deductible', 'cover limit' and 'reinstatement of cover' shall be outlined. In doing so, the inconsistent terminology regarding some of these concepts is to be pointed out.

I Ultimate net loss and losses to be aggregated

2.4 The concepts of ultimate net loss and individual loss shall be described below. The terminology for these two concepts is not uniform. In fact, the parties sometimes

---

1 *Lloyd's TSB General Insurance Holdings Ltd v Lloyd's Bank Group Insurance Co Ltd* [2003] UKHL 48, [2003] 4 All ER 43 [14] (Lord Hoffmann). See also Francis J Maloney III, 'The Application of "per-Occurrence" Deductible Provisions in First-Party Property Claims' (2002) 37 Tort and Insurance Law Journal 921, 921; Kristin Suga Heres and Patricia St. Peter, 'The "Number of Occurrences" Dispute of the Century' (2016) 46 Fall Brief.

2 *Scott v The Copenhagen Reinsurance Co (UK) Ltd* [2003] EWCA Civ 688, [2003] 2 All ER 190 [12] (Rix LJ).

3 Robert M Merkin, Laura Hodgson and Peter J Tyldesley, *Colinvaux's Law of Insurance* (5th edn, Sweet & Maxwell 2019) para 11–319; John Butler and Robert Merkin, *Butler and Merkin's Reinsurance Law*, vol 2 (Looseleaf, Sweet & Maxwell) para C–0221.

4 Merkin, Hodgson and Tyldesley (n 3) para 11–319; Butler and Merkin (n 3) para C–0221.

refer to them as claim and individual claims or occurrence and individual occurrences, respectively. Therefore, the specific meanings of these terms in the context of aggregation shall be examined.

1 The notion of 'loss' in general

2.5 In insurance and reinsurance, the notion of loss has a variety of different meanings.[5] In the *Dawson's Field Arbitration*, the arbitral tribunal noted that it was difficult and dangerous to attempt to define the term 'loss' in the context of insurance.[6]

2.6 As a general rule, it may be said, however, that a (re)insurer is only liable for losses proximately caused by the materialisation of a peril (re)insured against[7] that leaves it financially poorer than it was before.[8] In this sense, the word 'loss' bears the wider meaning of a financial detriment suffered by the insured or reinsured.[9] In indemnity insurance, the assured or reinsured is entitled to recover from the insurer or reinsurer the amount of its actual financial detriment.[10]

2.7 In non-marine insurance,[11] the insured or reinsured subject matter[12] may be totally or partially lost.[13] In either case, a court would determine the value of the insured or reinsured subject matter and put the insured or reinsured in the financial position it would have been in, had no loss occurred.[14] These rules apply in the context of primary insurance and reinsurance.[15]

2.8 Consequently, the insured is entitled to recover a sum of money that corresponds to the amount of its financial detriment.[16] More specifically, if the insured suffers a total loss, the amount recoverable corresponds to the value the insured subject matter had before the loss occurred. Where the loss is only partial, the amount recoverable is the difference between the value the insured subject matter had before the loss occurred and the value it has after the loss has occurred.[17]

---

5 Merkin, Hodgson and Tyldesley (n 3) para 11–340. Cf also Butler and Merkin (n 3) para C–0202.

6 Quoted by Rix J in *Kuwait Airways Corp v Kuwait Insurance Co SAK* [1996] 1 Lloyd's Rep 664 (Comm).

7 John Birds, Ben Lynch and Simon Paul, *MacGillivray on Insurance Law* (14th edn, Sweet & Maxwell 2018) para 21–001.

8 Malcolm A Clarke, *The Law of Insurance Contracts* (6th edn, Informa Law from Routledge 2009) para 16-2A.

9 Clarke (n 8) para 16–2A.

10 Clarke (n 8) para 28–1.

11 In marine insurance, there is the additional concept of 'constructive total loss'.

12 Birds, Lynch and Paul (n 7) para 35–026, where they note that '[t]he subject-matter of a contract of reinsurance is in many cases the subject-matter of the underlying contract of insurance (...)'.

13 Merkin, Hodgson and Tyldesley (n 3) para 11–001.

14 Clarke (n 8) para 28–2.

15 Birds, Lynch and Paul (n 7) paras 35–080 ff.

16 Merkin, Hodgson and Tyldesley (n 3) para 11–051. A distinction is to be drawn between valued and unvalued policies. In the case of valued policies, the insured is entitled to recover a predefined sum of money whereas an unvalued policy entitles the insured to recover the actual loss suffered.

17 Birds, Lynch and Paul (n 7) para 21–015.

2.9 By contrast, sometimes the term 'loss' refers to the deprivation of the insured subject matter.[18] In this regard, a loss consists in the insured's dispossession of a good[19] rather than in the insured's financial detriment.[20] In cases such as these, the insured or reinsured also merely has a right to be indemnified with a certain sum of money.

2.10 Yet, in the context of aggregation in excess of loss reinsurance, there are at least two different notions of loss, which are to be distinguished: ultimate net loss and individual losses to be aggregated.

2 The notion of 'ultimate net loss' in excess of loss reinsurance

2.11 In line with the House of Lords' decision in *Hill v Mercantile and General Reinsurance Co Plc*, the reinsurer's obligation to indemnify the reinsured arises if two conditions are met: first, the reinsured must prove that it is obliged to indemnify its original assured; secondly, the reinsured is required to prove that the reinsurer is liable under the contract of reinsurance.[21]

2.12 In this regard, the reinsured incurs a loss under the reinsurance agreement when its obligation to indemnify the original assured arises. This is the case when the reinsured's liability under the underlying contract has been established and quantified by judgment, arbitral award or binding settlement.[22] The term 'loss' in this sense refers to a financial detriment sustained by the reinsured.

2.13 Under an excess of loss reinsurance contract, the reinsurer covers the reinsured's loss 'only on a sum in excess of a particular figure on the risk'.[23] The reinsurer affords cover for the part of the loss that exceeds this particular figure.[24] To achieve this, the parties generally include a so-called 'liability clause' in which they define what a loss is and what deductible shall be applied to it.[25] Traditionally,

---

18 Clarke (n 8) para 16–2B.

19 Clarke (n 8) para 16–2B.

20 Cf *Kuwait Airways Corp v Kuwait Insurance Co SAK* (n 6) where Rix J held that when a party was deprived of an aircraft, the latter was only lost after a period of 'wait and see'; *Scott v The Copenhagen Reinsurance Co (UK) Ltd* (n 2) [73]–[77] (Rix LJ).

21 *Hill v Mercantile and General Reinsurance Co Plc* (1996) 1 WLR 1239 (HL) 1251 (Lord Mustill). It is to be noted, however, that 'the parties are free to agree on ways of proving whether these requirements are satisfied'. More specifically, the parties may do so by agreeing on a follow the settlements clause in their contract of reinsurance.

22 *Re Eddystone Marine Insurance Co* [1892] 2 Ch 423 (Comm) 427 f (Stirling J); Stephen Lewis, '"Pay as Paid" and the Ultimate Net Loss Clause' (1995) 3 International Insurance Law Review 308, 308; Merkin, Hodgson and Tyldesley (n 3) para 18–062.

23 Colin Edelman and Andrew Burns, *The Law of Reinsurance* (2nd edn, OUP 2013) para 1.49.

24 Edelman and Burns (n 23) para 1.49.

25 Regularly, they also define a cover limit. As pointed out in *Countrywide Assured Group Plc v Marshall* [2002] EWHC 2082 (Comm), [2003] 1 All ER 237 [13] (Morison J), multiple individual losses do not have to be aggregated the same way for the purposes of applying the deductible and the cover limit.

the reinsured's loss under the contract of reinsurance is referred to as 'ultimate net loss'.[26] Such a clause may read:

> *The Reinsurers shall only be liable if and when the Ultimate Net Loss sustained by the Reinsured in respect of interest coming within the scope of the Reinsuring Clause exceeds £3,000,000 or U.S. or Can. $6,000,000 each and every loss (…) arising out of one event (…).*[27]

2.14 The term 'ultimate net loss' may be defined as

> *(…) the sum actually paid by the Reinsured in settlement of losses or liability after making deductions for all recoveries, (…) and shall include all adjustment expenses arising from the settlement of claims (…).*[28]

2.15 As is obvious from these clauses, the term 'ultimate net loss' refers to the loss that is tested against the deductible as defined in the contract of reinsurance.[29] Since the clause contains aggregation language, the reinsured's ultimate net loss may be composed of multiple individual losses 'arising out of one event'.[30]

2.16 It appears to be imprecise, however, to say that the reinsured's ultimate net loss corresponds with 'the sum it actually paid in settlement of losses'. In fact, the reinsured's relevant loss under the contract of reinsurance, ie the loss to be tested against the deductible and the cover limit, depends on the aggregation mechanism contained in the reinsurance agreement.[31] As the aggregation mechanism in the underlying contract may differ from the one in the reinsurance policy,[32] the reinsured may pay more[33] in settling its inward claims than the amount of the loss to be tested

---

26 Klaus Gerathewohl, *Rückversicherung, Grundlagen und Praxis*, vol 2 (Verlag Versicherungswirtschaft eV 1979) 904, 912, 921; Marcel Grossmann, *Rückversicherung – Eine Einführung* (2nd edn, Institut für Versicherungswirtschaft an der Hochschule St Gallen 1982) 128; Lewis (n 22) 309; Jacquetta Castle, 'Reinsurance: Net Loss Clause' (1996) 4 International Insurance Law Review 133; Barlow Lyde and Gilbert LLP, *Reinsurance Practice and the Law* (Informa Law from Routledge 2009) para 18.23; Andreas Schwepcke and Alexandra Vetter, *Praxishandbuch: Rückversicherung* (VVW 2017) paras 957, 962, 991; Peter Liebwein, *Klassische und moderne Formen der Rückversicherung* (3rd edn, VVW 2018) 295; Stefan Pohl and Joseph Iranya, *The ABC of Reinsurance* (VVW 2018) 28; Butler and Merkin (n 3) paras C–0199 ff.

27 This liability clause was discussed in *Charter Reinsurance Co Ltd v Fagan* [1996] AC 313 (HL) 382 (Lord Mustill).

28 This definition of 'ultimate net loss' was considered in *Charter Reinsurance Co Ltd v Fagan* (n 27) 382 (Lord Mustill).

29 Cf Butler and Merkin (n 3) para C–0202.

30 Schwepcke and Vetter (n 26) para 957; Butler and Merkin (n 3) paras C–0219, C–0221. Additionally, the ultimate net loss may include costs related to the reinsured's efforts to settle the claims under the underlying contract. The reinsured's recoveries and all salvages as well as all claims upon other re-insurers may be deducted from that sum.

31 Cf Rob Merkin, 'The Christchurch Earthquakes Insurance and Reinsurance Issues' (2012) 18 Canterbury Law Review 119, 145, who states that '[a] typical XL reinsuring clause will indemnify the reinsured in respect of its "ultimate net loss", defined as the sum paid by the reassured in settlement of each and every loss (…). The key point is nevertheless the basis of aggregation, because that determines which losses can be added together to determine whether the trigger point for cover has been reached'.

32 Cf paras 7.21 ff.

33 Due to the principle of indemnity, the ultimate net loss in the reinsurance may not, however, be greater than the sum paid by the reinsured in the underlying contract.

against the deductible and the cover limit under the reinsurance agreement, ie the ultimate net loss.

2.17 In summary, the ultimate net loss is a financial loss that may be the product of aggregation, ie an aggregated loss. It is a loss that is incurred by the reinsured as opposed to the original assured.[34]

3 Individual losses to be aggregated

2.18 Where the contract of reinsurance contains an aggregation clause providing for the aggregation of losses based on causation,[35] the ultimate net loss incurred by the reinsured may be calculated by aggregating all the multiple individual losses arising from a unifying factor. First, it will be demonstrated that the relevant individual losses are suffered by the primary insured and not by the reinsured or the retrocessionaire in paying for the losses under their respective contracts of reinsurance. Second, two different approaches for determining an individual loss will be discussed.

3.1 Individual loss suffered by the primary insured

2.19 The individual losses are determined pursuant to the primary insurance relationship and not the reinsurance relationship.[36] To this effect, in *Caudle v Sharp*, the Court of Appeal held that '[t]he losses (...) in question are those affecting the original insured, rather than the 'loss' suffered by the insurer when he pays the claims'.[37]

2.20 The same is true when it comes to retrocession agreements. In order to determine the individual losses to be aggregated, it is necessary to look at the relationship between the primary assured and the primary insurer as opposed to the one between the retrocedent and the retrocessionaire.[38] This was confirmed by the Court of Appeal's judgment in *Mann v Lexington Insurance Co*.[39] This case concerned a chain of Indonesian supermarkets that were insured under one first-party insurance policy. This policy was reinsured and retroceded in the London Market. In the retrocession agreement, the parties provided for a deductible as well as a cover limit per occurrence.[40]

---

34 Cf Butler and Merkin (n 3) para C–0202. For the individual loss suffered by the original assured, see paras 2.19 ff.

35 This is in contrast to the aggregation of unrelated losses as in reinsurance contracts that operate on an aggregate basis, see for instance para 1.53.

36 Cf Barlow Lyde and Gilbert LLP (n 26) para 4.54, who state that it was the 'smaller original claims' that are aggregated into 'one reinsurance loss'; Terry O'Neill, Jan Woloniecki and Franziska Arnold-Dwyer, *The Law of Reinsurance in England and Bermuda* (5th edn, Sweet & Maxwell/Thomson Reuters 2019) para 5–117, observe that the aggregation of multiple claims under a primary insurance policy are also relevant for contracts of reinsurance.

37 *Caudle v Sharp* [1995] CLC 642 (CA) 648, 652 (Evans LJ).

38 Cf *Equitas Ltd v R and Q Reinsurance Co (UK) Ltd* [2009] EWHC 2787 (Comm), [2009] 2 CLC 706 [11] (Gross J).

39 *Mann v Lexington Insurance Co* [2000] EWCA Civ 256, [2000] CLC 1409, 1422 f (Waller LJ).

40 *Mann v Lexington Insurance Co* (n 39) 1414 (Waller LJ).

2.21 In the course of civil unrest, which preceded the Indonesian president's resignation, 22 of the insured stores were damaged. The primary insurers as well as the reinsurers paid separate claims in relation to each of the stores. By contrast, the retrocessionaire argued that the individual losses at the 22 stores were to be treated as one single loss that arose out of one occurrence.

2.22 It was undisputed that the relevant individual losses to which the aggregation clauses in the reinsurance and the retrocession contracts applied were suffered by the primary assureds, ie the owners of the supermarkets.[41]

2.23 The fact that the individual losses relevant in the context of aggregation are suffered by the primary insured is further confirmed in *Axa Reinsurance (UK) Ltd v Field*.[42] In his speech, Lord Mustill noted that where both the underlying contract and the reinsurance contract contain aggregation language, the parties do not necessarily intend the two clauses to have the same effect.[43] If the respective clauses have different effects, an aggregation gap will arise.[44] This means that the mode of adding together individual losses in the underlying contract differs from the mode of adding together individual losses in the reinsurance policy. If 'the parties intended the provisions for aggregation in the direct policy and in the reinsurance [contract] to be the same' they should, Lord Mustill explained, 'make sure that the aggregation clauses are the same'.[45]

2.24 If identical aggregation clauses in the direct policy and the reinsurance contract produce the same effect, they must add together the same individual losses. These can only be individual losses suffered by the original insured as only losses sustained by the primary assured–as opposed to losses sustained by a reinsured–exist under a policy of primary insurance.

2.25 In summary, the individual losses to be aggregated are losses affecting the original assured, rather than losses suffered by reinsureds or retrocedents when they pay out insurance or reinsurance money.

3.2 Determination of what constitutes an individual loss

2.26 In order to aggregate multiple individual losses, it is necessary to define and delimit one individual loss. In English law, different approaches for determining an individual loss have been adopted: insured unit and peoples' actions.

---

41 *Mann v Lexington Insurance Co* (n 39).

42 *Axa Reinsurance (UK) Ltd v Field* (1996) 1 WLR 1026 (HL).

43 *Axa Reinsurance (UK) Ltd v Field* (n 42) 1033 f (Lord Mustill).

44 As to the notion of 'aggregation gap' and the different means to deal with the adverse effects associated with such a gap, see paras 7.32 ff, 7.41 ff.

45 *Axa Reinsurance (UK) Ltd v Field* (n 42) 1034 (Lord Mustill).

a Insured Unit as The Basis of an Individual Loss

2.27 In the *Dawson's Field Arbitration*, the hijacking of four aircraft in 1970 was considered. One of the aircraft was destroyed in Cairo and the remaining were flown to Dawson's Field, where they were ultimately set on fire and destroyed.[46]

2.28 The case involved an excess of loss reinsurance agreement covering each and every loss arising out of one event in the excess of a particular sum. In this context, the arbitral tribunal was, first, required to determine the number of individual losses. It argued that if multiple aircraft were insured under one policy, the destruction of each insured unit, ie of each aircraft, was to be considered an individual loss.[47] Hence, the tribunal based its findings on one insured unit, ie on one risk.[48]

2.29 Depending on the type of cover, each insured unit is listed in the policy.[49] Often, the insured unit is, however, not defined in detail. In this regard, Kiln notes that providing a definition of one risk is a difficult task. He elaborates that '[i]n simpler times a single building within four walls, separated by a firebreak from other properties, was one risk. Now a large warehouse with a party wall trough the room may be two risks'.[50] The determination of an insured unit is, thus, a matter of contract construction.[51]

2.30 In *Mitsubishi Electric UK Ltd v Royal London Insurance (UK) Ltd*, an insurance policy relating to extensive building works in the City of London was to be construed. The deductibles provision stated that '[t]he first £250,000 of each and every loss in respect of any component part' shall be retained by the assured. Hence, the policy in question defined the relevant individual loss by reference to a 'component part'. Determining the relevant loss under this specific policy, thus, hinged upon the definition of what a 'component part' in a toilet module was.[52]

---

46 *Dawson's Field Arbitration*, quoted in: *Kuwait Airways Corp v Kuwait Insurance Co SAK* (n 6).

47 *Dawson's Field Arbitration*, quoted in: *Kuwait Airways Corp v Kuwait Insurance Co SAK* (n 6). Then a further question arose as to whether these individual losses all resulted from one single event and therefore were to be aggregated.

48 Cf also Klaus Gerathewohl, *Rückversicherung, Grundlagen und Praxis*, vol 1 (Verlag Versicherungswirtschaft eV 1976) 128. It is to be noted that in this context, the notion of 'risk' is not used to refer to an uncertainty about whether the insured peril will materialise. Nor is it used to indicate one reinsured original policy. Rather, the word refers to each insured unit; Grossmann (n 26) 121; Liebwein (n 26) 190.

49 See, for instance, *Kuwait Airways Corp v Kuwait Insurance Co SAK* (n 6), where the policy contained a schedule listing the 23 insured aircraft with their agreed values.

50 Robert Kiln, *Reinsurance in Practice* (4th edn, Witherby 1991) 194.

51 Cf Schwepcke and Vetter (n 26) para 916. It should be noted that if the contract of reinsurance contains a definition of 'loss', this definition does generally not determine what an individual loss is. Rather, as individual losses are suffered by the primary insured, determining the meaning of an individual loss should be undertaken based on the insured units described in the primary insurance policy.

52 *Mitsubishi Electric UK Ltd v Royal London Insurance (UK) Ltd* [1994] CLC 367 (CA) 371 (Sir Thomas Bingham MR).

2.31 The fact that what constitutes an individual loss is to be determined based on the insured unit does not mean that the individual loss is not financial in nature. On the contrary, each individual loss constitutes a financial detriment. Aggregation clauses provide for a mechanism to add together the financial detriments incurred through each individual loss for the purposes of determining the ultimate net loss.[53]

b Peoples' Action as The Basis of an Individual Loss

2.32 However, it is not always possible to express the insured subject matter as an insured unit. In both the contexts of first- and third-party insurance, there are often no insured units listed in the insurance policies.

2.33 In cases concerning aggregation clauses, the individual losses subject to aggregation are usually not explicitly determined.[54] In order to understand what an individual loss is, it, therefore, appears appropriate to analyse decisions concerning the definition of what constitutes one loss under insurance contracts that do not contain any aggregation clause. Whenever there is no aggregation clause in a contract of insurance, an individual loss must be the relevant loss.[55]

2.34 In *Glencore International AG v Alpina Insurance Co Ltd,* for instance, the Commercial Court was required to construe a policy providing cover against any risks of loss and damage to oil in which Glencore acquired an interest.[56]

2.35 After one of Glencore's business partners, MTI, misappropriated large quantities of oil over a period of many months, mainly by drawing without authority on stocks held to the order of Glencore, the Commercial Court was required to determine the number of losses. It expressly noted that the policy did not contain any aggregation language. Consequently, the court was required to determine the number of individual losses that had occurred.

2.36 The Commercial Court held that where 'goods are stolen on several occasions from the same location by the same person using the same method' a separate loss occurred on each occasion.[57] In the case in question, this meant that Glencore suffered a separate loss 'each time MTI drew oil from the bulk and disposed of it without authority'.[58] Rather than determining the individual losses by reference to insured units, the Commercial Court defined the individual losses by reference to the actions of

---

53 For the notion of 'ultimate net loss', see paras 2.11 ff.

54 An exception is the *Dawson's Field Arbitration*, quoted in: *Kuwait Airways Corp v Kuwait Insurance Co SAK* (n 6).

55 In fact, in the absence of an aggregation clause, individual losses are not to be aggregated, see *Mabey and Johnson Ltd v Ecclesiastical Insurance Office Plc* [2000] CLC 1570 (Comm). See also Merkin, Hodgson and Tyldesley (n 3) para 11–321.

56 *Glencore International AG v Alpina Insurance Co Ltd* [2003] EWHC 2792 (Comm), [2004] 1 All ER 766 [11] (Moore-Bick J).

57 *Glencore International AG v Alpina Insurance Co Ltd* (n 56) [293] (Moore-Bick J).

58 *Glencore International AG v Alpina Insurance Co Ltd* (n 56) [304] (Moore-Bick J).

those who caused the losses. As there were multiple separate acts of drawing oil from Glencore's stock, multiple separate individual losses had occurred.[59]

2.37 On a closer look and considering what the Commercial Court had stated *obiter*, this is remarkable. In fact, it noted *obiter* that where **several losses** were related, determining the number of losses was a complicated matter. For example, 'where an arsonist sets fire to two adjacent tanks in the course of a single attack', this might constitute one single loss. Similarly, the Commercial Court noted, 'if thieves enter a warehouse containing bagged goods which they remove using a number of different vehicles, (...) it is difficult to see how that could be regarded as more than one loss'. In both examples, the court stated that 'the **loss** occurred on one occasion in the course of a single enterprise'.[60]

2.38 This could mean one of two things: Either the Commercial Court may have decided that, despite the absence of aggregation language, multiple individual losses aggregate based on the unifying factor that they occurred on the same occasion in the course of a single enterprise.[61] Considering the decision in *Mabey and Johnson Ltd v Ecclesiastical Insurance Office Plc,* this would represent quite a conflicting approach. In fact, in the latter case, the Commercial Court expressly held that in the absence of an aggregation clause one cannot simply imply an aggregation mechanism.[62]

2.39 Alternatively, the Commercial Court may have decided that because the loss occurred on one occasion in the course of one enterprise, there was but one single big individual loss. Yet, this approach might be subject to a logical fallacy. If all the financial detriment incurred by the primary assured in the course of one action or one enterprise is to be considered one single individual loss, then it would never be possible to aggregate a number of losses resulting from the same act or event.[63] As there would be only one individual loss, there would be nothing to be aggregated. Determining an individual loss by reference to the actions out of which a claim arises undermines the concept of aggregation because those actions[64] are generally the factors upon which multiple individual losses are aggregated.

2.40 There are other English cases in which the issue of the number of losses under insurance agreements without aggregation clauses is discussed. In these cases, the courts held that if damage had been inflicted by the same person in multiple unrelated acts, each act causes a separate loss. More specifically, in *Pennsylvania Co for Insurances on Lives and Granting Annuities v Mumford*, the insurance policy before the court provided cover for all losses incurred because any securities as described in

---

59 *Glencore International AG v Alpina Insurance Co Ltd* (n 56) [304] (Moore-Bick J).

60 *Glencore International AG v Alpina Insurance Co Ltd* (n 56) [292] (Moore-Bick J).

61 Cf *Glencore International AG v Alpina Insurance Co Ltd* (n 56) [293] (Moore-Bick J).

62 *Mabey and Johnson Ltd v Ecclesiastical Insurance Office Plc* (n 55) 1573 f (Morison J). For more information on this aspect, see paras 3.5 ff.

63 This would at least be the case where so-called event-based aggregation is concerned. For more details as to the subject matter of event-based aggregation, see paras 3.27 ff and 4.1 ff.

64 In aggregation clauses, such an action is often referred to as an act, an event, an occurrence, an accident, etc. For more information regarding the unifying factors commonly used in aggregation clauses, see paras 3.25 ff.

the policy were stolen, misappropriated or made away with.[65] In this case, one of the assured's employees misappropriated securities belonging to four women on 41 different occasions. The court held that there was a separate loss for each of the 41 instances of misappropriation.[66] Accordingly, the Court of Appeal seems to have determined the number of individual losses by reference to the actions of those who have caused loss and damage.

2.41 Similarly, in *Dornoch Ltd v Mauritius Union Assurance Co Ltd*, a bank employee had drawn down client funds from their bank accounts on multiple instances without the clients' knowledge. The deductible clause referred to 'any one loss'. The Commercial Court stated that each transfer of money 'was a separate conscious act (...) against one or other of a range of different accounts'.[67] Hence, it held that each transfer represented a separate individual loss. In this instance, the Commercial Court determined an individual loss by reference to the actions of the person who caused loss and damage.

2.42 In summary, it is sometimes not possible to determine an individual loss by reference to an insured unit. On repeated occasions, English courts have defined one individual loss by reference to the actions of those who had caused the loss and damage. In this regard, it can be noted that legal uncertainty arises as to whether the actions or acts of those who cause loss and damage define one single loss or whether they constitute a unifying factor upon which multiple individual losses are to be aggregated.

4 The notion of 'claim'

4.1 The term 'claim' in general

2.43 The notion of 'claim' is often used for multiple different purposes in a single insurance or reinsurance contract.[68] Therefore, where the parties provide for a definition of the term in their contract of reinsurance, this definition is rarely suitable for every use of the term:[69]

2.44 As elaborated by Merkin, insurance policies only cover claims that relate to losses arising from the materialisation of an insured peril.[70] In *West Wake Price and Co v Ching*, the Commercial Court considered 'the primary meaning of the word 'claim'–whether used in a popular sense or in a strict legal sense is such as to attach it to the object that is claimed (...)'.[71] This meaning is confirmed by an entry in the

---

65 *Pennsylvania Co for Insurances on Lives and Granting Annuities v Mumford* [1920] 2 KB 537 (CA) 537. The policy in question was a Lloyd's Banks' and Trust Companies' Policy.

66 *Pennsylvania Co for Insurances on Lives and Granting Annuities v Mumford* (n 65) 547 (Warrington LJ).

67 *Dornoch Ltd v Mauritius Union Assurance Co Ltd (No 2)* [2007] EWHC 155 (Comm), [2007] Lloyd's Rep IR 350 [33] (Steel J).

68 See for instance *Standard Life Assurance Ltd v Oak Dedicated Ltd* [2008] EWHC 222 (Comm), [2008] 2 All ER 916 [97] (Tomlinson J); Butler and Merkin (n 3) para C–0242.

69 *Haydon v Lo and Lo* (1997) 1 WLR 198 (PC) 205 (Lord Lloyd); Clarke (n 8) para 17–4D; Merkin, Hodgson and Tyldesley (n 3) para 11–336.

70 Merkin, Hodgson and Tyldesley (n 3) para 11–336.

71 *West Wake Price and Co v Ching* [1957] 1 WLR 45 (QB) 55 (Devlin J).

Oxford English Dictionary, according to which the term 'claim' means '[a] demand for something due; an assertion of a right to something'.[72]

2.45 Another context is where an insurance or reinsurance policy is written on a claims-made basis and the insurer's or reinsurer's liability is triggered only if a claim is made against the primary assured within the policy period.[73] In this sense, the term 'claim' refers to a demand against the primary assured. Yet, in this instance, the focus does not lie on whether something is due but rather on whether the claim against the assured has been made within the currency of the policy.

2.46 The third option is that the term 'claim' may be used in the context of aggregation. In fact, an aggregation clause may provide for adding together individual claims into one single claim for the purposes of testing the latter against a deductible or a cover limit.[74]

4.2 The term 'claim' in aggregation clauses

2.47 For the purposes of this analysis, it is this third use of the term 'claim' that is of importance. For example, in *Lloyd's TSB General Insurance Holdings Ltd v Lloyd's Bank Group Insurance Co Ltd*, the House of Lords interpreted the following aggregation clause:

> If a series of third party **claims** shall result from any single act or omission (…) then, irrespective of the total number of **claims**, all such third party **claims** shall be considered to be a single third party claim for the purposes of the application of the deductible.[75]

2.48 In *Municipal Mutual Insurance Ltd v Sea Insurance Co Ltd*, Waller J at first instance noted that 'the question whether **claims** are separate or single must depend on the facts of the particular case and (…) on the words of the policy with which one is dealing'.[76] Stating this, Waller J did not try to determine what an individual claim was but rather to distinguish individual claims from an aggregated claim, which is composed of multiple individual claims. To this effect, he quoted from the Court of Appeal's judgment in *Thorman v New Hampshire Insurance Co (UK) Ltd*:

> An architect has separate contracts with separate building owners. The architect makes the same negligent mistakes in relation to each. The claims have a factor in common, namely the same negligent mistake, and to this extent they are related, but clearly they are separate claims (…).[77]

---

72 *Oxford English Dictionary* (100th edn, 2020), 'Claim'. See also *West Wake Price and Co v Ching* (n 71) 55 (Devlin J); O'Neill, Woloniecki and Arnold-Dwyer (n 36) para 5–115.

73 Merkin, Hodgson and Tyldesley (n 3) para 11–336; Butler and Merkin (n 3) para C–0243.

74 Merkin, Hodgson and Tyldesley (n 3) para 11–336. Cf also Butler and Merkin (n 3) para C–0247.

75 *Lloyd's TSB General Insurance Holdings Ltd v Lloyd's Bank Group Insurance Co Ltd* (n 1) [12] (Lord Hoffmann), [33] (Lord Hobhouse) (emphasis added). It should be noted that this case concerned a primary insurance policy. As the subject matter of aggregation appears to be the same in primary insurance and reinsurance, the case nevertheless bears relevance in the context of reinsurance.

76 *Municipal Mutual Insurance Ltd v Sea Insurance Co Ltd* [1996] CLC 1515 (Comm) 1521 (Waller J) (emphasis added).

77 *Thorman v New Hampshire Insurance Co (UK) Ltd* [1987] 1 Lloyd's Rep 7 (CA) 11 f (Sir John Donaldson MR).

2.49 It appears as if aggregation clauses referring to 'claims' instead of 'losses' are mostly used where third-party risks are insured or reinsured, as the case may be.[78] Professional liability policies in particular regularly contain aggregation clauses on an 'each and every claim' basis.[79] The reason for this is almost certainly that where third-party risks are concerned, a primary assured suffers a loss only if a third party has made a claim against the primary assured and the assured's liability for that loss has been established and quantified by judgment, arbitral award or binding settlement.[80]

2.50 Yet, it is important to note that aggregation clauses do not always use the term 'claim' instead of the term 'loss' where third-party risks are insured or re-insured. On the contrary, where third-party liability risks are involved, aggregation clauses often provide for an aggregation of multiple individual losses rather than multiple individual claims.[81]

2.51 In the context of aggregation, the relevant claim generally is a claim by the third party against the primary assured.[82] The term 'claim' refers to the sum of money sought by the third party.[83] The question of whether there is one or multiple claims must be determined based on the underlying facts and not the formulation of a claim by the third party.[84] Furthermore, the number of causes of action is not determinative for the number of claims.[85] For instance, where a third

---

78 *Countrywide Assured Group Plc v Marshall* (n 25) [3] (Morison J); *Lloyd's TSB General Insurance Holdings Ltd v Lloyd's Bank Group Insurance Co Ltd* (n 1) [8]–[10] (Lord Hoffmann); *Standard Life Assurance Ltd v Oak Dedicated Ltd* (n 68) [14] (Tomlinson J); *Beazley Underwriting Ltd v Travelers Co Inc* [2011] EWHC 1520 (Comm) [1] (Clarke J); *AIG Europe Ltd v Woodman* [2017] UKSC 18, [2018] 1 All ER 936 [9] (Lord Toulson SCJ); *Spire Healthcare Ltd v Royal and Sun Alliance Insurance Plc* [2018] EWCA Civ 317, [2018] Lloyd's Rep IR 425 [1] (Simon LJ); O'Neill, Woloniecki and Arnold-Dwyer (n 36) para 5–117. It is to be noted that some of these cases concern aggregation clauses in primary insurance contracts. Yet, they are also relevant in respect of the subject matter of aggregation in cases of reinsurance.

79 O'Neill, Woloniecki and Arnold-Dwyer (n 36) para 5–117.

80 Merkin, Hodgson and Tyldesley (n 3) para 21–081.

81 See for instance *Caudle v Sharp* (n 37); *Axa Reinsurance (UK) Ltd v Field* (n 42); *Brown (RE) v GIO Insurance Ltd* [1998] Lloyd's Rep IR 201 (CA); *Denby v English and Scottish Maritime Insurance Co Ltd; Yasuda Fire and Marine Co of Europe Ltd v Lloyd's Underwriting Syndicates no 209, 356* [1998] Lloyd's Rep IR 343 (CA), [1998] CLC 870; *IRB Brasil Resseguros SA v CX Reinsurance Co Ltd* [2010] EWHC 974 (Comm), [2010] Lloyd's Rep IR 560; *MIC Simmonds v Gammell* [2016] EWHC 2515 (Comm), [2016] Lloyd's Rep IR 693.

82 Cf Butler and Merkin (n 3) para C–0243; *Australia and New Zealand Bank Ltd v Colonial and Eagle Wharves Ltd* [1960] 2 Lloyd's Rep 241 (Comm).

83 In *Citibank NA v Excess Insurance Co Ltd* [1999] Lloyd's Rep IR 122 (Comm) 127 (Thomas J), it was stated that the underlying facts of a case were determinative of the question as to whether there was one claim or multiple claims and not the formulation of the claim by the third party. However, the Commercial Court clarified that it did not follow from this that there was a separate claim for each separate cause of action; *West Wake Price and Co v Ching* (n 71) 57 (Devlin J); Butler and Merkin (n 3) para C–0244.

84 *Haydon v Lo and Lo* (n 69) 204 (Lord Lloyd); *Citibank NA v Excess Insurance Co Ltd* (n 83) 127 (Thomas J).

85 In *Citibank NA v Excess Insurance Co Ltd* (n 83) 127 (Thomas J), it was stated that the underlying facts of a case were determinative of the question of whether there was one claim or multiple claims and not the formulation of the claim by the third party. However, the Commercial Court clarified that it did not follow from this that there was a separate claim for each separate cause of action; *Haydon v Lo and Lo* (n 69) 204 (Lord Lloyd); *West Wake Price and Co v Ching* (n 71) 57 (Devlin J); Butler and Merkin (n 3) para C–0244.

party brings a claim against a primary assured for misappropriating funds on a number of occasions, there is one single claim rather than one claim per act of misappropriation.[86]

2.52 As has been mentioned, aggregation clauses in reinsurance policies concerning third party liability sometimes contain references to individual losses rather than to individual claims.[87] In this context, it is unclear whether one individual claim can be equated with one individual loss. For instance, in *Glencore International AG v Alpina Insurance Co Ltd*, the cover limit of an insurance policy was defined by reference to 'any one loss'. In determining the number of individual losses, it was distinguished from the insurance policy before the Privy Council in *Haydon v Lo and Lo* which defined its cover limit by reference to 'any one claim'. In the former case, it was held that the insured incurred a separate loss with each act misappropriating his oil,[88] whereas it was determined in the latter case that multiple instances of misappropriating funds caused one single loss.[89] However, it must be noted that *Glencore International AG v Alpina Insurance Co Ltd* was not distinguished from *Haydon v Lo and Lo* on the grounds of a difference in the concepts of 'claim' and 'loss', but rather due to the fact that the former case concerned an all-risks property insurance agreement and the latter concerned a professional liability contract.[90]

2.53 In *IRB Brasil Resseguros SA v CX Reinsurance Co Ltd*, it was stated that the 'witness gave detailed evidence regarding the nature and history of the losses, the basis on which the original insured settled the claims with the US third party claimants (...)'.[91] In this instance, the terms 'loss' and 'claim' appear to have been used synonymously. Similarly, an aggregation clause discussed by the Commercial Court in *Countrywide Assured Group Plc v Marshall*[92] seems to have used the terms 'claim' and 'loss' synonymously. It read: '"ANY CLAIM" or "ANY LOSS" shall mean one occurrence or all occurrences of a series consequent upon or attributable to one source or originating cause'.[93]

---

86 *Haydon v Lo and Lo* (n 69) 204 ff (Lord Lloyd). This appears particularly notable because English courts have repeatedly held that where several unrelated acts of misappropriation cause loss and damage, each act of misappropriation causes a separate 'loss'. See for instance *Glencore International AG v Alpina Insurance Co Ltd* (n 56). In this case, *Haydon v Lo and Lo* was not distinguished based on the terms 'loss' and 'claim' but rather by reference to the fact that the former was 'an all risk policy on goods' and not 'a "claims made" professional indemnity policy'.

87 See para 2.50.

88 *Glencore International AG v Alpina Insurance Co Ltd* (n 56) [304] (Moore-Bick J).

89 *Haydon v Lo and Lo* (n 69) 206 (Lord Lloyd).

90 *Glencore International AG v Alpina Insurance Co Ltd* (n 56) [300]–[302] (Moore-Bick J). Cf also *Australia and New Zealand Bank Ltd v Colonial and Eagle Wharves Ltd* (n 82), where it seems to have been held that every act that causes a loss constitutes a separate claim. However, the case was distinguished from *Haydon v Lo and Lo* (n 69) as the former concerned an all-risks policy whereas the latter concerned a professional liability insurance.

91 In this context, see also *IRB Brasil Resseguros SA v CX Reinsurance Co Ltd* (n 81) [29] (Burton J), where it was stated that the 'witnesses gave detailed evidence regarding the nature and history of the losses, the basis on which the original insured settled the claims with the US third party claimants (...)'. It seems that the Commercial Court equated the terms 'losses' and 'claims'.

92 *Countrywide Assured Group Plc v Marshall* (n 25).

93 *Countrywide Assured Group Plc v Marshall* (n 25) [2] (Morison J).

2.54 Yet, it is impossible to conclusively say that an aggregation clause providing for adding together multiple individual claims produces the same effect as one that provides for a mechanism to aggregate multiple individual losses.

5 The notion of 'occurrence'

2.55 The term 'occurrence' is not used consistently in the context of aggregation clauses.[94] In fact, it may be said that the inconsistent usage of the word leads to misunderstandings as to the operation of aggregation mechanisms. A clarification of the meaning of the term shall be attempted below.

5.1 Misleading usage of the term 'occurrence'

2.56 Reinsurance contracts are often taken out on an 'occurrence' basis or on a 'losses occurring during' basis.[95] If a contract of reinsurance provides cover on such a basis, the reinsurer 'is liable to indemnify the [reinsured] in respect of loss and damage which occurs within the period of cover (...)'.[96] The losses occurring during basis provides a mechanism to allocate individual losses to a specific period of cover.[97] In this context, the term 'occurrence' focuses on the timing of a loss. As the time when the loss happens or occurs is paramount, the parties sometimes simply speak of 'occurrence' when in fact they mean 'loss'.

2.57 It appears that the terminology used in the context of allocating losses has sometimes also been used when it comes to the aggregation of losses. This may be illustrated well with the Court of Appeal's judgment in *Seele Austria GmbH and Co KG v Tokio Marine Europe Insurance Ltd*. In this case, the parties to an insurance contract[98] provided that '(...) the Insurer hereby agrees to indemnify the Insured (...) in respect of any **occurrence** of loss or damage or liability during the period of insurance'[99] and that the insured retained liability for '[t]he first £100,000 of each and every **occurrence** or series of occurrences of loss or damage arising out of any one event'.[100]

2.58 The parties used the term 'occurrence' to indicate 'loss' both in their loss allocation provision and in their aggregation clause. Using the parties' language, the Court of Appeal stated that '[o]ne must start by identifying the occurrences of

---

94 Cf Butler and Merkin (n 3) para C–0223.

95 *Wasa International Insurance Co Ltd v Lexington Insurance Co* [2009] UKHL 40, [2009] 4 All ER 909 [74] (Lord Collins); Barlow Lyde and Gilbert LLP (n 26) para 27.19; Schwepcke and Vetter (n 26) paras 548 ff; Liebwein (n 26) 274 ff; O'Neill, Woloniecki and Arnold-Dwyer (n 36) paras 5–126 f.

96 *Wasa International Insurance Co Ltd v Lexington Insurance Co* (n 95) [74] (Lord Collins).

97 For more details on the subject matter of allocating losses to the correct reinsurance period, see paras 6.5 ff.

98 The Court of Appeal was concerned with a primary insurance policy. However, it is equally relevant in the context of reinsurance.

99 *Seele Austria GmbH Co v Tokio Marine Europe Insurance Ltd* [2008] EWCA Civ 441 [3] (Waller LJ) (emphasis added).

100 *Seele Austria GmbH Co v Tokio Marine Europe Insurance Ltd* (n 99) [3] (Waller LJ) (emphasis added).

damage in respect of which the insured is entitled to be indemnified, since it is to these that the aggregation provisions apply'.[101]

2.59 Hence, the notion of 'occurrence' was used to designate the individual losses to be aggregated. Similarly, in *Caudle v Sharp*, the Court of Appeal interpreted an aggregation clause which appears to equate the terms 'loss' and 'occurrence' to some extent.[102] The clause read: 'For the purpose of this reinsurance the term "each and every loss" shall be understood to mean each and every loss and/or occurrence (...) arising out of one event'.[103]

2.60 In this case, the reinsurance contract provided that each and every occurrence that arises from the same event shall be aggregated. The individual units to be aggregated were termed 'occurrences'.[104] Again, the term 'occurrence' was used to indicate 'loss'.

5.2 Regular meaning of the term 'occurrence' in aggregation clauses

2.61 In the context of aggregation, however, the term 'occurrence' generally has a different meaning.[105] In fact, despite the contract clause used in *Caudle v Sharp* distinguishing between occurrences and events,[106] the Court of Appeal held that

> '[l]oss' in the reinsurance context means at first sight the loss suffered by the reinsured by reason of his liability to the original insured, falling within his 'ultimate net loss' as defined in the contract. The relevant occurrence, strictly, is the making of a claim or the discovery of a loss by the original insured, **but the word more readily means the occurrence out of which a claim arises**, for loss suffered by the original insured, such as storm damage, flood damage or the like, or in the case of professional indemnity losses, the negligent act or omission of the insured.[107]

2.62 In this passage, the Court of Appeal clarifies that in the context of aggregation the term 'occurrence' should not be used to indicate 'loss' but rather to denote a happening out of which one or multiple losses arise.[108] In line with this, the Commercial Court in *Kuwait Airways Corp v Kuwait Insurance Co SAK*, stated that '[a]n 'occurrence' (...) is not the same as a loss, for one occurrence may embrace a plurality of losses'.[109]

---

101 *Seele Austria GmbH Co v Tokio Marine Europe Insurance Ltd* (n 99) [54] (Moore-Bick LJ). It is to be noted that the relevant aggregation clause read '[t]he first £100,000 of each and every occurrence or series of occurrences of loss or damage arising out of any one event' [3]. Consequently, the terminology used by the Court of Appeal was based on the parties' language.

102 See *Caudle v Sharp* (n 37) 648, where Evans LJ noted that the terms 'loss' and 'occurrence' were equivalent.

103 *Caudle v Sharp* (n 37) 644 (Evans LJ).

104 As to the subject matter of individual losses to be aggregated, see paras 2.18 ff.

105 Cf Butler and Merkin (n 3) para C–0293, where they state that the term 'event' had a dual function: first, it determined whether or not the required event had occurred during the policy period. Secondly, it operated as a unifying factor. The same is true with regard to the term 'occurrence'.

106 Cf Clarke (n 8) para 17-4C3.

107 *Caudle v Sharp* (n 37) 648 (Evans LJ) (emphasis added).

108 Butler and Merkin (n 3) para C–0234.

109 *Kuwait Airways Corp v Kuwait Insurance Co SAK* (n 6).

2.63 In the same vein, it has repeatedly been held that the term 'occurrence' is interchangeable with the word 'event'.[110] More specifically, aggregation clauses usually provide that multiple individual losses be added together for the purposes of applying them to the deductible and the cover limit 'when they are linked by a unifying factor of some kind'.[111] An occurrence or an event can be such a unifying factor.[112] Therefore, it is of fundamental importance to distinguish between 'loss' and 'occurrence'.

2.64 In light of the aforementioned, it should be borne in mind that the parties to a reinsurance contract generally use the word 'occurrence' as a synonym for the term 'event' in terms concerning aggregation. In these cases, the parties agree that the unifying factor upon which individual losses shall be aggregated is an occurrence, a happening or an event.[113] Sometimes, however, the parties refer to the individual losses to be aggregated as 'individual occurrences'. Where this is the case, an occurrence is not to be understood as a unifying factor. Rather, the same rules apply as would have if the parties had used the term 'losses' to refer to the individual units to be aggregated.[114] It is, therefore, important to emphasise that the term 'occurrence' must be construed in the context of the contract in question.[115]

II Retention, deductible, excess point, attachment point

2.65 According to Pohl and Iranya, '[t]he backbone of every reinsurance program in a proportional or non-proportional treaty arrangement is the [c]edant's chosen retention'.[116] In the section below, the significance of the general concept of retention will be discussed. Thereafter, the terminology used in relation to the reinsured's retention in excess of loss reinsurance contracts as well as the relation between aggregation clauses and the reinsured's retention will be set out. Furthermore, the fact that the reinsured's retention may be variable will be addressed.

---

110 *Dawson's Field Arbitration*, as quoted in: *Kuwait Airways Corp v Kuwait Insurance Co SAK* (n 6); *American Centennial Insurance Co v INSCO Ltd* [1996] 1 LRLR 407 (Comm) 413 (Moore-Bick J); Barlow Lyde and Gilbert LLP (n 26) para 28.6; Kiran Soar, 'Interpretation of Wordings Key to Settling Aggregation Claims' [2010] LLID 7; Merkin, Hodgson and Tyldesley (n 3) para 11–324. See also *Aioi Nissay Dowa Insurance Co Ltd v Heraldglen Ltd and Advent Capital Ltd* [2013] EWHC 154 (Comm), [2013] 2 All ER 231 [20] (Field J); Clarke (n 8) para 17-4C3; Edelman and Burns (n 23) paras 4.55 ff.

111 *Lloyd's TSB General Insurance Holdings Ltd v Lloyd's Bank Group Insurance Co Ltd* (n 1) [14]–[15] (Lord Hoffmann); also quoted in: *Spire Healthcare Ltd v Royal and Sun Alliance Insurance Plc* (n 78) [23] (Simon LJ).

112 *Lloyd's TSB General Insurance Holdings Ltd v Lloyd's Bank Group Insurance Co Ltd* (n 1) [15] (Lord Hoffmann); Edelman and Burns (n 23) paras 4.52 ff.

113 Merkin, Hodgson and Tyldesley (n 3) para 11–325.

114 For the meanings of 'loss' and 'individual losses' and their relation, see paras 2.5 ff, 2.11 ff, 2.18 ff.

115 *Kuwait Airways Corp v Kuwait Insurance Co SAK* (n 6); *Mann v Lexington Insurance Co* (n 39) 1421 (Waller LJ); Butler and Merkin (n 3) para C–0237.

116 Pohl and Iranya (n 26) 160.

1 The concept of deductibles in general

2.66 Often, reinsureds cede a certain part of their risk to their reinsurer and retain the remaining part.[117] The portion of the risk that a reinsured does not cede to the reinsurer is termed 'retention'. In proportional reinsurance, the reinsured's retention is generally indicated as a percentage of the risk it assumed under the inward contract.[118] In non-proportional reinsurance, the reinsurer agrees to cover the part of a loss in excess of a particular figure on the risk.[119] The part of the loss below this figure is retained by the reinsured alone[120] or the reinsured together with another reinsurer.[121]

2.67 The reinsurer has a certain interest in knowing whether the reinsured retains a portion of the risk.[122] In *Kingscroft Insurance Co Ltd v Nissan Fire and Marine Insurance Co Ltd*, an expert witness stated that he regarded the 'retention as of considerable importance because it provides a measure of the reinsured's confidence in the business [it] is writing and provides a continuing incentive to underwrite responsibly'.[123]

2.68 The size of a retention is relevant for a number of reasons. First, as mentioned previously, the risk covered by the reinsured may represent more or less of an incentive to responsibly underwrite inward contracts.[124] Similarly, the reinsured will also behave differently in settling claims depending on the risk involved. In fact, the less exposure a reinsured has, the smaller is its incentive to defend claims made by the underlying assureds.[125] Secondly, the part of the risks retained by the reinsured is directly linked to its capital requirements as well as its liquidity.[126] Thirdly, depending on the size of the reinsured's retention, the extent of the reinsurer's liability varies. Consequently, the reinsurance premium is generally determined by taking into account the reinsured's retention.[127]

---

117 Barlow Lyde and Gilbert LLP (n 26) para 18.21.

118 Liebwein (n 26) 71.

119 Barlow Lyde and Gilbert LLP (n 26) para 4.45; Edelman and Burns (n 23) paras 1.49, 1.62.

120 *Lloyd's TSB General Insurance Holdings Ltd v Lloyd's Bank Group Insurance Co Ltd* (n 1) [30] (Lord Hobhouse). Cf also Barlow Lyde and Gilbert LLP (n 26) para 4.50; Edelman and Burns (n 23) para 1.36; Pohl and Iranya (n 26) 28.

121 *Lloyd's TSB General Insurance Holdings Ltd v Lloyd's Bank Group Insurance Co Ltd* (n 1) [30] (Lord Hobhouse); Barlow Lyde and Gilbert LLP (n 26) paras 18.21, 18.24.

122 Cf Pohl and Iranya (n 26) 160.

123 *Kingscroft Insurance Co Ltd v Nissan Fire and Marine Insurance Co Ltd* [1999] CLC 1875 (Comm) 1893 f (Moore-Bick J). See also Barlow Lyde and Gilbert LLP (n 26) para 18.20, who state that '[t]he presence and size of a retention is one way for the reinsurer to gauge exactly what the reinsured really thinks of the business originally accepted'.

124 *Kingscroft Insurance Co Ltd v Nissan Fire and Marine Insurance Co Ltd* (n 123) 1893 f (Moore-Bick J). See also Barlow Lyde and Gilbert LLP (n 26) para 18.20, who state that '[t]he presence and size of a retention is one way for the reinsurer to gauge exactly what the reinsured really thinks of the business originally accepted'.

125 Cf O'Neill, Woloniecki and Arnold-Dwyer (n 36) para 5–001.

126 Cf Gerathewohl (n 48) 143; Pohl and Iranya (n 26) 27, 161.

127 Gerathewohl (n 48) 174 ff.

2.69 Yet, despite the fact that it is quite common that the reinsured retains a certain part of its risk, the reinsured generally has a right to cede the entirety of it to one or multiple reinsurers.[128] In fact, under English law, there is no presumption and no term implied to the effect that the reinsured must retain any part of its risk.[129] In *Phoenix General Insurance Co of Greece SA v Halvanon Insurance Co Ltd*, Hobhouse J noted that there was 'no inconsistency between the idea of reinsurance and a nil retention'.[130] Consequently, the reinsured is only bound to retain a part of its risk if the contract of reinsurance contains an express warranty to this effect.[131] In *Assicurazioni Generali SpA v Arab Insurance Group (BSC)*, it was held that if it were stated in a line slip that the reinsured retained a certain percentage of the risk, this was merely a statement of fact and did not constitute a continuing warranty.[132]

2.70 By contrast, for example, under German and Swiss law, the reinsured's duty to retain a certain part of its risk is considered a trade usage.[133] Commentators argue that if the reinsured does not bear any of the risk it cannot be said to be 'insuring'. Thus, from a German perspective, the reinsured in such instances is considered to be a re-insurance intermediary rather than a primary insurer and reinsured.[134] Nevertheless, it is also the case under German law that the reinsured may cede the entirety of the risk if the reinsurer agrees.[135]

2.71 In the context of aggregation, the concept of retention is essential. The operation of the concept and its relation to the aggregation of losses shall, therefore, be addressed.

2 Terminology in excess of loss reinsurance and aggregation

2.72 Attempts are sometimes made to distinguish similar concepts in proportional and non-proportional reinsurance by using different terminology. However, such distinctions are not consistently observed in practice.[136] As the subject matter of ag-

---

128 Barlow Lyde and Gilbert LLP (n 26) para 18.21; Sieglinde Cannawurf and Andreas Schwepcke, '§ 8 Das Vertragsrecht der Rückversicherung' in Dieter W Lüer and Andreas Schwepcke (eds), *Rückversicherungsrecht* (CH Beck 2013) paras 44 f; O'Neill, Woloniecki and Arnold-Dwyer (n 36) para 6–035.

129 *Phoenix General Insurance Co of Greece SA v Halvanon Insurance Co Ltd* [1988] QB 216 (CA) 236, where Hobhouse J's first instance decision is transcribed; Barlow Lyde and Gilbert LLP (n 26) para 18.21; Cannawurf and Schwepcke (n 128) para 94; Schwepcke and Vetter (n 26) para 456; O'Neill, Woloniecki and Arnold-Dwyer (n 36) para 6–035.

130 *Phoenix General Insurance Co of Greece SA v Halvanon Insurance Co Ltd* (n 129) 236, where Hobhouse J's first instance decision is transcribed. See also Pohl and Iranya (n 26) 139.

131 Barlow Lyde and Gilbert LLP (n 26) para 18.21; Cannawurf and Schwepcke (n 128) para 94; O'Neill, Woloniecki and Arnold-Dwyer (n 36) para 6–035.

132 *Assicurazioni Generali SpA v Arab Insurance Group (BSC)* [2002] CLC 164 (Comm) 164, 171 f (Morison J).

133 Gerathewohl (n 48) 534; Cannawurf and Schwepcke (n 128) paras 93 f; Schwepcke and Vetter (n 26) paras 453 ff. Cf also Judgment of the Swiss Federal Supreme Court, *BGE 107 II 196* consideration 2, for the Swiss perspective.

134 Gerathewohl (n 48) 535; Schwepcke and Vetter (n 26) para 453; Pohl and Iranya (n 26) 160.

135 Gerathewohl (n 48) 537; Cannawurf and Schwepcke (n 128) para 93; Schwepcke and Vetter (n 26) para 454.

136 Birds, Lynch and Paul (n 7) para 35–016.

gregation is primarily an issue in excess of loss reinsurance, the reinsured's retention is described in light of the non-proportional business. Yet, some of the terms to be discussed may equally be used in proportional reinsurance and may bear the same or a slightly different meaning in the latter context.

2.73 In both facultative excess of loss reinsurance[137] and treaty excess of loss reinsurance,[138] the reinsurer agrees to indemnify the reinsured for the part of a loss that exceeds a predefined minimum figure,[139] ie a certain amount of money.[140] In *Charter Reinsurance Co Ltd (in Liquidation) v Fagan*, it was held that this minimum figure marked an excess point which triggered the reinsurer's liability.[141] The excess point is sometimes termed 'attachment point'.[142] The part of the loss that is below the excess or attachment point is the reinsured's retention,[143] deductible[144] or priority.[145] The part of the loss exceeding it is sometimes termed 'excess'.[146]

2.74 The reinsurer's ultimate net loss is generally tested against the excess or attachment point.[147] Regularly, this loss does not refer to a loss on an individual risk but rather to all losses arising out of a unifying factor of some kind.[148] In such a case, the part of the risk retained by the reinsured is sometimes referred to as a per event retention.[149]

2.75 To say that the reinsured must bear one deductible or retention per event is the equivalent of saying that all the individual losses arising out of one event are to be added

---

137 Edelman and Burns (n 23) para 1.49.

138 Edelman and Burns (n 23) para 1.62.

139 Barlow Lyde and Gilbert LLP (n 26) para 4.45; Edelman and Burns (n 23) paras 1.36, 1.49, 1.62; Birds, Lynch and Paul (n 7) para 35–015; Merkin, Hodgson and Tyldesley (n 3) para 18–004.

140 Cf Edelman and Burns (n 23) para 1.61.

141 *Charter Reinsurance Co Ltd (in Liquidation) v Fagan* (n 27) 341, where Mance J's first instance judgment was transcribed. See also Barlow Lyde and Gilbert LLP (n 26) para 4.45; Edelman and Burns (n 23) para 1.36.

142 *Charter Reinsurance Co Ltd (in Liquidation) v Fagan* (n 27) 390 (Lord Mustill); Munich Reinsurance America Inc, *Re-In-Sur-Ance: A Basic Guide to Facultative and Treaty Reinsurance* (2010) 22; O'Neill, Woloniecki and Arnold-Dwyer (n 36) para 7–014.

143 Barlow Lyde and Gilbert LLP (n 26) para 18.23; Pohl and Iranya (n 26) 27.

144 See, for instance, *Lloyd's TSB General Insurance Holdings Ltd v Lloyd's Bank Group Insurance Co Ltd* (n 1) [14], where Lord Hoffmann referred to a statement made by Moore-Bick J at first instance; *AIG Europe Ltd v Woodman* (n 78) [14] (Lord Toulson); *Spire Healthcare Ltd v Royal and Sun Alliance Insurance Plc* (n 78) [22]–[23] (Simon LJ); Edelman and Burns (n 23) para 1.62; Birds, Lynch and Paul (n 7) para 30–060; Pohl and Iranya (n 26) 27.

145 Pohl and Iranya (n 26) 27.

146 See, for instance, *Brown (RE) v GIO Insurance Ltd* (n 81) 202 (Waller LJ); *Countrywide Assured Group Plc v Marshall* (n 25) [13] (Morison J).

147 *Charter Reinsurance Co Ltd v Fagan* (n 27) 390; Pohl and Iranya (n 26) 28. For more information regarding the reinsurer's ultimate net loss, see paras 2.11 ff.

148 Pohl and Iranya (n 26) 31 f, where they refer to 'per event excess of loss'; Edelman and Burns (n 23) para 1.62. For more information regarding the difference between the reinsured's ultimate net loss and the individual losses to be aggregated, see paras 2.11 ff, 2.18 ff.

149 Pohl and Iranya (n 26) 161, depending on the unifying factor chosen by the parties, this may, of course, also be a per cause retention or per accident retention. Cf also Butler and Merkin (n 3) para C–021.

together to form one aggregated loss, which is then tested against the reinsured's deductible.[150] This means that, initially, the values of multiple individual losses are added together. Once this sum has been calculated, further expenses incurred by the reinsured in settling the inward claims are added to it and deductions for all recoveries are made, amounting to the reinsured's ultimate net loss.[151] The next step is to test whether the reinsured's deductible is exceeded and consequently the reinsurer's liability is triggered. This involves applying the reinsured's deductible to its ultimate net loss.[152]

2.76 This is perfectly summarised in *Lloyd's TSB General Insurance Holdings Ltd v Lloyd's Bank Group Insurance Co Ltd*, where Lord Hobhouse explained the relationship between the reinsured's deductible and the concept of aggregation with the following words:

> The (…) policy deductible, [is] the provision which states the level up to which the assured must self-insure (or insure elsewhere) before [it] has the right to recovery under the relevant policy. This provision may be qualified by an aggregation clause which enables the assured to aggregate self-insured losses together so as to exceed in aggregate the deductible and give a right of recovery.[153]

3 Variable excess

2.77 Contracts of reinsurance may provide that the reinsured's deductible is variable. In fact, the latter may vary depending on the reinsured's premium income. Further, the parties may provide that different deductibles apply with respect to different risks or perils.

3.1 Variation of deductible in relation to the net premium income

2.78 Instead of setting a predefined monetary sum as the applicable deductible,[154] the parties may provide for a more flexible mechanism. In particular, they may agree that the deductible applicable to a specific loss depends on factors such as the reinsured's premium income.

2.79 In *North Atlantic Insurance Co Ltd v Bishopsgate Insurance Ltd*, the Commercial Court dealt with a variable excess clause which provided that the reinsured's deductible was to be increased if its net premium income exceeded the estimated income.[155]

---

150 Cf Gerathewohl (n 48) 170 f; Edelman and Burns (n 23) para 4.52.

151 See, for instance, the clause discussed in *Charter Reinsurance Co Ltd v Fagan* (n 27) 382 f (Lord Mustill); Pohl and Iranya (n 26) 28.

152 *Charter Reinsurance Co Ltd v Fagan* (n 27) 390 (Lord Mustill); Pohl and Iranya (n 26) 28. For more information as to the reinsurer's ultimate net loss, see paras 2.11 ff.

153 *Lloyd's TSB General Insurance Holdings Ltd v Lloyd's Bank Group Insurance Co Ltd* (n 1) [30] (Lord Hobhouse).

154 Barlow Lyde and Gilbert LLP (n 26) para 4.45; Edelman and Burns (n 23) paras 1.36, 1.49, 1.62; Birds, Lynch and Paul (n 7) para 35–015; Merkin, Hodgson and Tyldesley (n 3) para 18–004.

155 *North Atlantic Insurance Co Ltd v Bishopsgate Insurance Ltd* [1998] 1 Lloyd's Rep 459 (Comm). See also Edelman and Burns (n 23) para 4.90.

2.80 If the monetary amount of the reinsured's deductible is flexible, this generally has no bearing on the aggregation mechanism. This is because the aggregation mechanism provides the mode of adding together multiple individual losses but does not itself define the figure against which the aggregated loss is tested.

3.2 Variation of deductible in relation to the reinsured risk or the peril reinsured against

2.81 It is equally possible that a reinsurance contract provides for different deductibles with respect to losses arising from different reinsured perils or with respect to different reinsured risks.[156] This may be appropriate where a variety of different risks or perils are reinsured and the probability of corresponding losses occurring differs from risk to risk or peril to peril.[157]

2.82 In 1976, Gerathewohl noted that, while it was uncommon, it sometimes happened that reinsurance contracts provided for different deductibles with respect to different risks or perils.[158] This was–he argued–because the compilation of statistics in this regard as well as the pricing of the reinsurance while taking into account different deductibles was utterly difficult.[159]

2.83 It may well be that this has changed with the increasing digitalisation of the insurance and reinsurance sector. In fact, it appears that it must be possible or at least become possible to provide for different deductibles depending on the reinsured risks and perils. This seems to be the equivalent of providing cover sublimits in relation to losses that occur to different risks or arise from different perils.[160]

2.84 If the parties to a contract of reinsurance agree on different deductibles with regard to different risks or perils, they may certainly also provide for different aggregation mechanisms with respect to these different deductibles.[161]

2.85 In such a case, the parties' agreement may be regarded as an indication that they do not intend for individual losses occurring to different groups of risks or arising from different perils[162] to be aggregated. If the contract of reinsurance is to be understood in this manner, the aggregation of individual losses will be undertaken separately for each deductible.

---

156 The term 'risk', in this sense, refers to the reinsured subject matter rather than the abstract danger of the materialisation of a peril.

157 Cf Gerathewohl (n 48) 157 ff.

158 Gerathewohl (n 48) 161.

159 Gerathewohl (n 48) 161.

160 See paras 2.91 ff.

161 Cf paras 2.94 f, where different aggregation mechanisms with regard to different sublimits are discussed.

162 Depending on whether different deductibles are agreed upon with respect to different risks or different perils.

III Cover, limit, cover limit

2.86 Excess of loss reinsurance policies may contain an overall cover limit as well as sublimits. In relation to both, the aggregation of losses is relevant.

1 Overall cover limit

2.87 The reinsurer's cover under an excess of loss reinsurance contract is regularly limited.[163] In *Lloyd's TSB General Insurance Holdings Ltd v Lloyd's Bank Group Insurance Co Ltd*, it was noted that reinsurance '[p]olicies (...) normally contain clauses which limit the liability of the insurer (...)'.[164] More specifically, such clauses may confine the reinsurer's liability to a certain monetary amount, the 'cover'.[165] The upper limit of the reinsurance cover is termed 'limit' or 'cover limit'.[166] In *Axa Reinsurance (UK) Ltd v Field*, Lord Mustill noted that provisions relating to limits were of cardinal importance in excess of loss reinsurance.[167]

2.88 Cover limits are generally applied to the reinsurer's ultimate net loss.[168] Frequently, the ultimate net loss does not refer to a loss on an individual risk but rather to an aggregated loss that consists of multiple individual losses.[169] In *Lloyd's TSB General Insurance Holdings Ltd v Lloyd's Bank Group Insurance Co Ltd*, Lord Hobhouse observed that (re-)insurance policies might provide 'a limit by reference to individual losses or claims but give the insurer the right to aggregate losses or claims so as to enable [it] to apply the limit to the aggregate'.[170]

2.89 To say that the individual losses may be aggregated to form one single loss, to which the cover limit applies, is the equivalent of saying that the cover limit in the contract of reinsurance applies per unifying factor, such as an event.[171]

2.90 Basically, this means that, first, the values of multiple individual losses are added together in accordance with the aggregation mechanism contained in the reinsurance contract.[172] Expenses incurred by the reinsured in settling its claims are then added to the

---

163 Barlow Lyde and Gilbert LLP (n 26) para 34.31; Edelman and Burns (n 23) para 4.52.

164 *Lloyd's TSB General Insurance Holdings Ltd v Lloyd's Bank Group Insurance Co Ltd* (n 1) [30] (Lord Hobhouse). It may be noted that the case dealt with a primary insurance policy rather than a re-insurance policy. Yet, the statement is equally applicable to contracts of reinsurance.

165 Barlow Lyde and Gilbert LLP (n 26) para 28.2; Edelman and Burns (n 23) para 4.52; Pohl and Iranya (n 26) 27.

166 *Lloyd's TSB General Insurance Holdings Ltd v Lloyd's Bank Group Insurance Co Ltd* (n 1) [30] (Lord Hobhouse); Gerathewohl (n 48) 208 ff, 241 ff; Barlow Lyde and Gilbert LLP (n 26) para 28.2; Edelman and Burns (n 23) para 4.52; Cannawurf and Schwepcke (n 128) para 369; Schwepcke and Vetter (n 26) para 858; Liebwein (n 26) 184, 192; Pohl and Iranya (n 26) 32.

167 *Axa Reinsurance (UK) Ltd v Field* (n 42) 1035 (Lord Mustill).

168 Pohl and Iranya (n 26) 28. For more information as to the reinsurer's ultimate net loss, see paras 2.11 ff.

169 Cf Schwepcke and Vetter (n 26) para 957.

170 *Lloyd's TSB General Insurance Holdings Ltd v Lloyd's Bank Group Insurance Co Ltd* (n 1) [30] (Lord Hobhouse).

171 Or, for that matter, to any unifying factor the aggregation clause may provide.

172 Cf Barlow Lyde and Gilbert LLP (n 26) para 34.32.

resulting sum of money. This new total amounts to the reinsured's ultimate net loss.[173] It is apparent that the reinsured's ultimate net loss hinges on the aggregation mechanism provided for in the reinsurance agreement. Second, it is to be tested whether the reinsured's ultimate net loss pierces the cover limit.[174] The reinsurer's liability is ultimately confined to the part of the ultimate net loss which exceeds the reinsured's retention but does not pierce the cover limit.

2 Sublimit

2.91 Reinsurance contracts often not only provide for overall cover limits but also for sublimits. If a reinsurance contract is taken out against a plurality of different perils, the parties may agree on a sublimit with respect to one particular peril. For instance, in a reinsurance contract taken out against the perils of earthquake and fire, the parties may agree on an overall cover limit as well as a sublimit for fire losses.

2.92 Similarly, multiple different assets or groups of assets may be reinsured under a contract of reinsurance. *Kuwait Airways Corp v Kuwait Insurance Co SAK* was concerned with reinsurance cover that had been bought for two different groups of assets. On the one hand, reinsurance was taken out for losses that occurred to the Kuwait Airways fleet of aircraft; on the other, losses to aircraft spares were reinsured.[175]

2.93 The reinsurance agreement provided for a cover limit of any one aircraft of 'US $300,000,000–any one occurrence, any one location'. By contrast, the policy provided for a cover limit with regard to the aircraft spare parts of 'US$10,000,000 any one item, US$30,000,000 any one sending and US$150,000,000 any one location'.[176] As can be seen from the clause discussed in *Kuwait Airways Corp v Kuwait Insurance Co SAK*, sublimits may also refer to losses that occur at any one location or in any one sending.

2.94 It has been discussed above that cover limits may apply to the aggregate of multiple individual losses.[177] This is equally true for sublimits. In fact, it is even possible that the mechanisms of aggregating individual losses differ in respect of different sublimits.[178]

2.95 An example is provided in the PRICL where a reinsured has taken out reinsurance for the perils of fire and tsunami. The overall cover limit is defined on the basis of the aggregate of all individual losses originating in one single cause. Further, the contract of reinsurance provides a specific sublimit for fire losses as well as a sublimit for tsunami losses.[179]

---

173 *Charter Reinsurance Co Ltd v Fagan* (n 27); Pohl and Iranya (n 26) 28.

174 Cf Pohl and Iranya (n 26) 28. For more information as to the reinsurer's ultimate net loss, see paras 2.11 ff.

175 *Kuwait Airways Corp v Kuwait Insurance Co SAK* (n 6).

176 *Kuwait Airways Corp v Kuwait Insurance Co SAK* (n 6).

177 See paras 2.88 ff.

178 See comments 23 f and illustrations 28 f to Article 5.2 PRICL and comments 24 f and illustrations 12 f to Article 5.3 PRICL.

179 See illustration 12 to Article 5.3 PRICL.

2.96 In such a case, the first step is to test whether the sublimits are exhausted. This is to say that the individual losses arising from the tsunami are added together and tested against the sublimit for tsunami losses. If the aggregated tsunami loss pierces the sublimit for tsunami losses, the part of the aggregated loss exceeding the sublimit is excluded from cover. Similarly, the individual losses arising from the fire are to be aggregated and tested against the sublimit for fire losses. The reinsurer is under no obligation to indemnify the reinsured for the part of the aggregated loss exceeding the sublimit for fire losses.

2.97 The second step is that the part of the aggregated tsunami loss and the part of the aggregated fire loss falling within their corresponding sublimits for tsunami and fire losses, respectively, may then be aggregated if both losses originate in the same cause, eg an earthquake. The resulting aggregated loss is to be tested against the overall cover limit.

3 Reinstatement of cover

2.98 Excess of loss reinsurance generally provide cover for a certain period of time, often one year.[180] Typically, full reinsurance cover is in place for any loss or aggregate loss that can be allocated to the relevant policy year.[181] The parties may, however, agree that the losses to be paid by the reinsurer exhaust the reinsurance cover, which is to the reinsurer's benefit.[182] Excess of loss reinsurance treaties regularly contain an annual aggregate limit[183] as well as a per loss limit.[184] Depending on the agreement, either limit may be exhausted.[185]

2.99 If a policy's cover is exhausted, the reinsured is left with no reinsurance cover for further losses during the relevant policy period. In order to avoid such a gap in cover, the parties may agree–sometimes in return for an additional premium[186]–on a reinstatement of the cover.[187] More specifically, a reinstatement of cover reactivates the reinsurance cover so that the reinsurer remains bound to indemnify the reinsured for further losses that exceed the deductible and remain within the cover limit.[188]

---

180 Robert M Merkin, *A Guide to Reinsurance Law* (Informa Law from Routledge 2007) 42.

181 Merkin (n 180) 58; Cannawurf and Schwepcke (n 128) para 371. Some authors appear to be of the opinion that the default rule is that claims paid by the reinsurer exhaust the reinsurance cover, see Liebwein (n 26) 285; Pohl and Iranya (n 26) 41. Barlow Lyde and Gilbert LLP (n 26) para 34.31, argue that the parties may agree on a limit per loss as well as a limit per aggregate. Only if the latter is exhausted, will the reinsurer cease to be liable for any further losses that are to be allocated to the relevant policy period.

182 Merkin (n 180) 56 ff; Barlow Lyde and Gilbert LLP (n 26) para 34.31; Liebwein (n 26) 285; Pohl and Iranya (n 26) 41.

183 Cf *Denby v English and Scottish Maritime Insurance Co Ltd; Yasuda Fire and Marine Co of Europe Ltd v Lloyd's Underwriting Syndicates no 209, 356* (n 81) 879 f (Hobhouse LJ), where an excess of loss reinsurance contract taken out on an aggregate basis is discussed.

184 Barlow Lyde and Gilbert LLP (n 26) para 34.31.

185 Grossmann (n 26) 131; Barlow Lyde and Gilbert LLP (n 26) para 34.31; Schwepcke and Vetter (n 26) para 877; Pohl and Iranya (n 26) 41.

186 Gerathewohl (n 48) 360; Merkin (n 180) 41 ff; Barlow Lyde and Gilbert LLP (n 26) para 34.34; Schwepcke and Vetter (n 26) para 878; Liebwein (n 26) 288 ff; Pohl and Iranya (n 26) 41 f.

187 Liebwein (n 26) 286.

188 Liebwein (n 26) 286. Cf Barlow Lyde and Gilbert LLP (n 26) para 34.34.

IV Different aggregation mechanisms for the purposes of deductible and cover limit

2.100 If a reinsurance policy contains an aggregation clause, multiple individual losses are to be added together for the purposes of applying deductible and cover limit to the ultimate net loss. Commonly, the mechanism of adding together individual losses to form one single aggregated loss is the same for the purposes of applying deductibles and cover limits to the ultimate net loss.[189]

2.101 Yet, as the parties may freely agree upon the structure of the reinsurance cover, they may provide for different aggregation mechanisms with regard to the reinsured's deductible and the reinsurer's cover limit.[190] Hence, whether individual losses are to be added together following the same rules essentially depends on the construction of the reinsurance agreement, ie 'upon the wording of the policy, and the circumstances which surrounded it being underwritten'.[191]

V Summary of the chapter

2.102 Aggregation clauses provide that multiple individual losses be treated as one single loss, which is then tested against the reinsured's deductible as well as the reinsurer's cover limit.[192] In this chapter, there has been no discussion of the question concerning the circumstances in which multiple individual losses are aggregated. Rather, the context in which the aggregation of losses takes place has been outlined.

2.103 First, a distinction has been drawn between an ultimate net loss and the individual losses to be aggregated. The former is incurred by the reinsured, whereas the latter are suffered by the primary assureds. What constitutes an individual loss is often determined on the basis of an insured unit under the primary insurance contract and consequently depends on the construction of the policy. Yet, English courts have repeatedly determined one loss by reference to the actions of those who caused the loss. This approach may, however, create legal uncertainty regarding the question of whether the actions of those who cause loss and damage represent one single loss or whether they constitute a unifying factor upon which multiple individual losses are to be aggregated.

2.104 Insurance and reinsurance agreements regularly provide for the aggregation of claims instead of losses. In this regard, it appears uncertain whether an aggregation clause providing for the adding together of multiple individual claims produces the same effect as one that provides for a mechanism to aggregate multiple individual losses. Further, the parties sometimes agree to aggregate individual

---

189 *Countrywide Assured Group Plc v Marshall* (n 25) [13] (Morison J).

190 *Countrywide Assured Group Plc v Marshall* (n 25) [13] (Morison J); Butler and Merkin (n 3) para C–0223. For policies where the aggregation mechanisms for the purposes of applying the deductible and cover limit to the ultimate net loss differed, see *AIG Europe Ltd v Woodman* (n 78); *Spire Healthcare Ltd v Royal and Sun Alliance Insurance Plc* (n 78).

191 *Countrywide Assured Group Plc v Marshall* (n 25) [13] (Morison J).

192 *Lloyd's TSB General Insurance Holdings Ltd v Lloyd's Bank Group Insurance Co Ltd* (n 1) [15] (Lord Hoffmann); *Scott v The Copenhagen Reinsurance Co (UK) Ltd* (n 2) [12] (Rix LJ). See also *Spire Healthcare Ltd v Royal and Sun Alliance Insurance Plc* (n 78) [23] (Simon LJ); Edelman and Burns (n 23) para 4.52.

occurrences. This may lead to confusion because the term 'occurrence' has a special meaning in the context of aggregating losses. In fact, it refers to a happening or event out of which multiple individual losses originate. Therefore, it appears unfavourable to use the term to designate the individual units to be added together.

2.105 Second, the concept of the reinsured's deductible and its heterogeneous terminology have been discussed. Reinsurance contracts sometimes refer to the reinsured's retention or priority instead of its deductible. However, it can be assumed that all three terms have the same meaning. Further, it has been analysed that the deductible applies to the reinsured's ultimate net loss which may be composed of multiple individual original losses as well as further costs.

2.106 Third, the concepts of 'overall cover limit', 'sublimit' and the 'reinstatement of cover' have been discussed and related to the aggregation of losses.

2.107 Finally, it has been set out that normally reinsurance contracts provide for one single aggregation mechanism that is applicable with regard to both the reinsured's deductible and the reinsurer's cover limit. However, the parties may deviate from what is normal and agree on different aggregation mechanisms for the purposes of deductible and cover limit.

CHAPTER 3

Features of aggregation clauses and causal requirements

3.1 In this chapter, it will first be demonstrated that aggregation mechanisms are impartial features. At the time the reinsurance contract is negotiated, it is generally not predictable to whose benefit they will work. Secondly, it will be outlined that multiple individual losses will not be aggregated unless the parties have explicitly provided for an aggregation mechanism in their contract. Finally, in the main part of the chapter, the unifying concept of causation will be analysed. The effects of the different terms used in aggregation clauses on causal requirements, in particular, will be examined. It will be argued that the 'jurisprudential riches'[1] on the point have not fostered legal certainty regarding the causal requirements in aggregation mechanisms.

I Aggregation clause as an impartial feature

3.2 An aggregation of losses cannot generally be said to be beneficial to the re-insured or the reinsurer. Rather, the party in whose interest it is to add together multiple individual losses depends on the profile of the losses and the structure of the cover.[2] In this vein, Lord Mustill noted that 'the favourable or unfavourable effect of [an aggregation] clause (…) may be impossible to determine in advance of the actual claims experience'.[3]

3.3 Aggregation clauses principally will operate in favour of the reinsured if the values of the individual losses fall below the deductible, whereas the aggregate of multiple individual losses exceeds the reinsured's retention and thereby triggers the reinsurer's liability.[4] By contrast, an aggregation of losses will be to the reinsurer's benefit if the aggregated loss pierces the cover limit and consequently caps the re-insurer's liability.[5] Thus, if the aggregation clause 'qualifies both a deductible clause

---

1 Terry O'Neill, Jan Woloniecki and Franziska Arnold-Dwyer, *The Law of Reinsurance in England and Bermuda* (5th edn, Sweet & Maxwell/Thomson Reuters 2019) para 7–013.

2 Colin Edelman and Andrew Burns, *The Law of Reinsurance* (2nd edn, OUP 2013) para 4.53.

3 *Axa Reinsurance (UK) Ltd v Field* (1996) 1 WLR 1026 (HL) 1035 (Lord Mustill).

4 *Municipal Mutual Insurance Ltd v Sea Insurance Co Ltd* [1998] EWCA Civ 546, [1998] CLC 957, 967 (Hobhouse LJ); *AIG Europe Ltd v Woodman* [2017] UKSC 18; [2018] 1 All ER 936 [14] (Lord Toulson SCJ); Edelman and Burns (n 2) para 4.53; O'Neill, Woloniecki and Arnold-Dwyer (n 1) para 5–096. See also Barlow Lyde and Gilbert LLP, *Reinsurance Practice and the Law* (Informa Law from Routledge 2009) para 28.2.

5 *Municipal Mutual Insurance Ltd v Sea Insurance Co Ltd* (n 4) 967 (Hobhouse LJ); *AIG Europe Ltd v Woodman* (n 4) [14] (Lord Toulson SCJ); Edelman and Burns (n 2) para 4.53; O'Neill, Woloniecki and Arnold-Dwyer (n 1) para 5–096. See also Barlow Lyde and Gilbert LLP (n 4) para 28.2.

DOI: 10.4324/9781003080480-3

and a limit clause, it may at times work in favour of the [reinsured] and at other times in favour of the [reinsurer]'.[6]

3.4 In *Lloyd's TSB General Insurance Holdings Ltd v Lloyd's Bank Group Insurance Co Ltd*, Lord Hobhouse, therefore, concluded that the construction of aggregation clauses should not be influenced by any need to protect the one party or the other. They were, instead, to be construed 'in a balanced fashion giving effect to the words used'.[7]

II The parties' agreement upon an aggregation clause

3.5 The parties to a reinsurance contract are free to decide whether they want to insert an aggregation clause into their agreement. If they omit to expressly provide for such a clause, no aggregation will be possible.[8]

3.6 More specifically, in *Mabey and Johnson Ltd v Ecclesiastical Insurance Office Plc,* the Commercial Court held that an implication of an aggregation clause was impossible because even in the absence of aggregation language the policy was 'clear and certain'.[9] Further, the parties cannot be taken to have intended to 'change the nature of the insurance' by implicitly agreeing on an aggregation clause. Moreover, there exists a variety of different aggregation clauses 'all of which are broadly designed to achieve the same result but which differ considerably in their detail'.[10] Hence, even if an implication were generally possible, it would by no means be clear what mechanism should be implied.[11] Similarly, the Commercial Court noted that it was sheer impossible to imply an aggregation clause by trade usage or market practice due to the number of different possible aggregation mechanisms.[12]

---

6 *Lloyd's TSB General Insurance Holdings Ltd v Lloyd's Bank Group Insurance Co Ltd* [2003] UKHL 48, [2003] 4 All ER 43 [30] (Lord Hobhouse).

7 *Lloyd's TSB General Insurance Holdings Ltd v Lloyd's Bank Group Insurance Co Ltd* (n 6) [30] (Lord Hobhouse); Mark Cannon, 'When Two Become One: Aggregation of Claims in Professional Indemnity Insurance' (IMC Insurance Market Conferences 2012) para 24 <http://imc-seminars.com/uploads/papers/Mark%20Cannon%20QC%20Paper.pdf> accessed 24 March 2020.

8 *Mabey and Johnson Ltd v Ecclesiastical Insurance Office Plc* [2000] CLC 1570 (Comm) 1573 f (Morison J), where professional indemnity insurance was concerned and it was held that no 'series provision' was to be implied. It is notable that the suggested series provision read: the insurer's liability was limited in the aggregate during that policy year to £2m in respect of 'all claims arising out of the same act of negligent omission or error or a series of such acts consequent upon or attributable to the same cause or original source (...)'. The clause under scrutiny appears to be a series provision as well as an aggregation clause; John Birds, Ben Lynch and Simon Paul, *MacGillivray on Insurance Law* (14th edn, Sweet & Maxwell 2018) para 30–060; Robert M Merkin, Laura Hodgson and Peter J Tyldesley, *Colinvaux's Law of Insurance* (Sweet & Maxwell 2019) para 11–321.

9 *Mabey and Johnson Ltd v Ecclesiastical Insurance Office Plc* (n 8) 1573 f (Morison J). It has been repeatedly held that a term may only be implied into a contract if without it the contract would not be workable, see for instance *Associated Japanese Bank (International) Ltd v Credit Du Nord SA* [1988] 1 WLR 255 (Comm) 263 (Steyn J); *Concord Trust v The Law Debenture Trust Corp Plc* [2005] UKHL 27, [2005] 1 WLR 1591 [37] (Lord Scott).

10 *Mabey and Johnson Ltd v Ecclesiastical Insurance Office Plc* (n 8) 1574 (Morison J).

11 *Mabey and Johnson Ltd v Ecclesiastical Insurance Office Plc* (n 8) 1574 (Morison J).

12 *Mabey and Johnson Ltd v Ecclesiastical Insurance Office Plc* (n 8) 1574 (Morison J).

3.7 Likewise, where the contract of reinsurance expressly provides for an aggregation clause based on which a series of losses are to be aggregated, 'the nature of the unifying factor', ie the 'factors which make them (...) a series must [generally] be expressed (...)'.[13] In this context, 'it may sometimes be necessary to imply a unifying factor'.[14]

3.8 However, in *Glencore International AG v Alpina Co Ltd*, it was held *obiter* that the simple word 'loss' may itself be an indication that the contract provides for an aggregation mechanism. The Commercial Court suggested that where 'several losses are related–as, for example, where an arsonist sets fire to two adjacent tanks in the course of a single attack' even in the absence of aggregation language, these losses may have to be regarded as one single loss.[15] The court explained that such losses might have to be aggregated based on 'the unifying factor (...) that the loss occurred on one occasion in the course of a single enterprise'.[16] In light of *Mabey and Johnson Ltd v Ecclesiastical Insurance Office Plc*,[17] this is remarkable.[18]

3.9 Butler and Merkin seem to support the view expressed by the Commercial Court's in *Glencore International AG v Alpina Co Ltd*. They opine that where a policy of insurance or reinsurance contained no aggregation clause, 'the overall structure of the agreement [would] determine' whether multiple individual losses were to be aggregated.[19] In their opinion, aggregation language is not necessarily required to provide for an aggregation mechanism in a contract of reinsurance.

3.10 In summary, the parties to a reinsurance contract cannot generally be taken to have agreed on an aggregation mechanism if they have not expressly provided for an aggregation clause in their reinsurance contract. By contrast, if they have provided for an aggregation clause, the aggregation clause's exact mode of operation, ie the workings of the mechanism, may–depending on the circumstances–be implied into a contract of reinsurance. Furthermore, even if a reinsurance policy initially does not appear to contain aggregation language, courts might unexpectedly identify an aggregation agreement.

---

13 *Lloyd's TSB General Insurance Holdings Ltd v Lloyd's Bank Group Insurance Co Ltd* (n 6) [26] (Lord Hoffmann).

14 *Lloyd's TSB General Insurance Holdings Ltd v Lloyd's Bank Group Insurance Co Ltd* (n 6) [26] (Lord Hoffmann).

15 *Glencore International AG v Alpina Insurance Co Ltd* [2003] EWHC 2792 (Comm), [2004] 1 All ER 766 [292] (Moore-Bick J).

16 *Glencore International AG v Alpina Insurance Co Ltd* (n 15) [293] (Moore-Bick J).

17 *Mabey and Johnson Ltd v Ecclesiastical Insurance Office Plc* (n 8) 1570 (Morison J), where the policy in question was an 'each and every claim' policy. In fact, if the word 'loss' is capable of containing an aggregation mechanism, the word 'claim' might equally be.

18 Instead of arguing that the word 'loss' itself incorporated an aggregation mechanism into the contract, the Commercial Court could have argued that the attack only produced one single loss so that nothing had to be aggregated. For more details as to the what constitutes one single loss, see paras 2.26 ff.

19 John Butler and Robert Merkin, *Butler and Merkin's Reinsurance Law*, vol 2 (Looseleaf, Sweet & Maxwell) para C–0251.

III Aggregation and the concept of causation

3.11 In *Scott v The Copenhagen* Reinsurance *Co (UK) Ltd,* Rix LJ stated that aggregation mechanisms determined whether it was appropriate to regard multiple individual losses as constituting a single loss for the purposes of aggregation under a specific policy.[20] This largely depended on whether they each are sufficiently linked to a unifying factor by being causally connected with it.[21]

3.12 The concept of causation and its role in the subject matter of aggregation is analysed below.

1 Causation in general

3.13 The concept of causation has stimulated much philosophical literature.[22] It is a complex concept that, in law as in life, is contextually variable.[23] In fact, causation is not one single, static concept 'to be mechanically applied without regard to the context in which the question arises'.[24] As Lord Hoffmann underlines, causal requirements are 'creatures of the law' and the causal requirement of one rule may differ from that of another.[25]

3.14 In *Environment Agency (formerly National Rivers Authority) v Empress Car Co (Abertillery) Ltd,* Lord Hoffmann, therefore, stated that 'one cannot give a common sense answer to a question of causation for the purpose of attributing responsibility under some rule without knowing the purpose and scope of the rule'.[26] As a consequence, he said, it was necessary to first identify the scope of the relevant rule before answering questions about causation.[27] Determining the relevant standard of causation in a specific case 'is not a question of common sense fact' but rather one of law.[28]

3.15 Determining causal requirements in the context of the aggregation of multiple individual losses, therefore, depends on the purpose and the scope of an aggregation clause.[29]

---

20 *Scott v The Copenhagen Reinsurance Co (UK) Ltd* [2003] EWCA Civ 688, [2003] 2 All ER 190 [68] (Rix LJ).

21 *Scott v The Copenhagen Reinsurance Co (UK) Ltd* (n 20) [68] (Rix LJ).

22 For further references, see O'Neill, Woloniecki and Arnold-Dwyer (n 1) para 7–015.

23 *US v Oberhellmann* (1991) 946 F2d 50 (United States Court of Appeals, Seventh Circuit) 53.

24 *Regina v Kennedy (No 2)* [2007] UKHL 38, [2007] 1 AC 269 [15].

25 Rt Hon Lord Hoffmann, 'Causation' in Richard Goldberg (ed), *Perspectives on Causation* (Hart Publishing 2011) 9.

26 *Environment Agency (formerly National Rivers Authority) v Empress Car Co (Abertillery) Ltd* [1999] 2 AC 22 (HL) 31 (Lord Hoffmann).

27 *Environment Agency (formerly National Rivers Authority) v Empress Car Co (Abertillery) Ltd* (n 26) 31 (Lord Hoffmann).

28 *Environment Agency (formerly National Rivers Authority) v Empress Car Co (Abertillery) Ltd* (n 26) 31 (Lord Hoffmann).

29 *Scott v The Copenhagen Reinsurance Co (UK) Ltd* (n 20) [68] (Rix LJ).

2 Purpose and scope of an aggregation clause

3.16 In *Lloyd's TSB General Insurance Holdings Ltd v Lloyd's Bank Group Insurance Co Ltd*, the House of Lords endorsed the Commercial Court's observation that the purpose of an aggregation clause was 'to enable two or more separate losses covered by the policy to be treated as a single loss for deductible or other purposes when they are linked by a unifying factor of some kind'.[30]

3.17 In *Scott v The Copenhagen Reinsurance Co (UK) Ltd*, the Court of Appeal noted that the function of an aggregation clause was 'to police the imposition of a limit by treating a plurality of linked losses as if they were one loss. For this purpose the losses [had] to be identified by a unifying concept (…)'.[31]

3.18 As a synthesis of these two judicial observations, it may be said that aggregation clauses provide a mechanism to add together multiple individual losses to form one single aggregated loss. This mechanism is primarily characterised by a 'unifying factor' or 'unifying concept' agreed upon by the parties.[32] The unifying concept inherent in event-[33] and cause-based[34] aggregation mechanisms is one of causation.

3.19 It should be noted that there is not just one single unifying concept. Rather, the parties to a contract of reinsurance may tailor a unifying concept to their needs. Varying unifying concepts generally differ in their causal requirements.[35]

3.20 In *Scott v The Copenhagen Reinsurance Co Ltd*, Rix LJ observed that the scope and purpose of the specific event-based aggregation clause concerned was defined by its wording and particularly the phrase 'arising out of one event'. He elaborated that a plurality of losses was to be aggregated only if they could be sufficiently linked to a single unifying event by being casually connected with it. From this, he inferred that '[t]he aggregation function of such a clause is antagonistic to a weak or loose causal relationship between the losses and the required unifying single event'.[36]

3.21 Consequently, '[t]he choice of language by which the parties designate the unifying [concept] in an aggregation clause is (…) of critical importance and can be expected to be the subject of careful negotiation'.[37]

---

30 *Lloyd's TSB General Insurance Holdings Ltd v Lloyd's Bank Group Insurance Co Ltd* (n 6) [14] (Lord Hoffmann). See also *Spire Healthcare Ltd v Royal and Sun Alliance Insurance Plc* [2018] EWCA Civ 317, [2018] Lloyd's Rep IR 425 [23] (Simon LJ).

31 *Scott v The Copenhagen Reinsurance Co (UK) Ltd* (n 20) [12] (Rix LJ).

32 *Lloyd's TSB General Insurance Holdings Ltd v Lloyd's Bank Group Insurance Co Ltd* (n 6) [14] (Lord Hoffmann); *Scott v The Copenhagen Reinsurance Co (UK) Ltd* (n 20) [12] (Rix LJ).

33 See, for instance, *Caudle v Sharp* [1995] CLC 642 (CA) 648 (Evans LJ).

34 See, for instance, *American Centennial Insurance Co v INSCO Ltd* [1996] 1 LRLR 407 (Comm) 414 (Moore-Bick J).

35 Cf Ken Louw and Deborah Tompkinson, 'Curiouser and Curiouser: The Meaning of "Event"' (1996) 4 International Insurance Law Review 6, 11. Cf also *American Centennial Insurance Co v INSCO Ltd* (n 34) 414 (Moore-Bick J).

36 *Scott v The Copenhagen Reinsurance Co (UK) Ltd* (n 20) [68] (Rix LJ).

37 *Lloyd's TSB General Insurance Holdings Ltd v Lloyd's Bank Group Insurance Co Ltd* (n 6) [17] (Lord Hoffmann).

3.22 The factors determining the causal requirements in a specific case are discussed below.

IV Factors determining causal requirements

1 Starting point

3.23 Typically, aggregation clauses define the relevant loss for making a claim under the contract of reinsurance. They define the term 'loss' as the sum of each and every loss 'arising out of one event'[38] or 'consequent on or attributable to one source or original cause'.[39] It can be inferred from this that aggregation clauses generally consist of four elements.

1. First, they mention 'each and every loss' and thereby refer to the individual losses to be aggregated.[40]
2. Secondly, they mention a unifying factor, such as 'event' or 'original cause', which provokes the individual losses to be aggregated.
3. Thirdly, they contain linking phrases[41] such as 'arising out of' or 'consequent on or attributable to'. Linking phrases indicate the relation between the unifying factor (no 2) and each individual loss to be aggregated (no 1).
4. Finally, they provide that the 'loss' as defined in the contract of reinsurance is the product of aggregating individual losses in accordance with the defined aggregation mechanism. The notion of 'loss' refers to the reinsured's so-called 'ultimate net loss'.[42]

3.24 The unifying factors[43] and linking phrases[44] both contribute to the determination of the causal requirements inherent in an aggregation mechanism.[45]

2 Unifying factors

3.25 If the parties to a reinsurance contract agree to provide for an aggregation mechanism, they will generally also agree on a unifying factor of some

---

38 For instance, *Caudle v Sharp* (n 33) 644.

39 For instance, *Spire Healthcare Ltd v Royal and Sun Alliance Insurance Plc* (n 30) [3] (Simon LJ).

40 See paras 2.18 ff.

41 The term 'linking phrase' has been chosen in accordance with *Standard Life Assurance Ltd v Ace European Group* [2012] EWHC 104 (Comm), [2012] 1 Lloyd's Rep IR 655 [262] (Eder J), where it is termed 'description of the link'; Clyde and Co, 'Aggregation Words' (*The Insurance Hub*, 26 April 2016) 1 ff <https://clydeco.com/uploads/Blogs/employment/Aggregation_Words_-_Clyde__Co.pdf> accessed 24 March 2020, refer to the link as 'connecting words'.

42 See paras 2.11 ff; it is to be noted that the reinsured's 'ultimate net loss' generally comprises expenses incurred in settling a claim under the underlying contract.

43 *Axa Reinsurance (UK) Ltd v Field* (n 3) 1035 (Lord Mustill); *Caudle v Sharp* (n 33) 648 (Evans LJ); Louw and Tompkinson (n 35) 11.

44 *Standard Life Assurance Ltd v Ace European Group* (n 41) [262] (Eder J); *Aioi Nissay Dowa Insurance Co Ltd v Heraldglen Ltd and Advent Capital Ltd* [2013] EWHC 154 (Comm), [2013] 2 All ER 231 [21] (Field J); Cannon (n 7) para 49.

45 James Roberts, 'Aggregation Triggers: The Wait Continues' (*The Insurance Hub*, 20 April 2016) <https://clydeco.com/blog/insurance-hub/article/aggregation-triggers-the-wait-continues> accessed 24 March 2020; Clyde and Co (n 41).

kind.[46] In *Lloyd's TSB General Insurance Holdings Ltd v Lloyd's Bank Group Insurance Co Ltd*, Lord Hoffmann observed that '[t]he choice of language by which the parties designate the unifying factor in an aggregation clause is (...) of critical importance and can be expected to be the subject of careful negotiation'.[47] In the same vein, Lord Mustill in *Axa Reinsurance (UK) Ltd v Field* stated that he believed that when construing an aggregation clause, 'the only safe course is to fall back on the words actually used, and to read them as they stand'.[48] Yet, Merkin notes that it should not be assumed that a single one of the terms used to describe unifying factors bore a consistent meaning across multiple policies or even within the same policy as there was a tendency by those who drafted insurance policies to use different words interchangeably and the same word in different ways.[49]

3.26 In any case, it is said that the words chosen to designate an aggregation clause's unifying factor have a significant bearing on the causal requirements between the individual losses to be aggregated and the unifying factor. Classically, contracts of (re-)insurance provide for unifying factors such as 'event',[50] 'originating cause' or 'original cause'[51], respectively.[52] A variety of

---

46 Cf Edelman and Burns (n 2) para 4.52.

47 *Lloyd's TSB General Insurance Holdings Ltd v Lloyd's Bank Group Insurance Co Ltd* (n 6) [17] (Lord Hoffmann). See also Edelman and Burns (n 2) para 4.54.

48 *Axa Reinsurance (UK) Ltd v Field* (n 3) 1036 (Lord Mustill).

49 Merkin, Hodgson and Tyldesley (n 8) para 11–320.

50 *Caudle v Sharp* (n 33) 644 (Evans LJ); *American Centennial Insurance Co v INSCO Ltd* (n 34) 412 ff (Moore-Bick J); *Axa Reinsurance (UK) Ltd v Field* (n 3) 1031 f (Lord Mustill); *Brown (RE) v GIO Insurance Ltd* [1998] Lloyd's Rep IR 201 (CA) 202 (Waller LJ); *Midland Mainline Ltd v Eagle Star Insurance Co Ltd* [2003] EWHC 1771 (Comm), [2004] Lloyd's Rep IR 22 [13] (Steel J). See Appendix to *Denby v English and Scottish Maritime Insurance Co Ltd; Yasuda Fire and Marine Co of Europe Ltd v Lloyd's Underwriting Syndicates no 209, 356* [1998] Lloyd's Rep IR 343 (CA), [1998] CLC 870; *Scott v The Copenhagen Reinsurance Co (UK) Ltd* (n 20) [6]–[7] (Rix LJ); *Equitas Ltd v R and Q Reinsurance Co (UK) Ltd* [2009] EWHC 2787 (Comm), [2009] 2 CLC 706 [30] (Gross J); *IRB Brasil Resseguros SA v CX Reinsurance Co Ltd* [2010] EWHC 974 (Comm), [2010] Lloyd's Rep IR 560 [11] (Burton J); *Aioi Nissay Dowa Insurance Co Ltd v Heraldglen Ltd and Advent Capital Ltd* (n 44) [2] (Field J); *MIC Simmonds v Gammell* [2016] EWHC 2515 (Comm), [2016] Lloyd's Rep IR 693 [7] (Sir Jeremy Cooke).

51 *Cox v Bankside Members Agency Ltd* [1995] CLC 671 (CA) 679 (Sir Thomas Bingham); *Municipal Mutual Insurance Ltd v Sea Insurance Co Ltd* (n 4) 959 (Hobhouse LJ); *Countrywide Assured Group Plc v Marshall* [2002] EWHC 2082 (Comm), [2003] 1 All ER 237 [3] (Morison J); *Lloyd's TSB General Insurance Holdings Ltd v Lloyd's Bank Group Insurance Co Ltd* (n 6) [12] (Lord Hoffmann); *Standard Life Assurance Ltd v Oak Dedicated Ltd* [2008] EWHC 222 (Comm), [2008] 2 All ER 916 [14] (Tomlinson J); *Standard Life Assurance Ltd v Ace European Group* (n 41) [255] (Eder J); *Tokio Marine Europe Insurance Ltd v Novae Corporate Underwriting Ltd* [2014] EWHC 2105 (Comm), [2014] Lloyd's Rep IR 638 [8] (Field J); *AIG Europe Ltd v OC320301 LLP* [2016] EWCA Civ 367, [2016] Lloyd's Rep IR 289 [8] (Longmore LJ); *Spire Healthcare Ltd v Royal and Sun Alliance Insurance Plc* (n 30) [3] (Simon LJ).

52 Deborah Tompkinson, 'Reinsurance: "Originating Cause" and "Event"' (1995) 3 International Insurance Law Review 82; Louw and Tompkinson (n 35) 6 ff; Jonathan Wright, 'Defining the Word "Event" in a Reinsurance Policy' (1997) 5 International Insurance Law Review 361; Barlow Lyde and Gilbert LLP (n 4) paras 28.7 ff, 28.37 ff; Kiran Soar, 'Interpretation of Wordings Key to Settling Aggregation Claims' [2010] LLID 7; Darlene K Alt, Nathan Hull and James Killelea, 'A Reinsurance Perspective: The Aggregation of Losses Following the Tohoku Earthquake and Tsunami' (2011) 22 Mealey's Litigation Report 1, 2; Rob Merkin, 'The Christchurch Earthquakes Insurance and Reinsurance Issues' (2012) 18 Canterbury Law Review 119, 145; Edelman and Burns (n 2) paras 4.52 ff, 4.59 ff; Clyde and Co (n 41) 8 ff, 10 ff; Merkin, Hodgson and Tyldesley (n 8) paras 11–324 ff, 11–335.

other terms such as 'occurrence',[53] 'accident',[54] 'act or omission',[55] 'catastrophe',[56] 'disaster'[57] and 'calamity'[58] are also sometimes mentioned in the context of aggregation. Therefore, the meanings associated with these terms in the context of aggregation are discussed below.

2.1 Event

3.27 It may be noted that the term 'event' is used in a variety of different contexts. The meaning of the word may change depending on the purpose it has in a given context.[59] In the following examination, focus is placed on the meaning of the term for aggregation purposes.

3.28 In *Caudle v Sharp*, Evans LJ stated that '[t]he Second World War, the One Hundred Years War and even the Ice Age' could all properly be said to be 'events'. He pointed out, however, that these were not 'relevant events' as it could not realistically be said that this kind of events was referred to in the aggregation clause concerned.[60]

3.29 Evans LJ opined that a relevant event comprised three elements: First, there needed to be a common factor which could properly be described as an event. Secondly, a causal link between the individual losses to be aggregated and this common factor was required. Thirdly, the said event should not be too remote from the individual losses, ie the causative link between the individual losses and the relevant event should not be too weak.[61]

---

53 *Kuwait Airways Corp v Kuwait Insurance Co SAK* [1996] 1 Lloyd's Rep 664 (Comm); *Mann v Lexington Insurance Co* [2000] CLC 1409 (CA).

54 *The South Staffordshire Tramways Co Ltd v The Sickness and Accident Assurance Association Ltd* [1891] 1 QB 402 (CA). For an American policy using the unifying factor of 'accident', see *National Liability and Fire Insurance Co v Itzkowitz* [2015] 624 FedAppx 758 (United States Court of Appeals for the Second Circuit) 759 f.

55 *Lloyd's TSB General Insurance Holdings Ltd v Lloyd's Bank Group Insurance Co Ltd* (n 6) [12] (Lord Hoffmann); *Standard Life Assurance Ltd v Oak Dedicated Ltd* (n 51) [14] (Tomlinson J); *Standard Life Assurance Ltd v Ace European Group* (n 41) [255] (Eder J); *AIG Europe Ltd v OC320301 LLP* (n 51) [8] (Longmore LJ); *AIG Europe Ltd v Woodman* (n 4) [1] (Lord Toulson SCJ).

56 *Caudle v Sharp* (n 33) 644 (Evans LJ); *Axa Reinsurance (UK) Ltd v Field* (n 3) 1031 f (Lord Mustill); *Denby v English and Scottish Maritime Insurance Co Ltd; Yasuda Fire and Marine Co of Europe Ltd v Lloyd's Underwriting Syndicates no 209, 356* (n 50) 873 (Hobhouse LJ); *IRB Brasil Resseguros SA v CX Reinsurance Co Ltd* (n 50) [11] (Burton J).

57 *Caudle v Sharp* (n 33) 644 (Evans LJ); *Axa Reinsurance (UK) Ltd v Field* (n 3) 1031 f (Lord Mustill); *Denby v English and Scottish Maritime Insurance Co Ltd; Yasuda Fire and Marine Co of Europe Ltd v Lloyd's Underwriting Syndicates no 209, 356* (n 50) 873 (Hobhouse LJ); *IRB Brasil Resseguros SA v CX Reinsurance Co Ltd* (n 50) [11] (Burton J).

58 *Caudle v Sharp* (n 33) 644 (Evans LJ); *Axa Reinsurance (UK) Ltd v Field* (n 3) 1031 f (Lord Mustill); *Denby v English and Scottish Maritime Insurance Co Ltd; Yasuda Fire and Marine Co of Europe Ltd v Lloyd's Underwriting Syndicates no 209, 356* (n 50) 873 (Hobhouse LJ); *IRB Brasil Resseguros SA v CX Reinsurance Co Ltd* (n 50) [11] (Burton J).

59 Butler and Merkin (n 19) para C–0230.

60 *Caudle v Sharp* (n 33) 648 (Evans LJ).

61 *Caudle v Sharp* (n 33) 648 (Evans LJ).

a Proper description of what can be described as event

3.30 If the only unifying factor available is something that cannot properly be described as an event, then the individual losses are not to be aggregated under an event-based aggregation mechanism.[62] It is, therefore, important to consider what can properly be termed an 'event'.

3.31 In *Axa* Reinsurance *(UK) Ltd v Field*, Lord Mustill famously characterised an event as 'something which happens at a particular time, at a particular place, in a particular way'.[63] In the context of natural disasters, tsunamis,[64] earthquakes[65] and hurricanes[66] may constitute events. Events may, however, also be man-made. In fact, the hijacking of an aircraft,[67] a terror attack,[68] an invasion of a country and seizure of its property,[69] the negligent underwriting of an insurance policy,[70] the destruction of property belonging to a third party,[71] the issuance of a speed restriction on a railway network[72] as well as a faulty installation of a window[73] have been considered events. In light of these cases, an event is something which of itself provokes one or multiple losses.[74]

3.32 By contrast, it has been held that a plan,[75] a decision,[76] a state of affairs,[77] a state of ignorance,[78] the lack of proper training of selling personnel,[79] the

62 *Scott v The Copenhagen Reinsurance Co (UK) Ltd* (n 20) [62] (Rix LJ). See also *Caudle v Sharp* (n 33) 648 f (Evans LJ); Butler and Merkin (n 19) para C–0221.

63 *Axa Reinsurance (UK) Ltd v Field* (n 3) 1035 (Lord Mustill).

64 See, for instance, Alt, Hull and Killelea (n 52).

65 See, for instance, Alt, Hull and Killelea (n 52); Merkin (n 52) 147. For a case to this extent, see *Moore v IAG New Zealand Ltd* [2019] NZHC 1549, [2020] Lloyd's Rep IR 167.

66 *Caudle v Sharp* (n 33) 648 f (Evans LJ).

67 See, for instance, *Aioi Nissay Dowa Insurance Co Ltd v Heraldglen Ltd and Advent Capital Ltd* (n 44).

68 *MIC Simmonds v Gammell* (n 50).

69 See, for instance, *Kuwait Airways Corp v Kuwait Insurance Co SAK* (n 53).

70 See, for instance, *Caudle v Sharp* (n 33).

71 See, for instance, *Dawson's Field Arbitration*, quoted in: *Kuwait Airways Corp v Kuwait Insurance Co SAK* (n 53); *Municipal Mutual Insurance Ltd v Sea Insurance Co Ltd* (n 4); *Mann v Lexington Insurance Co* (n 53).

72 *Midland Mainline Ltd v Eagle Star Insurance Co Ltd* (n 50).

73 *Seele Austria GmbH Co v Tokio Marine Europe Insurance Ltd* [2009] EWHC 255 (TCC), [2009] BLR 261.

74 *Caudle v Sharp* (n 33) 649 (Evans LJ); *American Centennial Insurance Co v INSCO Ltd* (n 34). It is to be noted, however, that the reinsurance agreement in question was only concerned with events 'affecting' underlying policies; Butler and Merkin (n 19) para C–0235.

75 *Dawson's Field Arbitration*, quoted in: *Kuwait Airways Corp v Kuwait Insurance Co SAK* (n 53); *Midland Mainline Ltd v Eagle Star Insurance Co Ltd* (n 50) [97] (Steel J); *Aioi Nissay Dowa Insurance Co Ltd v Heraldglen Ltd and Advent Capital Ltd* (n 44) [20] (Field J).

76 *Midland Mainline Ltd v Eagle Star Insurance Co Ltd* (n 50) [97] (Steel J). It may be noted, however, that in the *Dawson's Field Arbitration*, quoted in: *Kuwait Airways Corp v Kuwait Insurance Co SAK* (n 53), the arbitral tribunal considered the carrying out of a decision to blow up three aircraft one event. Similarly, in *IRB Brasil Resseguros SA v CX Reinsurance Co Ltd* (n 50) [46] (Burton J), it has been held that the determination each year to carry out its installation activities using asbestos was to be considered an event.

77 *Axa Reinsurance (UK) Ltd v Field* (n 3) 1035 (Lord Mustill); *Midland Mainline Ltd v Eagle Star Insurance Co Ltd* (n 50) [98] (Steel J); Merkin, Hodgson and Tyldesley (n 8) para 11–326.

78 *Caudle v Sharp* (n 33) 649 (Evans LJ).

79 *Countrywide Assured Group Plc v Marshall* (n 51) [15] (Steel J).

misunderstanding as to the results of a discussion[80] or the failure of putting in place an adequate system to protect stored goods[81] could not properly be described as events for the purposes of aggregation.

3.33 Furthermore, it appears to be controversial whether an omission can be considered an event.[82] In *Scott v The Copenhagen Reinsurance Co Ltd*, referring to *Caudle v Sharp*, Rix LJ stated that 'a negligent omission could not be an "event"'.[83] A closer look at the judgment in *Caudle v Sharp* reveals, however, that this general proposition is not supported by the Court of Appeal's decision. In *Caudle v Sharp*, the Court of Appeal held that an underwriter's 'blind spot' or 'his failure to conduct the necessary research and investigation' into a risk did not constitute an event as 'it did not constitute a negligent omission until [he] underwrote a relevant policy of insurance'. His liability was only triggered once he entered into a contract of insurance and no event had occurred until he became liable.[84]

3.34 Yet, a negligent omission may, in certain circumstances, directly trigger liability. In *Forney v Dominion Insurance Co Ltd*, Donaldson J considered a case where a solicitor was liable towards two clients. Each of his clients had claims against the estate of a deceased tortfeasor. It was the solicitor's duty to issue a writ or writs and initiate proceedings on their behalf against the estate of the deceased within a certain deadline. Yet, the solicitor had failed to so do. The question before the court was whether the solicitor's omissions to begin proceedings on behalf of each client against the estate of the deceased constituted one or two occurrences. As the solicitor could have issued one single writ for both clients, Donaldson J stated that the failure to issue a writ for the clients constituted a single occurrence.[85] In this respect, Louw and Tompkinson suggest that there were two different types of omissions. First, there was a pure omission which itself and without any further requirement of positive action caused harm. The failure to issue a writ was an omission of this type.[86] Secondly, there was a dormant omission which did not itself cause harm but rather required some further positive act or event in order to trigger the harm. An underwriter's failure to conduct the necessary research before entering into a

---

80 Cf *Caudle v Sharp* (n 33) 650, where Evans LJ stated, *obiter*, that the misinformation of an underwriter as to the scale of the asbestosis problem could be regarded as a causative event. It was, however, not a relevant event because it was too remote from the individual losses; *American Centennial Insurance Co v INSCO Ltd* (n 34) 414 (Moore-Bick J). Contrast, *Seele Austria GmbH Co v Tokio Marine Europe Insurance Ltd* [2008] EWCA Civ 441 [56], where Moore-Bick LJ seems to have suggested, *obiter*, that 'giving the workman wrong instructions' could be considered a single relevant event.

81 *Municipal Mutual Insurance Ltd v Sea Insurance Co Ltd* (n 4) 967 (Hobhouse LJ).

82 Edelman and Burns (n 2) para 4.55, argue that an omission cannot be an event; Louw and Tompkinson (n 35) 10, opine that an omission may–under certain circumstances–be considered an event.

83 *Scott v The Copenhagen Reinsurance Co (UK) Ltd* (n 20) [59] (Rix LJ).

84 *Caudle v Sharp* (n 33) 649 (Evans LJ).

85 *Forney v Dominion Insurance Co Ltd* [1969] 1 WLR 928 (QB) 933 (Donaldson J).

86 Louw and Tompkinson (n 35) 11.

contract does not itself cause harm. However, by taking the further action of entering into an insurance contract in his state of ignorance, the underwriter may cause harm.[87] Thus, Louw and Tompkinson argue that a pure omission can be an event for the purposes of aggregation, whereas a dormant omission cannot.[88] This approach seems to be more nuanced than the one promoted in *Scott v The Copenhagen Reinsurance Co Ltd*.[89]

3.35 Whether one or two events can be said to have occurred in a given case essentially depends on the viewpoint of the observer.[90] This was illustrated by the arbitral tribunal in the *Dawson's Field Arbitration*:

> The crews of a submarine and of ships which are attacked and sunk in a convoy would no doubt regard each attack and sinking as a separate occurrence. An admiral at Naval Headquarters might regard the whole attack and its results as one occurrence; a historian almost certainly would.[91]

3.36 In *Kuwait Airways Corp v Kuwait Insurance Co SAK*, this proposition was refined. It was held that 'the matter must be scrutinised from the point of view of an informed observer placed in the position of the assured'.[92] Hence, Rix J clarified and the Commercial Court in *Aioi Nissay Dowa Insurance Co Ltd v Heraldglen Ltd and Advent Capital Ltd* confirmed that it was not the viewpoint of any observer but the one of the involved primary insured that had to be considered in determining the number of events in a given case.[93]

3.37 In any case, not every event may be a relevant event for the purposes of aggregation.[94] In the search for a relevant event, one is to move back on the chains of causation culminating in the individual losses to be aggregated. Yet, for the purposes of aggregation, the 'infinite reach of the workings of causation' needs to be limited.[95] Evans LJ's second and third element deal with this limitation.[96]

---

87 Louw and Tompkinson (n 35) 11.

88 Louw and Tompkinson (n 35) 11.

89 *Scott v The Copenhagen Reinsurance Co (UK) Ltd* (n 20) [59] (Rix LJ).

90 *Dawson's Field Arbitration*, quoted in: *Kuwait Airways Corp v Kuwait Insurance Co SAK* (n 53).

91 *Dawson's Field Arbitration*, quoted in: *Kuwait Airways Corp v Kuwait Insurance Co SAK* (n 53).

92 *Kuwait Airways Corp v Kuwait Insurance Co SAK* (n 53).

93 *Kuwait Airways Corp v Kuwait Insurance Co SAK* (n 53); *Aioi Nissay Dowa Insurance Co Ltd v Heraldglen Ltd and Advent Capital Ltd* (n 44) [31] (Field J). It is to be noted, however, that Barlow Lyde and Gilbert LLP (n 4) para 28.6, seem not to make a distinction between the viewpoint of an ordinary observer and the point of view of an observer placed in the shoes of the primary insured.

94 *Caudle v Sharp* (n 33) 648 (Evans LJ); *Scott v The Copenhagen Reinsurance Co (UK) Ltd* (n 20) [63] (Rix LJ). Cf also *American Centennial Insurance Co v INSCO Ltd* (n 34) 413, where Moore-Bick J held that an event 'is not necessarily a relevant event for the purposes of art. VIII (...) which is concerned only with events, which affect policies issued by the reinsured'.

95 *Scott v The Copenhagen Reinsurance Co (UK) Ltd* (n 20) [63] (Rix LJ).

96 *Caudle v Sharp* (n 33) 648 (Evans LJ).

b Causative link and lack of remoteness

3.38 As to the second and third element of the concept of event, Evans LJ explained that an event did not have to be the proximate cause of individual losses.[97] He opined that '[s]ome wider test of causation' was to be applied.[98] Yet, the relevant event should not be too remote from the individual losses to be aggregated.[99]

3.39 In *Scott v The Copenhagen Reinsurance Co (UK) Ltd*, it was held that the function of the concept of remoteness was to separate relevant events from the irrelevant ones.[100] Rix LJ acknowledged, however, that 'the use of this tool is somewhat opaque'.[101] He elaborated that even though the causal requirements were looser than those of proximate cause, courts should 'look for a nearer and more relevant cause [rather] than for a more distant one'.[102] In other words, he suggested that the causative links between the individual losses to be aggregated and the relevant event had to be 'a significant rather than a weak one'.[103] In the same vein, he declared that the function of an event-based aggregation clause was 'antagonistic to a weak or loose causal relationship between the losses and the required unifying single event'.[104]

3.40 Yet, describing the required causal link as a significant rather than a weak or loose one still appears to be very vague and inappropriate for a clear standard of causal requirements in event-based aggregation mechanisms. In *Scott v The Copenhagen Reinsurance Co Ltd*, the Court of Appeal seems to have shared this view when it attempted to gain more precision in formulating the following rule:

> The relevant event is the *one event which should be regarded as the cause of [the individual losses to be aggregated] so as to make it appropriate to regard these losses as constituting for the purposes of aggregation under this policy one loss.*[105]

---

97 *Caudle v Sharp* (n 33) 648 (Evans LJ). It is to be noted, however, that by contrast to the predominant view, the Court of Appeal did not consider the notions of 'event' and 'occurrence' to be interchangeable. On the contrary, it noted that because the term 'occurrence' was capable of meaning the operation of the insured peril and, thus, could be said to be the individual losses' proximate cause and that this occurrence had itself arisen out of the relevant 'event', the causal relationship between the individual losses to be aggregated and the relevant event could not be one of proximate cause.

98 *Caudle v Sharp* (n 33) 648 (Evans LJ). In *Kuwait Airways Corp v Kuwait Insurance Co SAK* (n 53), it was consequently held that an event was not the same thing as a peril.

99 *Caudle v Sharp* (n 33) 648 (Evans LJ); *Kuwait Airways Corp v Kuwait Insurance Co SAK* (n 53).

100 *Scott v The Copenhagen Reinsurance Co (UK) Ltd* (n 20) [63] (Rix LJ). See also Barlow Lyde and Gilbert LLP (n 4) para 28.13.

101 *Scott v The Copenhagen Reinsurance Co (UK) Ltd* (n 20) [63] (Rix LJ).

102 *Scott v The Copenhagen Reinsurance Co (UK) Ltd* (n 20) [63] (Rix LJ).

103 *Scott v The Copenhagen Reinsurance Co (UK) Ltd* (n 20) [63] (Rix LJ). See also *MIC Simmonds v Gammell* (n 50) [30] (Sir Jeremy Cooke).

104 *Scott v The Copenhagen Reinsurance Co (UK) Ltd* (n 20) [68] (Rix LJ).

105 *Scott v The Copenhagen Reinsurance Co (UK) Ltd* (n 20) [68] (Rix LJ). In *MIC Simmonds v Gammell* (n 50) [29], Sir Jeremy Cooke held that the so-called unities test was 'an aid in determining whether the circumstances of the losses involve[d] such a degree of unity as to justify their being described as "arising out of one occurrence"'. More specifically, in *Kuwait Airways Corp v Kuwait Insurance Co SAK* (n 53), Rix J stated that the losses' circumstances must be scrutinised to see whether they involve such a degree of unity as to justify their being described as, or as arising out of, one occurrence. 'In assessing the degree of unity', he held that 'regard may be had to such factors as cause, locality and time and the intentions of human agents'. Yet, the unities test also involves a great deal of judgment

3.41 However, this rule appears to be circular. In fact, the assessment of whether the aggregation of multiple losses is appropriate should not be used to determine the standard of causation required in a specific case. The standard of causal requirements should be informative as to whether it is appropriate to aggregate multiple individual losses in a given case.

3.42 In *Kuwait Airways Corp v Kuwait Insurance Co SAK*, the Commercial Court exemplified the question of appropriateness. Rix J noted that an event was 'not the same thing as a peril' but that in determining the relevant event 'one may properly have regard to the context of the perils insured against'.[106] He elaborated that when the insured peril was the peril of war it was appropriate to describe the relevant event in broader terms.[107] Hence, the appropriateness of aggregating a plurality of individual losses may depend on the description of the peril (re-)insured against in the policy.

3.43 Yet, determining the relevant event by assessing the appropriateness of adding together multiple individual losses lowers any meaningful standard of causal requirements and exposes causal requirements in event-based aggregation mechanisms to pure exercises of judgment.[108]

3.44 In summary, it appears undisputed that the unifying factor of event contributes towards defining the causal requirements in event-based aggregation mechanisms. A meaningful standard of causal requirements can, however, not be deduced from the decisions on that point.[109] Consequently, there seems to be no legal certainty as to the causal requirements associated with the unifying factor of event.[110]

2.2 'Originating cause' and 'original cause'

3.45 Contracts of reinsurance sometimes aggregate on the basis of an 'originating cause or source' or 'one source or original cause'.[111] There appears to be no difference between the two variations of the unifying factor.[112]

---

and cannot offer any legal certainty as to the causal requirements in event-based aggregation mechanisms. The unities test is discussed in greater detail below, see paras 4.14 ff.

106 *Kuwait Airways Corp v Kuwait Insurance Co SAK* (n 53).

107 *Kuwait Airways Corp v Kuwait Insurance Co SAK* (n 53).

108 Cf *Scott v The Copenhagen Reinsurance Co (UK) Ltd* (n 20) [81] (Rix LJ); *MIC Simmonds v Gammell* (n 50) [28], [33], [36], [39] (Sir Jeremy Cooke). For more details on whether determining an event comes down to an exercise of judgment, see paras 4.81 ff.

109 According to Merkin (n 52) 146, '[t]he cases on "event" are borderline and often give rise to disagreements between first instance and appellate judges'.

110 Cf *Scott v The Copenhagen Reinsurance Co (UK) Ltd* (n 20) [68] (Rix LJ).

111 In respect of the term 'originating cause or source', see *Axa Reinsurance (UK) Ltd v Field* (n 3) 1032 (Lord Mustill); *Cox v Bankside Members Agency Ltd* (n 51) 679 (Sir Thomas Bingham); *Standard Life Assurance Ltd v Oak Dedicated Ltd* (n 51) [14] (Tomlinson J); *Standard Life Assurance Ltd v Ace European Group* (n 41) [255] (Eder J). For the phrase 'one source or original cause', see *Municipal Mutual Insurance Ltd v Sea Insurance Co Ltd* [1996] CLC 1515 (Comm) 959 (Hobhouse LJ); *Countrywide Assured Group Plc v Marshall* (n 51) [3] (Morison J). See also generally Robert M Merkin, *A Guide to Reinsurance Law* (Informa Law from Routledge 2007) 282; Barlow Lyde and Gilbert LLP (n 4) paras 28.37 ff; Edelman and Burns (n 2) para 4.59; Merkin, Hodgson and Tyldesley (n 8) para 11–335.

112 *Municipal Mutual Insurance Ltd v Sea Insurance Co Ltd* (n 4) 967 (Hobhouse LJ). Cf also *Countrywide Assured Group Plc v Marshall* (n 51) [15] (Morison J); Barlow Lyde and Gilbert LLP (n 4) para 28.49; Edelman and Burns (n 2) paras 4.59 ff. See also Merkin, Hodgson and Tyldesley (n 8) para 11–335.

3.46 In a similar fashion to the discussion about the unifying factor of event, it will first be dealt with what can properly be described as a cause in the context of cause-based aggregation mechanisms.[113] Thereafter, causal requirements associated with the unifying factors of 'originating cause' and 'original cause' will be analysed.

a Proper description of what can be described as cause

3.47 In *Axa Reinsurance (UK) Ltd v Field*, Lord Mustill famously compared the unifying factors of event and cause. He explained that

> *[t]he contrast is between 'originating' coupled with 'cause' (...) and 'event' (...). In [his] opinion these expressions are not at all the same (...). In ordinary speech, an event is something which happens at a particular time, at a particular place, in a particular way (...). A cause is to [his] mind something altogether less constricted. It can be a continuing state of affairs; it can be the absence of something happening.*[114]

3.48 In *Countrywide Assured Group Plc v Marshall*, for instance, the Commercial Court dealt with a case where an insurance company had become liable to its customers for misselling pensions. As a preliminary issue, it was to be determined 'whether on the proper construction of the [insurance policy], all the misselling claims (...) fall to be treated as one claim for the purposes of applying the limit of indemnity (...)'.[115] Morison J opined that a cause was 'not just "something altogether less constricted"' than an event as Lord Mustill had suggested. Rather, the term 'cause' fulfilled a different function. More specifically, he argued that the term 'event' described what had happened, whereas the word 'cause' described why something had happened.[116] The reason for the cases of misselling, he declared, was 'the lack of proper training of the selling agents and employees'.[117] Accordingly, Morison J concluded that the original cause, based on which an aggregation of all the misselling losses was possible, consisted of a lack of training.

3.49 In *Municipal Mutual Insurance Ltd v Sea Insurance Co Ltd*, the reinsured, Municipal Mutual Insurance, insured the Port of Sunderland. One of the latter's customers stored cranes at the port. Over a period of some three years, the cranes were vandalised in a succession of individual acts of pilferage for which the port was held liable.[118] Among the issues before the court was the question whether the losses resulting from these individual acts of pilferage could be aggregated and presented to the reinsurers as one single loss. Hobhouse LJ held that the individual losses resulted from one original cause, which was the port's lack of an 'adequate system to protect

---

113 For a discussion of the unifying factor of 'source', see paras 3.81 f.

114 *Axa Reinsurance (UK) Ltd v Field* (n 3) 1035 (Lord Mustill).

115 *Countrywide Assured Group Plc v Marshall* (n 51) [5] (Morison J).

116 *Countrywide Assured Group Plc v Marshall* (n 51) [15] (Morison J). See also Merkin (n 52) 145.

117 *Countrywide Assured Group Plc v Marshall* (n 51) [15] (Morison J).

118 *Municipal Mutual Insurance Ltd v Sea Insurance Co Ltd* (n 4) 961 (Hobhouse LJ).

the goods from pilferage and vandalism'.[119] Consequently, the lack of an adequate system to protect the goods from pilferage was the original cause based on which all the individual losses that occurred within one policy period were to be aggregated.

3.50 In the same vein, in *American Centennial Insurance Co v INSCO*, the Commercial Court stated, *obiter*, that 'where several people reach a common culpable misunderstanding as the result of discussions between them on which they all subsequently act it might be possible, depending on the facts of the case, to find in their discussions a single originating cause' of multiple negligent acts.[120] In other words, if the misunderstanding of multiple people has one single origin such as a discussion, this origin may be considered the originating cause for all the negligent acts and omissions that are committed based on the misunderstanding.

3.51 As an originating or original cause can lie in a state of affairs,[121] it might arguably also consist in a plan,[122] a decision[123] or a state of ignorance.[124] Generally, original or originating causes can be seen in any common origin of multiple individual losses to be aggregated.[125] It has even been suggested that the 'susceptibility of New Zealand to earthquakes could potentially be an originating cause'.[126] This is supported by Lord Mustill's analysis that the word 'originating' 'opens up the widest possible search for a unifying factor in the history of the losses which it is sought to aggregate'.[127]

3.52 Although the unifying factor of cause may be considered a lot wider than the unifying factor of event,[128] the Court of Appeal held in *Brown (RE) v GIO Insurance Ltd* that in some circumstances the terms 'event' and 'cause' may well refer 'precisely to the same thing, or at least to no different conclusion so far as aggregation is concerned'.[129] In fact, any event from which multiple individual claims arise can be considered their cause. Conversely, not every cause can be considered a relevant event for the purposes of aggregation.[130] For instance, each act of misselling may constitute a relevant event. At the same time, each act may also be considered the

---

119 *Municipal Mutual Insurance Ltd v Sea Insurance Co Ltd* (n 4) 967 (Hobhouse LJ).

120 *American Centennial Insurance Co v INSCO Ltd* (n 34) 414 (Moore-Bick J).

121 Louw and Tompkinson (n 35) 11. Cf also *Axa Reinsurance (UK) Ltd v Field* (n 3) 1035 (Lord Mustill); O'Neill, Woloniecki and Arnold-Dwyer (n 1) para 11–326; Butler and Merkin (n 19) para C–0239.

122 Cf *Dawson's Field Arbitration*, quoted in: *Kuwait Airways Corp v Kuwait Insurance Co SAK* (n 53); *Midland Mainline Ltd v Eagle Star Insurance Co Ltd* (n 50) [97] (Steel J); *Aioi Nissay Dowa Insurance Co Ltd v Heraldglen Ltd and Advent Capital Ltd* (n 44) [20] (Field J).

123 Cf *Midland Mainline Ltd v Eagle Star Insurance Co Ltd* (n 50) [97] (Steel J).

124 Cf *Caudle v Sharp* (n 33) 649 (Evans LJ).

125 Cf *Standard Life Assurance Ltd v Ace European Group* (n 41) [259] (Eder J).

126 Merkin (n 52) 145 f. Cf also *Moore v IAG New Zealand Ltd* (n 65).

127 *Axa Reinsurance (UK) Ltd v Field* (n 3) 1035 (Lord Mustill).

128 *Axa Reinsurance (UK) Ltd v Field* (n 3) 1035 (Lord Mustill); *Municipal Mutual Insurance Ltd v Sea Insurance Co Ltd* (n 4) 967 (Hobhouse LJ); *Countrywide Assured Group Plc v Marshall* (n 51) [15] (Morison J). Cf also *American Centennial Insurance Co v INSCO Ltd* (n 34) 413 f (Moore-Bick J).

129 *Brown (RE) v GIO Insurance Ltd* (n 50) 204 (Waller LJ).

130 Cf Louw and Tompkinson (n 35) 9; Merkin (n 52) 146.

cause of the corresponding loss. By contrast, although the lack of proper training of the selling personnel may constitute the losses' originating cause, it cannot be considered an event for the purposes of aggregation.[131]

b Causative link and limit of remoteness

3.53 In *American Centennial Insurance Co v INSCO Ltd*, the Commercial Court clarified that although the unifying factor of cause was one of 'a remote kind (...) it is still necessary for there to be some causative link between the originating cause and the loss and there must also be some limit to the degree of remoteness that is acceptable'.[132]

3.54 In *Axa Reinsurance (UK) Ltd v Field*, Lord Mustill explained that 'the word "originating" was in [his] view consciously chosen to open up the widest possible search for a unifying factor in the history of the losses which it is sought to aggregate'.[133]

3.55 Moreover, the words 'or source'[134] in an aggregation clause constitute an explicit alternative to the word 'cause' and further emphasise that the aggregation mechanism is wide and that multiple individual losses may be aggregated based on a remote factor.[135]

3.56 From these cases, it becomes clear that it is possible to 'look further back' and 'to use a remoter common fact' with the unifying factor of cause than it is with the unifying factor of event.[136] Yet, to borrow the words of Louw and Tompkinson, English courts have not given 'much assistance in determining where in the landscape between here and the infinity of remoteness'[137] a relevant cause may lie. Consequently, there appears to be no legal certainty as to the causal requirements associated with the unifying factor of originating or original cause.

2.3 Other unifying factors

a 'Occurrence'

3.57 As has been mentioned above, the notion of 'occurrence'[138] is not consistently used in the context of reinsurance contracts.

3.58 In some aggregation clauses, the term 'occurrence' refers to one of the individual units to be aggregated, ie to an individual loss.[139] For instance, it was held in *Tokio Marine Europe Insurance Ltd v Novae Corporate Underwriting Ltd* that the

---

131 Cf *Countrywide Assured Group Plc v Marshall* (n 51) [15] (Morison J).

132 *American Centennial Insurance Co v INSCO Ltd* (n 34) 414 (Moore-Bick J).

133 *Axa Reinsurance (UK) Ltd v Field* (n 3) 1035 (Lord Mustill).

134 For more information on the unifying factor of 'source', see paras 3.81 f.

135 *Standard Life Assurance Ltd v Ace European Group* (n 41) [259] (Eder J).

136 Louw and Tompkinson (n 35) 11. Cf also Butler and Merkin (n 19) para C–0241.

137 Louw and Tompkinson (n 35) 8. It is to be noted that these words have been used in the context of determining what can be considered a relevant event for the purposes of aggregation.

138 See paras 2.55 ff.

139 See paras 2.56 ff.

phrase 'loss occurrence' used in a retrocession agreement was to be construed the same way as the word 'occurrence' in the underlying contract of reinsurance. The Commercial Court elaborated that in the case at hand, the term 'occurrence' was defined to mean 'any one Occurrence or any series of Occurrences consequent upon or attributable to one source or original cause'.[140] Apparently, the court considered that the words 'occurrence' and 'loss occurrence' referred to the individual losses and that under the aggregation clause these losses were to be aggregated if they were attributable to the same source or cause.[141] In its reasoning, the Commercial Court held that the word 'loss occurrence' was not used in the sense of the unifying factor of event.[142]

3.59 As has been demonstrated above, however, the term 'occurrence' generally designates a unifying factor in the context of aggregation.[143] Where the term identifies a unifying factor, it is said to be interchangeable with the term 'event'.[144] Hence, the legal uncertainties associated with what can properly be considered an event[145] and the vagueness of the standard of the causal links[146] required between the individual losses to be aggregated and the unifying factor equally exist where the unifying factor is termed 'occurrence'.[147]

3.60 Thus, the meaning of the term 'occurrence' depends on the contractual context in which it is used.

---

140 *Tokio Marine Europe Insurance Ltd v Novae Corporate Underwriting Ltd* [2013] EWHC 3362 (Comm), [2014] 1 Lloyd's Rep IR 490 [51], [59] (Hamblen J).

141 *Tokio Marine Europe Insurance Ltd v Novae Corporate Underwriting Ltd* (n 140) [51]–[65] (Hamblen J).

142 *Tokio Marine Europe Insurance Ltd v Novae Corporate Underwriting Ltd* (n 140) [62] (Hamblen J).

143 See paras 2.61 ff.

144 *Dawson's Field Arbitration*, quoted in: *Kuwait Airways Corp v Kuwait Insurance Co SAK* (n 53); *American Centennial Insurance Co v INSCO Ltd* (n 34) 413 (Moore-Bick J); *Mann v Lexington Insurance Co* (n 53) 1411, where Walker J's first instance judgment is transcribed; *Aioi Nissay Dowa Insurance Co Ltd v Heraldglen Ltd and Advent Capital Ltd* (n 44) [20] (Field J); Barlow Lyde and Gilbert LLP (n 4) para 28.6; Malcolm A Clarke, *The Law of Insurance Contracts* (6th edn, Informa 2009) para 17–4C3; Soar (n 52); Edelman and Burns (n 2) paras 4.55 ff; Merkin, Hodgson and Tyldesley (n 8) para 11–324; Butler and Merkin (n 19) para C–0222. For an American authority in this regard, see *Newmont Mines Ltd v Hanover Insurance Co* (1986) 784 F2d 127 (United States Court of Appeals for the Second Circuit) 135.

145 See paras 3.30 ff.

146 See paras 3.38 ff.

147 Cf *Scott v The Copenhagen Reinsurance Co (UK) Ltd* (n 20) [68] (Rix LJ). In *Caudle v Sharp* (n 33), the Court of Appeal dealt with the following aggregation clause: 'For the purpose of this reinsurance the term "each and every loss" shall be understood to mean each and every loss and/or occurrence (…) arising out of one event'. At first sight, one might think that the terms 'loss' and 'occurrence' are equivalents under this aggregation clause. The Court of Appeal found, however, that the term 'occurrence' was 'at least capable of meaning the operation of the insured peril out of which the original loss arose, and that occurrence has itself arisen out of the relevant "event" (…)'. Accordingly, in light of this aggregation clause, the Court of Appeal considered it possible that the words 'event' and 'occurrence' had not been used interchangeably. This further complicates the question of the causal requirements as the required causal link between the 'event' and the 'occurrence' is not clear nor is the one between the 'occurrence' and the 'original loss'.

b 'Accident'

3.61 The parties sometimes use the term 'accident' in the context of clauses describing the applicable deductible or cover limit. Particularly in English law, the notion of 'accident' has, however, repeatedly been held not to operate as a unifying factor.

3.62 In *The South Staffordshire Tramways Co Ltd v The Sickness and Accident Assurance Association Ltd,* the courts dealt with a clause limiting the insurer's liability 'in respect of any one accident'.[148] The insured, a tramcar company, was held liable for personal injury to forty persons after one of its tramcars was overturned. At first instance, Day J considered that an accident was simply an event and that the tramcar's overturning constituted such an event which resulted in injuries to a large number of persons.[149] Consequently, all 40 losses resulting from the injuries were to be aggregated and the policy limit applied one single time to this aggregate. The Court of Appeal, however, overturned Day J's judgment. It held that each person suffered a separate accident so that there was no basis for an aggregation of the 40 individual losses.[150]

3.63 Similarly, in *Allen v London Guarantee and Accident Co Ltd,* the Commercial Court dealt with a clause providing that the insurer's cover limit was £300 for all claims 'in respect of or arising out of any one accident or occurrence'.[151] The insured's car struck one person, causing the latter to crash into a second person and left both injured. Phillimore J held that as two persons were injured, two separate accidents had befallen. However, he went on to state that there was, nevertheless, only one occurrence that took place. Hence, Phillimore J considered that an accident was not the same thing as an occurrence. The individual losses that arose from the injuries were to be aggregated on the basis that they arose out of the same occurrence.[152] By contrast, the term 'accident' did not operate as a unifying factor.

3.64 The term 'accident' was further considered in *Tioxide Europe Ltd v CGU International Insurance Plc.* Tioxide's product liability policy provided that '[t]he word loss wherever used in this policy, means an accident, including continuous or repeated exposure to the same general harmful conditions'.[153]

3.65 Tioxide manufactured two grades of white titanium dioxide pigments. The pigments were supplied for use in the manufacture of u-PVC compounds which in

---

148 *The South Staffordshire Tramways Co Ltd v The Sickness and Accident Assurance Association Ltd* (n 54).

149 *The South Staffordshire Tramways Co Ltd v The Sickness and Accident Assurance Association Ltd* (n 54) 405, where Day J's first instance decision is transcribed.

150 *The South Staffordshire Tramways Co Ltd v The Sickness and Accident Assurance Association Ltd* (n 54) 407 f (Bowen LJ).

151 *Allen v London Guarantee and Accident Co Ltd* (1912) 28 TLR 254 (Comm).

152 *Allen v London Guarantee and Accident Co Ltd* (n 151).

153 *Tioxide Europe Ltd v CGU International Insurance Plc* [2004] EWHC 216 (Comm), [2005] Lloyd's Rep IR 114 [34] (Langley J).

turn were to be used in the manufacture of doors and window frames. The pigments manufactured by Tioxide caused discolouration of the doors and window frames in which they were used. One of the questions before the Commercial Court was whether there was one single accident from which multiple individual losses had arisen.[154] The court held that each instance of discolouration constituted a separate accident and, hence, a separate loss.[155] Thus, the term 'accident' was not considered a unifying factor that justified adding together the losses associated with the individual cases of discolouration.[156]

3.66 In line with this, Merkin noted that an accident was 'the individual manifestation of a loss rather than the state of affairs which gave rise to those losses'.[157] The aforementioned decisions suggest that the notion of 'accident' is not to be considered a unifying factor for the purposes of aggregation.

3.67 Yet, in *Tioxide Europe Ltd v CGU International Insurance Plc*, the Commercial Court noted, *obiter*, that–depending on the circumstances–the term 'accident' could operate as unifying factor. More specifically, it stated that an 'an explosion or escape giving rise to a multiplicity of claims' may be considered an accident.[158]

3.68 In summary, it may be said that English courts have been reluctant to recognise the term 'accident' as a unifying factor. The Commercial Court suggested, however, that–depending on the circumstances–it could indeed operate as a unifying factor. The causal requirements associated with the unifying factor of 'accident' remain unclear.

---

154 *Tioxide Europe Ltd v CGU International Insurance Plc* (n 153) list of split issues following [83] (Langley J).

155 *Tioxide Europe Ltd v CGU International Insurance Plc* (n 153) [54] (Langley J).

156 *Tioxide Europe Ltd v CGU International Insurance Plc* (n 153) [53]–[54] (Langley J).

157 Merkin, Hodgson and Tyldesley (n 8) para 11–323. Yet, in Butler and Merkin (n 19) para C–0219, the authors argue that an 'accident' may constitute a unifying factor.

158 *Tioxide Europe Ltd v CGU International Insurance Plc* (n 153) [53] (Langley J). The case *Re Deep Vein Thrombosis Litigation* [2003] EWCA Civ 1005, [2004] QB 234, deals with the term of 'accident' within the meaning of Article 17 of the Warsaw Convention for the Unification of certain rules relating to international carriage by air. The issue before the Court of Appeal was not one of aggregation. Remarkably, the Court of Appeal considered that when determining the meaning of the term 'accident', Lord Mustill's definition in *Axa Reinsurance (UK) Ltd v Field* (n 3) 1035, of what constitutes an event in the context of aggregation can be applied. It is further to be noted that a number of American courts have held that the terms 'accident' and 'occurrence' were synonymous so that the term 'accident' operated as a unifying factor for the purposes of aggregation, see *The Arthur A Johnson Corp v Indemnity Insurance Co of North America* (1958) 6 AD2d 97 (Supreme Court, Appellate Division, First Department, New York) 101 f; *Hartford Accident and Indemnity Co v Edward Wesolowski* (1973) 33 NY2d 169 (Court of Appeals of New York) [6]; *Metropolitan Life Insurance Co v Aetna Casualty and Surety Co* (2001) 255 Conn 295 (Supreme Court of Connecticut) 14, 20. Some insurance policies even define the term 'occurrence' as an 'accident', see, for instance, *Stonewall Insurance Co v Asbestos Claims Management Corp* (1995) 73 F3d 1178 (United States Court of Appeals for the Second Circuit) 1213.

c 'Act or omission'

3.69 In some aggregation clauses, the parties designate 'one act or omission'[159] or 'any single act or omission'[160] as 'the' or 'one of the' unifying factors for the purposes of aggregation.

3.70 In *Lloyd's TSB General Insurance Holdings Ltd v Lloyd's Bank Group Insurance Co Ltd*, the House of Lords found that the phrase 'act or omission' was to be construed the same way in the aggregation provision as it was in the liability clause.[161] The latter insured against 'a breach "in respect of which civil liability arises on the part of the assured"'.[162] Hence, the relevant 'act or omission' was the conduct which triggered the primary insured's liability and not any 'act or omission which [was] causally more remote'.[163] Lord Hoffmann expressly stated that not '"any act or omission", but only and specifically an act or omission which [gave] rise to the civil liability in question' was to be considered a unifying factor for the purposes of aggregation.[164] The House of Lords, therefore, concluded that, in this instance, the required causal link between the individual losses to be aggregated and the unifying factor of 'act or omission' corresponded with the standard of proximate cause.[165] Lord Hoffmann noted that '[a]n act or omission could qualify as a unifying factor in respect of more than one loss only if it gave rise to civil liability in respect of both losses'.[166]

3.71 Although the House of Lords held that the causal link between the unifying factor of 'act or omission' and each of the individual losses corresponded with the standard of proximate cause, a careful reading of the decision renders it impossible to conclude that the unifying factor of 'act or omission' generally corresponds with the standard of proximate cause. Lord Hoffmann made clear that where the contract provides that 'any acts or omissions', rather than only acts or omissions giving rise to civil liability, may operate as unifying factors, causal requirements might be different.[167]

---

159 *AIG Europe Ltd v OC320301 LLP* (n 51) [8] (Longmore LJ); *AIG Europe Ltd v Woodman* (n 4) [1] (Lord Toulson SCJ). Cf also *Standard Life Assurance Ltd v Oak Dedicated Ltd* (n 51) [14] (Tomlinson J) and *Standard Life Assurance Ltd v Ace European Group* (n 41) [255] (Eder J), where the aggregation clauses used the unifying factor of 'any one act, error, omission (...)'.

160 *Lloyd's TSB General Insurance Holdings Ltd v Lloyd's Bank Group Insurance Co Ltd* (n 6) [12] (Lord Hoffmann).

161 *Lloyd's TSB General Insurance Holdings Ltd v Lloyd's Bank Group Insurance Co Ltd* (n 6) [43] (Lord Hobhouse).

162 *Lloyd's TSB General Insurance Holdings Ltd v Lloyd's Bank Group Insurance Co Ltd* (n 6) [20] (Lord Hoffmann).

163 *Lloyd's TSB General Insurance Holdings Ltd v Lloyd's Bank Group Insurance Co Ltd* (n 6) [20] (Lord Hoffmann).

164 *Lloyd's TSB General Insurance Holdings Ltd v Lloyd's Bank Group Insurance Co Ltd* (n 6) [25] (Lord Hoffmann).

165 *Lloyd's TSB General Insurance Holdings Ltd v Lloyd's Bank Group Insurance Co Ltd* (n 6) [43] (Lord Hobhouse). In respect of the fundamental principle of 'insurance law that the insurer is only liable for losses proximately caused by the peril' covered, see Birds, Lynch and Paul (n 8) para 21–001.

166 *Lloyd's TSB General Insurance Holdings Ltd v Lloyd's Bank Group Insurance Co Ltd* (n 6) [23] (Lord Hoffmann).

167 *Lloyd's TSB General Insurance Holdings Ltd v Lloyd's Bank Group Insurance Co Ltd* (n 6) [25] (Lord Hoffmann).

3.72 In *AIG Europe Ltd v Woodman*, the Supreme Court considered an aggregation clause containing a variety of different unifying factors one of which was 'one act or omission'.[168] It held that the words 'one act or omission' 'requires no further explanation'.[169] It seems that the unifying factor of 'one act or omission' was not the pertinent one in the case before the Supreme Court, which, therefore, declined to discuss it in detail. In light of Lord Hoffmann's speech in *Lloyd's TSB General Insurance Holdings Ltd v Lloyd's Bank Group Insurance Co Ltd*,[170] it should, however, not be assumed that the causal requirements associated with the phrase 'act or omission' were clear and undisputed.

3.73 In summary, depending on the context of the aggregation clause, the unifying factor of 'act or omission' might be associated with the causative standard of proximate cause. In such a case, the causal link between the unifying factor and each of the individual losses must be even stronger than where the parties use the unifying factor of event.[171] Yet, it might well be that the causative requirements associated with the unifying 'act or omission' are less strict in other circumstances.

d 'Catastrophe', 'disaster', 'calamity'

3.74 A further type of aggregation provisions contains the terms 'catastrophe', 'disaster' and 'calamity'.[172] They read:

> For the purpose of this reinsurance the term 'each and every loss' shall be understood to mean each and every loss and/or occurrence and/or catastrophe and/or disaster and/or calamity (...) arising out of one event.[173]

3.75 On its face, the wording of the clause suggests that a 'catastrophe', a 'disaster' or a 'calamity' assumes the same function as a loss or an occurrence. It is notable that not all of these terms operate as unifying factors. The unifying factor provided for in this clause is 'one event'.[174]

3.76 In *Caudle v Sharp*, where this clause was discussed, Evans LJ stated that 'on a strict reading of the clause, the "catastrophe and/or disaster and/or calamity" [was] treated as equivalent to the "loss and/or occurrence" and must itself have arisen out of one event'.[175] He noted, however, that in his view 'a strictly

---

168 *AIG Europe Ltd v Woodman* (n 4) [1] (Lord Toulson SCJ).

169 *AIG Europe Ltd v Woodman* (n 4) [15] (Lord Toulson SCJ).

170 *Lloyd's TSB General Insurance Holdings Ltd v Lloyd's Bank Group Insurance Co Ltd* (n 6) [25] (Lord Hoffmann).

171 For the causative link required in respect of the unifying factor of 'event', see paras 3.38 ff.

172 *Caudle v Sharp* (n 33) 644; *Axa Reinsurance (UK) Ltd v Field* [1995] CLC 1504 (CA) 1505 f, where Phillips J's first instance decision is transcribed; *Axa Reinsurance (UK) Ltd v Field* (n 3) 1029 (Lord Mustill); *Denby v English and Scottish Maritime Insurance Co Ltd; Yasuda Fire and Marine Co of Europe Ltd v Lloyd's Underwriting Syndicates no 209, 356* (n 50) 873 (Hobhouse LJ); *IRB Brasil Resseguros SA v CX Reinsurance Co Ltd* (n 50) [11] (Burton J).

173 *Caudle v Sharp* (n 33) 644 (Evans LJ).

174 *Caudle v Sharp* (n 33) 648 (Evans LJ).

175 *Caudle v Sharp* (n 33) 648 (Evans LJ).

literal meaning of the clause [was] not sufficient to give effect to the intentions of the parties (...)'.[176] By so saying, Evans LJ was presumably suggesting that the terms 'catastrophe', 'disaster' and 'calamity' operated as unifying factors, just like the term 'event', rather than as equivalents to the term 'loss'. If this was the case, it seems that multiple individual losses were to be aggregated if they all arose out of the same catastrophe, disaster or calamity.

3.77 Similarly, Merkin appears to regard the notions of 'catastrophe',[177] 'occurrence' and 'event' as synonymous, which he conceives as being used as unifying factors.[178] More precisely, he equated the phrases 'catastrophic occurrence' and 'catastrophic event'.[179] Merkin opines that there was room for argument as to whether a catastrophe such as an earthquake was an event or an occurrence for excess of loss treaty purposes.[180]

3.78 By contrast, Tompkinson seems to have a different understanding of the roles attributed to terms such as 'catastrophe', 'disaster' and 'calamity'. She affords the example of a hurricane damaging multiple different houses. In this scenario, she argues, each harmed house might constitute a separate occurrence, ie a separate 'incident of damage (loss)'.[181] Tompkinson does not explicitly state that each individual loss also constitutes a catastrophe, disaster or calamity. She notes, however, that the terms 'occurrence', 'catastrophe', 'disaster' and 'calamity' were alternative phrases that are meant to assume the same role within the aggregation mechanism.[182]

3.79 In any case, it appears doubtful whether the distinction between the terms 'event', 'occurrence', 'catastrophe', 'disaster' and 'calamity' is useful.[183] In fact, 'if each word is to be afforded a separate and distinct meaning, much splitting of hairs will be required'.[184] Furthermore, there is no authority for the proposition that these different terms each come with a distinguishable concept of causation. In line with what has been previously discussed, the term 'occurrence', in the context of aggregation, generally refers to a unifying factor and is interchangeable with the term 'event'.[185] Arguably, the terms 'catastrophe', 'disaster' and 'calamity' are to be

---

176 *Caudle v Sharp* (n 33) 648 (Evans LJ).

177 This is presumably also true with regard to the terms 'calamity' and 'disaster'.

178 Merkin (n 52) 144 f.

179 Merkin (n 52) 144 f.

180 Merkin (n 52) 147. Cf also *Moore v IAG New Zealand Ltd* (n 65) where Dunningham J held that the original earthquake was the 'cause' of two aftershocks, both of which were considered to be 'events' for the purpose of the aggregation clause under consideration.

181 Deborah Tompkinson, 'Jabberwocky: Recent Decisions on the Meaning of "Event" and "Occurrence" in the English Courts' (1995) 3 International Insurance Law Review 82, 82.

182 Tompkinson (n 181) 82.

183 Tompkinson (n 181) 82.

184 Tompkinson (n 181) 82, views the terms 'occurrence', 'catastrophe', 'disaster' and 'calamity' as synonymous, but distinguishes them from the term 'event'.

185 See paras 2.61 ff, 3.59.

equated with the terms 'event' and 'occurrence'.[186] If so, all these terms would be used to designate an aggregation mechanism's unifying factor.

3.80 In summary, there appear to be different views as to the roles terms such as 'catastrophe', 'disaster' and 'calamity' assume in aggregation mechanisms. The Court of Appeal has noted that a strictly literal reading of typical aggregation clauses equating such terms with the term 'loss' would not reflect the parties' intention. Furthermore, there appears to be no legal authority that attributes different meanings to the notions of 'occurrence', 'catastrophe', 'disaster' and 'calamity' in the context of aggregation. Hence, the proliferation of terms does not foster legal certainty but rather further dispels it.

e 'Source'

3.81 Particularly in the context of cause-based aggregation, the parties sometimes agree to aggregate individual losses on the basis that they stem from the same 'source'.[187] In *Standard Life Assurance Ltd v Ace European Group*, it was observed by the Commercial Court that the word 'source' was an 'explicit alternative to "cause"'.[188]

3.82 Commonly, the unifying factor of 'source' is coupled with the unifying factor of 'cause'. There seem to be no legal authorities distinguishing the causative potencies of the two unifying factors. They are, instead, to be read in combination so that one standard of causation results from the phrases 'originating cause or source' and 'one source or original cause'.[189]

2.4 The special case of series clauses

3.83 Aggregation clauses sometimes use the unifying factors of a 'related series of acts or omissions',[190] a 'series of related acts or omissions'[191] or a 'series of related matters or transactions'.[192] Aggregation clauses using unifying factors of this kind are referred to as series clauses.[193]

---

186 It may be noted, however, that a sub-group of the International Underwriting Association considered that the word 'catastrophe' provided more flexibility than the word 'event', see 'IUA 01–033 Definition of Loss Occurrence (Hours Clause) – Commentary' para 4.2 <http://iuaclauses.co.uk/site/cms/contentDocumentLibraryView.asp?chapter=5> accessed 24 March 2020.

187 *Municipal Mutual Insurance Ltd v Sea Insurance Co Ltd* (n 4) 959, 961 (Hobhouse LJ); *Countrywide Assured Group Plc v Marshall* (n 51) [3] (Morison J); *Standard Life Assurance Ltd v Oak Dedicated Ltd* (n 51) [14] (Tomlinson J); *Beazley Underwriting Ltd v Travelers Co Inc* [2011] EWHC 1520 (Comm) [28] (Clarke J); *Standard Life Assurance Ltd v Ace European Group* (n 41) [255] (Eder J); *Tokio Marine Europe Insurance Ltd v Novae Corporate Underwriting Ltd* (n 140) [51] (Hamblen J); *Spire Healthcare Ltd v Royal and Sun Alliance Insurance Plc* (n 30) [3] (Simon LJ).

188 *Standard Life Assurance Ltd v Ace European Group* (n 41) [259] (Eder J).

189 *Municipal Mutual Insurance Ltd v Sea Insurance Co Ltd* (n 4) 967 (Hobhouse LJ). Cf also Butler and Merkin (n 19) para C–0240.

190 *Lloyd's TSB General Insurance Holdings Ltd v Lloyd's Bank Group Insurance Co Ltd* (n 6) [12] (Lord Hoffmann).

191 *AIG Europe Ltd v Woodman* (n 4) [1] (Lord Toulson SCJ).

192 *AIG Europe Ltd v Woodman* (n 4) [1] (Lord Toulson SCJ).

193 Barlow Lyde and Gilbert LLP (n 4) paras 28.75 ff; Merkin, Hodgson and Tyldesley (n 8) paras 11–341 ff. For cases from other jurisdictions dealing with the term 'series', see *The Distillers Co Biochemicals (Australia) Pty Ltd v Ajax Insurance Co Ltd* (1974) 130 CLR 1 (HCA); *Bank of*

3.84 Where the parties agree on a series clause, they deem that multiple individual losses are to be aggregated if they result from events, acts, omissions, transactions or matters that are related and form a series.[194] Yet, it is important to note that series clauses are not to be read in isolation.[195] In *Lloyd's TSB General Insurance Holdings Ltd v Lloyd's Bank Group Insurance Co Ltd*, Lord Hoffmann pointed out that '[w]hen one speaks of events being "related" or forming a "series", the nature of the unifying [element] which makes them related or a series must be expressed or implied by the sentence in which the words are used'.[196] Thus, series clauses are always to be construed in light of the wider context of the aggregation clause and other related provisions.[197]

3.85 Therefore, it seems impossible to attribute an established meaning to phrases such as 'related series of acts or omissions', 'series of related acts or omissions' and 'series of related matters or transactions'. From the fact that the parties use a series clause, no inference can be made as to the broadness of the aggregation mechanism. Any of the phrases mentioned are capable of forming part of a very broad or a very narrow aggregation mechanism. In fact, the broadness of the aggregation mechanism entirely depends on the unifying element that makes multiple events, acts, omissions, transactions or matters related or a series.[198] Series clauses regularly fail, however, to expressly describe this element.

3.86 Moreover, although it has been held in *Lloyd's TSB General Insurance Holdings Ltd v Lloyd's Bank Group Insurance Co Ltd* that sometimes it might 'be necessary to imply [the] unifying [element] from the general context,[199] it appears to be utterly difficult to so. Consequently, the insurance and reinsurance markets are left with no legal certainty as to the operation of unifying factors that are based on series of events, acts, omissions, transactions or matters.

a *Lloyd's TSB General Insurance Holdings Ltd v Lloyd's Bank Group Insurance Co Ltd*

3.87 In *Lloyd's TSB General Insurance Holdings Ltd v Lloyd's Bank Group Insurance Co Ltd*, the House of Lords dealt with a case where salesmen sold personal pension schemes without adequate advice about the risks, advantages and

---

Queensland Ltd v AIG Australia Ltd [2019] NSWCA 190, [2019] Lloyd's Rep IR 639; *Moore v IAG New Zealand Ltd* (n 65).

194 Cannon (n 7) para 38. It is to be noted that Merkin (n 52) n 106, argues that the series clause is the professional indemnity equivalent of an hours clause.

195 Cannon (n 7) para 40.

196 *Lloyd's TSB General Insurance Holdings Ltd v Lloyd's Bank Group Insurance Co Ltd* (n 6) [26] (Lord Hoffmann).

197 Cannon (n 7) para 40.

198 *Countrywide Assured Group Plc v Marshall* (n 51) [14], where Morison J stated the following: 'When is an occurrence part of a series of occurrences? To form part of a series there must be some connecting factor which links occurrences which would otherwise be separate'.

199 *Lloyd's TSB General Insurance Holdings Ltd v Lloyd's Bank Group Insurance Co Ltd* (n 6) [26] (Lord Hoffmann).

disadvantages to a number of employees. The underlying reason for these cases of misselling was primarily 'the inadequacy of the training and monitoring' of the salesmen by the companies employing them.[200] By failing to provide adequate training to their salesmen and monitoring them, the company breached the LAUTRO rules. As a breach of the LAUTRO rules was actionable under the Financial Services Act 1986,[201] 22,000 persons who invested in the personal pension schemes filed action against the company.[202] Most of the claims were for relatively small amounts. None of the claims exceeded £35,000. In total, however, the company paid out more than £125 million in compensation.[203]

3.88 The question before their Lordships was 'whether the (...) companies [could] recover any part' of the damages paid under their contract of insurance.[204] As the relevant deductible amounted to £1 million, 'each and every claim'[205] and the individual losses did not exceed £35,000, the issue at hand primarily revolved around the construction of the aggregation clause contained in the contract of insurance:

> *If a series of third party claims shall result from any single act or omission (or related series of acts or omissions) then, irrespective of the total number of claims, all such third party claims shall be considered to be a single third party claim for the purposes of the application of the deductible.*[206]

3.89 The question pertained to the meanings of 'act or omission' and '(related series of acts or omissions)'.[207] Lord Hoffmann and Lord Hobhouse both agreed with the Court of Appeal that the phrase 'act or omission' in the aggregation clause had the same meaning as the phrase 'act or omission' in the insuring clause.[208] It was stated that 'an "act or omission" must be something which constitutes the investor's cause of action. It cannot mean an act or omission which is causally more remote'.[209] Consequently, '[a]n act or omission could qualify as a unifying factor in respect of more than one loss only if it gave rise to civil liability in respect of both losses'.[210] Lord

---

200 *Lloyd's TSB General Insurance Holdings Ltd v Lloyd's Bank Group Insurance Co Ltd* (n 6) [5] (Lord Hoffmann).

201 The Financial Services Act 1986 has since been repealed and replaced by the Financial Services and Markets Act 2000.

202 *Lloyd's TSB General Insurance Holdings Ltd v Lloyd's Bank Group Insurance Co Ltd* (n 6) [6] (Lord Hoffmann).

203 *Lloyd's TSB General Insurance Holdings Ltd v Lloyd's Bank Group Insurance Co Ltd* (n 6) [7] (Lord Hoffmann).

204 *Lloyd's TSB General Insurance Holdings Ltd v Lloyd's Bank Group Insurance Co Ltd* (n 6) [8] (Lord Hoffmann).

205 *Lloyd's TSB General Insurance Holdings Ltd v Lloyd's Bank Group Insurance Co Ltd* (n 6) [11] (Lord Hoffmann).

206 *Lloyd's TSB General Insurance Holdings Ltd v Lloyd's Bank Group Insurance Co Ltd* (n 6) [12] (Lord Hoffmann).

207 *Lloyd's TSB General Insurance Holdings Ltd v Lloyd's Bank Group Insurance Co Ltd* (n 6) [18] (Lord Hoffmann).

208 *Lloyd's TSB General Insurance Holdings Ltd v Lloyd's Bank Group Insurance Co Ltd* (n 6) [20] (Lord Hoffmann), [43] (Lord Hobhouse).

209 *Lloyd's TSB General Insurance Holdings Ltd v Lloyd's Bank Group Insurance Co Ltd* (n 6) [20] (Lord Hoffmann).

Hoffmann clarified that the act or omission which gave rise to the company's civil liability was each salesman's failure to give best advice. Hence, it was not possible to aggregate multiple individual losses on the basis of an 'act or omission'.[211]

3.90 The House of Lords then turned to the question of whether an aggregation of the individual losses was possible on the basis of the unifying factor of '(related series of acts or omissions)'. In this regard, Lord Hoffmann criticised the Court of Appeal that had ruled that acts or omissions could be considered a 'related series' if they had a 'single underlying cause', a 'common origin' or if they were 'the same omission' which had occurred on more than one occasion.[212] More specifically, Lord Hoffmann analysed that by designating 'an act or omission which gives rise to the civil liability in question' as unifying factor, the parties had chosen a unifying factor which is even narrower than 'any one event'.[213] Lord Hoffmann and Lord Hobhouse regarded it as unlikely that the parties intended to abrogate this narrow aggregation basis and produce 'a clause in which the unifying factor is as broad as one could possibly wish' by adding a series language in parenthesis.[214]

3.91 Lord Hobhouse stated that under the unifying factor of '(related series of acts or omissions)' the individual losses 'still [had] to result from something done or omitted as between the relevant "consultant" and the relevant third party'. He found that the fact that the company employing the salesmen failed to 'ensure' that the salesmen were properly trained and monitored did not relate the separate acts of misselling.[215] With a view to making sense of the unifying factor, Lord Hobhouse gave the example of a consultant who prepared a document which misrepresented the merits of the pension scheme he was endeavouring to sell and gave that document to a number of interested people. His Lordship concluded that each act of giving the misleading document to an investor would be a distinct act. However, the acts could be considered a 'related series' from which 'a series of third party claims' had resulted.[216] As no such document was handed out to the investors in the case before the House of Lords, Lord Hobhouse rejected the idea that the individual acts of misselling constituted 'a related series of acts' due to which an aggregation of the individual losses was not possible.

---

210 *Lloyd's TSB General Insurance Holdings Ltd v Lloyd's Bank Group Insurance Co Ltd* (n 6) [23] (Lord Hoffmann).

211 *Lloyd's TSB General Insurance Holdings Ltd v Lloyd's Bank Group Insurance Co Ltd* (n 6) [23] (Lord Hoffmann).

212 *Lloyd's TSB General Insurance Holdings Ltd v Lloyd's Bank Group Insurance Co Ltd* (n 6) [24] (Lord Hoffmann).

213 *Lloyd's TSB General Insurance Holdings Ltd v Lloyd's Bank Group Insurance Co Ltd* (n 6) [25] (Lord Hoffmann).

214 *Lloyd's TSB General Insurance Holdings Ltd v Lloyd's Bank Group Insurance Co Ltd* (n 6) [25] (Lord Hoffmann), [51] (Lord Hobhouse).

215 *Lloyd's TSB General Insurance Holdings Ltd v Lloyd's Bank Group Insurance Co Ltd* (n 6) [46] (Lord Hobhouse).

216 *Lloyd's TSB General Insurance Holdings Ltd v Lloyd's Bank Group Insurance Co Ltd* (n 6) [46] (Lord Hobhouse).

3.92 Lord Hoffmann noted that 'the nature of the unifying factor or factors which makes them related or a series must be expressed or implied' by the aggregation clause.[217] Analysing the aggregation language, his Lordship concluded that the only unifying element 'which the clause itself provide[d] for describing the acts or omissions in the parenthesis as "related" and a "series" [was] that they "result[ed]" in a series of third party claims. In other words, the unifying element [was] a common causal relationship'.[218] It was not enough that one act resulted in one individual loss and another act in another loss, as there would be no causal element relating the different acts.[219]

3.93 Lord Hoffmann, however, reserved his opinion as to the example given by Lord Hobhouse. He would not be inclined to accept, he stated, that multiple acts of handing out a document misrepresenting the merits of the pension scheme were to be considered a series simply because these acts were very similar.[220] Lord Hoffmann concluded that the series clause under consideration could 'only mean that the acts or events form[ed] a related series if they together resulted in each of the claims'.[221] In fact, this was the case if 'liability under each of the aggregated [losses] [could not] be attributed to a single act or omission but [could] be attributed to the same acts or omissions acting in combination'.[222] He illustrated the unifying factor of '(related series of acts or omissions)' by amending the example afforded by Lord Hobhouse: a person distributed a document misrepresenting the merits of a pension scheme to multiple people. The person distributing the document did not act in negligence, but someone else who ought to have corrected him did. It was a person's distribution of the documents and another person's failure to correct him together that caused each of the individual losses.[223] His Lordship concluded that the individual losses in the case at hand did not arise from a combination of different acts and/or omissions and were, thus, not to be aggregated.[224]

3.94 In summary, the meaning of the unifying factor of '(related series of acts or omissions)' depends on what makes the acts and omissions a related series. Lord Hoffmann and Lord Hobhouse agreed that the plurality of individual losses in the case at hand was not to be aggregated as the acts and omissions leading to these losses did not form a related series. By contrast, their Lordships differed in their opinions as to what constitutes a related series. In Lord Hobhouse's view, multiple acts or omissions

---

217 *Lloyd's TSB General Insurance Holdings Ltd v Lloyd's Bank Group Insurance Co Ltd* (n 6) [26] (Lord Hoffmann).

218 *Lloyd's TSB General Insurance Holdings Ltd v Lloyd's Bank Group Insurance Co Ltd* (n 6) [27] (Lord Hoffmann).

219 *Lloyd's TSB General Insurance Holdings Ltd v Lloyd's Bank Group Insurance Co Ltd* (n 6) [27] (Lord Hoffmann).

220 *Lloyd's TSB General Insurance Holdings Ltd v Lloyd's Bank Group Insurance Co Ltd* (n 6) [28] (Lord Hoffmann).

221 *Lloyd's TSB General Insurance Holdings Ltd v Lloyd's Bank Group Insurance Co Ltd* (n 6) [27] (Lord Hoffmann).

222 *Lloyd's TSB General Insurance Holdings Ltd v Lloyd's Bank Group Insurance Co Ltd* (n 6) [27] (Lord Hoffmann).

223 *Lloyd's TSB General Insurance Holdings Ltd v Lloyd's Bank Group Insurance Co Ltd* (n 6) [29] (Lord Hoffmann).

224 *Lloyd's TSB General Insurance Holdings Ltd v Lloyd's Bank Group Insurance Co Ltd* (n 6) [29] (Lord Hoffmann).

formed a series if they originated in a common mistake such as the formulation of a document. Lord Hoffman considered multiple acts or omissions to be a related series only if they had jointly caused all of the individual losses to be aggregated.

3.95 In *AIG Europe Ltd v Woodman*, it was held that professional indemnity insurers, in particular, had slightly amended their series clauses in the aftermath of the House of Lords' decision in *Lloyd's TSB General Insurance Holdings Ltd v Lloyd's Bank Group Insurance Co Ltd*. However, this amendment did not render the point of difference between Lord Hobhouse and Lord Hoffmann academic.[225] Depending on whether Lord Hobhouse or Lord Hoffmann is followed, the operation of the respective series clause will be fundamentally different. This leaves the market with substantial legal uncertainty with regard to the unifying factor of a '(related series of acts or omissions)'.

b *Countrywide Assured Group Plc v Marshall*

3.96 *Countrywide Assured Group Plc v Marshall* represents another case of misselling of pensions. In this case, the Commercial Court was required to interpret the phrase '(...) all occurrences of a series consequent upon or attributable to one source or originating cause'.[226] More specifically, the case before the Commercial Court revolved around the issue whether an insurer was liable where multiple individual losses arose as a result of the misselling of pensions between 1988 and 1994. As a preliminary issue, the following question was tried: 'Whether on the proper construction of the [policy] all the misselling claims (...) fall to be treated as one claim for the purposes of applying the limit of indemnity (...)'.[227]

3.97 In relation to the aggregation clause under consideration in *Countrywide Assured Group Plc v Marshall*, the question was whether multiple occurrences formed a series.[228] Yet, this question was not of paramount importance, as multiple individual losses were not simply to be aggregated because they formed a series. Rather, an aggregation was only possible if the series of losses was consequent upon or attributable to one source or originating cause. Therefore, the question as to whether multiple individual losses formed a series was dealt with only briefly.

3.98 Morison J held that, to form part of a series, there must have been a connecting element which links the occurrences that would otherwise be separate.[229] Referring to the Australian case of *The Distillers Co Biochemicals (Australia) Pty Ltd v Ajax Insurance Co Ltd*,[230] Morison J found that multiple occurrences formed one series if they were of a

---

225 *AIG Europe Ltd v Woodman* (n 4) [16] (Lord Toulson SCJ).

226 *Countrywide Assured Group Plc v Marshall* (n 51) [3] (Morison J).

227 *Countrywide Assured Group Plc v Marshall* (n 51) [5] (Morison J).

228 *Countrywide Assured Group Plc v Marshall* (n 51) [14] (Morison J). It may be noted that the terms 'occurrence' and 'loss' had been conflated to some degree in the aggregation clause in question.

229 *Countrywide Assured Group Plc v Marshall* (n 51) [14] (Morison J). It may be noted that Morison J used the word 'occurrence' instead of 'loss'. Arguably, he did so because these terms had been conflated to some degree in the aggregation clause concerned.

230 *The Distillers Co Biochemicals (Australia) Pty Ltd v Ajax Insurance Co Ltd* (1974) 130 CLR 1 (HCA).

sufficiently similar kind.[231] As all the individual losses resulted from the misselling of pensions, Morison J regarded them as sufficiently similar to qualify as forming a series.[232]

3.99 Thus, in *Countrywide Assured Group Plc v Marshall*, the mere fact that each individual loss was the result of an act of misselling made them a series. This is in contrast to the conclusion reached in *Lloyd's TSB General Insurance Holdings Ltd v Lloyd's Bank Group Insurance Co Ltd* where Lord Hoffmann expressly held that the fact that the breaches of duty were the same was not sufficient for the individual acts to form a series.[233] It should, however, be noted that Lord Hoffmann came to this conclusion by considering the wider context of the aggregation clause which was substantially different from the one before the Commercial Court in *Countrywide Assured Group Plc v Marshall*.

3.100 The conclusion that may be drawn from this is, again, that it is impossible to determine whether multiple acts form a series without having regard to the wider context of the aggregation clause under consideration.

c *AIG Europe Ltd v Woodman*

3.101 In 2012, Cannon discussed the phrase 'the same act or omission in a series of related matters or transactions'.[234] He argues that the term 'related' had 'an entirely different function' in this phrase than in the series clause under consideration in *Lloyd's TSB General Insurance Holdings Ltd v Lloyd's Bank Group Insurance Co Ltd*. More specifically, it is not a number of separate acts or omissions that are required to be related under such a clause, but rather a number of different transactions or matters.[235]

3.102 In analysing how the matters and transactions have to be related to each other for the purposes of the series clause, Cannon notes that 'related' did not mean 'similar' but 'connected'.[236] For instance, Cannon argues, a contract to purchase land and the loan, secured by mortgage, of the money to fund the purchase could be said to be related matters or transactions.[237] By contrast, where a firm of engineers had re-hashed the same flawed design for a number of different clients under different contracts, those contracts were not 'related matters or transactions' merely

---

231 *Countrywide Assured Group Plc v Marshall* (n 51) [14] (Morison J).

232 *Countrywide Assured Group Plc v Marshall* (n 51) [14] (Morison J). For the meaning of the term 'series' cf also *Ritchie v Woodward* [2016] NSWSC 1715 [587] where Emmet AJA stated that '[t]he use of the word "series" [...] suggests a number of events of a sufficiently similar kind following each other in temporal succession'; *Moore v IAG New Zealand* (n 65) [31] where Dunningham J held that 'one may speak of there being a series when more than one event of the same or similar type happens within a limited time period. There need be no greater connection between the events than that they are, in some way, similar'; *Bank of Queensland Ltd v AIG Australia Ltd* (n 193) [85]–[94] (Macfarland JA).

233 *Lloyd's TSB General Insurance Holdings Ltd v Lloyd's Bank Group Insurance Co Ltd* (n 6) [25] (Lord Hoffmann).

234 Cannon (n 7) para 46.

235 Cannon (n 7) para 46.

236 Cannon (n 7) para 47.

237 Cannon (n 7) para 47.

because the same defective design was at the root of all the losses that occurred to the different clients.[238] In such a case, the various individual losses might have resulted from the same cause, but not from the same or similar acts in a series of related matters or transactions.[239]

3.103 In 2017, the exact phrase discussed by Cannon in 2012 came before the Supreme Court. In *AIG Europe Ltd v Woodman*, 214 investors in a project to develop holiday resorts on a plot near Izmir, Turkey, and in a similar project at Marrakech, Morocco, brought actions against a defunct firm of solicitors.[240] The solicitors devised a legal mechanism for the financing of foreign developments by private investors who would have security over the developed land.[241] The investors would either grant loans to the developers of the holiday resort or alternatively purchase holiday properties. The funds advanced by the investors would initially be held by the solicitors in an escrow account. The solicitors were instructed not to release the funds to the developers unless and until the value of the assets protecting the investments was sufficient to cover them.[242] Although the developers had not been able to buy the site in Izmir where the holiday resort was planned to be built nor to purchase the shares of the company that owned the site where the Marrakech resort was to be constructed, the solicitors had released all the investors' funds to the developers.[243]

3.104 In *AIG Europe Ltd v Woodman*, the question was whether the solicitors' professional indemnity insurance was liable for the losses that resulted from the solicitors' mistakes. The solicitors' professional indemnity insurance was limited to £3 million in respect of each claim. The investors' claims amounted to over £10 million in total. Therefore, the insurers argued that all the individual losses suffered by the 214 investors were to be aggregated so that its own liability was limited to £3 million in total.[244] More specifically, the insurers' case was that all the investors' claims arose from 'similar acts or omissions in a series of related matters or transactions'.[245]

3.105 At first instance,[246] Teare J found that the investors' losses did arise from similar acts or omissions but rejected the argument that they formed 'a series of related matters or transactions'. In his view, 'a series of related matters or transactions' referred to a number of transactions or matters which were conditional or dependent on each other. In the case at hand, he argued, there were separate

---

238 Cannon (n 7) para 48.

239 Cannon (n 7) para 48.

240 *AIG Europe Ltd v Woodman* (n 4) [3] (Lord Toulson SCJ).

241 *AIG Europe Ltd v Woodman* (n 4) [4] (Lord Toulson SCJ).

242 *AIG Europe Ltd v Woodman* (n 4) [4] (Lord Toulson SCJ).

243 *AIG Europe Ltd v Woodman* (n 4) [7] (Lord Toulson SCJ).

244 *AIG Europe Ltd v Woodman* (n 4) [9] (Lord Toulson SCJ).

245 *AIG Europe Ltd v Woodman* (n 4) [10] (Lord Toulson SCJ).

246 *AIG Europe Ltd v OC320301 LLP* [2015] EWHC 2398 (Comm), [2016] Lloyd's Rep IR 147 [31], [42] (Longmore LJ).

contracts with the developers and each of the investors and those contracts were not mutually conditional nor mutually dependent.[247]

3.106 Upon appeal, the Court of Appeal criticised Teare J. It held that for the purposes of the aggregation clause, it was not required for the various transactions to have a relationship with some outside connecting factor.[248] The Court of Appeal found that the series clause required an 'intrinsic' relationship between the transactions. The court further stated that what would be 'intrinsic' depended on the circumstances of the release of the funds by the solicitors to the developers.

3.107 The Supreme Court clarified that, under the unifying factor of 'a series of related matters or transactions', aggregation was not possible simply on the basis that the individual losses arose from repeated similar negligent acts or omissions. Rather, the losses were to be aggregated only 'if there [was] a real connection between the transactions in which they occurred'.[249] Moreover, it distinguished the unifying factor of '(related series of acts or omissions)' under consideration in *Lloyd's TSB General Insurance Holdings Ltd v Lloyd's Bank Group Insurance Co Ltd* from the unifying factor of 'a series of related matters or transactions' with which the Supreme Court was concerned in the case at hand.[250] The Supreme Court noted that the Court of Appeal's requirement that there be an 'intrinsic' relationship between the matters or transactions was too vague.[251] Rather, the individual losses suffered by the investors were to be aggregated if the matters or transactions that resulted in the losses were somehow interconnected.[252] Determining whether a number of transactions or matters were related was a fact sensitive exercise of judgment.[253]

3.108 The Supreme Court first held that it was necessary to identify the relevant matters or transactions. The Court of Appeal had considered the release of funds from the escrow account to the developers as relevant transactions. In contrast, the Supreme Court regarded the 'investment[s] in a particular development scheme under a contractual agreement' as the relevant transactions.[254] The Supreme Court then determined whether the relevant transactions were related. It concluded that the transactions of the investors who participated in the Izmir project and those of the investors participating in the Marrakech project were related, respectively.[255] The transactions were considered related because they shared the common underlying objective of the execution of a particular development project.[256] Hence, all the

---

247 *AIG Europe Ltd v Woodman* (n 4) [11] (Lord Toulson SCJ).
248 *AIG Europe Ltd v OC320301 LLP* (n 51) [19] (Longmore LJ).
249 *AIG Europe Ltd v Woodman* (n 4) [18] (Lord Toulson SCJ).
250 *AIG Europe Ltd v Woodman* (n 4) [19] (Lord Toulson SCJ).
251 *AIG Europe Ltd v Woodman* (n 4) [21] (Lord Toulson SCJ).
252 *AIG Europe Ltd v Woodman* (n 4) [22] (Lord Toulson SCJ).
253 *AIG Europe Ltd v Woodman* (n 4) [22] (Lord Toulson SCJ).
254 *AIG Europe Ltd v Woodman* (n 4) [23] (Lord Toulson SCJ).
255 *AIG Europe Ltd v Woodman* (n 4) [24] (Lord Toulson SCJ).
256 *AIG Europe Ltd v Woodman* (n 4) [26] (Lord Toulson SCJ).

losses suffered by the investors in the Izmir project and all the losses suffered by the investors in the Marrakech project were to be aggregated, respectively.

3.109 By contrast, the losses suffered by the investors in the Izmir project were not to be aggregated with the losses suffered by the investors in the Marrakech project. The Supreme Court noted that the projects bore a striking similarity but considered this not to suffice for an aggregation under the series clause.[257] The two development projects were separate and unconnected as they related to different sites and different groups of investors.

3.110 In summary, there appear to be multiple factors contributing to substantial legal uncertainty with regard to the operation of aggregation mechanisms that are based on the unifying factor of 'a series of related matters or transactions'. First, the meaning of the term 'transaction' in a specific case appears to be disputable. Secondly, the Supreme Court considered the question of whether a number of transactions were related to be a fact sensitive exercise of judgment. It is, therefore, impossible to label an aggregation mechanism using the unifying factor of 'a series of related matters or transactions' as either broad or narrow.

3 Linking phrases

3.111 In addition to unifying factors, linking phrases[258] also contribute to the determination of the causal requirements inherent in an aggregation mechanism.[259] Common linking phrases are 'arising out of', 'arising from', 'consequent upon', 'attributable to', 'in connection with' and 'resulting from'. It is important to note that phrases such as these are also used in contexts other than that of aggregating losses.[260]

3.112 As has already been mentioned, English courts have repeatedly held that it is impossible 'to give an informed answer to a question of causation without knowing the purpose and the scope of the rule'.[261] For example, using the words 'arising out of' in one context provides for the causal requirement of 'proximate cause',[262] whereas it refers to a 'somewhat weaker causal connection', rather than 'dictate a proximate cause test, in other circumstances'.[263] Similarly, depending on the context, the phrase 'attributable to' sometimes describes a wider causal requirement than

---

257 *AIG Europe Ltd v Woodman* (n 4) [27] (Lord Toulson SCJ).

258 *Standard Life Assurance Ltd v Ace European Group* (n 41) [262] (Eder J); *Aioi Nissay Dowa Insurance Co Ltd v Heraldglen Ltd and Advent Capital Ltd* (n 44) [21] (Field J); Cannon (n 7) para 49.

259 Roberts (n 45); Clyde and Co (n 41) 1 ff.

260 *Beazley Underwriting Ltd v Travelers Co Inc* (n 187) [120]–[127] (Clarke J). *The Cultural Foundation v Beazley Furlonge Ltd* [2018] EWHC 1083 (Comm), [2018] WLR (D) 289 [163] (Andrew Henshaw QC).

261 *Environment Agency (formerly National Rivers Authority) v Empress Car Co (Abertillery) Ltd* (n 26) 31 (Lord Hoffmann); *Scott v The Copenhagen Reinsurance Co (UK) Ltd* (n 20) [68] (Rix LJ); *Beazley Underwriting Ltd v Travelers Co Inc* (n 187) [125], [127] (Clarke J); *The Cultural Foundation v Beazley Furlonge Ltd* (n 260) [163] (Andrew Henshaw QC).

262 *Coxe v Employers' Liability Assurance Corp Ltd* [1916] 2 KB 629 (Comm) 634 (Scrutton J).

263 *Beazley Underwriting Ltd v Travelers Co Inc* (n 187) [128] (Clarke J).

'proximate cause', whereas it refers precisely to the causal requirement of 'proximate cause'[264] at other times.

3.113 Consequently, only case law discussing phrases such as 'arising out of' or 'attributable to' in the context of aggregation may have a bearing on the determination of the effect a linking phrase has on an aggregation mechanism.[265]

3.1 'Arising out of' and 'arising from'

3.114 The linking phrases of 'arising out of' and 'arising from' are used in combination with both the unifying factors of 'event' and 'cause'.[266] In *Axa Reinsurance (UK) Ltd v Field*, Lord Mustill distinguished two aggregation mechanisms respectively containing the causal connectors of 'arising out of' and 'arising from'. However, the distinction drawn between the two aggregation clauses was based on the different unifying factors rather than on the linking phrases.[267]

3.115 In the *Dawson's Field Arbitration*, the arbitral tribunal noted that its view about the meaning of 'arising out of' might have been coloured by its understanding of the notion of 'occurrence', ie of the unifying factor concerned.[268] Thus, the meaning of the linking phrase of 'arising out of'[269] and the causative effect it affords to an aggregation mechanism may depend on the unifying factor with which it is coupled.[270]

3.116 In *Caudle v Sharp*, the Court of Appeal held that an aggregating event does not have to be 'the direct and proximate cause of the original insured loss'. Evans LJ considered that the phrase 'arising out of' did not indicate the same causal requirement as the one of 'proximate cause' but that 'some wider test of causation' was to be applied.[271] Evans LJ went on to hold that '[t]here [was] no express, restriction on remoteness, provided the loss [could] be said to have "arisen out of" the event, but, some restriction must be inferred (…)'.[272]

3.117 In *Scott v The Copenhagen Reinsurance Co Ltd*, Rix LJ stated that 'the causative link inherent in the words "arising from", when coupled with the

---

264 *Beazley Underwriting Ltd v Travelers Co Inc* (n 187) [126]–[127] (Clarke J), explicitly drawing this distinction.

265 *Scott v The Copenhagen Reinsurance Co (UK) Ltd* (n 20) [68] (Rix LJ); *Beazley Underwriting Ltd v Travelers Co Inc* (n 187) [127] (Clarke J); *The Cultural Foundation v Beazley Furlonge Ltd* (n 260) [163] (Andrew Henshaw QC).

266 Cf *Axa Reinsurance (UK) Ltd v Field* (n 3) 1031 f (Lord Mustill).

267 *Axa Reinsurance (UK) Ltd v Field* (n 3) 1035 (Lord Mustill). In fact, the aggregation clause contained in the primary insurance contract stated that all individual losses 'arising from one originating cause' were to be aggregated. By contrast, the aggregation clause in the reinsurance contract provided that all individual losses 'arising out of one event' were to be aggregated.

268 *Dawson's Field Arbitration*, quoted in: *Scott v The Copenhagen Reinsurance Co (UK) Ltd* (n 20) [52] (Rix LJ).

269 Arguably, the same is true for the causal connector of 'arising from'.

270 This is also suggested in *Scott v The Copenhagen Reinsurance Co (UK) Ltd* (n 20) [65] (Rix LJ).

271 *Caudle v Sharp* (n 33) 648 f (Evans LJ).

272 *Caudle v Sharp* (n 33) 649 (Evans LJ).

expression "one event", should be regarded as a relatively strong and significant link (...)'.[273] Accordingly, even though the causative requirement may be weaker than the one of 'proximate cause', the causative link between the individual losses and the unifying factor 'has to be a significant rather than a weak one'.[274]

3.118 It may be deduced from these cases that the linking phrases of 'arising out of' and 'arising from' play a substantial role in determining an aggregation mechanism's causal requirements. However, it appears to be impossible to deduce abstract and meaningful implications as to the linking phrases' actual and precise causative potencies. Consequently, their roles in and effects on an aggregation mechanism remain vague and unpredictable.

3.2 'Consequent upon or attributable to'

3.119 Particularly in cause-based aggregation mechanisms, the parties regularly provide for the linking phrase of 'consequent (up)on or attributable to'.[275] However, there seem to be no case authorities regarding the effect such a linking phrase has on an aggregation mechanism. Rather, judicial discussions about causal requirements of aggregation mechanisms containing such phrasing generally focus on the unifying factor's causative effect.[276]

3.120 In *Beazley Underwriting Ltd v Travelers Co Inc*, the Commercial Court touched on the causative effect of the phrase 'attributable to'.[277] In fact, one of the parties involved in this case referred to *Lloyd's TSB General Insurance Holdings Ltd v Lloyd's Bank Group Insurance Co Ltd*[278] where Lord Hoffmann discussed the aggregation mechanism dealt with in *Municipal Mutual Insurance Ltd v Sea Insurance Co Ltd*.[279] However, rather than having determined the causative effect of the linking phrase of 'attributable to', Lord Hoffman seems to have discussed the causative potency of the unifying factor of 'cause'.

3.121 Thus, the role in and effects of the linking phrase of 'consequent upon or attributable to' on an aggregation mechanism remain unclear.

---

273 *Scott v The Copenhagen Reinsurance Co (UK) Ltd* (n 20) [65] (Rix LJ).

274 *Scott v The Copenhagen Reinsurance Co (UK) Ltd* (n 20) [63] (Rix LJ); *Beazley Underwriting Ltd v Travelers Co Inc* (n 187) [125] (Clarke J); *The Cultural Foundation v Beazley Furlonge Ltd* (n 260) [163] (Andrew Henshaw QC).

275 *Municipal Mutual Insurance Ltd v Sea Insurance Co Ltd* (n 4) 959, 966 (Hobhouse LJ); *Countrywide Assured Group Plc v Marshall* (n 51) [3] (Morison J); *Spire Healthcare Ltd v Royal and Sun Alliance Insurance Plc* (n 30) [3] (Simon LJ); Clyde and Co (n 41) 4. Cf also *Standard Life Assurance Ltd v Ace European Group* (n 255) [255] (Eder J); *AIG Europe Ltd v OC320301 LLP* (n 51) [21], [51] (Longmore LJ). For a case under New York law, see *World Trade Center Properties LLC v Hartford Fire Insurance Co* (2003) 345 F 154 (United States Court of Appeals for the Second Circuit) 180.

276 *Municipal Mutual Insurance Ltd v Sea Insurance Co Ltd* (n 4) 967 (Hobhouse LJ); *Countrywide Assured Group Plc v Marshall* (n 51) [15] (Morison J).

277 *Beazley Underwriting Ltd v Travelers Co Inc* (n 187) [126] (Clarke J).

278 *Lloyd's TSB General Insurance Holdings Ltd v Lloyd's Bank Group Insurance Co Ltd* (n 6) [15]–[16] (Lord Hoffmann).

279 *Beazley Underwriting Ltd v Travelers Co Inc* (n 187) [126] (Clarke J); Clyde and Co (n 41) 4. For the aggregation mechanism referred to, see *Municipal Mutual Insurance Ltd v Sea Insurance Co Ltd* (n 4) 966 (Hobhouse LJ).

3.3 'In connection with'

3.122 In *Standard Life Assurance Ltd v ACE European Group*, the Commercial Court discussed the causative effect of the following aggregation language: 'All claims (...) arising from or in connection with or attributable to any one act, error, omission or originating cause or source (...) shall be considered to be a single third party claim (...)'.[280]

3.123 Eder J specifically referred to the linking phrase of 'in connection with'. He stated that

> *[n]ot only does the clause in the Policy use the expression 'originating cause or source', but the description of the link required between the 'originating cause or source' and the claims which it is sought to aggregate is worded in the broadest possible terms (...). The phrase '***in connection with***' is extremely broad and indicates that it is not even necessary to show a **direct** causal relationship between the claims and the state of affairs identified as their 'originating cause or source', and that some form of connection between the claims and the unifying factor is all that is required.*[281]

3.124 Eder J notes that aggregation mechanisms using the liking phrase of 'in connection with' did not require a direct causal relationship between the individual losses to be aggregated and the unifying factor. Aggregation would be possible if there were some other form of connection between the individual losses and the unifying factor.[282] It is not entirely clear, however, whether Eder J intended to suggest that the required connection is to consist of an indirect causal relationship between the individual losses and the unifying factor or whether the unifying concept is not based on causation altogether in such a case.

3.125 Therefore, the linking phrase of 'in connection with' certainly provides for a very broad aggregation of losses. If a causative link between the individual losses to be aggregated and the unifying factor were required, a very loose link would be sufficient. However, the precise effect of such a linking phrase on an aggregation mechanism remains obscure.

3.4 'Shall result from'

3.126 In *Lloyd's TSB General Insurance Holdings Ltd v Lloyd's Bank Group Insurance Co Ltd*, the House of Lords dealt with the following aggregation clause:

> *If a series of third party claims* **shall result from** *any single act or omission (or related series of acts or omissions) then, irrespective of the total number of claims, all such third party claims shall be considered to be a single third party claim for the purpose of the application of the deductible.*[283]

---

280 *Standard Life Assurance Ltd v Ace European Group* (n 41) [255] (Eder J).

281 *Standard Life Assurance Ltd v Ace European Group* (n 41) [262] (Eder J; emphasis added).

282 *Standard Life Assurance Ltd v Ace European Group* (n 41) [262] (Eder J); Clyde and Co (n 41) 4 f. See also O'Neill, Woloniecki and Arnold-Dwyer (n 1) para 5–087.

283 *Lloyd's TSB General Insurance Holdings Ltd v Lloyd's Bank Group Insurance Co Ltd* (n 6) [12] (Lord Hoffmann; emphasis added).

3.127 This aggregation clause provides for different unifying factors. Both 'any single act or omission' and '(related series of acts or omissions)' figure as unifying factors.[284]

3.128 In his speech, Lord Hoffmann examined the factors which make acts or omissions related or a series.[285] He noted that 'the only unifying [concept] which the clause itself provide[d] for describing the acts or omissions (...) as "related" and a "series" [was] that they "resulted" in a series of third party claims'.[286] He went on to state that the linking phrase of 'shall result from' provided for a 'common causal relationship'.[287] In Lord Hoffmann's view, as long as each of the individual losses could be attributed to multiple 'acts or omissions acting in combination', they were to be aggregated.[288]

3.129 By contrast, Lord Hoffmann did not assess the required strength of the causal relationship between the acts and each of the losses. Consequently, the causative effect that the linking phrase of 'shall result from' affords to an aggregation mechanism remains unclear.

V Summary of the chapter

3.130 This chapter began with two general features of aggregation mechanisms. First, it has been demonstrated that aggregation mechanisms are impartial. As one cannot predict in whose benefit an aggregation mechanism will ultimately operate before an actual claims experience, there is no reason to construe an aggregation clause in favour of one party or the other. Secondly, it has been set forth that aggregation is not something that is inherent in every reinsurance contract. If the parties wish to add together certain individual losses to form one single loss for the purposes of deductible and cover limit, they must expressly provide for an aggregation clause in their contract.

3.131 The main part of the chapter deals with the concept of causation and its role in the subject matter of aggregation. In this regard, it has been noted that the causal requirements inherent in an aggregation mechanism essentially depend on the words used in the aggregation clause. More specifically, aggregation clauses generally refer to so-called unifying factors and use linking phrases. Unifying factors and linking phrases are both said to be determinative of an aggregation mechanism's causal requirements.

3.132 Most frequently, aggregation clauses designate either an 'event' or an 'originating cause' as the relevant unifying factor. Courts have held that the term

---

284 *Lloyd's TSB General Insurance Holdings Ltd v Lloyd's Bank Group Insurance Co Ltd* (n 6) [26] (Lord Hoffmann).

285 *Lloyd's TSB General Insurance Holdings Ltd v Lloyd's Bank Group Insurance Co Ltd* (n 6) [26] (Lord Hoffmann).

286 *Lloyd's TSB General Insurance Holdings Ltd v Lloyd's Bank Group Insurance Co Ltd* (n 6) [26]–[27] (Lord Hoffmann).

287 *Lloyd's TSB General Insurance Holdings Ltd v Lloyd's Bank Group Insurance Co Ltd* (n 6) [27] (Lord Hoffmann).

288 *Lloyd's TSB General Insurance Holdings Ltd v Lloyd's Bank Group Insurance Co Ltd* (n 6) [27], [29] (Lord Hoffmann).

'event' was much narrower than the phrase 'originating cause'. Consequently, so-called event-based aggregation mechanisms call for a stronger causal link between the individual losses to be aggregated and the unifying factor than cause-based aggregation mechanisms. However, courts have never succeeded in deriving a clear standard of causation from the respective unifying factors.

3.133 Similarly, linking phrases have been used to describe causal requirements in certain cases. However, courts have never succeeded in deducing a clear standard of causation from different linking phrases. Rather, it appears that the effect a specific linking phrase has on an aggregation mechanism's causal requirements mostly depends on the judgment of the person construing the relevant aggregation clause.

3.134 Therefore, even when the profile of the individual losses and the structure of the reinsurance cover is known, it is practically impossible to predict how an aggregation clause will operate. In other words, aggregation clauses are surrounded by considerable legal uncertainty.

CHAPTER 4

Event-based aggregation in focus

4.1 In the last chapter, it was identified that the unifying concept in event-based aggregation mechanisms is one of causation.[1] It has been explained that the unifying factor as well as the linking phrase provided for in an aggregation clause together determine an aggregation mechanism's causal requirements. In this chapter, it will be demonstrated that substantial legal uncertainty revolves around causal requirements of event-based aggregation mechanisms under English law. To reduce the legal uncertainty which is inherent in event-based aggregation, courts have developed the so-called 'unities test' which itself is a further source of legal uncertainty. It will be argued that the determination of whether a plurality of losses aggregates under an event-based aggregation mechanism purely comes down to an exercise of judgment.

4.2 Moreover, two instruments created to avoid this legal uncertainty shall be examined. So-called 'hours clauses' and 'sole judge clauses' shall be put under scrutiny. It will be argued that while hours clauses are meant to reduce the legal uncertainty concerning event-based aggregation mechanisms, they lack legal certainty themselves. By contrast, sole judge clauses may–to some degree–reduce legal uncertainty. Yet, particularly reinsurers will be reluctant to accept such clauses, as they place them at the mercy of the reinsureds.

4.3 Thereafter, the event-based aggregation mechanism provided for in the recently developed PRICL 2019 will be summarised. As the PRICL are a brand-new legal instrument, courts and arbitral tribunals have had no opportunity to discuss the mechanism yet. Therefore, the presentation of the relevant provision, Article 5.2 PRICL, shall be limited to outlining the goals the PRICL Project Group seeks to achieve with the rule.

I Event-based aggregation in English law

4.4 Event-based aggregation clauses seem to be common in reinsurance contracts concluded in the UK. As demonstrated above, the causative requirements inherent in event-based aggregation mechanisms depend on the unifying factor as well as the linking phrase contained in the aggregation clause.[2]

---

1 See paras 3.38 ff.

2 See paras 3.24, 3.111 ff.

DOI: 10.4324/9781003080480-4

1 Typical unifying factors and linking phrases

4.5 Typically, event-based aggregation clauses provide for the unifying factor of 'event'.[3] As has been discussed,[4] the term 'occurrence' is generally used inter-changeably with the term 'event' in the context of aggregating losses.[5] If so, the term 'occurrence' used in an event-based aggregation mechanism operates as a unifying factor.

4.6 Similarly, it has been observed that there seems to be no legal authority for the proposition that the terms 'occurrence', 'catastrophe', 'disaster' and 'calamity' each come with a distinguishable concept of causation.[6] As the term 'occurrence' is used interchangeably with the term 'event', this may also be true of the terms 'catastrophe', 'disaster' and 'calamity'. In fact, any catastrophe, disaster or calamity can easily be described as an event.[7] In direct insurance policies, the terms 'accident' and 'happening' are often used interchangeably with the term 'event'.[8] This might also be appropriate in the context of reinsurance.[9]

4.7 Moreover, the unifying factor of 'event' is typically coupled with the linking phrases of 'arising from' or 'arising out of' in event-based aggregation clauses.[10]

---

3 *Caudle v Sharp* [1995] CLC 642 (CA) 644 (Evans LJ); *Axa Reinsurance (UK) Ltd v Field* (1996) 1 WLR 1026 (HL) 1031 f (Lord Mustill); *Brown (RE) v GIO Insurance Ltd* [1998] Lloyd's Rep IR 201 (CA) 207 (Chadwick LJ); *Denby v English and Scottish Maritime Insurance Co Ltd; Yasuda Fire and Marine Co of Europe Ltd v Lloyd's Underwriting Syndicates no 209, 356* [1998] Lloyd's Rep IR 343 (CA), [1998] CLC 870, 873 (Hobhouse LJ); *Scott v The Copenhagen Reinsurance Co (UK) Ltd* [2003] EWCA Civ 688, [2003] 2 All ER 190 [6] (Rix LJ); *IRB Brasil Resseguros SA v CX Reinsurance Co Ltd* [2010] EWHC 974 (Comm), [2010] Lloyd's Rep IR 560 [11] (Burton J); *Aioi Nissay Dowa Insurance Co Ltd v Heraldglen Ltd and Advent Capital Ltd* [2013] EWHC 154 (Comm), [2013] 2 All ER 231 [7] (Field J); *MIC Simmonds v Gammell* [2016] EWHC 2515 (Comm), [2016] Lloyd's Rep IR 693 [10] (Sir Jeremy Cooke).

4 See paras 2.63, 3.59.

5 *Dawson's Field Arbitration*, quoted in: *Kuwait Airways Corp v Kuwait Insurance Co SAK* [1996] 1 Lloyd's Rep 664 (Comm); *American Centennial Insurance Co v INSCO Ltd* [1996] 1 LRLR 407 (Comm) 413 (Moore-Bick J). Cf also *Aioi Nissay Dowa Insurance Co Ltd v Heraldglen Ltd and Advent Capital Ltd* (n 3) [20] (Field J); Barlow Lyde and Gilbert LLP, *Reinsurance Practice and the Law* (Informa Law from Routledge 2009) para 28.6; Malcolm A Clarke, *The Law of Insurance Contracts* (6th edn, Informa Law from Routledge 2009) para 17-4C3; Kiran Soar, 'Interpretation of Wordings Key to Settling Aggregation Claims' [2010] LLID 7; Colin Edelman and Andrew Burns, *The Law of Reinsurance* (2nd edn, OUP 2013) paras 4.55 ff; Robert M Merkin, Laura Hodgson and Peter J Tyldesley, *Colinvaux's Law of Insurance* (5th edn, Sweet and Maxwell 2019) para 11–324. For an American authority in this regard, see *Newmont Mines Ltd v Hanover Insurance Co* [1986] 784 F2d 127 (United States Court of Appeals for the Second Circuit) 135.

6 See para 3.79.

7 Not just any event may be considered a 'catastrophe', a 'disaster' or a 'calamity'. Yet, if an aggregation clause designates its unifying factor with one of these terms, it must be assumed that the parties intended to aggregate multiple individual losses following an event-based aggregation mechanism. It may be noted, however, that a sub-group of the International Underwriting Association considered that the word 'catastrophe' provided more flexibility than the word 'event', see 'IUA 01–033 Definition of Loss Occurrence (Hours Clause) - Commentary' para 4.2 <http://iuaclauses.co.uk/site/cms/contentDocumentLibraryView.asp?chapter=5> accessed 24 March 2020.

8 John Butler and Robert Merkin, *Butler and Merkin's Reinsurance Law*, vol 2 (Looseleaf, Sweet & Maxwell) para C–0223.

9 Butler and Merkin (n 8) para C–0223, who seem to doubt that it is appropriate to use these terms interchangeably.

10 *Caudle v Sharp* (n 3) 644 (Evans LJ); *Axa Reinsurance (UK) Ltd v Field* (n 3) 1031 f (Lord Mustill);

2 Lack of legal certainty as to the causal requirements in event-based aggregation

4.8 It has been established that unifying factors and linking phrases both contribute to the determination of causal requirements associated with aggregation mechanisms.[11] It has also been discussed that the unifying factor of 'event'[12] and the linking phrases of 'arising out of' or 'arising from'[13] are both insufficiently certain to define the causative link required.

4.9 In respect of event-based aggregation, courts have held that multiple individual losses are to be aggregated even if the event is remoter than the proximate cause.[14] In *Caudle v Sharp*, Evans LJ noted that '[t]here is no express restriction of remoteness, provided the loss or occurrence can be said to have "arisen out of" the event (...)'.[15]

4.10 Yet, not everything that can be described as an event can realistically be said to be the kind of event referred to in aggregation clauses.[16] For this reason, Evans LJ held that 'some restriction [of remoteness] must (...) be inferred' into the aggregation mechanism in order to reflect the parties' intentions.[17] In this regard, Rix LJ noted in *Scott v The Copenhagen Reinsurance Co (UK) Ltd* that the concept of remoteness was used 'as a tool to limit the otherwise infinite reach of the workings of causation'.[18] He elaborated that if a 'merely weak causal connection is required, there is in principle no limit to the theoretical possibility of tracing back to the causes of causes'.[19]

4.11 In *Caudle v Sharp*, Evans LJ did not offer much assistance in determining where in the landscape between the proximate cause and the infinity of remoteness the applicable standard of causation comes to lie.[20] In *Kuwait Airways Corp v Kuwait Insurance Co SAK*, it has been held that, in determining this standard, the peril (re-) insured against is to be taken into account.[21] Further, the causative potencies of the

---

Dawson's Field Arbitration, quoted in: *Kuwait Airways Corp v Kuwait Insurance Co SAK* (n 5); *Brown (RE) v GIO Insurance Ltd* (n 3) 207 (Chadwick LJ); *Denby v English and Scottish Maritime Insurance Co Ltd; Yasuda Fire and Marine Co of Europe Ltd v Lloyd's Underwriting Syndicates no 209, 356* (n 3) 873 (Hobhouse LJ); *Scott v The Copenhagen Reinsurance Co (UK) Ltd* (n 3) [6] (Rix LJ); *IRB Brasil Resseguros SA v CX Reinsurance Co Ltd* (n 3) [11] (Burton J); *Aioi Nissay Dowa Insurance Co Ltd v Heraldglen Ltd and Advent Capital Ltd* (n 3) [7] (Field J); *MIC Simmonds v Gammell* (n 3) [10] (Sir Jeremy Cooke).

11 See para 3.24.

12 See paras 3.38 ff.

13 See paras 3.114 ff.

14 *Caudle v Sharp* (n 3) 648 f (Evans LJ); *Scott v The Copenhagen Reinsurance Co (UK) Ltd* (n 3) [63] (Rix LJ); *MIC Simmonds v Gammell* (n 3) [35] (Sir Jeremy Cooke).

15 *Caudle v Sharp* (n 3) 649 (Evans LJ).

16 Barlow Lyde and Gilbert LLP (n 5) para 28.13.

17 *Caudle v Sharp* (n 3) 649 (Evans LJ).

18 *Scott v The Copenhagen Reinsurance Co (UK) Ltd* (n 3) [63] (Rix LJ).

19 *Scott v The Copenhagen Reinsurance Co (UK) Ltd* (n 3) [68] (Rix LJ).

20 Ken Louw and Deborah Tompkinson, 'Curiouser and Curiouser: The Meaning of "Event"' (1996) 4 International Insurance Law Review 6, 8.

21 *Kuwait Airways Corp v Kuwait Insurance Co SAK* (n 5).

linking phrase 'arising out of' and the unifying factor of 'event' may be inter-dependent.[22] Finally, in *Scott v The Copenhagen Re Co (UK) Ltd,* Rix LJ found that there was 'a significant rather than a weak' causal link between the event and the individual losses inherent in an event-based aggregation mechanism.[23]

4.12 As discussed previously,[24] one can probably not deduce a meaningful standard of causation from these case authorities. In fact, the concept of a significant rather than a weak causal link taking into account the peril (re-)insured against appears to be extremely vague. It is difficult, perhaps impossible, to abstractly define a standard of causation that allows for pinpointing the relevant events on the chain of causation.[25] It is perhaps for this reason that Rix LJ stated in his judgment that the question became: 'Is there one event which should be regarded as the cause of [a plurality of losses] so as to make it appropriate to regard these losses as constituting for the purposes of ag-gregation (...) one loss?'[26]

4.13 Rix LJ admitted that the question whether multiple individual losses arose out of one event could 'only be answered by finding and considering all the relevant facts carefully, and then conducting an exercise of judgment'.[27] Accordingly, it is essentially a question of judgment as to whether it is appropriate to aggregate a plurality of losses. In an attempt to dispel at least some legal uncertainty in the context of event-based aggregation mechanisms, Rix LJ noted that this exercise of judgment could be assisted by the unities test.[28]

3 Unities test and its shortcomings

4.14 Presumably aware of the legal uncertainty inherent in event-based aggrega-tion mechanisms, some arbitral tribunals and English courts have used the unities test to assess whether multiple individual losses were to be aggregated.[29]

4.15 The unities test was developed in the course of the *Dawson's Field Arbitration.*[30] In the *Dawson's Field Arbitration,* it was held that the question '[w]hether or not something which produce[d] a plurality of loss or damage [could] properly be described as one occurrence (...) involve[d] the question of degree of

---

22 *Dawson's Field Arbitration,* quoted in: *Scott v The Copenhagen Reinsurance Co (UK) Ltd* (n 3) [52] (Michael Kerr QC).

23 *Scott v The Copenhagen Reinsurance Co (UK) Ltd* (n 3) [63] (Rix LJ).

24 See paras 3.38 ff.

25 Cf Barlow Lyde and Gilbert LLP (n 5) para 28.39.

26 *Scott v The Copenhagen Reinsurance Co (UK) Ltd* (n 3) [68] (Rix LJ). It has been discussed above that this seems to be a circular rule, see para 3.41.

27 *Scott v The Copenhagen Reinsurance Co (UK) Ltd* (n 3) [81] (Rix LJ).

28 *Scott v The Copenhagen Reinsurance Co (UK) Ltd* (n 3) [81] (Rix LJ).

29 *Kuwait Airways Corp v Kuwait Insurance Co SAK* (n 5); *Mann v Lexington Insurance Co* [2000] CLC 1409 (CA) 1423 (Waller LJ); *Aioi Nissay Dowa Insurance Co Ltd v Heraldglen Ltd and Advent Capital Ltd* (n 3) [9], [18]–[23], [28]–[32] (Field J). Cf also *MIC Simmonds v Gammell* (n 3) [29] (Sir Jeremy Cooke); Barlow Lyde and Gilbert LLP (n 5) paras 28.16; Edelman and Burns (n 5) paras 4.56 ff; Sieglinde Cannawurf and Andreas Schwepcke, '§ 8 Das Vertragsrecht der Rückversicherung' in Dieter W Lüer and Andreas Schwepcke (eds), *Rückversicherungsrecht* (CH Beck 2013) para 363; Butler and Merkin (n 8) para C–0222.

30 *Dawson's Field Arbitration,* quoted in: *Kuwait Airways Corp v Kuwait Insurance Co SAK* (n 5).

unity in relation to cause, locality, time and, if initiated by human action, the circumstances and purposes of the persons responsible'.[31] In other words, the 'losses' circumstances must be scrutinised to see whether they involve such a degree of unity as to justify their being described as, or arising out of, one occurrence'.[32] In determining whether there was sufficient unity, 'such factors as cause, locality and time and the intentions of the human agents' are to be taken into account.[33]

4.16 The following analysis will examine whether the unities test is capable of determining a standard of causation inherent in event-based aggregation mechanisms. It will further explore whether it may assist in determining whether the aggregation of a plurality of losses is appropriate in a given case.

3.1 Scope and significance of the unities test

4.17 In the *Dawson's Field Arbitration* where the unities test was developed,[34] the arbitral tribunal dealt with an aggregation of losses for 'any one occurrence'.[35] Likewise, in *Kuwait Airways Corp v Kuwait Insurance Co SAK*, where Rix J revisited the test, the aggregation mechanism concerned was per 'any one occurrence'.[36] Consequently, the unities test was first applied in the context of aggregation mechanisms using the unifying factor of occurrence.

4.18 In *Scott v The Copenhagen Re Co (UK) Ltd*, one of the parties argued that it was inappropriate to apply the unities test in relation to aggregation clauses providing for an aggregation of losses 'arising out of one event'. More specifically, the party argued that, in construing the phrase 'arising out of one event', 'a more traditional causal approach' than a test by reference to the 'unities' was to be taken.[37] The Court of Appeal disagreed and held that whether multiple losses arose from one event could only be determined by 'considering all the relevant facts carefully' and that the unities test could be of assistance to do so.[38] Irrespective of whether the unifying factor is 'any one occurrence' or 'one event', it is the unities test that is commonly applied in the context of event-based aggregation mechanisms.[39] By

---

31 *Dawson's Field Arbitration*, quoted in: *Kuwait Airways Corp v Kuwait Insurance Co SAK* (n 5).

32 *Kuwait Airways Corp v Kuwait Insurance Co SAK* (n 5).

33 *Kuwait Airways Corp v Kuwait Insurance Co SAK* (n 5). Cf also Butler and Merkin (n 8) para C–0222.

34 *Kuwait Airways Corp v Kuwait Insurance Co SAK* (n 5); Barlow Lyde and Gilbert LLP (n 5) para 28.17; Edelman and Burns (n 5) para 4.57.

35 *Dawson's Field Arbitration*, quoted in: *Kuwait Airways Corp v Kuwait Insurance Co SAK* (n 5); likewise quoting *Dawson's Field Arbitration*, *Scott v The Copenhagen Reinsurance Co (UK) Ltd* (n 3) [51]–[53] (Michael Kerr QC).

36 *Kuwait Airways Corp v Kuwait Insurance Co SAK* (n 5).

37 *Scott v The Copenhagen Reinsurance Co (UK) Ltd* (n 3) [29] (Rix LJ).

38 *Scott v The Copenhagen Reinsurance Co (UK) Ltd* (n 3) [81] (Rix LJ).

39 *Dawson's Field Arbitration*, quoted in: *Kuwait Airways Corp v Kuwait Insurance Co SAK* (n 5); *Kuwait Airways Corp v Kuwait Insurance Co SAK* (n 5); *Mann v Lexington Insurance Co* (n 29) 1422 f (Waller LJ); *Scott v The Copenhagen Reinsurance Co (UK) Ltd* (n 3) [81]–[82] (Rix LJ); *Midland Mainline Ltd v Eagle Star Insurance Co Ltd* [2003] EWHC 1771 (Comm), [2004] Lloyd's Rep IR 22 [99]–[100] (Steel J); *IRB Brasil Resseguros SA v CX Reinsurance Co Ltd* (n 3) [46] (Burton J); *Aioi Nissay Dowa Insurance Co Ltd v Heraldglen Ltd and Advent Capital Ltd* (n 3) [19]–[23] (Field J); *MIC Simmonds v Gammell* (n 3) [29] (Sir Jeremy Cooke).

contrast, the unities test appears to have never been applied in the context of cause-based aggregation mechanisms.[40]

4.19 It is to be noted, however, that arbitral tribunals and English courts have not always applied the unities test in dealing with event-based aggregation mechanisms.[41] It appears to be uncertain in which cases the unities test can be considered the right test for the determination of an aggregation problem.

4.20 Furthermore, even if the unities test is considered by an arbitral tribunal or a court, it is by no means certain what its significance is in determining whether multiple individual losses are to be aggregated. In *Aioi Nissay Dowa Insurance Co Ltd v Heraldglen Ltd and Advent Capital Ltd,* the Commercial Court reported that the arbitral tribunal had 'accepted that the unities test was the correct way' to determine whether the individual losses had resulted from one or two events[42] and held that the tribunal 'accurately summarised the law relating to the unities'.[43] By contrast, Rix LJ stated in *Scott v The Copenhagen Re Co (UK) Ltd* that, in determining whether multiple losses arose out of one event, 'all the relevant facts' were to be considered carefully but the decision involved an exercise of judgment. He elaborated that this exercise of judgment could be assisted by the unities test.[44] It seems as though the Court of Appeal did not apply the unities test to conclusively determine questions of aggregation in this case. In the same vein, the Commercial Court explicitly stated in *MIC Simmonds v Gammell* that

> [t]he 'unities' are merely an aid in determining whether the circumstances of the losses involved such a degree of unity as to justify their being described as 'arising out of one occurrence'.[45]

4.21 It further held that the arbitrators 'fully understood the test that they had to apply in deciding on the question of aggregation'.[46] They had to determine whether a sufficient causal link between the individual losses to be aggregated and the event existed.[47] In the event that such a sufficient causal connection could be identified, the conduct of the unities test became legally superfluous.[48]

---

40 See, for instance, *Cox v Bankside Members Agency Ltd* [1995] CLC 671 (CA); *Municipal Mutual Insurance Ltd v Sea Insurance Co Ltd* [1996] CLC 1515 (Comm); *American Centennial Insurance Co v INSCO Ltd* (n 5); *Countrywide Assured Group Plc v Marshall* [2002] EWHC 2082 (Comm), [2003] 1 All ER 237; *Spire Healthcare Ltd v Royal and Sun Alliance Insurance Plc* [2018] EWCA Civ 317, [2018] Lloyd's Rep IR 425.

41 *Caudle v Sharp* (n 3); *Axa Reinsurance (UK) Ltd v Field* (n 3). Cf also *Seele Austria GmbH Co v Tokio Marine Europe Insurance Ltd* [2008] EWCA Civ 441, [2009] 1 All ER 171.

42 *Aioi Nissay Dowa Insurance Co Ltd v Heraldglen Ltd and Advent Capital Ltd* (n 3) [18] (Field J).

43 *Aioi Nissay Dowa Insurance Co Ltd v Heraldglen Ltd and Advent Capital Ltd* (n 3) [37] (Field J).

44 *Scott v The Copenhagen Reinsurance Co (UK) Ltd* (n 3) [81] (Rix LJ).

45 *MIC Simmonds v Gammell* (n 3) [29] (Sir Jeremy Cooke).

46 *MIC Simmonds v Gammell* (n 3) [27] (Sir Jeremy Cooke).

47 *MIC Simmonds v Gammell* (n 3) [28]–[36] (Sir Jeremy Cooke).

48 *MIC Simmonds v Gammell* (n 3) [29] (Sir Jeremy Cooke).

4.22 In summary, the unities test bears relevance only in the context of event-based aggregation mechanisms. However, the unities test was not deemed relevant and applicable by the courts in all the cases where event-based aggregation mechanisms were concerned. Furthermore, in the cases where the unities test was considered relevant, the same importance has not always been attached to it. Consequently, there exists substantial uncertainty regarding the unities test's significance in event-based aggregation mechanisms.

3.2 Purpose of the unities test

4.23 In chapter 3, it was set forth that, in Evans LJ's view, an event-based aggregation mechanism presupposes three different requirements. First, there must be something that can properly be described as an event. Secondly, there must be a causal connection between the event and each of the individual losses to be aggregated. Thirdly, the event should not be too remote from the individual losses. Hence, an event can be considered a relevant event only if the causal links between it and each of the individual losses are not too weak.[49]

4.24 In the *Dawson's Field Arbitration*, where the unities test was developed, it was held that

> *[w]hether or not something which produces a plurality of loss or damage can **properly be described as one occurrence** (…) involves the question of degree of unity in relation to cause, locality, time and, if initiated by human action, the circumstances and purposes of the persons responsible.*[50]

4.25 The phrase 'properly be described as' calls to mind Evan LJ's first requirement. The unities test appears to have been used to determine whether the circumstances from which the individual losses arose can be considered one single as opposed to two or multiple events.[51] In the same vein, Rix LJ noted in *Scott v The Copenhagen Re Co (UK) Ltd* that the unities were reminiscent of Lord Mustill's description that an event was 'something which happens at a particular time, at a particular place, in a particular way'.[52] However, the determination that something can properly be described as one single event cannot solve the issue. Even if the application of the unities test results in establishing that one sole event produced all the individual losses, it is still not clear whether this event is a relevant one.[53] As Evans LJ mentioned, not every event is a relevant event for the purposes of aggregation. Rather, it is only where a certain causal

---

49 *Caudle v Sharp* (n 3) 648 (Evans LJ). For more details, see paras 3.29, 3.38 ff.

50 *Dawson's Field Arbitration*, quoted in: *Kuwait Airways Corp v Kuwait Insurance Co SAK* (n 5) (emphasis added).

51 Barlow Lyde and Gilbert LLP (n 5) para 28.6, who state that '[w]hether or not something which produces a plurality of loss or damage can be described as an event/occurrence depends on the position and viewpoint of the observer and involves an examination of the degree of unity among the losses in relation to their cause, locality, time and, intention (commonly known as the "unities")'; Darlene K Alt, Nathan Hull and James Killelea, 'A Reinsurance Perspective: The Aggregation of Losses Following the Tohoku Earthquake and Tsunami' (2011) 22 Mealey's Litigation Report 1, 2.

52 *Scott v The Copenhagen Reinsurance Co (UK) Ltd* (n 3) [65] (Rix LJ). For Lord Mustill's description of an event, see *Axa Reinsurance (UK) Ltd v Field* (n 3) 1035.

53 See para 3.39.

link between the event and each individual loss exists that it may be considered a relevant event.[54] In other words, if the unities test only helps determine whether Evans LJ's first requirement has been met, his second and third requirement would still have to be addressed by another test.

4.26 Yet, it is sometimes opined that the unities test is used to test the causative requirements between the individual losses to be aggregated and the unifying event.[55] Hence, according to some commentators, the unities test actually serves to determine whether Evans LJ's second and third requirement have been fulfilled and is used as a means to determine whether the causal connections between the event and each individual loss justify an aggregation in a specific case. However, it appears rather unclear how the relevant causative standard should be determined by applying the unities test.

4.27 More specifically, it is not possible to define the standard of causation required nor to determine whether the required standard of causation is met in a given case due to the fact that the circumstances of the individual losses (or for that matter the losses themselves[56]) involve spatial and temporal proximity.[57] For instance, it is impossible to deduce the required standard of causation from the fact that three aircraft were destroyed in consecutive explosions in close proximity more or less simultaneously.[58] Further, the concept of 'unity of cause'[59] seems to only require that there are causative links between the event and each of the individual losses but does not concern the strength of these links. This requirement is, therefore, not capable of determining the required standard of causation that justifies an aggregation of a plurality of losses. Nor does it assist in determining whether the required standard has been met in a given case. Lastly, the criterion of 'unity of intent'[60] also cannot assist in defining the standard of causation in an aggregation mechanism. More specifically, the fact that a hijacker has made a single decision to blow up three aircraft[61] does not afford any insight as to the strength of the causative link between each of the individual losses and the event of destroying the aircraft.

4.28 It would perhaps be more straightforward to admit that it is very hard, maybe impossible, to define an abstract test which is capable of determining a standard of causation for event-based aggregation mechanisms. In fact, it was admitted in *Scott v The Copenhagen Re Co (UK) Ltd* that the relevant question was whether there was 'one event which should be regarded as the cause [of a plurality of] losses so as to make it appropriate to regard [them] as constituting for the purposes

---

54 *Caudle v Sharp* (n 3) 648 (Evans LJ).

55 Barlow Lyde and Gilbert LLP (n 5) para 28.16; Edelman and Burns (n 5) para 4.56.

56 See, for instance, Edelman and Burns (n 5) para 4.58, where it is said that the unities test assesses the proximity of the individual losses rather than the circumstances of the losses.

57 Rather, the fact that the losses' circumstances involved unity of location and time reflects a certain correlation among a set of common circumstances and multiple individual losses.

58 Cf the *Dawson's Field Arbitration*, quoted in: *Kuwait Airways Corp v Kuwait Insurance Co SAK* (n 5).

59 See paras 4.57 ff.

60 See paras 4.65 ff.

61 *Dawson's Field Arbitration*, quoted in: *Kuwait Airways Corp v Kuwait Insurance Co SAK* (n 5).

of aggregation (…) one loss'.[62] Rix LJ held that this determination involved an exercise of judgment in which the unities test could be of assistance.[63] Consequently, Evans LJ's test as set forth in *Caudle v Sharp*[64] has been replaced rather than concretised by applying the unities test.

4.29 It is to be noted that replacing Evans LJ's test with the unities test means testing whether there are causal links between the event and the individual losses. The strength of the causal links is, however, not assessed using the unities test. Instead, it assesses whether the losses' circumstances involve a certain degree of correlation, ie proximity in time, location, and intention. Where a court or arbitral tribunal considers the correlation strong enough, it will hold that an aggregation of the losses is justified.

4.30 In summary, the unities test's task does not appear to be undisputed.[65] According to judicial authority, the unities test does not aim at determining a standard of causation inherent in an event-based aggregation mechanism but rather at determining whether something can properly be described as an event.[66] By contrast, some scholars purport that the unities test is actually used to determine the standard of causation associated with an event-based aggregation mechanism.[67] In any case, it appears to be unclear how the unities test should be capable of achieving this.

3.3 Operation of the unities test

a Subject matter of the unities test

4.31 Developing the unities test in the *Dawson's Field Arbitration*, the arbitral tribunal held that whether a plurality of losses could properly be described as one occurrence 'involve[d] the question of degree of unity in relation to cause, locality, time and, if initiated by human action, the circumstances and purposes of the persons responsible'.[68] This statement leaves open, however, the subject matter that should be in unity.

4.32 The *Dawson's Field Arbitration* arose out of the hijacking of four aircraft in 1970 by members of the Popular Front for the Liberation of Palestine. One aircraft was flown to Cairo and destroyed there; the other three were flown to Dawson's Field, a remote airstrip in Jordan, and blown up there. The question before the arbitrator was whether the three losses, ie the destruction of the three aircraft at Dawson's Field, arose out of one single or multiple events.[69] The arbitral tribunal concluded that the

---

62 *Scott v The Copenhagen Reinsurance Co (UK) Ltd* (n 3) [68] (Rix LJ).

63 *Scott v The Copenhagen Reinsurance Co (UK) Ltd* (n 3) [81] (Rix LJ).

64 *Caudle v Sharp* (n 3) 648 (Evans LJ).

65 This is well illustrated by Barlow, Lyde and Gilbert (n 5) paras 28.6, 28.16, who argue in one instance that the unities test aims at determining what can be considered an event and, in another instance, propound that the causal link between the event and the individual losses is tested by reference to the 'unities'.

66 See para 4.25.

67 See para 4.26.

68 *Dawson's Field Arbitration*, quoted in: *Kuwait Airways Corp v Kuwait Insurance Co SAK* (n 5).

69 *Dawson's Field Arbitration*, quoted in: *Kuwait Airways Corp v Kuwait Insurance Co SAK* (n 5).

destruction of the different aircraft constituted one single event as they were blown up 'in close proximity more or less simultaneously, within the time span of a few minutes, and as a result of a single decision to do so (...)'.[70] Consequently, the arbitral tribunal focused on whether the acts that had caused the loss of the individual aircraft occurred in spatial, temporal and intentional proximity. By contrast, it did not test whether the individual losses themselves occurred in spatial, temporal and intentional proximity.

4.33 Rix J applied the unities test in *Kuwait Airways Corp v Kuwait Insurance Co SAK.* In this case, the question before the Commercial Court was whether the seizure of 15 Kuwaiti aircraft by Iraqi forces and the fact that the aircraft were subsequently flown to Iraq constituted one single or multiple events. Rix J stated that it was the circumstances surrounding the losses that must be scrutinised to see whether they involved the degree of unity required.[71] In his 'findings of fact regarding the circumstances of the aircraft's loss' he held, for example, that 'the aircraft were [all] lost on 2 August' and that therefore there was unity of time.[72] Consequently, according to Rix J, the unities test did not consist of assessing whether the acts that had caused the losses involved a certain degree of unity, but rather whether the individual losses occurred in temporal, spatial and intentional proximity to one another. In the same vein, the Commercial Court in *Aioi Nissay Dowa Insurance Co Ltd v Heraldglen Ltd and Advent Capital Ltd* could not find an error of law in the arbitral tribunal applying the unities test and, for the purposes of unity of time, assessing when the individual losses occurred.[73]

4.34 Similarly, referring to *Mann v Lexington Insurance*[74] where the Court of Appeal was faced with the question whether the deliberate orchestration of a civil unrest which resulted in riot damage to 22 supermarket stores constituted one single event, Edelman and Burns argue that since the individual losses occurred at different locations and at different times there was no unity of location or unity of time.[75] Hence, they also appear to be of the view that the unities test examines whether the individual losses rather than the acts that resulted in these losses involve unity.

4.35 However, it may be noted that the Court of Appeal was not very explicit in *Mann v Lexington Insurance.* In fact, Waller LJ at first held that '[w]hat caused the losses [were] acts of rioters over a wide area, at different locations, and over two days'.[76] The Court of Appeal appears to have focused on the question whether the acts that caused the losses were at the core of the unities test rather than the losses themselves. In the next paragraph of the judgment, however, Waller LJ stated that it 'seem[ed] to [him] difficult to conceive of a situation in which if the [damaged] properties were some distance apart, and if there was lack of unity of time, there

---

70 *Dawson's Field Arbitration*, quoted in: *Kuwait Airways Corp v Kuwait Insurance Co SAK* (n 5).

71 *Kuwait Airways Corp v Kuwait Insurance Co SAK* (n 5).

72 *Kuwait Airways Corp v Kuwait Insurance Co SAK* (n 5).

73 *Aioi Nissay Dowa Insurance Co Ltd v Heraldglen Ltd and Advent Capital Ltd* (n 3) [22] (Field J).

74 *Mann v Lexington Insurance Co* (n 29).

75 Edelman and Burns (n 5) para 4.58.

76 *Mann v Lexington Insurance Co* (n 29) 1423 (Waller LJ).

could still be one occurrence (…)'.[77] Here, Waller LJ's unities test shifted its focus from whether the acts leading to the losses occurred in spatial and temporal proximity to whether the losses themselves occurred in spatial and temporal proximity.

4.36 Admittedly, it will not make any difference in many cases whether the acts that caused the losses or the losses themselves are examined for unity. Taking the case of the *Dawson's Field Arbitration*,[78] it seems to be irrelevant to distinguish the question of whether the three acts of blowing up three aircraft at Dawson's Field involved spatial, temporal and intentional proximity from the one of whether the individual losses of the aircraft at Dawson's Field occurred in spatial, temporal and intentional proximity. The acts of destroying the aircraft as well as the losses of the aircraft occurred simultaneously, in spatial proximity and as the result of one decision to do so.

4.37 However, in some cases, the acts that result in the individual losses may not be conducted at the same place and time as the occurrence of the individual losses. For instance, a cyber attack launched in the UK might result in numerous losses at different locations throughout China and at different times. If the unities test is applied to determine whether the cyber attack constitutes one single event from which a plurality of losses arose, it is very important to know whether the unities test focuses on whether all the acts of hacking occurred in the UK during a certain period of time or whether it aims at determining whether the individual losses sustained by the hacked entity throughout China took place in spatial and temporal proximity. Self-evidently, these two different approaches may lead to substantially different results.

4.38 In summary, it is not entirely clear what the subject matter is of the unities test. More specifically, it is unclear whether the unities test focuses on the acts that lead to multiple individual losses or on the losses themselves. This results in a lack of legal certainty, in particular, in cases where acts that provoke multiple losses are not undertaken at the same place and time as the losses' occurrence.

b Unity of time

4.39 One aspect of the unities test is 'unity of time'. If the circumstances of a plurality of losses involve unity of time, this is an indication that it might be appropriate to regard the individual losses as constituting one loss for the purposes of aggregation.[79]

4.40 Unity of time means that the circumstances of the individual losses involve temporal proximity. However, the concept of unity of time or temporal proximity is extremely vague and provides courts and arbitral tribunals with ample opportunity to reach result-oriented judgments. In fact, an analysis of judicial authorities dealing with the matter suggests that it is equally possible to find that there is unity of time or to hold that there is no unity of time regardless of the circumstances of a case.

---

77 *Mann v Lexington Insurance Co* (n 29) 1423 (Waller LJ).

78 *Dawson's Field Arbitration*, quoted in: *Kuwait Airways Corp v Kuwait Insurance Co SAK* (n 5).

79 Cf *Kuwait Airways Corp v Kuwait Insurance Co SAK* (n 5); *Aioi Nissay Dowa Insurance Co Ltd v Heraldglen Ltd and Advent Capital Ltd* (n 3) [22] (Field J).

4.41 As has been mentioned previously, in the *Dawson's Field Arbitration,* three aircraft were hijacked, flown to Dawson's Field and later blown up one after the another 'more or less simultaneously, within the time span of a few minutes'.[80] It is interesting to note that when conducting the unities test, the arbitral tribunal considered the time span between the first and third explosion of the aircraft relevant in assessing whether there was unity of time. As the explosions took place within a few minutes of each other, the arbitrators held that they involved unity of time. Consequently, it did not deem important at what time the aircraft were hijacked and flown to Dawson's Field.

4.42 *Aioi Nissay Dowa Insurance Co Ltd v Heraldglen Ltd and Advent Capital Ltd* was a case dealing with the consequences of the terror attack on the World Trade Center on 11 September 2001. The question before the Commercial Court was whether the arbitral award holding that the attack consisted of two separate events rather than one single event was correct in law. In application of the unities test, the arbitrators took the view that 'it was right to look at the whole period from check-in and passenger scrutiny to the collapse of each Tower and not just from the time each flight took off'.[81] The Tribunal concluded that, although 'there were clearly similarities in the timing of the events from the commencement of the flights to contact with the Towers', there was no unity of time.[82] The Commercial Court affirmed this arbitral finding. In contrast to the *Dawson's Field Arbitration,* the arbitral tribunal deemed even the time before the hijackings of the aircraft, and not merely when the aircraft and properties were finally destroyed and people were killed, as relevant in the conduct of the unities test.[83]

4.43 The comparison between the *Dawson's Field Arbitration and Aioi Nissay Dowa Insurance Co Ltd v Heraldglen Ltd and Advent Capital Ltd* reveals that the unities test essentially depends on the definition of the period of time under scrutiny. If, in *Aioi Nissay Dowa Insurance Co Ltd v Heraldglen Ltd and Advent Capital Ltd,* the relevant period of time had been deemed the time from the impact of the first aircraft in one tower to the impact of the second aircraft in the other tower–which was 16 minutes–one could arguably have found unity of time.

4.44 Further, *Midland Mainline Ltd v Eagle Star Insurance Co Ltd* was a case following the derailment of a passenger train in 2000, where four passengers were killed and a number of others were seriously injured.[84] In the aftermath of the

---

80 *Dawson's Field Arbitration,* quoted in: *Kuwait Airways Corp v Kuwait Insurance Co SAK* (n 5).

81 *Aioi Nissay Dowa Insurance Co Ltd v Heraldglen Ltd and Advent Capital Ltd* (n 3) [22] (Field J).

82 *Aioi Nissay Dowa Insurance Co Ltd v Heraldglen Ltd and Advent Capital Ltd* (n 3) [22] (Field J).

83 It may be noted, however, that the losses arising in respect of the three aircraft in the *Dawson's Field Arbitration* were the individual losses to be aggregated, whereas the individual losses in *Aioi Nissay Dowa Insurance Co Ltd v Heraldglen Ltd and Advent Capital Ltd* consisted of property damage, personal injury and third party liability claims and that the 'infliction of personal injury and death started in the case of each aircraft shortly after they were hijacked and continued until at least the collapse of each of the Towers', see *Aioi Nissay Dowa Insurance Co Ltd v Heraldglen Ltd and Advent Capital Ltd* (n 3) [22] (Field J); *Dawson's Field Arbitration,* quoted in: *Kuwait Airways Corp v Kuwait Insurance Co SAK* (n 5).

84 *Midland Mainline Ltd v Eagle Star Insurance Co Ltd* (n 39) [5] (Steel J).

disaster, the operator of the railway network repeatedly imposed emergency speed restrictions on its network. These measures caused disruptions for the train-operating companies which resulted in losses in revenue and increased working costs.[85] The question before the Commercial Court was 'whether there was one occurrence or event in the form of the overall impact of the implementation of the [emergency speed restrictions over a period of 36 months] or whether the imposition of each individual emergency speed restriction was a separate occurrence or event'.[86] As the emergency speed restrictions were consistently imposed over a period of 36 months, the Commercial Court held that there could not be said to have been unity of time[87] so that each instance of an emergency speed restriction constituted a separate event.

4.45 By contrast, one of the questions before the Commercial Court in *IRB Brasil Resseguros SA v CX Reinsurance Co Ltd* was whether the installation of insulation material containing asbestos for many years and resulting in more than 318,000 claims constituted one single event.[88] The Commercial Court upheld the arbitral tribunal's finding that 'the loss each year stemmed from a single [event], being [the company's] liability arising from their installation activities'.[89] More specifically, the Commercial Court found that 'the Arbitrators were entitled to conclude that the determination of [the company] each year to carry out its installation activities was an annual "aggregating" event (…) and met the test of unity in the citation from Kuwait'.[90] In *IRB Brasil Resseguros SA v CX Reinsurance Co Ltd*, the Commercial Court went so far as to decide that a substantial number of different acts of installations throughout a year involved a degree of unity of time so as to justify their being described as arising out of one event.

4.46 Comparing *Midland Mainline Ltd v Eagle Star Insurance Co Ltd* with *IRB Brasil Resseguros SA v CX Reinsurance Co Ltd* reveals that there is no determinable standard of unity of time. Rather, courts and arbitral tribunals will be able to find arguments to justify why the losses' circumstances involve unity of time as well as reasons for why there cannot be said to be unity of time in a certain case.

4.47 Consequently, it may be concluded that the concept of unity of time does not provide any legal certainty in the subject matter of event-based aggregation mechanisms. This is so, firstly, because the test largely depends on the period of time deemed relevant and, secondly, because there cannot be said to be an objective standard of temporal proximity that provides legal certainty.

---

85 *Midland Mainline Ltd v Eagle Star Insurance Co Ltd* (n 39) [10] (Steel J).

86 *Midland Mainline Ltd v Eagle Star Insurance Co Ltd* (n 39) [73] (Steel J).

87 *Midland Mainline Ltd v Eagle Star Insurance Co Ltd* (n 39) [99] (Steel J).

88 *IRB Brasil Resseguros SA v CX Reinsurance Co Ltd* (n 3) [26] (Burton J).

89 *IRB Brasil Resseguros SA v CX Reinsurance Co Ltd* (n 3) [46] (Burton J), quoting the arbitration award.

90 *IRB Brasil Resseguros SA v CX Reinsurance Co Ltd* (n 3) [46] (Burton J).

c Unity of location

4.48 Another aspect of the unities test is 'unity of location'. If the circumstances surrounding a plurality of losses' involve unity of location, this is an indication that it might be appropriate to regard all the corresponding individual losses as constituting one loss for the purpose of event-based aggregation.[91] Unity of location means that the individual losses' circumstances involve spatial proximity.

4.49 In a number of cases, the circumstances of the losses have not been deemed to involve unity of location. For instance, it has been held that there was no unity of location where 22 stores in Indonesia were damaged by rioters as the stores 'were at locations some distance apart'.[92] When dealing with the question whether the circumstances of the losses involved unity of location, Waller LJ, in this case, further discussed the hypothetical case that a plurality of stores 'were damaged by the same typhoon at their different locations (...)'.[93] Even in this case, he argued, there would be a strong argument that there was 'a lack of unity of place', and that each store as it was damaged would constitute a separate occurrence.[94] In another matter, it has been held that the imposition of emergency speed restrictions at different locations in a railway network did not involve unity of location.[95]

4.50 By contrast, there are cases where courts and arbitral tribunals have concluded that there was unity of location. For example, it has been held that the destruction of three different aircraft in close proximity involved unity of location.[96] In a further case, it was held that each year's installation of insulation material at a variety of different places constituted one aggregating event and met the unities test.[97]

4.51 On the basis of these authorities, it appears difficult to identify an abstract rule governing the test of whether there is unity of location in a specific case. As with the concept of unity of time, the concept of unity of location is, in fact, extremely flexible and provides courts and arbitral tribunals with extensive opportunity to reach result-oriented decisions. A more detailed comparison of two cases may illustrate this finding well.

4.52 In *Aioi Nissay Dowa Insurance Co Ltd v Heraldglen Ltd and Advent Capital Ltd*, the Commercial Court discussed the arbitral tribunal's finding that the attacks on the World Trade Center on 11 September 2001 involved no unity of location. The

---

91 Cf *Kuwait Airways Corp v Kuwait Insurance Co SAK* (n 5); *Aioi Nissay Dowa Insurance Co Ltd v Heraldglen Ltd and Advent Capital Ltd* (n 3) [23] (Field J).

92 *Mann v Lexington Insurance Co* (n 29) 1423 (Waller LJ).

93 *Mann v Lexington Insurance Co* (n 29) 1422 (Waller LJ).

94 *Mann v Lexington Insurance Co* (n 29) 1422 (Waller LJ).

95 *Midland Mainline Ltd v Eagle Star Insurance Co Ltd* (n 39) [99] (Steel J).

96 *Dawson's Field Arbitration*, quoted in: *Kuwait Airways Corp v Kuwait Insurance Co SAK* (n 5). It may be noted that the arbitral tribunal stated that the aircraft did not become total losses by virtue of the hijacking. Hypothetically, however, if they had become total losses by hijacking, then the losses could not be aggregated, because the aircraft were hijacked at widely separated localities.

97 *IRB Brasil Resseguros SA v CX Reinsurance Co Ltd* (n 3) [46] (Burton J). It is to be noted, however, that the Commercial Court did not specifically address the question of whether there was unity of location in this case. Instead, it generally stated that the unities test was met.

arbitral tribunal had argued that although 'the Twin Towers were located in close proximity to one another and were part of a single property complex', the circumstances of the losses did not involve unity of location. The arbitral tribunal elaborated that '[e]ach Tower was a separate building, albeit connected by a single mall'.[98] The Commercial Court ruled that the arbitral tribunal was entitled to find that there was no sufficient unity of location.[99]

4.53 In this regard, it is notable that the arbitral tribunal dealt exclusively with the question whether the Twin Towers were located in spatial proximity. By contrast, it did not assess whether the locations at which the hijackers had boarded the aircraft before the attacks or where passengers had died during the flights involved spatial proximity.[100]

4.54 In *Kuwait Airways Corp v Kuwait Insurance Co SAK*, the Commercial Court had to decide whether the invasion of Kuwait by Iraqi forces, bringing Kuwait airport under their control and finally flying 15 Kuwaiti aircraft to Iraq constituted one event. All the aircraft were seized at and flown away from Kuwait airport. Rix J noted that the parties rightly agreed that whatever happened at Kuwait airport involved unity of location.[101]

4.55 At the time, however, Kuwait airport was not contained in one single building. It consisted of a complex of buildings, a variety of aircraft stands and airfields. Further, the airport site consisted of an area at least as big as the land where the World Trade Center was situated. Yet, by contrast to *Aioi Nissay Dowa Insurance Co Ltd v Heraldglen Ltd and Advent Capital Ltd*, the spaciousness of the relevant area or the number of buildings were not deemed determinative in *Kuwait Airways Corp v Kuwait Insurance Co SAK*.

4.56 Consequently, as with the concept of unity of time, the concept of unity of location is so vague that it must be concluded to be incapable of providing any legal certainty. It appears that it is possible to find arguments for and against a finding of unity of location irrespective of the facts of a case.

---

98 *Aioi Nissay Dowa Insurance Co Ltd v Heraldglen Ltd and Advent Capital Ltd* (n 3) [23] (Field J).

99 *Aioi Nissay Dowa Insurance Co Ltd v Heraldglen Ltd and Advent Capital Ltd* (n 3) [38] (Field J).

100 Cf *Aioi Nissay Dowa Insurance Co Ltd v Heraldglen Ltd and Advent Capital Ltd* (n 3) [23] (Field J). This seems particularly notable because in their assessment of whether there was unity of time, the arbitrators deemed the time from passenger scrutiny to the collapse of the towers relevant as 'the infliction of personal injury and death started in the case of each aircraft shortly after they were hijacked and continued until at least the collapse of each of the Towers'.

101 *Kuwait Airways Corp v Kuwait Insurance Co SAK* (n 5). It is to be noted, however, that the aggregation clause in question provided for losses in 'any one occurrence, any one location'. In this regard, the parties agreed that Kuwait airport was to be regarded as 'one location'. In fact, the parties' agreement did not relate to the unifying factor of 'any one occurrence' but rather to the unifying factor of 'any one location'. There does not seem to be any legal authority that deems the unities test applicable in cases where the unifying factor is 'any one location'. Yet, when Rix J subsequently applied the unities test to deal with the unifying factor of 'any one occurrence', he assumed that the parties had agreed that there was but one single location (unity of location) for the purpose of the unities test as well.

d Unity of cause

4.57 A further aspect of the unities test is 'unity of cause'. Referring to the *Dawson's Field Arbitration* and *Caudle v Sharp*, the Court of Appeal stated in *Scott v The Copenhagen Re Co (UK) Ltd* that in the context of an event-based aggregation mechanism, 'a plurality of losses is to be regarded as a single aggregated loss if they can be sufficiently linked to a single unifying event by being causally connected with it'.[102] The concept of unity of cause incorporates the need for a causal relationship between the aggregating event and the individual losses into the unities test.

4.58 In *Aioi Nissay Dowa Insurance Co Ltd v Heraldglen Ltd and Advent Capital Ltd*, the arbitral tribunal simplistically stated that by assessing whether there was unity of cause, it was to be asked 'what was the cause of the losses'.[103] Yet, it has been pointed out, both in *Caudle v Sharp* and in *Scott v The Copenhagen Re Co (UK) Ltd*, that not every event that is causative for all the individual losses can be considered a relevant event for the purposes of aggregation.[104] Consequently, it is the purpose of a standard of causation 'to separate out relevant from irrelevant' events.[105]

4.59 It is uncertain whether the concept of 'unity of cause' merely aims at determining whether there are causative links between an event and each of the individual losses or whether the concept is further directed at separating the relevant event from irrelevant ones.

4.60 In *Kuwait Airways Corp v Kuwait Insurance Co SAK*, Rix J stated in the context of the appropriation of 15 Kuwaiti aircraft by Iraqi forces that there was 'unity of cause, for, whichever of the insured perils [was] the appropriate one, it operate[d] alike in respect of all aircraft'.[106] Hence, the relevant event was not specifically identified. Rather, Rix J stated that it was irrelevant which of the insured perils was the appropriate one, as in each case there were causative connections with the individual losses. Thus, the concept of 'unity of cause' was apparently merely used to determine whether there were causal links between the event and each of the 15 lost aircraft. However, the test was not used to determine which of multiple candidates was the relevant event for the purposes of aggregation.

4.61 By contrast, the arbitral tribunal found in *Aioi Nissay Dowa Insurance Co Ltd v Heraldglen Ltd and Advent Capital Ltd* that the terror attacks on the World Trade Center constituted 'two separate causes (...) because there were two separate

---

102 *Scott v The Copenhagen Reinsurance Co (UK) Ltd* (n 3) [68] (Rix LJ).

103 *Aioi Nissay Dowa Insurance Co Ltd v Heraldglen Ltd and Advent Capital Ltd* (n 3) [21] (Field J).

104 *Caudle v Sharp* (n 3) 648 (Evans LJ); *Scott v The Copenhagen Reinsurance Co (UK) Ltd* (n 3) [63] (Rix LJ).

105 *Scott v The Copenhagen Reinsurance Co (UK) Ltd* (n 3) [63]. It may be noted that Rix LJ considered that the concept of 'remoteness' is a tool used to separate out relevant from irrelevant events. In this analysis, the concept of remoteness is considered a part of the concept of causation. In fact, it determines the required strength of a causal link.

106 *Kuwait Airways Corp v Kuwait Insurance Co SAK* (n 5).

hijackings of two separate aircraft'.[107] It further elaborated that it was not satisfied that 'there was any basis, at least in the context of analysing unity of cause, for concluding that there was any factor amounting to an event of sufficient causative relevance to override the conclusion that two separate hijackings caused the separate loss and damage'.[108] In the course of the assessment of whether there was unity of cause, the arbitral tribunal apparently analysed different possible events as well as the strength of its causal links with the individual losses. It concluded that the hijackings of the two aircraft were to be considered the relevant events and that there was no other 'event of sufficient causative relevance to override this conclusion'.[109] Consequently, the concept of unity of cause was used in this case to test whether there were causal links between an event and the individual losses to be aggregated and it seems to also have been used to determine which of multiple candidates was the relevant event.

4.62 In any case, the arbitral tribunal's analysis in determining the relevant event has not been disclosed. More specifically, the arbitral tribunal did not disclose why it considered the individual hijackings rather than the coordinated attack or the killings of individual people on the aircraft as the relevant events. Nevertheless, the Commercial Court ruled that the arbitral tribunal was entitled to so find.[110]

4.63 Further, the Commercial Court noted in *Midland Mainline Ltd v Eagle Star Insurance Co Ltd* that the 'implementation of instructions' to impose emergency speed restrictions after a passenger train had derailed, was to some degree causative for the losses of revenue and increased working costs suffered by the train-operating companies. More specifically, however, the discoveries of the individual damage to different parts of the rails were considered causative for emergency speed restrictions being issued. The restrictions were not imposed as a unitary programme to the entire railway network.[111] In this case, the concept of unity of cause was undoubtedly used to determine whether there was a causative link between the implementation of instructions and the losses that arose out of the emergency speed restrictions. It remains unclear, however, whether the concept of unity of cause was also used to test the strength of the causative links in question with a view to separating relevant from irrelevant events.

4.64 Consequently, the purpose of the unity of cause as an element of the unities test is uncertain. In at least one instance, the concept of unity of cause was merely used to determine whether there were causative links between an event and a plurality of losses. In at least one other case, the concept was used to determine which of multiple candidates was to be considered the relevant event for the purposes of aggregation due to sufficient causal relevance. In any case, there is no judicial authority discussing how the concept of unity of cause would operate in separating relevant from irrelevant events. Thus, the concept of unity of cause does not provide any legal certainty; instead, it creates additional uncertainty.

---

107 *Aioi Nissay Dowa Insurance Co Ltd v Heraldglen Ltd and Advent Capital Ltd* (n 3) [21] (Field J).

108 *Aioi Nissay Dowa Insurance Co Ltd v Heraldglen Ltd and Advent Capital Ltd* (n 3) [21] (Field J).

109 *Aioi Nissay Dowa Insurance Co Ltd v Heraldglen Ltd and Advent Capital Ltd* (n 3) [21] (Field J).

110 *Aioi Nissay Dowa Insurance Co Ltd v Heraldglen Ltd and Advent Capital Ltd* (n 3) [37] (Field J).

111 *Midland Mainline Ltd v Eagle Star Insurance Co Ltd* (n 39) [100] (Steel J).

e Unity of intent

4.65 As was held in the *Dawson's Field Arbitration*, if a plurality of losses have been 'initiated by human action, the circumstances and purposes of the persons responsible' form a further aspect of the unities test.[112] Rix J reformulated the proposition by stating that '[i]n assessing the degree of unity regard may be had to such [a factor as] (...) the intentions of the human agents'.[113]

4.66 The concept of 'unity of intent', too, seems to be a rather vague concept. It does not appear to be entirely clear what the human agents' intentions must be in order to form unity of intent. More specifically, does the unity of intent require that the human agents intend to cause multiple individual losses? Alternatively, is it sufficient that they intend to commit an act which can be considered an event and thereby run the risk of causing losses?

4.67 In respect of the appropriation of 15 Kuwaiti aircraft by Iraqi forces, the Commercial Court found that it was President Saddam Hussein's goal, from the outset, to deprive Kuwait of its dominion over the aircraft and 'to take Kuwait's wealth by force'. The act of depriving Kuwait by force directly amounted to a number of losses.[114] Consequently, it may be said that President Saddam Hussein directly intended to induce a plurality of losses which amounted to unity of intent. In the *Dawson's Field Arbitration*, the arbitral tribunal similarly found that the hijackers had made one single decision to blow up three hijacked aircraft.[115] Hence, it was the hijackers' intention to induce multiple individual losses.

4.68 In *Midland Mainline Ltd v Eagle Star Insurance Co Ltd*, by contrast, the owner of a railway network issued instructions to impose emergency speed restrictions on various parts of its network following the derailment of a passenger train. These emergency speed restrictions resulted in losses in revenue and increased working costs for the train-operating companies. The Commercial Court held that '[t]he justification for the [emergency speed restrictions] was the discovery of individual incidents of [gauge corner cracking, a defect in the rails] of sufficient severity to call for action (...)'.[116] It appears evident that neither the instructions to issue emergency speed restrictions nor the issuing of such restrictions were intended to induce losses to the train-operating companies. Rather, these measures were taken to prevent further derailments. Consequently, the owner of the railway network cannot be said to have intended to induce a plurality of losses to the train-operating companies. The Commercial Court nevertheless concluded that there was unity of intent.[117]

---

112 *Dawson's Field Arbitration*, quoted in: *Kuwait Airways Corp v Kuwait Insurance Co SAK* (n 5).

113 *Kuwait Airways Corp v Kuwait Insurance Co SAK* (n 5).

114 *Kuwait Airways Corp v Kuwait Insurance Co SAK* (n 5).

115 *Dawson's Field Arbitration*, quoted in: *Kuwait Airways Corp v Kuwait Insurance Co SAK* (n 5).

116 *Midland Mainline Ltd v Eagle Star Insurance Co Ltd* (n 39) [100] (Steel J).

117 *Midland Mainline Ltd v Eagle Star Insurance Co Ltd* (n 39) [100]. Steel J expressly held that 'there is a degree of unity of (...) intent'.

4.69 Considering the aforementioned judicial authorities, it may be said that there is substantial uncertainty as to what human agents must intend in order for there to be unity of intent.

4.70 Further, in applying the unities test in *Aioi Nissay Dowa Insurance Co Ltd v Heraldglen Ltd and Advent Capital Ltd*, the arbitral tribunal considered the 'circumstances and purposes of the persons responsible' in the attacks on the World Trade Center.[118] In other words, the arbitral tribunal assessed whether there was unity of intent. In this regard, the arbitrators acknowledged 'that the hijackings were the result of a co-ordinated plot paid for by Al Qaeda but observed that it was clear from the judicial authorities that a conspiracy or plan [could not] of itself constitute an occurrence or an event (…)'.[119] In so finding, the arbitral tribunal seems to have lost sight of the fact that although human agents' intentions and decisions can never properly be described as an event,[120] the concept of unity of intent forms part of the unities test and is used to determine whether it is justified to aggregate a plurality of losses. By stating that there was no unity of intent because a plot can simply not constitute an event, the arbitral tribunal denied the concept of unity of intent its role within the unities test.

4.71 As with the other elements of the unities test, the concept of unity of intent is, consequently, also far from clear and fosters substantial uncertainty in the construction of event-based aggregation mechanisms.

3.4 Summary of the unities test's shortcomings

4.72 This analysis has shown that the unities test–as known today–is incapable of assessing whether it is justified to aggregate a plurality of losses in a specific case. In fact, the test itself suffers from a variety of different shortcomings.

4.73 First, not all courts that dealt with event-based aggregation mechanisms deem the unities test relevant and applicable. There does not appear to be any guidance from judicial authority as to where it is applicable and where it is not.

4.74 Secondly, it appears to be disputed whether the unities test merely aims at determining whether a certain happening can properly be described as an event or whether it aims at determining the standard of causation inherent in a specific aggregation mechanism. Even if the latter were the case, it is not evident how the unities test would determine such a standard by considering factors such as locality, time and the intentions of human agents. Indeed, these factors are rather aspects of correlation than aspects of causation.

4.75 Thirdly, it is uncertain whether the test assesses the unity of acts in order to determine whether they constitute one event or whether it assesses if the resulting losses are in unity. This shortcoming causes substantial uncertainty, in

---

118 *Aioi Nissay Dowa Insurance Co Ltd v Heraldglen Ltd and Advent Capital Ltd* (n 3) [20] (Field J).

119 *Aioi Nissay Dowa Insurance Co Ltd v Heraldglen Ltd and Advent Capital Ltd* (n 3) [20] (Field J).

120 *Midland Mainline Ltd v Eagle Star Insurance Co Ltd* (n 39) [97] (Steel J). It may be noted, however, that in the *Dawson's Field Arbitration*, quoted in: *Kuwait Airways Corp v Kuwait Insurance Co SAK* (n 5), the arbitral tribunal considered the carrying out of a decision to blow up three aircraft one event.

particular, in cases where the acts that provoke multiple losses are not undertaken at the same place and time as the occurrence of the losses.

4.76 Fourthly, the concept of unity of time largely depends on the period of time under scrutiny. Further, it cannot be said that there is an objective standard of what constitutes unity of time. Hence, the concept is too vague to provide legal certainty.

4.77 Fifthly, the concept of unity of location largely depends on the spatial area under scrutiny. Further, it cannot be said that there is an objective standard of what constitutes unity of location. Therefore, substantial legal uncertainty exists around the concept of unity of location.

4.78 Sixthly, it is not clear whether the concept of unity of cause is merely used to determine whether there are causal links between an event and a plurality of losses or whether the concept aims at separating the relevant from irrelevant events for the purposes of aggregation.

4.79 Seventhly, it is uncertain what unity of intent means. It is unclear whether human agents must intend to cause multiple individual losses or whether it is sufficient that they intend to commit a certain act which constitutes an event.

4.80 Therefore, the unities test–as it is known today–seems to be incapable of determining whether it is justified to aggregate a plurality of individual losses in a certain case. Rather than reducing legal uncertainty in the subject matter, it appears to create even more.

4 Exercise of judgment

4.81 As it is very difficult to precisely determine the causal requirements on which an aggregation mechanism is based,[121] 'cases on "event" are borderline and often give rise to disagreement between first instance and appellate judges'.[122] In any case, courts have recognised that assessing whether multiple losses are to be aggregated involves an exercise of judgment.[123]

4.82 More specifically, determining whether something can properly be described as an event[124] as well as where on the chain of causation culminating in the individual losses to be aggregated a relevant event[125] must lie in order to justify an aggregation of the losses is very difficult and depends to a large degree on the

---

121 See paras 4.8 ff.

122 Rob Merkin, 'The Christchurch Earthquakes Insurance and Reinsurance Issues' (2012) 18 Canterbury Law Review 119, 146.

123 In *Midland Mainline Ltd v Eagle Star Insurance Co Ltd* (n 39) [82], Steel J held that the assessment of whether there was one event 'was to be made both analytically and as a matter of intuition and common sense'; *Scott v The Copenhagen Reinsurance Co (UK) Ltd* (n 3) [81] (Rix LJ). In *Aioi Nissay Dowa Insurance Co Ltd v Heraldglen Ltd and Advent Capital Ltd* (n 3) [37], Field J noted that determining the different unities involved an exercise of judgment; *MIC Simmonds v Gammell* (n 3) [36], [39] (Sir Jeremy Cooke).

124 See paras 3.30 ff.

125 See paras 3.38 ff.

judgment of the person interpreting the aggregation clause.[126] The unities test is said to assist in exercising this judgment.[127] While the unities test aims at determining whether the circumstances of a plurality of losses justify their aggregation,[128] it ultimately merely constitutes a set of guidelines,[129] which itself requires an exercise of judgment.[130] Hence, the unities test is incapable of guiding the process of exercising judgment. In fact, rather than dispelling legal uncertainty, the unities test causes additional unpredictability. The fact that questions of event-based aggregation are mostly decided in an exercise of judgment may further be illustrated by two examples of the reinsurance litigation following the attacks on the World Trade Center on 11 September 2001.

4.83 In *MIC Simmonds v Gammell*, an arbitral tribunal dealt with a case in which the owner of the land where the Twin Towers were situated became subject of two sets of claims. In one set of claims, the owner became liable towards the relatives of employees who had been at the site of the World Trade Center at the time of the terror attacks and had been struck by or became trapped under the debris (Workers Compensation Claims).[131] In the other set of claims, persons involved in the clean-up operations following the attacks had claimed to have suffered personal injury which the owner of the land could have averted by providing adequate protective equipment such as respirators and adequate training (Respiratory Claims).[132] The dispute centred on whether the individual workers' compensation claims and the respiratory claims were to be aggregated because they all arose out of one single event.[133]

4.84 The arbitral tribunal concluded that the attack on the World Trade Center constituted one single event.[134] Once the attack had been identified as an event, the tribunal discussed whether there was sufficient causal connection between the event and each individual loss.[135] The arbitral tribunal found that there were significant causal links. Thus, it considered an aggregation of all the individual losses–whether Workers Compensation Claims or Respiratory Claims–as justified.[136] In an appeal against the arbitral award, the Commercial Court found no error of law on the part of the arbitrators and thus affirmed their arbitral award.[137]

4.85 By contrast, in further legal proceedings following the attacks on the World Trade Center, an arbitral tribunal had to decide whether a large number of claims,

---

126 *Scott v The Copenhagen Reinsurance Co (UK) Ltd* (n 3) [81] (Rix LJ).

127 *Scott v The Copenhagen Reinsurance Co (UK) Ltd* (n 3) [81] (Rix LJ).

128 *Kuwait Airways Corp v Kuwait Insurance Co SAK* (n 5).

129 *MIC Simmonds v Gammell* (n 3) [29] (Sir Jeremy Cooke).

130 *Aioi Nissay Dowa Insurance Co Ltd v Heraldglen Ltd and Advent Capital Ltd* (n 3) [37] (Field J).

131 *MIC Simmonds v Gammell* (n 3) [8] (Sir Jeremy Cooke).

132 *MIC Simmonds v Gammell* (n 3) [8] (Sir Jeremy Cooke).

133 *MIC Simmonds v Gammell* (n 3) [6] (Sir Jeremy Cooke).

134 *MIC Simmonds v Gammell* (n 3) [27]–[28], [30] (Sir Jeremy Cooke).

135 *MIC Simmonds v Gammell* (n 3) [30] (Sir Jeremy Cooke).

136 *MIC Simmonds v Gammell* (n 3) [30] (Sir Jeremy Cooke).

137 *MIC Simmonds v Gammell* (n 3) [38] (Sir Jeremy Cooke).

such as personal injury claims, wrongful death claims, property and business interruption claims, directly resulting from the attacks were to be aggregated. In *Aioi Nissay Dowa Insurance Co Ltd v Heraldglen Ltd and Advent Capital Ltd*, the Commercial Court held that the arbitrators had not committed an error of law when deciding that the attacks did not constitute one single but rather two distinct events as there were two successful hijackings of two separate aircraft.[138]

4.86 In both cases, the respective tribunals were required to decide whether multiple individual losses resulting from the attacks on the World Trade Center were to be aggregated. Both tribunals discussed their cases in light of the 'essential relevant authorities on the point of aggregation'.[139] Yet, their conclusions were diametrically opposed. It is submitted that this is evidence of the fact that determining what can properly be described as an event and whether there is a sufficient causal link between an event and the individual losses is an exercise of pure judgment.

5 Approaches to avoid legal uncertainty

4.87 Depending on the class of insurance, the parties to reinsurance contracts have sought different means to reduce the legal uncertainty inherent in event-based aggregation mechanisms. In property excess of loss reinsurance contracts, the parties have provided for so-called hours clauses. In other instances, the parties have sought to avoid the legal uncertainty existing around event-based aggregation mechanisms by providing for a so-called sole judge clause in their contract of reinsurance.[140]

5.1 Hours clauses

a Purpose of hours clauses

4.88 Hours clauses are often used in property excess of loss reinsurance contracts[141] reinsuring against natural catastrophes[142] or terrorism and political

---

138 *Aioi Nissay Dowa Insurance Co Ltd v Heraldglen Ltd and Advent Capital Ltd* (n 3) [40] (Field J).

139 *Aioi Nissay Dowa Insurance Co Ltd v Heraldglen Ltd and Advent Capital Ltd* (n 3) [3] (Field J); *MIC Simmonds v Gammell* (n 3) [20] (Sir Jeremy Cooke).

140 It may be noted that the excess of loss reinsurance contracts before the Court of Appeal in *Brown (RE) v GIO Insurance Ltd* (n 3) had been concluded before 1988. At that time, the parties to the contract could not have been aware of the legal uncertainties that resulted from court rulings and arbitral awards that were decided later. Accordingly, they could not have intended to dispel legal uncertainty created by these later decisions.

141 Barlow Lyde and Gilbert LLP (n 5) para 28.84.

142 Barlow Lyde and Gilbert LLP (n 5) para 28.84; Merkin, Hodgson and Tyldesley (n 5) para 11–356; Butler and Merkin (n 8) para C-0248/4; 'IUA 01–018 Hours Clause (NP61)' <http://www.iuaclauses.co.uk/site/cms/contentDocumentLibraryView.asp?chapter=9&category=59> accessed 1 March 2019; 'IUA 01–023 United Kingdom Hours Clause (NP65)' <http://www.iuaclauses.co.uk/site/cms/contentDocumentLibraryView.asp?chapter=9&category=59> accessed 1 March 2019; 'IUA 01–033 Definition of Loss Occurrence (Hours Clause) - Commentary' <http://www.iuaclauses.co.uk/site/cms/contentDocumentLibraryView.asp?chapter=5> accessed 1 March 2019; 'IUA 01–034 Definition of Loss Occurrence (Hours Clause)' <http://www.iuaclauses.co.uk/site/cms/contentDocumentLibraryView.asp?chapter=5> accessed 1 March 2019; 'LMA5223 Definition of Loss Occurrence (with Freeze Aggregate Extension)' (London Market Association 2015) <http://www.lmalloyds.com/LMA/Underwriting/Non-Marine/Property_Reinsurance/LMA/Underwriting/Non-Marine/PRBP/Property_Reinsurance.aspx?hkey=c34153bf-b969-4e53-a433-012644640a4a> accessed 1 March 2019; 'LMA5224 Definition of Loss Occurrence (Risk)' (London Market Association 2015) <http://www.lmalloyds.com/LMA/Underwriting/

---

violence.[143] According to Soar, hours clauses were developed to dispel uncertainties concerning aggregation mechanisms.[144] They aim at more closely describing the unifying factor upon which a plurality of individual losses is to be aggregated.[145] More specifically, hours clauses determine that multiple individual losses aggregate if they–subject to a specified period of time–all result from one single catastrophe.[146]

4.89 Multiple different wordings[147] that are based on different unifying factors exist. There are, eg, hours clauses using an 'event',[148] an 'act',[149] a 'manifestation of a peril'[150] or a 'catastrophe'[151] as their basis.

4.90 In 2012, the International Underwriting Association's Hours Clause Drafting Sub-Group presented its model hours clause, IUA 01–033, accompanied by a commentary. This hours clause was further developed and revised in February 2018. The work culminated in model clause IUA 01–034. This model clause focuses on the aggregation of losses following a natural disaster but also provides for a rule in respect of riots, civil commotions and malicious damage. Model clause IUA 01–034 reads as follows:

> *The words 'Loss Occurrence' shall mean all individual losses arising out of and directly occasioned by one catastrophe. However, the duration and extent of any 'Loss Occurrence' so defined shall be limited to:*
>
> a. *[72] consecutive hours as regards a hurricane, a typhoon, a cyclone, windstorm;*

Non-Marine/Property_Reinsurance/LMA/Underwriting/Non-Marine/PRBP/Property_Reinsurance.aspx?hkey=c34153bf-b969-4e53-a433-012644640a4a> accessed 1 March 2019.

143 'Hiscox War, Terrorism and Political Violence Insurance' <https://www.awris.com/Clauses/S&T%20andor%20PV%20business/Hiscox%20WTPV%20180507.pdf> accessed 4 March 2019; 'LMA 3030 - Terrorism Insurance - Physical Loss or Physical Damage Wording' <https://www.lmalloyds.com/LMA/Wordings/lma3030.aspx> accessed 4 March 2019; 'LMA 3092 - Physical Loss or Physical Damage - Riots, Strikes, Civil Commotion, Malicious Damage, Terrorism and Sabotage Insurance'; Andreas Schwepcke and Alexandra Vetter, *Praxishandbuch: Rückversicherung* (VVW 2017) para 918, who opine that hours clauses appear 'to be workable in the case of reinsurance of property against named perils, but, it is difficult to draft an hours clause which accommodates such diverse human loss-causative agents as negligent Lloyd's underwriters and aggressive Iraqi dictators'.

144 Soar (n 5).

145 Barlow Lyde and Gilbert LLP (n 5) para 28.84. Cf also Merkin, Hodgson and Tyldesley (n 5) para 11–356.

146 Barlow Lyde and Gilbert LLP (n 5) para 28.85.

147 Barlow Lyde and Gilbert LLP (n 5) para 28.87.

148 'Hiscox War, Terrorism and Political Violence Insurance' (n 143); 'LMA 3092 - Physical Loss or Physical Damage - Riots, Strikes, Civil Commotion, Malicious Damage, Terrorism and Sabotage Insurance' (n 143).

149 'LMA 3030 - Terrorism Insurance - Physical Loss or Physical Damage Wording' (n 143).

150 'IUA 01–018 Hours Clause (NP61)' (n 142); 'IUA 01–019 Loss Occurrence (NP64)' <http://www.iuaclauses.co.uk/site/cms/contentDocumentLibraryView.asp?chapter=9&category=59> accessed 1 March 2019; 'IUA 01–023 United Kingdom Hours Clause (NP65)' (n 142).

151 'IUA 01–033 Definition of Loss Occurrence (Hours Clause) - Commentary' (n 142); 'IUA 01–034 Definition of Loss Occurrence (Hours Clause)' (n 142); 'LMA5223 Definition of Loss Occurrence (with Freeze Aggregate Extension)' (n 142); 'LMA5224 Definition of Loss Occurrence (Risk)' (n 142).

b. *[72] consecutive hours as regards earthquake, seaquake, tsunami, tidal wave and/or volcanic eruption;*

c. *[72] consecutive hours as regards pluvial flood due to heavy precipitation;*

d. *[168] consecutive hours as regards fluvial flood due to the overflowing of one or several rivers or one or several rivers together with other waterbodies;*

e. *[72] consecutive hours as regards flooding due to storm surge;*

f. *[72] consecutive hours and within the limits of one city, town or village as regards riots, civil commotions and malicious damage;*

g. *[168] consecutive hours as regards any 'Loss Occurrence' of whatsoever nature which does not consist of or include individual loss or losses from any of the perils previously stated;*

and no individual loss from whatever insured peril, which occurs outside of these periods or areas, shall be included in that 'Loss Occurrence'.

Where such a Loss Occurrence consists of or includes losses from two or more insured perils, the duration of each insured peril contributing losses to such a 'Loss Occurrence' shall not exceed the relevant period of consecutive hours specified herein for that peril. Only one such period of consecutive hours for each insured peril may contribute to each Loss Occurrence so designated. The maximum number of consecutive hours for the entire Loss Occurrence consisting of or including a combination of insured perils shall be the number of consecutive hours specified for the applicable insured peril with the highest number of consecutive hours.

The Reinsured may choose the date and time when any such period of consecutive hours commences and if any catastrophe is of greater duration than the above periods, the Reinsured may divide that catastrophe into two or more 'Loss Occurrences', provided no two periods overlap and provided no period commences earlier than the date and time of the happening of the first recorded individual loss to the Reinsured in that catastrophe.

This clause shall not extend coverage beyond the business specified as covered by this {Response} and shall not replace, override or modify any other terms, clauses or conditions in this {Response}.[152]

4.91 In the following section, the operation of hours clauses and problems associated with such clauses will be discussed on the basis of the IUA 01–034 model hours clause.

b Operation of hours clauses

4.92 Clause IUA 01–034 defines the term 'Loss Occurrence'. It provides that one loss occurrence is composed of all individual losses that arise from one catastrophe. In other words, the term 'Loss Occurrence' corresponds with what has been termed as the re-insured's ultimate net loss (minus the reinsured's expenses for settling the claims).[153] The clause specifies that the duration of one loss occurrence shall be limited to a certain number of hours. The applicable hourly limit depends on the peril that caused the plurality of losses.[154] All individual losses that result from a catastrophe and occur within the applicable period of time are to be aggregated.

---

152 'IUA 01–034 Definition of Loss Occurrence (Hours Clause)' (n 142) quoted with permission from the International Underwriting Association.

153 See paras 2.11 ff.

154 'IUA 01–034 Definition of Loss Occurrence (Hours Clause)' (n 142).

4.93 The hours clause does not determine the reinsured perils. Only if the contract of reinsurance covers losses resulting from a specific peril will the time limit with regard to this peril in the hours clause operate. The clause's closing paragraph specifically clarifies that the hours clause is not intended to extend cover in any way.[155] Furthermore, the list of perils provided for in the hours clause is not an exhaustive one.[156] Rather, point (g) of the first paragraph of IUA 01–034 provides a time limit for the aggregation of losses resulting from insured perils that are not specifically named in the hours clause.[157]

4.94 The unifying factor used in this clause is 'one catastrophe'. It is important to note, however, that a peril named in the hours clause is not the same thing as a catastrophe.[158] It is, namely, possible that a catastrophe 'includes losses which result from one or more named perils'.[159] By contrast to its predecessor IUA 01–033, IUA 01–034 contains language dealing with loss occurrences consisting of a combination of insured perils.[160]

4.95 Moreover, for the purposes of IUA 01–033, the International Underwriting Association's Hours Clause Drafting Sub-Group considered whether it should use the unifying factor of 'event' in place of 'catastrophe' as the former term was often used in aggregation clauses in the London market. Yet, it decided to use the term 'catastrophe' because in contrast to the term 'event' the former term provided additional flexibility.[161] IUA 01–034 abided by that decision.[162]

4.96 Only losses that are attributable to one and the same catastrophe are aggregated. Thus, losses resulting from two different catastrophes, which both occur at the same time, are not to be aggregated.[163] For instance, if two or more separate windstorms occur in quick succession, only those losses resulting from the same windstorm may be aggregated, whereas losses that arise from different windstorms may not.[164]

---

155 'IUA 01–034 Definition of Loss Occurrence (Hours Clause)' (n 142). Cf also 'IUA 01–033 Definition of Loss Occurrence (Hours Clause) - Commentary' (n 142) para 14.1.

156 Cf 'IUA 01–033 Definition of Loss Occurrence (Hours Clause) - Commentary' (n 142) para 16, which is still relevant for IUA 01–034.

157 'IUA 01–034 Definition of Loss Occurrence (Hours Clause)' (n 142).

158 Anthony Dickinson, 'Hours Clause: Definition of Loss Occurrence' (2009) IUA Circular 116/09 3 <http://www.iuaclauses.co.uk/site/cms/contentDocumentView.asp?chapter=5> accessed 1 March 2019.

159 Dickinson (n 158) 3.

160 See 'IUA 01–034 Definition of Loss Occurrence (Hours Clause)' (n 142), which provides that '[w]here a loss occurrence consists of (…) losses from two or more insured perils, the duration of each insured peril contributing losses to such a "Loss Occurrence" shall not exceed the relevant period of consecutive hours specified (…) for that peril. The maximum number of consecutive hours for the entire Loss Occurrence consisting of or including a combination of insured perils shall be the number of consecutive hours specified for the applicable insured peril with the highest number of consecutive hours'.

161 'IUA 01–033 Definition of Loss Occurrence (Hours Clause) - Commentary' (n 142) para 4.2.

162 'IUA 01–034 Definition of Loss Occurrence (Hours Clause)' (n 142).

163 Dickinson (n 158) 3.

164 Dickinson (n 158) 3.

4.97 In any case, under model clause IUA 01–034, it is up to the reinsured to choose when–for the purposes of defining a loss occurrence–the indicated period of time starts to run.[165] If a catastrophe is of longer duration than the period of time indicated in the hours clause, the reinsured may present two aggregated losses to its reinsurer. It may, for that matter, divide the unifying factor of catastrophe into two or more instances. All the individual losses that arose from the catastrophe within one indicated period of time may be aggregated. Individual losses that occur after the elapse of this period of time may be aggregated if they, in turn, occurred during another period of time of the same length. Furthermore, the first and second period of time may not overlap and the first period of time may not be chosen to start before the occurrence of the first recorded individual loss.[166]

c Problems with hours clauses

4.98 The International Underwriting Association has deemed one of its model clauses preceding IUA 01–034 'very successful'.[167] It considered, however, that 'over the years there ha[d] inevitably been losses which ha[d] prompted questions about its operation'.[168] Since then, it has refined its model clauses repeatedly.

4.99 There is no English authority dealing with hours clauses in detail.[169] In fact, there appears to be substantial uncertainty as to their interpretation.

4.100 First and foremost, it has been set forth that 'a catastrophe is not the same thing as a peril' and that only losses from one and the same catastrophe are aggregated.[170] This begs the question of what constitutes one catastrophe. Barlow Lyde and Gilbert write that the purpose of the hours clause was 'to address one of the most persistent difficulties encountered in handling property excess of loss catastrophe claims, namely, how to define clearly (...) the basis upon which the reinsured may aggregate losses arising from one occurrence'.[171] Insofar as the hours clause does not provide for a clear definition of what constitutes one catastrophe, this specific difficulty is not even addressed. Irrespective of the time periods indicated in the hours clause, the vexing question of whether there were one or multiple catastrophes which caused the individual losses, hence, remains.

4.101 Secondly, the meaning of the phrase 'directly occasioned by' appears unclear.[172] In fact, this phrase seems to provide that a specific causal link between the unifying catastrophe and each individual loss is required. Yet, the hours clause remains silent as to the applicable standard of causation. In its circular 116/09, the International Underwriting Association explains that there must be a direct causal relationship. The

---

165 'IUA 01–034 Definition of Loss Occurrence (Hours Clause)' (n 142). See also Barlow Lyde and Gilbert LLP (n 5) para 28.89.

166 'IUA 01–034 Definition of Loss Occurrence (Hours Clause)' (n 142).

167 Dickinson (n 158) 1.

168 Cf Dickinson (n 158) 1.

169 Barlow Lyde and Gilbert LLP (n 5) para 28.86; Dickinson (n 158) 9.

170 Dickinson (n 158) 3.

171 Barlow Lyde and Gilbert LLP (n 5) para 28.84; Soar (n 5), states that 'the "hours clause" was developed to remove the uncertainties surrounding the application of cause and event wording'.

172 Barlow Lyde and Gilbert LLP (n 5) para 28.86.

purpose of this was to 'ensure that a claim could not be made for losses that [were] so far down a chain of events as to be considered too remote from the cause'.[173] It is certainly possible that multiple individual losses occur in temporal proximity while the causative connections between the catastrophe and each of the individual losses differ substantially. For instance, an earthquake may be a catastrophe that causes multiple individual losses. A number of individual losses may directly arise from the earthquake. At the same time, the earthquake may provoke a tsunami which, in turn, causes further individual losses. The force of the tsunami may, in turn, provoke a short circuit that also results in individual losses. Although the individual earthquake losses, the tsunami losses and the fire losses all occurred in temporal proximity, they cannot be said to involve the same degree causal proximity to the seismic catastrophe, ie the earthquake.

4.102 It may be deduced from this that both event-based aggregation mechanisms using an hours clause and those not providing for an hours clause come with an uncertain standard of causation. The temporal limitation provided for in the hours clause does not aim at and is not capable of overcoming the difficulties associated with the required degree of causation inherent in event-based aggregation mechanisms. The fact that the aggregation of a plurality of individual losses is temporally limited is, thus, merely to be considered an addition to the causal requirements that narrows down the aggregation mechanism.

4.103 Thirdly, when dealing with the question whether a specific individual loss occurred within the applicable period of time, a problem of timing may arise.[174] This is particularly so when the reinsured divides the catastrophe into two or multiple instances.[175] In fact, it will not always be easy to identify when exactly an individual loss occurred and, thus, to which period of time it relates.[176] For instance, if a windstorm moves over Europe and causes individual losses over a period of 100 hours, the reinsured may, under the model clause IUA 01–034, aggregate all individual losses that occurred during a period of 72 hours. After this period has elapsed, a second period of 72 hours starts to run. It may be difficult to identify at what time each individual loss occurred and thus whether it relates to the first or the second instance.[177]

4.104 In summary, hours clauses have not yet been fully tested by English courts. Irrespective of this, they do not seem to be capable of fully dispelling legal uncertainties associated with event-based aggregation mechanisms.

d *Tokio Marine Europe Insurance Ltd v Novae Corporate*

4.105 Hours clauses generally define the term 'occurrence' or 'loss occurrence' and use unifying factors such as 'catastrophe',[178] 'event',[179] 'act' or 'manifestation of an

---

173 Dickinson (n 158) 6.

174 Cf Barlow Lyde and Gilbert LLP (n 5) para 28.91.

175 See para 4.97.

176 Cf Barlow Lyde and Gilbert LLP (n 5) para 28.91.

177 Cf Barlow Lyde and Gilbert LLP (n 5) para 28.91.

178 See, for instance, IUA01–033; IUA 01–034; LMA 5223; LMA 5224.

179 See, for instance, LMA 3092.

original insured peril'.[180] Hence, they are mostly used in the context of event-based aggregation mechanisms.[181]

4.106 By contrast, hours clauses appear to be used rather seldomly in cause-based aggregation mechanisms. Yet, it may be that a reinsurance contract contains a cause-based aggregation clause as well as an event-based hours clause.[182] This begs the question of the relation between the hours clause and the aggregation clause.[183] In *Tokio Marine Europe Insurance Ltd v Novae Corporate Underwriting Ltd*, the Commercial Court touched upon this question.[184] In this case, the following aggregation clause was incorporated into the retrocession agreement between the retrocedent TMEI and the retrocessionaire Novae: 'Occurrence' means 'any one Occurrence or any series of Occurrences consequent upon or attributable to one source or original cause'.[185]

4.107 Further, the retrocession agreement also contained the following hours clause:

> *All loss, destruction or damage ... caused by inundation from the sea or the rising, overflowing or breaking of boundaries of any lake, pond, reservoir, river, stream or other body of water, all whether or not driven by wind, and occurring during a period of seventy two consecutive hours ... shall be deemed to have been caused by a single Occurrence.*[186]

4.108 Hence, the aggregation mechanism contained in this retrocession agreement is composed of a cause-based aggregation clause as well as an event-based hours clause. It is worth noting two aspects of this aggregation mechanism. First, both the hours clause and the aggregation clause use the term 'occurrence' but define it differently. Secondly, the term 'occurrence' is not designated as the unifying factor in the aggregation clause. It is, instead, 'one source or original cause' that is the unifying factor. By contrast, the term 'occurrence' may be understood to operate as the unifying factor in the hours clause.[187] Consequently, there are potentially at least two different unifying factors in the aggregation mechanism.

4.109 It is not surprising that the parties to the retrocession agreement favoured different interpretations of the aggregation mechanism.[188] The retrocessionaire, Novae, argued that the hours clause overrides the aggregation clause to the effect that the individual losses should be aggregated on the basis of any one occurrence as

---

180 See, for instance, IUA 01–018 (NP61); IUA 01–019 (NP64); IUA 01–023 (NP65).

181 Cf paras 2.61 ff, 3.59.

182 Merkin, Hodgson and Tyldesley (n 5) para 11–357.

183 Cf *Tokio Marine Europe Insurance Ltd v Novae Corporate Underwriting Ltd* [2013] EWHC 3362 (Comm), [2014] Lloyd's Rep IR 490 [100] (Hamblen J).

184 *Tokio Marine Europe Insurance Ltd v Novae Corporate Underwriting Ltd* (n 183) [99]–[104] (Hamblen J).

185 *Tokio Marine Europe Insurance Ltd v Novae Corporate Underwriting Ltd* (n 183) [51], [53] (Hamblen J).

186 *Tokio Marine Europe Insurance Ltd v Novae Corporate Underwriting Ltd* (n 183) [102] (Hamblen J).

187 *Tokio Marine Europe Insurance Ltd v Novae Corporate Underwriting Ltd* (n 183) [102] (Hamblen J).

188 Butler and Merkin (n 8) para C-0248/4.

defined in the hours clause.[189] The retrocedent, TMEI, on the other hand, contended that the hours clause is overridden by the aggregation clause and that the individual losses should be aggregated if they are consequent upon or attributable to one source or original cause.[190]

4.110 The Commercial Court was not required to and did not decide whether the hours clause prevailed over the aggregation clause or *vice versa*.[191] This is a question of constructing the retrocession agreement, which appears quite challenging, because there is one aggregation mechanism using conflicting unifying factors. The parties to re-insurance contracts are well advised to avoid using multiple incompatible unifying factors in one aggregation mechanism as this adds even more legal uncertainty as to the operation of the aggregation mechanism.

5.2 Sole judge clauses

4.111 It has been demonstrated that aggregation mechanisms based on 'each and every loss and/or series of losses arising out of one event' may be controversial.[192] There is, in fact, often considerable debate about the definition of an 'event' and the causal requirements associated with it.

4.112 With a view to dispel the legal uncertainties inherent in event-based aggregation mechanisms and 'to save endless litigation about the point',[193] so-called sole judge clauses have been developed. A typical sole judge clause might read as follows: 'The Reassured shall be the sole judge as to what constitutes each and every loss and/or one event'.[194]

4.113 A sole judge clause does not modify the event-based aggregation mechanism itself. It complements the aggregation provision with an agreement to leave it to the reinsured to decide whether a plurality of losses can properly be said to arise out of any single event.[195] By so doing, the parties confer the right to the reinsured to decide mixed questions of fact and law.[196]

4.114 Whether and to what extent this is permitted by the law was considered in *Brown (RE) v GIO Insurance Ltd*.[197] This was one of the legal proceedings following *Deeny v Gooda Walker*[198] and *Arbuthnot v Feltrim*.[199] In these cases Lloyd's Members'

---

189 *Tokio Marine Europe Insurance Ltd v Novae Corporate Underwriting Ltd* (n 183) [103] (Hamblen J).

190 *Tokio Marine Europe Insurance Ltd v Novae Corporate Underwriting Ltd* (n 183) [101], [104] (Hamblen J).

191 *Tokio Marine Europe Insurance Ltd v Novae Corporate Underwriting Ltd* (n 183); Merkin, Hodgson and Tyldesley (n 5) para 11–357.

192 See paras 4.4 ff. In respect of problems associated with series clauses, see paras 3.83 ff.

193 *Brown (RE) v GIO Insurance Ltd* (n 3) 206 (Waller LJ).

194 *Brown (RE) v GIO Insurance Ltd* (n 3). Another wording that has been used is: 'The Reassured's definition of each and every loss and/or event shall be final and binding on the Reinsurers hereon'.

195 *Brown (RE) v GIO Insurance Ltd* (n 3) 208 (Chadwick LJ).

196 *Brown (RE) v GIO Insurance Ltd* (n 3) 208 (Chadwick LJ).

197 *Brown (RE) v GIO Insurance Ltd* (n 3).

198 *Deeny v Gooda Walker Ltd* [1994] CLC 1224 (Comm).

199 *Arbuthnot v Feltrim Underwriting Agencies Ltd* [1995] CLC 437.

Agents were held liable for negligently underwriting insurance policies. The Members' Agents were covered for their liability under E&O insurance policies underwritten by, among others, Syndicate 702. Syndicate 702, in turn, bought excess of loss reinsurance cover for losses resulting from their E&O insurance policies.[200] With 'the commercial objective of avoiding unnecessary cost and expense in the settlement of reinsurance claims', Syndicate 702 complemented the aggregation provisions with sole judge clauses.[201]

4.115 First, the Court of Appeal noted that the sole judge rule was to be construed to the effect that 'as a matter of fact and construction of the reinsurance contract' the re-insured was given the power to decide whether multiple losses arose from one or multiple events for the purposes of aggregation.[202] It observed that a sole judge clause was an agreement to leave to the reinsured the decision as to what the facts were in a specific case and whether, from 'the combination of [these] facts', it may be concluded that multiple losses arose out of one single event.[203] The Court of Appeal held that, in principle, such agreements were valid. More specifically, it held that 'a sensible commercial bargain, made between parties experienced in their field' should not be vitiated unless 'there [was] some clearly identifiable element of public policy which require[d] that to be done'.[204] As long as the reinsured was bound to use his decision-making power in a reasonable fashion, sole judge clauses were not contrary to public policy and, thus, were valid.[205]

4.116 The Court of Appeal further considered the question of whether the re-insured's decision was unreasonable. Waller LJ noted that where a decision upon fact and construction had been left to one of the parties, this decision could not be considered unreasonable simply because the reinsurer could show that a court would have decided differently. A decision was unreasonable, according to Waller LJ, only if it could not even be argued that multiple losses arose from one single event when the matter came to be considered by a court.[206]

---

200 It may be noted that the primary insurance contract was taken out on the basis of 'any one occurrence (...) arising from one originating cause', whereas the reinsurance contracts provided for an aggregation on the basis of 'each and every loss (...) arising out of one event', see *Brown (RE) v GIO Insurance Ltd* (n 3). In *Cox v Bankside Members Agency Ltd* (n 40), it was held that each underwriter's negligent approach to the underwriting constituted one originating cause. In *Axa Reinsurance (UK) Ltd v Field* [1995] CLC 1504 (CA), the Court of Appeal held that an originating cause was essentially the same thing as an event. This is why in *Brown (RE) v GIO Insurance Ltd* (n 3), the Commercial Court at first instance held that the reinsured's decision to view the negligent approach to the overall underwriting as one single event was correct. Subsequently, however, the House of Lords overturned the Court of Appeal's judgment in *Axa Reinsurance (UK) Ltd v Field* (n 3) and clarified that an originating cause was something altogether less constricted than an event and that a state of mind could not constitute an event. It is for this reason that the reinsurers before the Court of Appeal in *Brown (RE) v GIO Insurance Ltd* (n 3) argued that the negligent approach to the overall process of underwriting might constitute an originating cause but not one single event; see also Barlow Lyde and Gilbert LLP (n 5) paras 28.80 ff.

201 *Brown (RE) v GIO Insurance Ltd* (n 3) 208 (Chadwick LJ).

202 *Brown (RE) v GIO Insurance Ltd* (n 3) 206 (Waller LJ).

203 *Brown (RE) v GIO Insurance Ltd* (n 3) 209 (Chadwick LJ).

204 *Brown (RE) v GIO Insurance Ltd* (n 3) 208 f (Chadwick LJ).

205 *Brown (RE) v GIO Insurance Ltd* (n 3) 206 (Waller LJ), 209 (Chadwick LJ).

206 *Brown (RE) v GIO Insurance Ltd* (n 3) 207 (Waller LJ).

4.117 In applying the sole judge clause, the reinsured had decided that the 'overall underwriting of an individual underwriter caused by his negligent approach' was one single event which resulted in multiple instances of negligent underwritings.[207] The reinsurer argued that it had been held in *Axa Reinsurance Plc v Field*[208] and in *Caudle v Sharp*[209] that, as a matter of law, a state of mind could not constitute an event within the meaning of aggregation clauses so that the reinsured's decision was to be considered unreasonable.[210]

4.118 The Court of Appeal stated that its finding that a negligent approach to the process of underwriting constituted one event does not mean that 'the state of mind of each individual underwriter was an "event"'.[211] Furthermore, in Waller LJ's opinion, it was a reasonable view 'that the overall underwriting of an individual underwriter caused by his negligent approach was an event from which all the losses arose'.[212] The Court of Appeal accordingly concluded that the reinsured's relevant decision was not unreasonable.[213]

4.119 Where a sole judge clause is used, the pertinent question becomes whether the reinsured's decision is reasonable.[214] It appears difficult to grasp the extent of the right conferred upon the reinsured to exercise his own judgment. As Butler and Merkin state, there is legal uncertainty as to whether the reinsured is required to take the reinsurer's interest into consideration when making its decision.[215]

4.120 Consequently, a sole judge clause may be an effective tool to dispel some of the legal uncertainty inherent in an event-based aggregation mechanism and, thus, to avoid endless legal proceedings about the question of correct aggregation.[216] However, as the extent of the reinsured's right to exercise his own judgment seems to be unclear, some legal uncertainty persists. Furthermore, sole judge clauses largely put the reinsurers at the reinsureds' mercy. Clearly, the decision as to whether to use a sole judge clause is a commercial decision, weighing up the risks of costly litigation about the correct aggregation of multiple losses and those of paying more re-insurance claims because the reinsured–not unreasonably–interpreted the aggregation clause in its own favour.

---

207 *Brown (RE) v GIO Insurance Ltd* (n 3) 207 (Waller LJ).

208 *Axa Reinsurance (UK) Ltd v Field* (n 3).

209 *Caudle v Sharp* (n 3).

210 *Brown (RE) v GIO Insurance Ltd* (n 3) 205 (Waller LJ).

211 *Brown (RE) v GIO Insurance Ltd* (n 3) 206 (Waller LJ).

212 *Brown (RE) v GIO Insurance Ltd* (n 3) 207 (Waller LJ).

213 *Brown (RE) v GIO Insurance Ltd* (n 3) 207 (Waller LJ), 210 (Chadwick LJ). It may be noted that in *IRB Brasil Resseguros SA v CX Reinsurance Co Ltd* (n 3) the annual decision to carry out installations using asbestos was considered one single event. Consequently, it might be argued that the negligent planning of underwriting activities equally constituted one single event.

214 Butler and Merkin (n 8) para C–0250.

215 Butler and Merkin (n 8) para C–0250.

216 Barlow Lyde and Gilbert LLP (n 5) para 28.83.

6 Summary of event-based aggregation under English law

4.121 Causal requirements inherent in event-based aggregation mechanisms are said to be determined by both the unifying factor and the linking phrase used in the aggregation clause. Courts have held that the causal link between an event and each individual loss to be aggregated must be a strong rather than a weak one. However, no meaningful standard of causation can be deduced from legal authorities so that substantial legal uncertainty exists around event-based aggregation mechanisms. In line with this, courts have held that deciding a question of aggregation involved an exercise of judgment.

4.122 With the aim of structuring this exercise of judgment, it has been held that the unities test may assist in determining whether it is justified to aggregate a plurality of losses in a specific case. Yet, the unities test appears to be incapable of this. It is so vague that it actually provides arbitral tribunals and courts with ample opportunity to reach result-oriented judgments. In any case, the unities test has not dispelled any of the legal uncertainty concerning event-based aggregation mechanisms. The reinsurance market has further tried to avoid legal uncertainty by developing hours clauses and sole judge clauses. The former, again, come with a lot of room for interpretation. The latter appear to be capable of reducing the legal uncertainty inherent in event-based aggregation mechanisms to some extent. Yet, this comes at the price of putting the reinsurer at the reinsured's mercy to a certain degree.

4.123 Consequently, 'there is now an embarrassment of jurisprudential riches' as O'Neill and Woloniecki call it,[217] substantial legal uncertainty with regard to event-based aggregation exists under English law. In awareness of the existence of such uncertainty, Article 5.2 PRICL was drafted to provide the reinsurance market with more legal certainty in this field. This article will be discussed in greater detail below.

II Event-based aggregation under Article 5.2 PRICL

1 What the PRICL are

4.124 The reinsurance industry is genuinely international.[218] More often than not, reinsurance contracts regulate cross-border transactions.[219] There is, however, no uniform reinsurance contract law. The current balance of power in the reinsurance markets enables the party seeking reinsurance cover to choose the law applicable to the reinsurance contract. The reinsured or, for that matter, the reinsurance broker often chooses the law of the country or federal state where the reinsured is based.[220]

---

217 Terry O'Neill, Jan Woloniecki and Franziska Arnold-Dwyer, *The Law of Reinsurance in England and Bermuda* (5th edn, Sweet & Maxwell/Thomson Reuters 2019) para 7–013.

218 Robert M Merkin, *A Guide to Reinsurance Law* (Informa Law from Routledge 2007) 380; Barlow Lyde and Gilbert LLP (n 5) para 3.1; Dieter Looschelders, '§ 9 Das IPR der Rückversicherung' in Dieter W Lüer and Andreas Schwepcke (eds), *Rückversicherungsrecht* (CH Beck 2013) para 68.

219 Barlow Lyde and Gilbert LLP (n 5) para 20.1.

220 Helmut Heiss, 'From Contract Certainty to Legal Certainty for Reinsurance Transactions: The Principle of Reinsurance Contract Law (PRICL)' [2018] Scandinavian Studies of Law 92, 99.

Hence, the meaning of the contractual terms will regularly be determined in light of the law of the country or federal state where the reinsured has its place of business.

4.125 On the European mainland and in Scandinavia, national insurance contract acts often exclude reinsurance contracts from their scopes of application.[221] In these countries, reinsurance contracts are governed by general contract law rules which typically do not address reinsurance-specific issues.[222] As these jurisdictions often do not regulate reinsurance-specific questions, substantial legal uncertainty exists.

4.126 By contrast, the scope of respective insurance legislation in England and the US generally extend to reinsurance contracts.[223] Yet, many aspects of English (re-)insurance contract law do not correspond to, for example, New York (re-)insurance contract law. For instance, aggregation clauses are construed differently in England and the US.[224] According to Staring and Hansell, a number of states use the so-called 'proximate cause' test, whereas the state of New York, for example, applies the 'unfortunate event' test to determine questions of aggregation.[225] Both of these tests are unknown under English law. Consequently, an underwriter who uses the same wording in contracts that are subject to different governing laws must conclude that his words have substantially different meanings depending on the applicable law.[226] Due to the fact that reinsurance companies generally do business with primary insurers from a variety of different countries,[227] it is virtually impossible for them to assess the meanings of their contracts of reinsurance under the respective governing laws. Hence, the laws applicable to reinsurance contracts entail substantial legal uncertainty for one or both parties to the contract.[228]

4.127 With a view to offering the reinsurance industry a set of uniform reinsurance contract law rules, the Universities of Zurich, Frankfurt am Main and Vienna initiated the development of the PRICL.[229] The Principles are elaborated by academics from a large variety of countries.[230] The drafting committee is advised by leading primary insurers, reinsurers, reinsurance brokers as well as special advisors who

---

221 See, for instance, section 186 of the Austrian Insurance Contract Act; Article 54 of the Belgian Insurance Contract Act; Article 7:927 of the Dutch Civil Code; section 1(3) of the Finnish Insurance Contract Act; Article L 111-1 of the French Insurance Contract Act; section 209 of the German Insurance Contract Act; Article 63 of the Liechtenstein Insurance Contract Act; Article 4 of the Luxembourg Insurance Contract Act; Article 101(1) of the Swiss Insurance Contract Act. Contrast Articles 1928 ff of the Italian Civil Code and Articles 77 ff of the Spanish Insurance Contract Act.

222 See, for instance, Judgment of the Swiss Federal Supreme Court of 17 January 2014, *BGE 140 III 115* consideration 6.3.

223 Explanatory Notes to the Insurance Act 2015, para 36. Cf also Graydon Shaw Staring and Dean Hansell, *Law of Reinsurance* (Thomson Reuters Westlaw 2018) para 1:2.

224 Staring and Hansell (n 223) para 15:4.

225 Staring and Hansell (n 223) para 15:4.

226 Heiss (n 220) 99.

227 Heiss (n 220) 99.

228 Heiss (n 220) 95 ff.

229 Heiss (n 220) 101 f.

230 Austria, Belgium, Brazil, France, Germany, Italy, Japan, Singapore, South Africa, Switzerland, United Kingdom and United States of America.

consult the drafters in relation to specific matters, such as arbitration, internationally mandatory law and the unification of private law.[231]

4.128 Moreover, the development of the Principles is conducted in cooperation with the International Institute for the Unification of Private Law (UNIDROIT), which is one of the leading institutions in the field of the unification of law.[232] Over many years, UNIDROIT has developed and refined its Principles of International Commercial Contracts (PICC), a new version of which was published in 2016. The PICC contain 'general rules for international commercial contracts'.[233]

4.129 Under Article 1.1.2 PRICL, issues that are not settled by the PRICL shall be settled in accordance with the PICC. In other words, the PRICL refer to the PICC for issues that are not specific to reinsurance contracts.[234] Together, the PRICL and the PICC form a comprehensive set of uniform rules dedicated to foster legal certainty in the reinsurance industry.[235] It is the PRICL Project Group's goal to provide the market with a package of neutral rules that are available to all industry participants. In pursuing this goal, both the PRICL and the PICC are accompanied by an official commentary as well as illustrations.[236]

4.130 It is important to note that the PRICL are not intended to be enacted as an international treaty, nor are they intended to be implemented in national legislation.[237] Rather, the PRICL may be classified as soft law comprised of a set of non-binding legal rules.[238] Consequently, if the parties to a contract of reinsurance wish their agreement to be governed by the PRICL, they have to agree on the applicability of the PRICL.[239]

4.131 In chapter 5 of the PRICL, there are three provisions dealing with the aggregation of losses. Article 5.1 PRICL sets the foundation for the Principles' event-based aggregation mechanism provided for in Article 5.2 as well as their cause-based aggregation mechanism described in Article 5.3.[240]

2 The general concept of Article 5.2 PRICL

4.132 Article 5.2 PRICL reads as follows:

> 1. *Where the parties agree on an event-based aggregation in a contract reinsuring first-party insurance policies, all losses that occur as a direct*

---

231 Heiss (n 220) 101.

232 Heiss (n 220) 102.

233 Preamble of the Unidroit Principles of International Commercial Contracts 2016.

234 Article 1.1.2 PRICL. See also Heiss (n 220) 103.

235 Cf Heiss (n 220) 101 f.

236 Heiss (n 220) 103.

237 Heiss (n 220) 105.

238 Heiss (n 220) 108.

239 Heiss (n 220) 105 f.

240 See paras 4.132 ff, 5.11 ff.

consequence of the same materialization of a peril reinsured against shall be considered as arising out of one event.

2. *Where the parties agree on an event-based aggregation in a contract reinsuring third-party liability insurance policies, all losses that occur as a direct consequence of the same act, omission or fact giving rise or allegedly giving rise to the primary insured's liability shall be considered as arising out of one event.*

4.133 This provision only operates if the parties have agreed on an event-based aggregation mechanism in their contract of reinsurance.[241] Article 5.2 PRICL basically offers simple and abstract rules for determining whether multiple separate losses are to be aggregated under an event-based aggregation mechanism. More specifically, it describes what can be considered the relevant event.[242] It further provides that if such an event is directly causative for each of the multiple individual losses, they are to be aggregated.[243]

4.134 Accordingly, the PRICL recognise that an aggregation is only possible if the aggregating event is causally linked to each of the separate losses to be aggregated.[244] However, Article 5.2 PRICL is based on the finding that it is utterly difficult, probably impossible, to abstractly define a standard of causation that allows moving back on the chain of causation and objectively identifying the relevant unifying event.[245] In the PRICL, an attempt has been made to simplify Evans LJ's test of determining whether something can properly be described as an event and if so whether it can be considered a relevant event satisfying a rather vague[246] test of causation.[247]

4.135 As set out above, English judicial authorities have repeatedly acknowledged that the unifying factors 'event' and 'occurrence' are used interchangeably in the context of the aggregation of losses.[248] Moreover, it has further been demonstrated that there is no legal authority distinguishing the terms 'catastrophe', 'disaster' and 'calamity' from the term 'occurrence'.[249] In fact, Tompkinson has pointed out that '[i]f each word is to be afforded a separate and distinct meaning, much splitting of hairs will be required'.[250] For this reason, she argued that it was reasonable to equate these terms.[251] Furthermore, it has been discussed that English courts have been reluctant to recognise the term 'accident' as a unifying factor.[252] By contrast, US courts have repeatedly

---

241 Comment 4 to Article 5.1 PRICL.

242 For more details, see paras 4.140 ff, 4.146 ff.

243 See paras 4.151 ff.

244 Comment 4 to Article 5.2 PRICL.

245 See para 4.12.

246 *Environment Agency (formerly National Rivers Authority) v Empress Car Co (Abertillery) Ltd* (1998) 2 AC 22 (HL) 31 (Lord Hoffmann).

247 *Caudle v Sharp* (n 3) 648 (Evans LJ).

248 See paras 2.63, 3.59.

249 See paras 3.79, 4.6.

250 Deborah Tompkinson, 'Jabberwocky: Recent Decisions on the Meaning of "Event" and "Occurrence" in the English Courts' (1995) 3 International Insurance Law Review 82, 82.

251 Tompkinson (n 250) 82.

252 See paras 3.61 ff.

recognised the terms 'occurrence' and 'accident' as synonymous in the context of the aggregation of losses.[253]

4.136 In line with this, Article 5.2 PRICL not only applies if the parties have used the unifying factor of 'event' in their contract of reinsurance. Rather, the terms of 'occurrence', 'catastrophe', 'disaster', 'calamity' and 'accident' are considered interchangeable with the term 'event' under the PRICL. Thus, whenever an aggregation mechanism is based on either of these unifying factors, Article 5.2 PRICL is pertinent.[254]

4.137 Moreover, it has been discussed that the linking phrases of 'arising out of' or 'arising from' are commonly used in the context of event-based aggregation mechanisms.[255] In English law, linking phrases are said to contribute to the determination of the causal requirements inherent in an aggregation mechanism.[256] In this regard, it has been concluded, however, that it appears to be impossible to deduce abstract and meaningful implications as to the causative potencies of the linking phrases of 'arising out of' and 'arising from' in the context of the aggregation of losses.[257] For this reason, the linking phrase used in the aggregation clause is not considered under Article 5.2 PRICL. As long as the parties provide for an event-based aggregation mechanism, the causal requirements provided for by Article 5.2 PRICL will apply.[258]

3 Determination of an event

4.138 With a view to determining the relevant event for the purposes of the aggregation of losses, there is a reference in Article 5.2 PRICL to the original insurance policies and a distinction is drawn between the reinsurance[259] of first-party and third-party contracts.[260]

3.1 Reinsurance of first-party insurance policies

4.139 First-party insurance policies provide protection against losses suffered by the primary insured to his own property or profit from designated perils.[261] In other words, the

---

253 See, for instance, *Hartford Accident and Indemnity Co v Edward Wesolowski* (1973) 33 NY2d 169 (Court of Appeals of New York) [6]; *Stonewall Insurance Co v Asbestos Claims Management Corp* (1995) 73 F3d 1178 (United States Court of Appeals for the Second Circuit) 1213; *Re Prudential Linse Inc v American Steamship Owners Mutual* (1998) 156 F3d 65 (United States Court of Appeals for the Second Circuit); *Metropolitan Life Insurance Co v Aetna Casualty and Surety Co* (2001) 255 Conn 295 (Supreme Court of Connecticut) 324; *World Trade Center Properties LLC v Hartford Fire Insurance Co* (2003) 345 F 154 (United States Court of Appeals for the Second Circuit) 188; *Appalachian Insurance Co v General Electric Co* (2007) 863 NE2d 994 (Court of Appeals of New York) 1000.

254 Comment 1 to Article 5.2 PRICL.

255 See para 4.7.

256 See paras 3.24, 3.111 ff.

257 See paras 3.1114 ff.

258 For the causal requirements provided for by Article 5.2 PRICL, see paras 4.138 ff, 4.151 ff.

259 In the case of a retrocession agreement, the distinction still applies to the underlying primary insurance policy that was reinsured and subsequently retroceded.

260 For a distinction to that extent, see, for instance, *Newmont Mines Ltd v Hanover Insurance Co* (n 5) 136 f; *World Trade Center Properties LLC v Hartford Fire Insurance Co* (n 253) 188.

261 Jon A Baumunk, 'New York's Unfortunate Event Test: Its Application Prior to the Events of 9/11' (2003) 39 California Western Law Review 323, 337.

primary insurer's obligation to pay insurance money arises where a designated peril has materialised and caused loss to the primary insured. If the primary insurer has bought reinsurance cover for losses arising from the materialisation of the said peril, the reinsurer's obligation to reimburse the primary insurer ensues. Consequently, the focus in Article 5.2(1) PRICL, in respect of the reinsurance of first-party insurance policies, is placed on the materialisation of a reinsured peril.

4.140 More specifically, Article 5.2(1) PRICL provides that an event is the materialisation of a reinsured peril. This is supported by Tompkinson who, as early as in 1995, suggested that the term 'event' could be 'interpreted to mean "materialisation of an insured peril"'.[262] Furthermore, the International Underwriting Association's model aggregation clause IUA 01–019 (NP64) provides that 'a loss occurrence shall consist of all individual insured losses (...) which are the direct and immediate result of the sudden violent physical manifestation and operation of one and the same (...) insured peril'.[263] The approach taken under Article 5.2(1) PRICL is also in line with Walker J's finding that that 'there is light to be gleaned (...) from the nature of the perils insured against (...)',[264] with Rix J's statement that in determining a question of aggregation 'one may properly have regard to the context of the perils insured against'[265] as well as Lord Hoffmann's widely accepted view that 'it is impossible to give an informed answer to a question of causation when attributing responsibility under some rule without knowing the purpose and scope of the rule'.[266]

4.141 This approach appears to simplify each step of Evans LJ's test.[267] First, the often controversial question of whether something can properly be described as an event[268] can be avoided and replaced by the question of whether a peril reinsured against has materialised. This latter question is one that must be answered anyway as the policy of reinsurance does not provide cover unless a peril reinsured against has materialised.

4.142 In many cases, the challenging question will be whether a peril has materialised in one single or multiple instances. Particularly when it comes to natural perils, it 'is expedient to resort to scientific data in order to determine the number of instances a peril has materiali[s]ed'.[269] For instance, an earthquake and related aftershocks may, in geological terms, be classified as one seismic event.[270] Further, the question of whether a man-made peril, such as a terror attack, has materialised in one or multiple instances

---

262 Tompkinson (n 250) 82. It may be noted, however, that Tompkinson distinguished the terms 'event' and 'occurrence'.

263 'IUA 01–019 Loss Occurrence (NP64)' (n 150).

264 Walker J's judgment at first instance is transcribed in: *Mann v Lexington Insurance Co* (n 29) 1411.

265 *Kuwait Airways Corp v Kuwait Insurance Co SAK* (n 5).

266 *Environment Agency (formerly National Rivers Authority) v Empress Car Co (Abertillery) Ltd* (n 246) 29 (Lord Hoffmann).

267 See para 3.29.

268 See paras 3.30 ff.

269 Comment 9 to Article 5.2 PRICL.

270 Cf Merkin (n 122) 147.

is to be determined from the perspective of reasonable parties at the time the contract of reinsurance was concluded.[271]

4.143 Secondly, Evan LJ's second question, ie whether an event is the relevant event as it is sufficiently causally linked to each of the individual losses,[272] may likewise be avoided. While Article 5.2(1) PRICL requires that the individual losses are each a 'the direct consequence' of the aggregating event, there is no overly vague standard of causation involved.[273]

4.144 Yet, the approach taken by Article 5.2(1) PRICL seems to conflict with the English law position. In fact, the Court of Appeal held in *Caudle v Sharp* that the unifying event does not have to be a reinsured peril.[274] Similarly, the Commercial Court noted in *Kuwait Airways Corp v Kuwait Insurance Co SAK* that '[a]n occurrence [was] not the same thing as a peril'.[275] Yet, in neither of the two cases did the courts explain why an event is not the same thing as the materialisation of a peril reinsured against.[276] In light of the lack of any judicial justification and the simplification that is achieved by Article 5.2(1) PRICL, the PRICL create more legal certainty in the industry and may, thus, be preferred over the current English position.

3.2 Reinsurance of third-party insurance policies

4.145 Third-party insurance contracts provide cover for losses resulting from the primary insured's legal liability towards a third party.[277] A primary insured's liability may, for instance, be triggered if he injures another person, damages other people's property[278] or otherwise causes financial harm to a third party. Consequently, there are generally no designated perils at the centre of third-party insurance contracts.[279] Therefore, the focus in Article 5.2(2) PRICL is on the liability triggering wrongdoing.

4.146 Article 5.2(2) PRICL provides that the primary insured's wrongful act, omission or fact[280] giving rise to his liability is the unifying event. In the same vein, Evans LJ noted in *Caudle v Sharp* that the relevant occurrence was 'the occurrence out of which a claim arises, for loss suffered by the original insured, such as (...) the

---

271 Comment 10 to Article 5.2 PRICL.
272 See paras 3.38 ff.
273 For details as to the requirement of 'direct consequence', see paras 4.151 ff.
274 *Caudle v Sharp* (n 3) 648 (Evans LJ). It is to be noted, however, that the Court of Appeal held that a unifying event must not be 'an insured peril under the original contract of insurance'. By contrast, Article 5.2 PRICL refers to the perils reinsured against for the determination of unifying events.
275 *Kuwait Airways Corp v Kuwait Insurance Co SAK* (n 5). Cf also *Mann v Lexington Insurance Co* (n 29) 1422 (Waller LJ).
276 Cf Louw and Tompkinson (n 20) 8.
277 Cf Baumunk (n 261) 332.
278 Clarke (n 5) para 17-4C1.
279 Cf Butler and Merkin (n 8) para C–0221.
280 According to comment 14 to Article 5.2 PRICL, it is not only a wrongful act or omission that may trigger a primary insured's liability. In cases of strict liability, a mere fact may give rise to the primary insured's liability. Therefore, Article 5.2(2) PRICL provides that such a liability triggering fact may constitute an aggregating event.

negligent act or omission of the insured'.[281] In *American Centennial Insurance Co v INSCO Ltd,* the Commercial Court similarly held that an event-based aggregation clause was 'only concerned with events or occurrences which give rise to a liability under underlying policies'.[282] Under New York law, it has likewise been held that 'courts should look to the event for which the insured is held liable, not some point further back in the causal chain'.[283]

4.147 The approach taken in the PRICL appears to reduce the complexity of Evans LJ's test.[284] First, if the event is seen in the act, omission or fact for which the primary insured is held liable, the often controversial question of what can properly be considered an event can be avoided. Secondly, the very difficult assessment as to whether an event is the relevant one as it is sufficiently causative for each of the individual losses can equally be avoided if courts need not look further back in the chain of causation than the primary insured's liability triggering wrongdoing or fact. While it is required under Article 5.2(2) PRICL that each individual loss is 'the direct consequence' of the aggregating event, there is no overly vague standard of causation involved.[285]

4.148 It may be noted, however, that there are English judicial authorities where this approach was not followed. In *IRB Brasil Resseguros SA v CX Reinsurance Co Ltd,* the Commercial Court dealt with a case where the primary insured triggered its liability by installing products containing asbestos over a long period of time.[286] In this case, the Commercial Court upheld an arbitral tribunal's finding that the primary insured's determination to install products containing asbestos over a 20-year period constituted an event.[287] The primary insured's liability certainly did not arise from its determination to install such products; it arose from its acts of installing the contaminated products. Consequently, it was not the liability triggering act, but rather the decision to commit multiple such acts that was considered the aggregating event in this case.

4.149 The situation was similar in *MIC Simmonds v Gammell,* a case following the terror attacks on the World Trade Center that came before the Commercial Court. Claims by workers who were at the World Trade Center at the time of the terror attacks and were either struck by or became trapped under the debris were made against the owner of the land on which the Twin Towers had stood. The owner of the land faced further claims by firemen, policemen and volunteers who were engaged in the clean-up operations at the site and thereby suffered personal injury because the owner of the land had not provided them with adequate protective equipment during

---

281 *Caudle v Sharp* (n 3) 648 (Evans LJ).

282 *American Centennial Insurance Co v INSCO Ltd* (n 5) 413 (Moore-Bick J). It is to be noted, however, that the aggregation clause in question referred to events 'affecting' the policies issued by the primary insurer.

283 *Stonewall Insurance Co v Asbestos Claims Management Corp* (n 253) 1213.

284 Evan LJ's test is described at para 3.29.

285 For details as to the requirement of 'direct consequence', see paras 4.151 ff.

286 *IRB Brasil Resseguros SA v CX Reinsurance Co Ltd* (n 3) [26] (Burton J).

287 *IRB Brasil Resseguros SA v CX Reinsurance Co Ltd* (n 3) [46] (Burton J).

the clean-up operations.[288] In this case, the Commercial Court upheld an arbitral tribunal's decision that all individual claims against the landowner were to be aggregated no matter whether they resulted from the attacks themselves or the negligent exposure of the injured to harmful conditions.[289] However, the landowner's liability was not triggered by the terror attacks on the Twin Towers. It was triggered by failing to protect its workers from being struck by or becoming trapped under the debris and by negligently omitting to provide clean-up workers with adequate protective equipment. Hence, it was the attacks that were not even conducted by the landowner, not the liability-triggering omissions, that were considered one unifying event in this case.

4.150 Hence, there seems to be a legal uncertainty under English law as to whether only a liability triggering wrongdoing or fact can be the relevant event or whether in such cases courts may look farther back in the causal chain for a unifying event. Irrespective of this legal uncertainty, the approach taken in Article 5.2(2) PRICL appears sensible for three reasons: First and foremost, the provision simplifies event-based aggregation mechanisms in the context of the reinsurance of third-party insurance policies. Secondly, the approach taken in the PRICL has ample judicial support both in English law as well as in New York law. Thirdly, as opposed to cause-based aggregation, event-based aggregation is supposed to be a narrow concept.[290] By ensuring that courts do not look farther back in the causal chain in the search of a unifying event than the liability triggering act, omission or fact, the aggregation mechanism does not become too loose.

4 The requirement of 'direct consequence'

4.151 Both paragraphs of Article 5.2 PRICL provide that only those losses that occur as a 'direct consequence' of the relevant event are to be aggregated. This is in line with, for example, the International Underwriting Association's model aggregation clause IUA 01–019 (NP64).[291]

4.152 It begs the question, however, what the phrase 'direct consequence' means and what standard of causation can be deduced from it. In line with English authorities[292] on the subject matter of aggregation, it is not required under Article 5.2 PRICL that an event is the proximate cause of individual losses for these to be aggregated.[293]

---

288 *MIC Simmonds v Gammell* (n 3) [6]–[8] (Sir Jeremy Cooke).

289 *MIC Simmonds v Gammell* (n 3) [36] (Sir Jeremy Cooke).

290 *Axa Reinsurance (UK) Ltd v Field* (n 3) 1035 (Lord Mustill); Edelman and Burns (n 5) paras 4.59, 4.61. Cf also Merkin (n 122) 145.

291 'IUA 01–019 Loss Occurrence (NP64)' (n 150), provides that '[f]or the purposes of this Agreement a loss occurrence shall consist of all individual insured losses in respect of any single risk which are the direct and immediate result of the sudden violent physical manifestation and operation of one and the same original insured peril'.

292 *Caudle v Sharp* (n 3) 648 (Evans LJ); *Scott v The Copenhagen Reinsurance Co (UK) Ltd* (n 3) [63] (Rix LJ); *MIC Simmonds v Gammell* (n 3) [30], [35] (Sir Jeremy Cooke).

293 Comment 17 to Article 5.2 PRICL.

4.153 More specifically, the relevant event does not necessarily have to be the last happening immediately preceding the occurrence of the loss.[294] If the materialisation of a peril, ie an event, directly results in the materialisation of another peril reinsured against, then all individual reinsured losses which directly result from the latter materialisation shall be deemed a direct consequence of the unifying event even where this event is not their proximate cause. This seems to be in line with the International Underwriting Association's model aggregation clause IUA 01–019 (NP64).[295] In more illustrative terms, imagine that first-party property insurance is taken out against the perils of earthquake and tsunami. The peril of earthquake materialises and causes multiple separate losses. At the same time, the earthquake provokes a tsunami which, in turn, also causes multiple individual losses. As the materialisation of the peril of earthquake resulted in the materialisation of the peril of tsunami, all losses–no matter whether they arose from the earthquake or the tsunami–are to be considered the earthquake's direct consequences.[296]

4.154 Furthermore, the requirement of 'direct consequence' in Article 5.2 PRICL appears to be much less vague than the causal requirements described in English law.[297] In fact, as the official commentary in the PRICL states '[a] loss may be considered an event's direct consequence if it can be considered an inevitable effect of the relevant aggregating event'.[298] This would not be the case if an independent intervening factor decisively contributes to the occurrence of a loss and thereby breaks the chain of causation.[299] Hence, as long as the chain of causation between each of the individual losses and the relevant event is not broken by a decisively intervening factor, the losses are considered the event's direct consequences.

4.155 Accordingly, it is important to determine what intervening factors may break the chain of causation. In this regard, the official commentary in the PRICL sets forth that, where a person was capable of and under the duty to prevent an event from resulting in a plurality of losses, a failure to live up to this duty would constitute an intervening factor breaking the chain of causation (*conditio cum qua non*).[300] An example is provided by applying Article 5.2(2) PRICL to the facts of *MIC Simmonds v Gammell*,[301] where a landowner has taken out third-party liability insurance. Two aircraft crash into the buildings situated on his land and thereby injure some of his employees. In the time after the crashes, the landowner–although under a duty to do so–fails to provide workers engaging in the clean-up operations with adequate protective equipment which results in bodily harm suffered by these workers. Under Article 5.2(2) PRICL, losses suffered by the landowner's employees who were injured

---

294 Comment 19 to Article 5.2 PRICL.

295 'IUA 01–019 Loss Occurrence (NP64)' (n 150).

296 See, for instance, illustration 16 to Article 5.2 PRICL. For a case dealing with earthquakes, see *Moore v IAG New Zealand Ltd* [2019] NZHC 1549, [2020] Lloyd's Rep IR 167.

297 For the causal requirements in English law, see paras 3.38 ff, 4.8 ff.

298 Comment 18 to Article 5.2 PRICL.

299 Comment 18 to Article 5.2 PRICL.

300 Comment 20 to Article 5.2 PRICL.

301 *MIC Simmonds v Gammell* (n 3).

at the time of the crashes and losses suffered by the workers engaging in the clean-up operations cannot be aggregated. This is because it was virtually impossible for the landowner to protect his employees at the site when the airplanes crashed into the World Trade Center, whereas it obviously violated its duty to protect the clean-up workers by failing to equip them with respirators. Had the landowner equipped the clean-up workers with respirators, they would not have suffered bodily harm. The landowner's omission, therefore, constitutes an intervening factor breaking the chain of causation and turning the losses suffered by the clean-up workers into merely indirect consequences of the landowner's liability in respect of the aircraft crashes.[302]

4.156 An intervening factor breaking the chain of causation may also lie in a happening which occurs independently of the unifying event (*conditio sine qua non*).[303] For instance, a primary insured takes out first-party property insurance against the peril of flood and environmental pollution. A vessel spills a significant amount of oil into the sea near the coast. Some days later, a windstorm occurs, blows some of the oil into a river and eventually causes a flood. Losses that were incurred due to the flood and environmental pollution losses resulting from the oil in the river cannot be aggregated under Article 5.2(1) PRICL. Had the vessel not accidently spilled oil prior to the materialisation of the peril of flood, the water bursting the riverbanks would not have been contaminated and could not have polluted the adjacent land. The oil spillage constitutes an intervening factor breaking the chain of causation and turning the environmental pollution losses into merely indirect consequences of the flood.[304]

4.157 It is to be noted, however, that not every happening that contributes to the occurrence of a loss is to be considered an intervening factor. Under Article 5.2 PRICL, only happenings that decisively interfere with the occurrence of the losses are regarded as relevant interfering factors.[305] For instance, common circumstances at the place and time where the reinsured peril materialises are not considered as having broken the chain of causation even if they may have slightly supported the occurrence of the losses. Take for example the case where a primary insured has taken out third-party liability insurance. He negligently sets a fire which–due to the common windy circumstances–spreads and causes multiple individual losses. The commonly windy weather cannot be considered a decisively intervening factor that breaks the chain of causation. Therefore, under Article 5.2(2) PRICL, the individual fire losses are to be aggregated.[306]

4.158 Thus, the requirement of 'direct consequence' cannot be said to be an overly vague standard of causation. Rather, the requirement simply ensures that individual losses cannot be aggregated if their development was decisively influenced by a factor

---

302 For the same example, see illustration 20 to Article 5.2 PRICL.

303 Comment 21 to Article 5.2 PRICL.

304 For the same example, see illustration 22 to Article 5.2 PRICL.

305 Comment 22 to Article 5.2 PRICL.

306 For the same example, see illustration 26 to Article 5.2 PRICL.

extraneous to the materialisation of a peril under paragraph 1 or the primary insured's liability triggering act, omission or fact under paragraph 2.

III Summary of the chapter

4.159 In English law, there is–what O'Neill and Woloniecki call–'an embarrassment of jurisprudential riches' on the subject matter of aggregation,[307] and substantial legal uncertainty exists in respect of causal requirements in event-based aggregation mechanisms.

4.160 It is said that both unifying factors and linking phrases contained in an aggregation clause contribute to the determination of the standard of causation inherent in an aggregation mechanism. Yet, it is not possible to deduce a meaningful causal standard from the unifying factor of 'event' or from the linking phrases of 'arising out of' and 'arising from'.

4.161 In light of the legal uncertainties associated with event-based aggregation mechanisms, English courts have held that multiple losses are to be aggregated if the circumstances of the losses so justify. In the same vein, it has been stated that the task of determining whether multiple individual losses are to be aggregated was essentially an exercise of judgment.

4.162 Furthermore, the unities test is said to assist judges and arbitrators in exercising their judgment in an analytical fashion. However, conducting the unities test itself involves an exercise of judgment. Moreover, it is so vague as to cause additional, rather than reduce legal uncertainty in the context of event-based aggregation.

4.163 In order to reduce said legal uncertainty, the parties have resorted to using so-called hours clauses and sole judge clauses. There seem to be no English authorities dealing with the interpretation of hours clauses. Yet, it has been demonstrated that they involve substantial interpretational uncertainty. By contrast, sole judge clauses appear to reduce the need to litigate questions of aggregation. However, by agreeing to a sole judge clause, the reinsurer largely puts itself at the reinsured's mercy. Thus, a sole judge clause may not always be a viable means to reduce the complexity of event-based aggregation mechanisms.

4.164 An alternative to the English law position is offered in Article 5.2 PRICL where a distinction is drawn between the reinsurance of first-party and third-party insurance policies. Paragraph 1 provides that where the reinsurance of first-party insurance policies is concerned, an event is the materialisation of a reinsured peril. With regard to the reinsurance of third-party insurance policies, paragraph 2 provides that an event consists of the primary insured's liability triggering act, omission or fact. By so doing, the questions of whether something can properly be described as an event and whether it might be the relevant event are avoided by Article 5.2 PRICL.

4.165 Furthermore, while the aggregation mechanism described in Article 5.2 PRICL recognises that multiple individual losses are only aggregated if they have a

---

307 O'Neill, Woloniecki and Arnold-Dwyer (n 217) para 7–013.

causal connection with the aggregating event, Article 5.2 PRICL does not provide for an overly vague standard of causation.

4.166 Therefore, if parties to a reinsurance contract wish to have greater legal certainty with regard to their event-based aggregation mechanism, they may consider–as the case may be–to agree upon the applicability of Article 5.2 PRICL or to incorporate Article 5.2 PRICL into their contract of reinsurance.

CHAPTER 5

Cause-based aggregation in focus

5.1 In this chapter, it will be discussed that, in English law, there is substantial legal uncertainty regarding the causal requirements of cause-based aggregation mechanisms. Thereafter, Article 5.3 PRICL will be presented. It will be examined whether Article 5.3 PRICL is capable of reducing legal uncertainty in the context of cause-based aggregation mechanisms.

I Cause-based aggregation in English law

5.2 Cause-based aggregation clauses are more common in direct insurance policies than in contracts of reinsurance.[1] Yet, as *Municipal Mutual Insurance Ltd v Sea Insurance Co Ltd* demonstrates, cause-based aggregation clauses are sometimes used in contracts of reinsurance.[2] This is particularly so if the primary insurance contract's aggregation clause is incorporated into the reinsurance contract.[3]

5.3 In any case, the causative requirements inherent in cause-based aggregation mechanisms depend on the unifying factor as well as the linking phrase contained in the aggregation clause.[4]

1 Typical unifying factors and linking phrases

5.4 Typically, cause-based aggregation clauses provide for the unifying factors of either 'originating cause or source'[5] or 'one source or original cause'.[6] Courts have treated the two variations as equivalent.[7] In *Standard Life Assurance Ltd v Ace*

---

1 Barlow Lyde & Gilbert LLP, *Reinsurance Practice and the Law* (Informa Law from Routledge 2009) paras 28.38, 28.40.

2 *Municipal Mutual Insurance Ltd v Sea Insurance Co Ltd* [1998] EWCA Civ 546, [1998] CLC 957 (CA) 961 (Hobhouse LJ).

3 *Municipal Mutual Insurance Ltd v Sea Insurance Co Ltd* (n 2) 961 (Hobhouse LJ).

4 See paras 3.24, 3.45 ff, 3.114 ff, 3.119 ff.

5 See, for instance, *Cox v Bankside Members Agency Ltd* [1995] CLC 671 (CA) 679 (Sir Thomas Bingham); *Axa Reinsurance (UK) Ltd v Field* [1996] 1 WLR 1026 (HL) 1032 (Lord Mustill); *Standard Life Assurance Ltd v Oak Dedicated Ltd* [2008] EWHC 222 (Comm), [2008] 2 All ER 916 [14] (Tomlinson J); *Standard Life Assurance Ltd v Ace European Group* [2012] EWHC 104 (Comm), [2012] 1 Lloyd's Rep IR 655 [255] (Eder J). Cf also *American Centennial Insurance Co v INSCO Ltd* [1996] LRLR 407 (Comm) 414 (Moore-Bick J).

6 Cf *Municipal Mutual Insurance Ltd v Sea Insurance Co Ltd* (n 2) 959 (Hobhouse LJ); *Countrywide Assured Group Plc v Marshall* [2002] EWHC 2082 (Comm), [2003] 1 All ER 237 [3] (Morison J).

7 *Municipal Mutual Insurance Ltd v Sea Insurance Co Ltd* (n 2) 967 (Hobhouse LJ). Cf also *Countrywide*

DOI: 10.4324/9781003080480-5

European Group, the Commercial Court noted that 'the words "or source"' were an 'explicit alternative to "cause"'.[8] Yet, there seem to be no legal authorities distinguishing between the concepts of 'cause' and 'source' in cause-based aggregation mechanisms.[9]

5.5 The unifying factor of 'cause' is most typically coupled with the linking phrase of 'consequent upon or attributable to'.[10] There appear to be no legal authorities distinguishing between the concepts of 'consequent upon' and 'attributable to', although the latter phrase, in contrast to the former, does not necessarily indicate a causal connection.[11] The linking phrase of 'arising from' has equally been used in the context of cause-based aggregation.[12]

2 Lack of legal certainty as to the causal requirements in cause-based aggregation

5.6 It has been pointed out[13] that, in English law, the concept of 'cause' is much less constricted than the concept of 'event'[14] and that the word 'cause' describes why something has happened, whereas the word 'event' refers to what has happened.[15] An event is something that happens at a particular place, in a particular way at a particular time, whereas a cause is not something that necessarily happens.[16] A cause may consist in a mere state of affairs.[17] Arguably, a unifying cause may further be constituted by a plan,[18] a decision,[19] a state

---

Assured Group Plc v Marshall (n 6) [15] (Morison J); Barlow Lyde & Gilbert LLP (n 1) para 28.49; Colin Edelman and Andrew Burns, *The Law of Reinsurance* (2nd edn, OUP 2013) paras 4.59 ff; Robert M Merkin, Laura Hodgson and Peter J Tyldesley, *Colinvaux's Law of Insurance* (Sweet & Maxwell 2019) para 11–335.

8   *Standard Life Assurance Ltd v Ace European Group* (n 5) [259] (Eder J).

9   See paras 3.81f.

10 See, for instance, *Municipal Mutual Insurance Ltd v Sea Insurance Co Ltd* (n 2) 966 (Hobhouse LJ); *Countrywide Assured Group Plc v Marshall* (n 6) [3] (Morison J); *Tokio Marine Europe Insurance Ltd v Novae Corporate Underwriting Ltd* [2014] EWHC 2105 (Comm), [2014] Lloyd's Rep IR 638 [8] (Field J); *Spire Healthcare Ltd v Royal & Sun Alliance Insurance Plc* [2018] EWCA Civ 317, [2018] Lloyd's Rep IR 425 [3] (Simon LJ). Alternatively, the unifying factor of 'cause' is often coupled with 'arising from or in connection with or attributable to', see, for instance, *Standard Life Assurance Ltd v Oak Dedicated Ltd* (n 5) [14] (Tomlinson J); *Beazley Underwriting Ltd v Travelers Co Inc* [2011] EWHC 1520 (Comm) [28] (Clarke J); *Standard Life Assurance Ltd v Ace European Group* (n 5) [255] (Eder J).

11 It is to be noted, however, that the concept of causation is inherent in the unifying factors of cause and source so that where the linking phrase of 'attributable to' is coupled with either of these unifying factors, the unifying concept would still be one of causation.

12 *Cox v Bankside Members Agency Ltd* (n 5) 679 (Sir Thomas Bingham); *Axa Reinsurance (UK) Ltd v Field* (n 5) 1031 (Lord Mustill).

13 See paras 3.47 ff, 3.53 ff.

14 *Axa Reinsurance (UK) Ltd v Field* (n 5) 1035 (Lord Mustill).

15 *Countrywide Assured Group Plc v Marshall* (n 6) [15] (Morison J).

16 *Axa Reinsurance (UK) Ltd v Field* (n 5) 1035 (Lord Mustill).

17 *Axa Reinsurance (UK) Ltd v Field* (n 5) 1035 (Lord Mustill).

18 *Aioi Nissay Dowa Insurance Co Ltd v Heraldglen Ltd and Advent Capital Ltd* [2013] EWHC 154 (Comm), [2013] 2 All ER 231 [20] (Field J).

19 Cf *Midland Mainline Ltd v Eagle Star Insurance Co Ltd* [2003] EWHC 1771 (Comm), [2004] Lloyd's Rep IR 22 [98] (Steel J).

of ignorance,[20] the mere propensity of an individual to act in a certain way[21] or the susceptibility of a region to a natural disaster.[22]

5.7 Any event from which multiple individual losses arise may be considered the losses' cause. Therefore, an event is always also a cause.[23] By contrast, not every cause constitutes an event.[24] Clearly, there may be causes that provoke an event which, in turn, then results in multiple individual losses. For instance, a common culpable misunderstanding as to the result of discussions within a group of selling agents may be considered a cause upon which each of them subsequently acts and triggers their employer's liability.[25] Each act of misselling can be considered an event that results in losses. Consequently, each act of misselling can also be considered the losses' cause. By contrast, the selling agents' misunderstanding is not an event, but it is the events' cause.[26]

5.8 In contrast to event-based aggregation mechanisms, cause-based aggregation mechanisms make it possible to look further back in the chain of causation for a unifying factor.[27] In *Standard Life Assurance Ltd v Ace European Group,* the Commercial Court noted that a cause-based aggregation mechanism made it possible to trace back losses to wherever a common origin could reasonably be found.[28] In *Axa Reinsurance (UK) Ltd v Field*, Lord Mustill stated that the word originating coupled with the word cause opened up 'the widest possible search for a unifying factor in the history of the individual losses that are sought to be aggregated.[29]

5.9 However, the Commercial Court clarified in *American Centennial Insurance Co v INSCO* that, although an originating cause was a unifying factor of a remote kind, there still must 'be some limit to the degree of remoteness that is acceptable'.[30] In other words, it is not sufficient that a plurality of losses have a common origin. An aggregation of the individual losses is only possible if their common factor is not too remote.

5.10 There seems to be no guidance as to where this limit of remoteness lies in English law. Accordingly, the decision as to whether a cause is too remote and,

---

20 *Caudle v Sharp* [1995] CLC 642 (CA) 649 (Evans LJ).

21 Rob Merkin, 'The Christchurch Earthquakes Insurance and Reinsurance Issues' (2012) 18 Canterbury Law Review 119, 146; Merkin, Hodgson and Tyldesley (n 7) para 11–335.

22 Merkin (n 21) 145 f.

23 Cf *Brown (RE) v GIO Insurance Ltd* [1998] Lloyd's Rep IR 201 (CA) 204 (Waller LJ); Ken Louw and Deborah Tompkinson, 'Curiouser and Curiouser: The Meaning of "Event"' (1996) 4 International Insurance Law Review 6, 9; Merkin (n 21) 146.

24 Cf Louw and Tompkinson (n 23) 9; Merkin (n 21) 146.

25 *American Centennial Insurance Co v INSCO Ltd* (n 5) 414 (Moore-Bick J).

26 Cf *American Centennial Insurance Co v INSCO Ltd* (n 5) 414 (Moore-Bick J).

27 Louw and Tompkinson (n 23) 11.

28 *Standard Life Assurance Ltd v Ace European Group* (n 5) [259] (Eder J).

29 *Axa Reinsurance (UK) Ltd v Field* (n 5) 1035 (Lord Mustill).

30 *American Centennial Insurance Co v INSCO Ltd* (n 5) 414 (Moore-Bick J).

therefore, cannot serve as a unifying cause for the purposes of aggregation is dependent on how judges and arbitrators feel about exercising their judgment. In the context of cause-based aggregation, there is, in fact, not even any such thing as a unities test that is meant to guide the process of exercising this judgment. This allows courts and arbitral tribunals to reach purely result-oriented conclusions. Thus, there is substantial legal uncertainty concerning the causal requirements inherent in cause-based aggregation mechanisms.

II Cause-based aggregation under Article 5.3 PRICL

1 The general concept of Article 5.3 PRICL

5.11 Article 5.3 PRICL reads as follows:

1. *Where the parties agree on a cause-based aggregation in a contract reinsuring first-party insurance policies, all losses that occur as the direct consequence of one or multiple events within the meaning of Article 5.2 paragraph (1) shall be considered as arising out of one common cause if it was reasonably foreseeable that a cause of this kind could give rise to such an event.*

2. *Where the parties agree on a cause-based aggregation in a contract reinsuring third-party liability insurance policies, all losses that occur as the direct consequence of one or multiple events within the meaning of Article 5.2 paragraph (2) shall be considered as arising out of one common cause if it was reasonably foreseeable that a cause of this kind could give rise to such an event.*

5.12 It is to be noted that this provision only operates if the parties have agreed on a cause-based aggregation mechanism in their reinsurance contract.[31] However, Article 5.3 PRICL applies not only where the parties have used the unifying factor of cause, but equally where their aggregation clause refers to the unifying factor of source.[32] Thus, whenever an aggregation mechanism is based on either or both of these unifying factors, Article 5.3 PRICL is pertinent.[33]

5.13 In Article 5.3 PRICL, rules are outlined regarding the question of whether a plurality of losses are to be added together for presenting a claim to the reinsurer based on a cause-based aggregation mechanism. For the same reason as Article 5.2 PRICL, a distinction is drawn in Article 5.3 PRICL between the reinsurance of first-party and third-party insurance policies.[34]

5.14 Moreover, it is acknowledged in the PRICL that a cause-based aggregation of multiple individual losses is only possible if there is a causal link between the aggregating cause and each of the individual losses to be aggregated.[35] As has been demonstrated, the linking phrase of consequent upon or attributable to is commonly used in the context of

---

31 Comment 5 to Article 5.1 PRICL.

32 Comment 2 to Article 5.3 PRICL.

33 Comment 2 to Article 5.3 PRICL.

34 See paras 4.139 ff, 4.145 ff.

35 Comment 6 to Article 5.3 PRICL.

cause-based aggregation mechanisms.[36] It has, however, been concluded that it is impossible to deduce a clear standard of causation from this linking phrase.[37] Thus, no regard is had in Article 5.3 PRICL to linking phrases contained in aggregation clauses. As long as the parties provide for a cause-based aggregation mechanism, the standard of causation provided for in Article 5.3 PRICL applies.

5.15 As in English law,[38] the concept of cause-based aggregation under the PRICL is wider than the concept of event-based aggregation.[39] Thus, in the search of an aggregating cause, under Article 5.3 PRICL, one is allowed to move farther back in the chain of causation than one would be in respect of an event within the meaning of Article 5.2 PRICL.[40] For the determination of the unifying cause in a specific case, Article 5.3 PRICL provides for a three-step analysis.

5.16 First, where the reinsurance of first-party insurance policies is concerned, the instances of materialised perils are to be identified. Similarly, with regard to the reinsurance of third-party insurance policies, the liability triggering acts, omissions or facts are to be determined. In other words, it is required under Article 5.3 PRICL that one or multiple events within the meaning of Article 5.2 PRICL are identified and pinpointed on the chain of causation.[41]

5.17 Secondly, having completed the first step, one is to move farther back in the chain of causation in the search of a unifying cause.[42] If no cause can be found to have triggered one or multiple events, each instance of materialised peril or liability triggering act, omission or fact is to be considered a unifying cause under Article 5.3 PRICL.[43]

5.18 By contrast, if there is a cause that triggered multiple different events which, in turn, resulted in a plurality of losses, the third step is to test whether said cause is a relevant cause for the purposes of cause-based aggregation. Article 5.3 PRICL provides that a cause is a relevant cause if, at the time of the conclusion of the reinsurance contract, it was reasonably foreseeable that 'in the ordinary course of things (...) a cause of this kind would lead to an event of the kind under consideration, ie an instance of materialized peril (article 5.2(1)) or an act, omission or fact that triggers the primary insured's liability (article 5.2(2))'.[44]

---

36 See para 5.5.

37 See paras 3.119 ff.

38 *Axa Reinsurance (UK) Ltd v Field* (n 5) 1035 (Lord Mustill); *Countrywide Assured Group Plc v Marshall* (n 6) [15] (Morison J); Barlow Lyde & Gilbert LLP (n 1) para 28.6; Merkin (n 21) 145; Colin Edelman and Andrew Burns (n 7) para 4.59.

39 Comment 5 to Article 5.3 PRICL.

40 Comment 8 to Article 5.3 PRICL.

41 Comment 7 to Article 5.3 PRICL.

42 Comment 8 to Article 5.3 PRICL. Cf *Moore v IAG New Zealand Ltd* [2019] NZHC 1549, [2020] Lloyd's Rep IR 167 where Dunningham J considered that an earthquake was a 'cause' that provoked two subsequent 'events', ie two aftershocks.

43 Comment 8 to Article 5.3 PRICL. For more information as to why this is so, see para 5.7.

44 Comment 13 to Article 5.3 PRICL.

5.19 If a relevant cause can be identified in a particular case, all individual losses that originate from any event which, in turn, was triggered by this cause are to be aggregated.

2 Reference to the concept of event in Article 5.3 PRICL

5.20 It has been noted that for the determination of a unifying cause, Article 5.3 PRICL refers to the concept of event within the meaning of Article 5.2 PRICL.[45] In the following section, it is to be laid out why it is important to define cause-based aggregation mechanisms by reference to the concept of event.

5.21 Under the PRICL cause-based and event-based aggregation mechanisms, both operate on a unifying concept of causation.[46] Cause-based aggregation is, however, broader than event-based aggregation and makes it possible to look farther back in the chain of causation in the search of a unifying factor.[47]

5.22 On this basis, parties intending to facilitate the aggregation of individual losses are advised to provide for a cause-based rather than an event-based aggregation mechanism in their contract of reinsurance.[48] Yet, even if they do so, courts and arbitral tribunals would not necessarily apply a broader aggregation mechanism than an aggregation mechanism based on an event. As has been discussed, a cause and an event 'may well be precisely the same thing' in some circumstances under English law, so that favouring a cause-based over an event-based aggregation mechanism may not lead to a different conclusion.[49]

5.23 More specifically, any event that causes multiple individual losses may be considered the losses' cause.[50] As there is no guidance in English law as to the required degree of causation between the unifying cause and the individual losses to be aggregated, courts and arbitral tribunals might or might not find that the materialisation of a peril reinsured against or a liability triggering act, omission or fact, ie an event within the meaning of Article 5.2 PRICL, is the losses' common cause. In so doing, a court or arbitral tribunal might deny that a common cause found farther back in the chain of causation is the relevant cause within the meaning for Article 5.3 PRICL. Courts or arbitral tribunals would thereby equate cause-based with event-based aggregation mechanisms and potentially disrespect the parties' choice of a 'broader' concept of aggregation.

5.24 The aim of Article 5.3 PRICL is to ensure that the parties' choice in favour of a broader aggregation mechanism over an aggregation mechanism based on any one event is respected. In pursuing this goal, both paragraphs of Article 5.3 PRICL refer to the notion of event within the meaning of Article 5.2 in the process of determining

---

45 See para 5.16.

46 Comment 16 to Article 5.1 PRICL.

47 Comment 8 to Article 5.3 PRICL.

48 Barlow Lyde & Gilbert LLP (n 1) para 28.6; Merkin (n 21) 145; Edelman and Burns (n 7) para 4.59.

49 *Brown (RE) v GIO Insurance Ltd* (n 23) 204 (Waller LJ).

50 Cf *Brown (RE) v GIO Insurance Ltd* (n 23) 204 (Waller LJ); Louw and Tompkinson (n 23) 9; Merkin (n 21) 146.

a unifying cause. More specifically, Article 5.3 PRICL provides that if a cause gives rise to one or multiple events which, in turn, trigger a plurality of individual losses, all of the individual losses–no matter from which event they arose–are to be aggregated.[51] By so doing, Article 5.3 PRICL instructs courts and arbitral tribunals not to be satisfied that an instance of materialised peril or a liability triggering act, omission or fact is the relevant unifying cause, but to look farther back in the chain of causation in the search of a unifying cause.

5.25 Certainly, there will not always be a cause that triggered multiple different instances of materialised perils or liability triggering acts, omissions or facts. In such cases, each instance of materialised peril or liability triggering act, omission or fact is to be considered a unifying cause within the meaning of Article 5.3 PRICL.[52] Yet, it will often be possible to identify a cause that triggered multiple different instances of materialised perils[53] or liability triggering acts, omissions or facts.[54] By instructing courts and arbitral tribunals to look for such a unifying cause, Article 5.3 PRICL upholds the parties' choice for a wide aggregation mechanism.[55]

5.26 As in English law,[56] the situation under Article 5.3 PRICL is that not just any cause can be a relevant cause for the purposes of aggregation. Rather, if the causal links between the aggregating cause and the instances of materialised perils or liability triggering acts, omissions or facts are too weak, there will not be any unifying cause for the purposes of Article 5.3 PRICL. In order to test whether a cause is too remote so as to operate as unifying factor, Article 5.3 PRICL uses the concept of 'reasonable foreseeability'.

3 The requirement of 'reasonable foreseeability'

5.27 By introducing the concept of 'reasonable foreseeability', the PRICL address the problem of how much farther back in the chain of causation than a materialised peril or a liability triggering act, omission or fact one must look in order to find a unifying cause.[57] In other words, the concept of 'reasonable

---

51 It may be noted that, under Article 5.2 PRICL, individual losses are only to be aggregated if they are an event's direct consequence. The same is true under Article 5.3 PRICL. While Article 5.3 PRICL provides for a broader aggregation mechanism, it does not broaden the scope of the aggregation 'downstream' to the effect that individual losses that are only loosely connected with an instance of materialised peril or a liability triggering act, omission or fact are aggregated. However, it does broaden the scope 'upstream' to the effect that a cause further back in the chain of causation that triggered multiple instances of materialised perils or liability triggering acts, omissions or facts may operate as unifying cause.

52 Comment 8 to Article 5.3 PRICL.

53 In other words, an event within the meaning of Article 5.2(1) PRICL.

54 In other words, an event within the meaning of Article 5.2(2) PRICL.

55 Cf comment 9 to Article 5.3 PRICL, which states that it was 'important not to give a court or arbitral tribunal the leeway to consider the materiali[s]ation of a peril reinsured against or the liability triggering act, omission or fact as the relevant cause within the meaning of Article 5.3. Otherwise, the parties' choice for a broader aggregation mechanism would be disregarded'.

56 See, for instance, *American Centennial Insurance Co v INSCO Ltd* (n 5) 414 (Moore-Bick J).

57 Comment 12 to Article 5.3 PRICL.

foreseeability' is used to provide guidance as to whether a cause is too remote so as to be acceptable as a basis upon which a plurality of losses are to be aggregated.[58]

5.28 In Article 5.3 PRICL, it is stated that 'a cause may be considered the unifying factor for the purposes of aggregation, if it was reasonably foreseeable to the parties that–in the ordinary course of things–a cause of this kind would lead to an event of the kind under consideration, ie an instance of materiali[z]ed peril (...) or an act, omission or fact that triggers the primary insured's liability'.[59] The question of whether it was foreseeable that a certain cause would provoke a specific event is to be analysed from the perspective of a reasonable person in the circumstances of the parties at the time they agreed upon the aggregation mechanism and in light of the ordinary course of things.[60]

5.29 The commentary on Article 5.3 PRICL elaborates that the concept of foreseeability does not correspond with the concept of foreseeability in tort law, general contract law or insurance law.[61] These branches of law use the concept of foreseeability as a limit to liability.[62] Under Article 5.3 PRICL, the concept of reasonable foreseeability is not necessarily used to limit the reinsurer's liability. If it is not reasonably foreseeable that a particular cause would provoke a certain event, this cause cannot be considered a unifying cause under Article 5.3 PRICL. As a consequence, the number of losses to be aggregated may decrease. This is, however, not to be equated with limiting the reinsurer's liability. In fact, this may mean that the reinsurer is confronted with multiple claims not piercing the reinsurance cover limit, instead of one single claim surpassing the reinsurance policy limit. Depending on the circumstances, a narrower aggregation may, therefore, lead to broader liability for the reinsurer.[63]

5.30 It has been noted that Article 5.3 PRICL uses the concept of reasonable foreseeability to limit how much farther back beyond an instance of materialised peril or a liability triggering act, omission or fact one may look in the search of a unifying factor. Accordingly, the concept of reasonable foreseeability aims at defining a standard of causation. Yet, an exercise of judgment appears to be involved in determining whether it was reasonably foreseeable that a particular cause would lead to an event of the sort under consideration.[64] In this regard, the standard of reasonable foreseeability appears to afford courts and arbitral tribunals with ample opportunity to reach result-oriented rather than objectively predictable decisions on the question of aggregation.[65]

---

58 Comment 12 to Article 5.3 PRICL.
59 See also comment 13 to Article 5.3 PRICL.
60 Comments 15 f to Article 5.3 PRICL.
61 Comments 17 f to Article 5.3 PRICL.
62 Comment 18 to Article 5.3 PRICL.
63 Comment 19 to Article 5.3 PRICL.
64 Comment 20 to Article 5.3 PRICL.
65 Comment 20 to Article 5.3 PRICL.

5.31 Under Article 5.3 PRICL and by contrast to English law,[66] however, a cause is defined by reference to an event within the meaning of Article 5.2 PRICL and the concept of reasonable foreseeability offers courts and arbitral tribunals some guidance in exercising their judgment. Hence, the operation of cause-based aggregation mechanisms governed by Article 5.3 PRICL may be more predictable than cause-based aggregation mechanisms subject to English law.

III Summary of the chapter

5.32 Traditionally, cause-based aggregation mechanisms use the unifying factors of 'originating cause or source' or 'one source or original cause' and the linking phrase of 'consequent upon or attributable to'. The standard of causation inherent in cause-based aggregation mechanisms is said to be defined by the unifying factor and the linking phrase used in the aggregation clause.

5.33 In light of the English authorities on the subject matter, it appears to be clear that cause-based aggregation mechanisms are broader than event-based aggregation mechanisms. It has been noted that the word 'originating' coupled with the word 'cause' 'opens up the widest possible search for a unifying factor in the history of the individual losses'.[67] It has, thus, been suggested that a unifying cause has allowed tracing back losses to wherever a common origin could reasonably be found.[68] Yet, it has equally been held that even though an 'originating cause' was a unifying factor of a remote kind, the degree of remoteness between the unifying factor and the individual losses to be aggregated still needs to be limited.

5.34 In English law, however, there appears to be no concept of limitation on the acceptable degree of remoteness in cause-based aggregation. The question of whether a cause is too remote so as to operate as a unifying factor in a given case seems to be one that has been left entirely to the courts' or arbitral tribunals' exercise of judgment. As the unities test does not apply in the context of cause-based aggregation, courts and arbitral tribunals have no guidance in their exercise of judgment, which opens up ample opportunity for courts and arbitral tribunals to reach result-oriented decisions.

5.35 The aim of Article 5.3 PRICL is to reduce the legal uncertainty inherent in cause-based aggregation mechanisms. It provides the market with rules that are meant to guide courts and arbitral tribunals in determining the required standard of causation between the unifying causes and the individual losses to be aggregated. In order to ensure that cause-based aggregation is broader than event-based aggregation, the standard of causation inherent in cause-based aggregation mechanisms is defined in Article 5.3 PRICL by reference to the concept of 'event' within the meaning of Article 5.2 PRICL. In fact, it is ensured under Article 5.3 PRICL that one looks farther back than the materialisation of a peril or the liability triggering act, omission or fact in the search of a unifying cause. The concept of 'reasonable foreseeability' addresses the question of how much farther back one is to look.

---

66 See para 5.10.

67 *Axa Reinsurance (UK) Ltd v Field* (n 5) 1035 (Lord Mustill).

68 *Standard Life Assurance Ltd v Ace European Group* (n 5) [259] (Eder J).

5.36 Clearly, the determination of whether a cause is acceptable as a unifying factor or whether it is too remote so as to justify an aggregation of a plurality of losses is an exercise of judgment under Article 5.3 PRICL. Therefore, cause-based aggregation mechanisms under Article 5.3 PRICL bear legal uncertainty and provide courts and arbitral tribunals with the opportunity to reach result-oriented judgments. Yet, both the definition of a unifying cause by reference to the definition of an 'event' as well as the concept of 'reasonable foreseeability' provide courts and arbitral tribunals with analytical guidance. Considering this, Article 5.3 PRICL may be capable of reducing legal uncertainty in cause-based aggregation.

PART II

AGGREGATION ISSUES IN THE RELATIONSHIP BETWEEN THE REINSURER AND THE REINSURED

CHAPTER 6

Aggregation and allocation

6.1 The aim of this chapter is to distinguish between the concept of aggregation of losses and the concept of allocation of losses. In the following sections, it will be demonstrated that both concepts are used to determine whether a loss is within the scope of the reinsurance cover in a specific case. However, they respond to different aspects of the scope of cover. Thereafter, the concept of loss allocation will briefly be presented before the relation between the concepts of aggregation and allocation shall be addressed.

I Concepts respond to different aspects of scope of cover

1 Quantitative scope of cover and aggregation

6.2 As elaborated above, in non-proportional reinsurance, the reinsurer provides cover for the amount of a loss exceeding the reinsured's deductible up to a specified cover limit.[1] Accordingly, specifying the applicable deductible and cover limit in a given case means defining the quantitative scope of a reinsurance cover.[2]

6.3 In an aggregation clause, the parties to a reinsurance contract agree that, under certain circumstances, multiple individual losses will be aggregated and are to be considered as one single loss, which is then tested against the reinsured's deductible and the reinsurer's cover limit.[3]

6.4 Hence, the concept of aggregation is used to determine whether a loss falls within the quantitative scope of reinsurance cover so as to trigger the reinsurer's liability.

2 Temporal scope of cover and allocation

6.5 Allocating losses means determining which of multiple reinsurance policies responds to a specific loss. It is to be tested whether a loss falls within the scope of the reinsurance cover of a particular contract. This involves questions such as whether the loss results from a reinsured peril,[4] whether the reinsurance contract extends to

---

1 See para 1.34.

2 Andreas Schwepcke and Alexandra Vetter, *Praxishandbuch: Rückversicherung* (VVW 2017) para 858. Cf also Klaus Gerathewohl, *Rückversicherung, Grundlagen und Praxis*, vol 1 (Verlag Versicherungs wirts chaft eV 1976) 187; Peter Liebwein, *Klassische und moderne Formen der Rückversicherung* (3rd edn, VVW 2018) 184, 191.

3 Barlow Lyde and Gilbert LLP, *Reinsurance Practice and the Law* (Informa Law from Routledge 2009) para 28.1.

4 Cf Gerathewohl (n 2) 743.

the geographic location where the loss occurred,[5] whether the loss occurred within the reinsurance period[6] and whether the loss triggers the reinsurer's liability from a quantitative perspective.[7]

6.6 In practice, however, disputes regarding the concept of loss allocation primarily revolve around the question of the temporal scope of the reinsurance cover.[8] More specifically, it is sometimes difficult to determine when exactly a loss attaches to the reinsurance contract. Correspondingly, it is equally difficult to determine whether a loss falls within the temporal scope of one reinsurance contract or another. The latter question primarily arises where the reinsured has been on risk for multiple years and has taken out different reinsurance cover[9] over this time.[10]

6.7 The extent of a reinsurer's exposure depends substantially on whether a loss is within a given temporal scope of cover. This, in turn, depends on the mechanism of allocating losses.[11] In fact, different allocation mechanisms have been developed for reinsurance contracts.

II Different mechanisms of allocation in reinsurance

6.8 In treaty reinsurance, the reinsurance period and the insurance periods of the underlying policies are generally not the same.[12] Reinsurance treaties are commonly taken out per calendar year, whereas primary insurance periods may start and expire on any day in the year.[13] This begs the question whether a loss under a primary insurance policy that was entered into in calendar year 1 is reinsured under a treaty that incepts on 1 January of calendar year 2 if the loss has occurred in calendar year 2.[14]

6.9 In this regard, Lord Mance noted that excess of loss reinsurance responds either to losses occurring during the reinsurance period or to losses occurring during the period of policies attaching during the reinsurance period.[15] The majority of excess of loss reinsurance policies are taken out on a 'losses occurring during' basis.[16]

---

5 Cf Gerathewohl (n 2) 766.

6 Cf Gerathewohl (n 2) 726.

7 Cf *Teal Assurance Co Ltd v WR Berkley Insurance (Europe) Ltd* [2013] UKSC 57, [2013] 4 All ER 643.

8 Barlow Lyde and Gilbert LLP (n 3) paras 27.1 ff; Eberhard Witthoff, '§ 15 Schadenbearbeitung in der Rückversicherung' in Dieter W Lüer and Andreas Schwepcke (eds), *Rückversicherungsrecht* (CH Beck 2013) para 116; Robert M Merkin, Laura Hodgson and Peter J Tyldesley, *Colinvaux's Law of Insurance* (Sweet & Maxwell 2019) para 18–089.

9 As long as multiple consecutive reinsurance contracts exist it is irrelevant whether this is with different reinsurers or with the same reinsurer.

10 Merkin, Hodgson and Tyldesley (n 8) para 18–089.

11 Terry O'Neill, Jan Woloniecki and Franziska Arnold-Dwyer, *The Law of Reinsurance in England and Bermuda* (5th edn, Sweet & Maxwell/Thomson Reuters 2019) para 5–126.

12 Gerathewohl (n 2) 726.

13 Gerathewohl (n 2) 726.

14 Gerathewohl (n 2) 726.

15 *Wasa International Insurance Co Ltd v Lexington Insurance Co* [2009] UKHL 40, [2009] 4 All ER 909 [41] (Lord Mance); Gerathewohl (n 2) 733 f; O'Neill, Woloniecki and Arnold-Dwyer (n 11) paras 5–127 f.

16 Barlow Lyde and Gilbert LLP (n 3) para 27.19; Gerathewohl (n 2) 734. Cf also Liebwein (n 2) 274.

The concepts of 'losses occurring during' and 'risks attaching during' determine the temporal scope of the reinsurance cover. However, they do not do so conclusively.

6.10 In *Balfour v Beaumont*, it was held that '[w]here, (...), the reinsurance [was] on a losses occurring basis the reinsurer [was] undertaking to indemnify the reassured in respect of all losses occurring during the specified period of reinsurance (...)' and that it was 'quite irrelevant when the original policy came into effect or when its term expired. The only question [was] whether the loss occurred during the period of the reinsurance'.[17] By contrast, a reinsurance contract on a 'risks attaching during' basis provides cover for underlying insurance contracts that are entered into during the reinsurance period.[18]

6.11 Upon a closer examination, both concepts are primarily used to determine the set of primary insurance policies that are reinsured.

1 'Losses occurring during' and temporal scope of reinsurance cover

6.12 In order to recover under a reinsurance contract which has been taken out on a 'losses occurring during' basis, the reinsured must–on the balance of probabilities–prove that a loss occurred during the reinsurance period.[19] Whether a loss can be said to have occurred during the reinsurance period is a question of fact.[20]

6.13 This begs the question of whether the losses occurring during basis refers to a loss incurred by the original insured under a primary insurance policy or to a loss incurred by the reinsured under the reinsurance treaty. In *Youell v Bland Welch and Co Ltd*, it was held that, under a reinsurance contract taken out on a losses occurring during basis, the reinsurer was 'obliged to pay [its] share of the loss suffered by the **reinsured**, if it occurred during the period when the reinsurance contract was in force'.[21] Hence, in English law, a loss is incurred under a treaty of reinsurance when the reinsured's liability has been established and quantified either by judgment, arbitral award or a reasonable and binding settlement.[22] Accordingly, the Court of Appeal considered in *Youell v Bland Welch and Co Ltd* that it was the point in time when the reinsured's loss occurred and not when the original loss occurred that was the relevant point in time for allocating a loss to a reinsurance treaty taken out on a losses occurring during basis.[23]

---

17 *Balfour v Beaumont* [1984] 1 Lloyd's Rep 272 (CA).

18 O'Neill, Woloniecki and Arnold-Dwyer (n 11) para 5–128.

19 *Municipal Mutual Insurance Ltd v Sea Insurance Co Ltd* [1998] EWCA Civ 546, [1998] CLC 957, 969 (Hobhouse LJ); Barlow Lyde and Gilbert LLP (n 3) para 27.19; Witthoff (n 8) para 119.

20 *Municipal Mutual Insurance Ltd v Sea Insurance Co Ltd* (n 19) 969 (Hobhouse LJ); Witthoff (n 8) para 119.

21 *Youell v Bland Welch and Co Ltd (No 1)* [1992] 2 Lloyd's Rep 127 (CA) (emphasis added). Likewise referring to the reinsured's and not the original loss, *Wasa International Insurance Co Ltd v Lexington Insurance Co* (n 15) [76] (Lord Collins); Stefan Pohl and Joseph Iranya, *The ABC of Reinsurance* (VVW 2018) 38. Cf also O'Neill, Woloniecki and Arnold-Dwyer (n 11) para 5–127.

22 Merkin, Hodgson and Tyldesley (n 8) para 18–062, with further references; John Butler and Robert Merkin, *Butler and Merkin's Reinsurance Law*, vol 2 (Looseleaf, Sweet & Maxwell) para C–0202.

23 It may be noted that this conclusion seems to be in line with *Municipal Mutual Insurance Ltd v Sea Insurance Co Ltd* (n 19) 962, 969, where Hobhouse LJ considered the point in time when the physical loss occurred as the relevant loss occurrence for the purposes of allocating a loss under a contract of

6.14 Yet, the reinsured's liability is not necessarily triggered when the primary insured incurs the physical loss or damage. This is because the parties to the primary insurance contract may specify another trigger for the primary insurer's (reinsured's) liability. More specifically, the primary insurance policy may provide that the primary insurer's (reinsured's) liability is triggered when a loss is discovered, when a loss is reported or when a claim is made.[24] In the US long-tail business, in particular, the so-called triple trigger theory often applies. Under this theory, a primary insurance contract responds to a loss if it was in force either at the time of initial exposure, during continued exposure of the insured or a third party to hazardous conditions or at the time of the loss manifestation.[25] Hence, the point in time when the reinsured incurs liability, ie when it incurs a loss, may depend on the trigger provided for in the primary insurance contract.

6.15 Consequently, the phrase 'losses occurring during' provided for in a re-insurance treaty is not necessarily referring to the occurrence of the original physical loss.[26] The phrase merely defines the set of primary insurance policies that are re-insured under the treaty. Whenever the reinsured suffers a loss, the reinsurance contract is activated. Where, for example, the primary insurance contract uses a claims-made trigger, the reinsured suffers a loss only when a claim has been made in the primary insurance context.[27] Therefore, under the reinsurance contract, a loss does not occur when the physical loss occurs under the primary insurance contract–even though the reinsurance treaty is taken out on a losses occurring during basis–but when a claim is made under the primary insurance contract.[28]

6.16 It is to be noted, however, that a contract of reinsurance may define the losses to be allocated to it independently of the underlying contract. For instance, the reinsurance contract interpreted in *Caudle v Sharp* provided that 'the reinsurers are liable for losses discovered or claims made, by or against the original insured, during the period of reinsurance cover, irrespective of the date on which the loss itself may have occurred'.[29] In this case, the reinsurance contract itself contained a trigger.

6.17 To sum up, the phrase 'losses occurring during' in a reinsurance treaty should

---

reinsurance. This is so because the underlying contract provided that the reinsured's liability would be triggered when a physical loss occurred. Similarly, in *Wasa International Insurance Co Ltd v Lexington Insurance Co* (n 15), the House of Lords stated that the relevant loss occurrence was the reinsured's loss occurrence. In this case, the reinsured became liable to indemnify its primary insured for all the environmental pollution damage whenever it occurred. Accordingly, the reinsured's liability appears to have arisen when the physical damage occurred; Butler and Merkin (n 22) para C–0293.

24 Liebwein (n 2) 278.

25 Malcolm A Clarke, *The Law of Insurance Contracts* (6th edn, Informa Law from Routledge 2009) para 17-4C2.

26 Cf Barlow Lyde and Gilbert LLP (n 3) para 18.11, who note that 'losses discovered' or 'claims made' clauses may be used to determine the date of loss where the reinsurance treaty provides cover on a 'losses occurring during' basis.

27 *Caudle v Sharp* [1995] CLC 642 (CA) 651 f (Evans LJ); Barlow Lyde and Gilbert LLP (n 3) para 18.11. Cf also Liebwein (n 2) 275 in connection with 132 and n 759; O'Neill, Woloniecki and Arnold-Dwyer (n 11) para 5–112.

28 Cf Liebwein (n 2) 275 in connection with 132 and n 759.

29 *Caudle v Sharp* (n 27) 652 f (Evans LJ).

generally not be considered a trigger. This is because the 'losses occurring during' basis on its own does not, in general, determine the temporal scope of the reinsurance cover. It determines the underlying policies that are reinsured under a contract of reinsurance. The reinsurance agreement's temporal scope of cover, thus, to some extent depends on the terms of the underlying insurance policy.

2 'Risks attaching during' and temporal scope of reinsurance cover

6.18 If reinsurance treaties are taken out on a 'risks attaching during' basis, primary insurance policies that are entered into (or renewed) during the reinsurance period are relevant.[30] More specifically, the reinsurance treaty provides cover for losses that occur after the reinsurance term has ended if the relevant primary insurance contract has been entered into during the reinsurance period.[31] By contrast, they do not provide cover for losses that occur during the reinsurance period if the primary insurance contract has been entered into before the reinsurance period has started to run.

6.19 Consequently, the risks attaching during basis is used to determine the set of primary insurance policies that are reinsured. By doing so, it defines the reinsurance treaty's temporal scope of application. However, whether a specific loss is covered under the treaty equally depends on the primary insurance policy's temporal scope of application.

6.20 Where the primary insurance contract uses a claims-made trigger, for example, a claim must be made in the primary insurance context in order to activate the primary insurer's (reinsured's) liability. This may be long after a physical loss has occurred. In such a case, the reinsurer's liability is triggered if the relevant primary insurance policy has been entered into during the reinsurance period and a claim has been made in the context of the original insurance.

6.21 In summary, the phrase 'risks attaching during' on its own does not determine the temporal scope of the reinsurance cover. In order to fully understand the temporal scope of a contract of reinsurance, the trigger used in the underlying insurance policy must be analysed. The question whether a loss is to be allocated to the reinsurance agreement depends substantially on the terms of the primary insurance policy.

III Relation between aggregation and allocation

1 Possible conflict between aggregation and allocation

6.22 With an aggregation clause, the parties to a reinsurance contract agree that multiple individual losses are to be aggregated if they all result from a specified unifying factor. A reinsurance contract's temporal scope of cover defines whether the timing of the loss was of the kind required to provide cover for the loss under the specific contract.

6.23 A reinsurance contract's temporal scope of cover is often defined independently

---

30 Gerathewohl (n 2) 733 f; Schwepcke and Vetter (n 2) paras 544 ff; O'Neill, Woloniecki and Arnold-Dwyer (n 11) para 5–128; Liebwein (n 2) 129 ff, 273 f. Cf also Marcel Grossmann, *Rückversicherung – Eine Einführung* (2nd edn, Institut für Versicherungswirtschaft an der Hochschule St Gallen 1982) 129.

31 Liebwein (n 2) 130; O'Neill, Woloniecki and Arnold-Dwyer (n 11) para 5–128.

of the aggregation clause. Basically, the underlying question is whether multiple in-dividual losses are to be allocated to the correct policy period so that the losses that are so allocated can subsequently be aggregated or whether multiple losses are to be ag-gregated and this aggregate is subsequently to be allocated to the correct policy year. In more illustrative words, the question is whether multiple individual losses are to be grouped together to one big balloon and this balloon is then to be attached to one policy year or whether multiple small individual balloons are to be attached to a policy year and only those balloons that are attached to the same policy year may ultimately be aggregated.[32]

2 Allocation before aggregation

2.1 *Municipal Mutual Insurance Ltd v Sea Insurance Co Ltd*

6.24 In *Municipal Mutual Insurance Ltd v Sea Insurance Co Ltd*, the Court of Appeal dealt with a facultative excess of loss reinsurance contract.

6.25 Cranes left at the port of Sunderland 'by a company called Concorde were vandalised by a succession of individual acts of pilferage' during a period of some 18 months.[33] Concorde brought action against the Port of Sunderland for not putting in place a system to protect its goods that were stored at the port. Municipal insured the Port of Sunderland under a primary insurance policy that was renewed annually. Sea Insurance Co Ltd reinsured Municipal Mutual Insurance Ltd under three consecutive facultative reinsurance contracts, each of 12 months' duration.[34] The reinsured, Municipal, paid out insurance money to the Port of Sunderland and sought to recover a certain amount from its reinsurers.[35]

6.26 The reinsurance slips each indicated that the reinsurance period lasted '12 months at 24 June 1986'.[36] Further, as the reinsurance contracts were designed to be back-to-back with the primary insurance contract, the primary insurance policy's limit of liability clause was incorporated into the reinsurance contracts.[37] The provision read:

[A]ll sums which the insured may become legally liable to pay ... for ... loss or damage caused to property ... provided that such ... loss or damage is caused by any act of commission or omission negligence or error of judgment by the insured or their servants or employees ... and arises during any period of insurance under this policy.[38]

6.27 The contracts of reinsurance contained aggregation clauses providing that the limit of liability was to be applied 'to compensation payable, "in respect of or arising

---

32 This illustrative depiction was used by Christian Lang, Swiss Re, at the 5th PRICL workshop, taking place in Vienna from 15 to 18 January 2018.

33 *Municipal Mutual Insurance Ltd v Sea Insurance Co Ltd* (n 19) 962 (Hobhouse LJ).

34 *Municipal Mutual Insurance Ltd v Sea Insurance Co Ltd* (n 19) 962 (Hobhouse LJ). The three contracts of reinsurance, ie the slips, were taken out for 1986–87, 1987–88 and 1988–89, respectively.

35 *Municipal Mutual Insurance Ltd v Sea Insurance Co Ltd* (n 19) 957 (Hobhouse LJ).

36 *Municipal Mutual Insurance Ltd v Sea Insurance Co Ltd* (n 19) 958 (Hobhouse LJ). The provisions in the second and third contract were adapted according to the respective year of cover.

37 *Municipal Mutual Insurance Ltd v Sea Insurance Co Ltd* (n 19) 957 (Hobhouse LJ).

38 *Municipal Mutual Insurance Ltd v Sea Insurance Co Ltd* (n 19) 966 (Hobhouse LJ).

out of any one occurrence or in respect of or arising out of all occurrences of a series consequent on or attributable to one source or original cause'".[39]

6.28 The Court of Appeal first held that the individual acts of pilferage were 'attributable to a single source or original cause', ie the lack of an adequate system to protect the cranes from pilferage and vandalism, and were, thus, to be aggregated.[40]

6.29 The Court of Appeal then had to make sense of the reinsurance periods. It held that '[w]hen the relevant cover is placed on a time basis, the stated period of time is fundamental and must be given effect to. It is for that period of risk that the premium payable is assessed'.[41]

6.30 Without directly addressing the conflict between the concept of aggregation and the concept of allocation, the Court of Appeal held that, if a contract of reinsurance was taken out on a time basis, individual losses had to first be allocated to a policy year. Only losses that were allocated to the same policy year could then be aggregated.[42] Hence, if multiple individual losses occurred during different reinsurance periods, they cannot be aggregated even if they are attributable to one source or original cause.

2.2 *Caudle v Sharp*

6.31 In *Caudle v Sharp*, the Court of Appeal dealt with excess of loss reinsurance treaties.[43]

6.32 Between 1980 and 1982, the managing agent of the Outhwaite syndicate underwrote 32 run-off insurance contracts on behalf of the syndicate. The contracts resulted in enormous losses for the Outhwaite syndicate. These losses were initially borne by the syndicate's members. They subsequently brought an action against the managing agent, Mr Outhwaite, for having negligently written the risks.[44] Mr Sharp was Mr Outhwaite's professional indemnity insurer. Under this primary insurance professional indemnity policy, Mr Sharp paid claims totalling £7,375,891. Some of these claims were made in 1985, others in 1987. Mr Sharp then sought to recover this amount under four contracts of reinsurance.[45]

6.33 The reinsurance treaties contained the following reinsurance period clause:

This reinsurance covers all losses as herein defined occurring during the period commencing with 1 January 1985 and ending with 31 December, 1985 both days inclusive, local standard time at the place where the loss occurs.[46]

6.34 The reinsurance treaties also contained aggregation clauses defining the term 'each and every loss': 'For the purpose of this reinsurance the term "each and every

---

39 *Municipal Mutual Insurance Ltd v Sea Insurance Co Ltd* (n 19) 966 (Hobhouse LJ).

40 *Municipal Mutual Insurance Ltd v Sea Insurance Co Ltd* (n 19) 967 (Hobhouse LJ).

41 *Municipal Mutual Insurance Ltd v Sea Insurance Co Ltd* (n 19) 968 (Hobhouse LJ).

42 *Municipal Mutual Insurance Ltd v Sea Insurance Co Ltd* (n 19) 967 (Hobhouse LJ).

43 *Caudle v Sharp* (n 27) 644 f (Evans LJ).

44 *Caudle v Sharp* (n 27) 643 (Evans LJ).

45 *Caudle v Sharp* (n 27) 643 (Evans LJ).

46 *Caudle v Sharp* (n 27) 645 (Evans LJ).

loss" shall be understood to mean each and every loss (...) and/or series of losses (...) arising out of one event'.[47]

6.35 Moreover, it is to be noted that the primary insurance policy was taken out on a claims-made basis,[48] whereas the reinsurance treaties were designed on a losses occurring during basis.[49]

6.36 The Court of Appeal identified two relevant questions. The first was whether the original losses incurred under 32 separate run-off policies can be aggregated. If this were answered in the affirmative, the second question would be whether the losses that occurred[50] in 1987 could be aggregated with losses that had occurred[51] in 1985 if they all arose from the same event.[52]

6.37 As to the first question, the Court of Appeal concluded that Mr Outhwaite's ignorance in underwriting the 32 run-off policies could not be considered an event within the meaning of the aggregation clause. Consequently, the underwritings of the run-off policies were considered 32 separate events so that the corresponding losses could not be aggregated.

6.38 On the basis of the court holding that the individual losses could not be aggregated, the second question did not arise in respect of the case concerned.[53] Nevertheless, the court pronounced, *obiter*, its opinion on the issue. Generally, a plurality of losses that arise out of one particular event are to be aggregated. However, if–under a primary insurance policy taken out on a claims-made basis–the different underlying claims were made in 1985 and 1987 respectively, they may not be allocated to the same reinsurance period. Only claims made in 1985 could be allocated to the reinsurance treaty in question. The Court of Appeal noted that there was 'no justification (...) for (...) extending the reinsurance cover so as to bring within its scope claims made or losses discovered after the cover has expired'.[54]

6.39 The court arrived at this conclusion even though the reinsurance treaties contained an 'extension of protection clause'. This clause provided that

> *[i]f this reinsurance should expire whilst a loss (...) arising out of one event is in progress, it is agreed that subject to the other conditions of this reinsurance, the reinsurers shall pay their proportion of the entire loss or damage, provided that the loss (...) arising out of one event commenced before the time of expiration of this reinsurance.*[55]

---

47 *Caudle v Sharp* (n 27) 644 (Evans LJ).

48 *Caudle v Sharp* (n 27) 644 (Evans LJ).

49 This results from the reinsurance period clause, *Caudle v Sharp* (n 27) 652 f (Evans LJ).

50 Under the reinsurance treaties, a loss occurred when for the purpose of the primary insurance policy a claim was made.

51 Under the reinsurance treaties, a loss occurred when for the purpose of the primary insurance policy a claim was made.

52 Cf *Caudle v Sharp* (n 27) 643 (Evans LJ) where the second question is put slightly differently.

53 *Caudle v Sharp* (n 27) 650 (Evans LJ).

54 *Caudle v Sharp* (n 27) 653 (Evans LJ).

55 *Caudle v Sharp* (n 27) 644 (Evans LJ).

6.40 The Court of Appeal reasoned that such a clause could easily be applied to a case of physical damage. More specifically, where the primary insurance policy and the reinsurance contract were both taken out on a losses occurring during basis, it was sensible to aggregate multiple individual losses that resulted from a hurricane even if some of them occurred after the expiry of the reinsurance period.[56] By contrast, it held that the parties may not have intended to apply the clause in the case of professional indemnity insurance on a claims-made basis. The Court of Appeal stated that applying an extension of protection clause to such cases could 'have a dramatic effect. The reinsurance cover [would be] extended to include all claims arising out of the particular act of negligence, whenever they [might] be made, provided that one claim at least [was] made during the period of cover'.[57] It concluded that 'entire loss' meant 'the whole of the loss subsequently established in respect of that claim', so that there was no justification for reading the clause as extending the cover so as to bring within its scope claims made after the reinsurance cover had expired.[58]

6.41 Consequently, the Court of Appeal noted that only losses that occurred[59] during one period of reinsurance might be aggregated.[60] The fact that the parties had used an extension of protection clause did not, in general, change the situation where the underlying insurance policy was a third-party liability insurance.[61] Hence, losses that occur outside the reinsurance period cannot be aggregated with losses occurring during the period even if they all arise from the same event.[62] If the parties wish to aggregate individual losses that are *prima facie* to be allocated to different policy years, this must be expressed in the contract of reinsurance very clearly.[63]

2.3 *Pacific Dunlop Ltd v Swinbank*

6.42 In the Australian case *Pacific Dunlop Ltd v Swinbank*, the Supreme Court of Victoria Court of Appeal was confronted with a primary excess of loss liability insurance policy. The insured, Pacific Dunlop (more precisely, its subsidiary), produced coronary pacemaker leads which were designed to convey electronic signals to the patients' hearts. In 1994, the insured voluntarily recalled all unimplanted devices. Subsequently, patients to whom such coronary pacemakers had been implanted sought compensation for injury caused by an actual fracture of the device or the need to explant the device due to its susceptibility to fracture.

6.43 The relevant insurance contract contained an aggregation clause as well as an insurance period clause. The aggregation provision read:

---

56 *Caudle v Sharp* (n 27) 652 (Evans LJ).

57 *Caudle v Sharp* (n 27) 652 (Evans LJ).

58 *Caudle v Sharp* (n 27) 653 (Evans LJ).

59 Under the reinsurance treaties, a loss occurred when for the purpose of the primary insurance policy a claim was made.

60 *Caudle v Sharp* (n 27) 653 (Evans LJ).

61 *Caudle v Sharp* (n 27) 652.

62 *Caudle v Sharp* (n 27) 653.

63 Butler and Merkin (n 22) para C–0206.

An Occurrence or series of Occurrences arising directly from a common cause or condition shall be deemed to be one Occurrence regardless of the number of persons or organisations who sustain Personal Injury Property Damage or Advertising Injury. All such Occurrences shall be deemed to have occurred on the day of the first of such Occurrences.[64]

6.44 The period of insurance was stated to last 'from 4.00 p.m. Australian Eastern Standard Time on 30 September 1992 to 4.00 p.m. Australian Eastern Standard Time on 30 September 1993'.[65]

6.45 In the proceedings before the first instance court, the insurer contested that the individual third-party claims constitute a 'series of occurrences'. Before the appellate court, however, the insurer did not forcefully uphold its contention, so that the individual third-party losses were treated as a series of occurrences.[66] The appellate court had to decide whether an individual third-party loss that occurred outside the insurance period formed part of the relevant series of occurrences.[67]

6.46 The issue before the appellate court basically came down to the question of whether the concept of aggregation prevailed over the concept of allocation. In this regard, the court emphasised that it was a question of construction of the aggregation clause and the date deeming provision.[68] More specifically, the question to be determined was whether by stating that 'all such Occurrences shall be deemed to have occurred on the day of the first of such Occurrences' the parties intended to extend the cover beyond the period of insurance.[69]

6.47 The court held that the insurance policy was essentially shaped 'as one that [was] calculated to afford insurance cover to [the insured] by way of indemnity over a distinct, limited and finite portion of time, marked out at each end to the very minute, and designated as "the Period of Insurance"'. It went on to state that the relevant policy insured against 'liability for the consequences of a particular event (called an "Occurrence") happening within that particularly specified time frame'.[70] The court concluded that 'the scope of indemnity [was not] "controlled" by the requirements of the aggregation clause'.[71]

6.48 In reaching its conclusion, the court was explicitly aware of the fact that its interpretation rendered the sentence '[a]ll such Occurrences shall be deemed to have occurred on the day of the first of such Occurrences' nugatory in the context of product liability.[72]

6.49 Consequently, the Supreme Court of Victoria Court of Appeal acknowledged that the question of whether an aggregation clause controlled an allocation clause or

64 *Pacific Dunlop Ltd v Swinbank* (2001) 11 ANZ Insur Cases 61–496 (Supreme Court of Victoria Court of Appeal) [11] (Tadgell JA).
65 *Pacific Dunlop Ltd v Swinbank* (n 64) [2] (Tadgell JA).
66 *Pacific Dunlop Ltd v Swinbank* (n 64) [18] (Tadgell JA).
67 *Pacific Dunlop Ltd v Swinbank* (n 64) [19] (Tadgell JA).
68 *Pacific Dunlop Ltd v Swinbank* (n 64) [18]–[19] (Tadgell JA).
69 Cf *Pacific Dunlop Ltd v Swinbank* (n 64) [19] (Tadgell JA).
70 *Pacific Dunlop Ltd v Swinbank* (n 64) [23] (Tadgell JA).
71 *Pacific Dunlop Ltd v Swinbank* (n 64) [24] (Tadgell JA).
72 *Pacific Dunlop Ltd v Swinbank* (n 64) [26] (Tadgell JA).

vice versa was a question of contract interpretation. Hence, it is generally up to the parties to extend the insurance period by means of an aggregation clause. However, if they intend to do so, this must be expressed very clearly as the court deemed the insurance period clause to be defining the essential nature of the policy.[73]

2.4 Scholarly opinion on the importance of the allocation mechanism for aggregation

6.50 Gerathewohl agrees with the judiciary findings presented[74] in an example:[75] An excess of loss treaty was in place for the year 1976. The reinsured had two primary insurance policies in place, one that incepted on 1 July 1975 and the other that started to run on 1 January 1976. Losses occurred on 2 January 1976 and affected both primary insurance policies.

6.51 If the reinsurance treaty were taken out on a losses occurring during basis, it would not matter when the primary insurance policies incepted or when their term expired. By contrast, it would be important that both policies were in force at the time the losses occurred. As both primary insurance policies were in force on 2 January 1976, they were both reinsured under the treaty for losses that occurred on this day. Consequently, the individual losses would be aggregated.

6.52 If the reinsurance were, however, taken out on a risks attaching during basis, the time when the primary insurance policy incepted would be fundamental. In the example, the first policy incepted on 1 July 1975, ie before the reinsurance period began. The second policy incepted on 1 January 1976, ie within the reinsurance period. Consequently, the losses under the first policy cannot be said to be within the temporal scope of the reinsurance cover, whereas those under the second one can. Gerathewohl, thus, opines that losses under the first policy cannot be aggregated with losses under the second one even if they all resulted from one single event.[76]

6.53 In essence, Gerathewohl opines that multiple individual losses must first be allocated to a reinsurance period. Only losses that are allocated to the same period of reinsurance may be aggregated.

IV Aggregation and allocation under the PRICL

6.54 The PRICL follow the English rule on this point. More specifically, '[o]nly individual losses that are allocated to the same reinsurance period may be aggregated' under the PRICL.[77] Consequently, if multiple individual losses are allocated to different reinsurance periods, they cannot be aggregated even if they all arose from the same event or cause.[78]

---

73 Butler and Merkin (n 22) para C–0206.

74 *Pacific Dunlop Ltd v Swinbank* (n 64) [18]–[19] (Tadgell JA). See also *Caudle v Sharp* (n 27) 652 f (Evans LJ); *Municipal Mutual Insurance Ltd v Sea Insurance Co Ltd* (n 19) 967 ff (Hobhouse LJ). Contrast, Jacques Bourthoumieux, 'La notion d'événement dans les traités de réassurance en excédent de sinistres' (1969) 40 Revue générale des assurances terrestres 457, 460.

75 Gerathewohl (n 2) 734.

76 Gerathewohl (n 2) 734.

77 Comment 7 to Article 5.1 PRICL.

78 Comment 7 to Article 5.1 PRICL.

V Summary of the chapter

6.55 The concept of allocating losses and the concept of aggregating losses are both used to determine whether a loss is within the scope of the reinsurance cover in a specific case. The concept of aggregation deals with the question of whether multiple individual losses can be grouped together and presented to the reinsurer as one single loss with regard to the reinsured's deductible and the reinsurer's cover limit.[79] This question is essential in determining whether a loss is within the quantitative scope of the reinsurance cover. By contrast, the concept of allocating losses is used to determine whether a loss can be allocated to a specific policy year, ie whether it is within the temporal scope of the reinsurance cover.

6.56 Where a reinsurance contract contains an aggregation clause that provides for the aggregation of multiple individual losses if they result from one common unifying factor, there may be situations where these losses are *prima facie* to be allocated to different reinsurance periods. Consequently, the aggregation mechanism may conflict with the allocation mechanism.

6.57 It is a question of contract construction whether multiple individual losses are to be aggregated before the aggregated loss is allocated to a policy year or *vice versa*. Yet, English and Australian case law suggests that where the parties take out a reinsurance contract on a time basis, the reinsurance period is of fundamental importance. The parties are generally assumed to have agreed that multiple individual losses are to first be allocated to a reinsurance period and that only losses that are allocated to the same policy year may be aggregated.[80]

6.58 In *Caudle v Sharp*, the reinsurance treaties were interpreted as providing for a prevalence of the concept of allocation over the concept of aggregation even though they contained an extension of protection clause.[81] By contrast to a first-party insurance context, in particular, extension of protection clauses in reinsurance contracts reinsuring third-party risks may have no effect. In *Pacific Dunlop Ltd v Swinbank*, the court held that the parties to a reinsurance contract had not provided for an allocation of losses subject to prior aggregation by agreeing that 'all such Occurrences shall be deemed to have occurred on the day of the first of such Occurrences' even though the first occurrence was within the reinsurance period.[82]

6.59 Consequently, if the parties to a reinsurance contract intend to aggregate individual losses first and to allocate the aggregated product to a reinsurance period subsequently, they have to make this intention very clear.

6.60 Gerathewohl's example illustrates well that because, in general, only losses that are to be allocated to the same reinsurance period may be aggregated, the relevant allocation mechanism is important. Depending on whether the parties provide

---

79 Barlow Lyde and Gilbert LLP (n 3) para 28.1.

80 *Municipal Mutual Insurance Ltd v Sea Insurance Co Ltd* (n 19).

81 *Caudle v Sharp* (n 27).

82 *Pacific Dunlop Ltd v Swinbank* (n 64).

for an allocation on a losses occurring during basis or a risks attaching during basis, the reinsurance cover may differ substantially in a given case.[83]

6.61 In line with the English position, aggregation under the PRICL is only possible for losses that are allocated to the same reinsurance period.

---

83 Gerathewohl (n 2) 734.

CHAPTER 7

Aggregation and the principle of back-to-back

7.1 In this chapter, the relation between the concept of back-to-back cover and the concept of the aggregation of losses will be discussed.

7.2 As Lord Mustill stated in *Axa Reinsurance (UK) Ltd v Field*, provisions relating to limits are of cardinal importance in the case of excess of loss reinsurance.[1] Aggregation clauses are such provisions. Aggregation mechanisms may be provided for in both the underlying contract and the contract of reinsurance.

7.3 Therefore, the relation between the aggregation mechanisms in the two contracts is essential. According to the principle of back-to-back cover, the scope and the nature of cover of the underlying contract and the contract of reinsurance are the same. Yet, this principle only applies to proportional reinsurance.[2] The aggregation of losses, however, is primarily relevant in excess of loss reinsurance, ie non-proportional reinsurance.[3] Consequently, the relation between the aggregation clauses in the inward and the outward contracts will be discussed.

I The concept of back-to-back cover

7.4 As a basis for this discussion, the concept of back-to-back cover will be laid out. This includes a presentation of the presumption of back-to-back cover in proportional reinsurance as well as ways to rebut that presumption. Further, it will be set forth that the presumption of back-to-back cover does not extend to non-proportional reinsurance, such as excess of loss reinsurance.

1 Presumption of back-to-back cover in proportional facultative reinsurance

7.5 The relation between the reinsurance contract and the underlying contract is of fundamental importance.[4] In cases of proportional facultative reinsurance, the reinsurer covers a portion of the risk that the underlying insurer has assumed.[5] Where

---

1 *Axa Reinsurance (UK) Ltd v Field* (1996) 1 WLR 1026 (HL) 1035 (Lord Mustill).

2 *Axa Reinsurance (UK) Ltd v Field* (n 1) 1033 f (Lord Mustill); John Birds, Ben Lynch and Simon Paul, *MacGillivray on Insurance Law* (14th edn, Sweet & Maxwell 2018) para 35–067; Robert M Merkin, Laura Hodgson and Peter J Tyldesley, *Colinvaux's Law of Insurance* (12th edn, Sweet & Maxwell 2019) para 18–060.

3 See paras 1.38, 1.42, 1.43 ff, 1.58.

4 Terry O'Neill, Jan Woloniecki and Franziska Arnold-Dwyer, *The Law of Reinsurance in England and Bermuda* (5th edn, Sweet & Maxwell/Thomson Reuters 2019) para 4–003.

5 Özlem Gürses, *Reinsuring Clauses* (Informa Law from Routledge 2010) para 2.82.

the reinsured and the reinsurer each cover a portion of the original risk, it is said to be commercially sensible that 'the scope and nature of the cover afforded [by the reinsurance] is the same as the cover afforded by the insurance'.[6] If the covers provided by the two contracts are co-extensive, they are considered to be back-to-back.[7]

7.6 Whether the underlying contract and the reinsurance contract are back-to-back depends on the construction of the reinsurance contract.[8] Consequently, in determining whether the reinsurance contract follows the underlying contract is a matter of the parties' intent.[9]

7.7 According to Lord Collins, 'in proportional facultative reinsurance the starting point for the construction of the reinsurance policy is that the scope and nature of the cover in the reinsurance is co-extensive with the cover in the insurance'.[10] In this regard, Lord Griffiths in *Forsikringsaktieselskapet Vesta v Butcher*[11] noted that:

> *[i]n the ordinary course of business reinsurance is referred to as 'back-to-back' with the insurance, which means that the reinsurer agrees that if the insurer is liable under the policy the reinsurer will accept liability to pay whatever percentage of the claim he has agreed to reinsure. A reinsurer could, of course, make a special contract with an insurer and agree only to reinsure some of the risks covered by the policy of insurance, leaving the insurer to bear the full cost of the other risks. [Such a contract would] be wholly exceptional, a departure from the normal understanding of the back-to-back nature of reinsurance and would require to be spelt out in clear terms.[12]*

7.8 Consequently, there is a legal presumption under English law that the covers provided in the underlying insurance contract and the proportional facultative re-insurance contract are back-to-back.[13] This can be illustrated by the cases of

---

6 *Groupama Navigation et Transports v Catatumbo CA Seguros* [2000] EWCA Civ 220, [2000] 2 All ER 193; *Wasa International Insurance Co Ltd v Lexington Insurance Co* [2009] UKHL 40, [2009] 4 All ER 909 [58], [60] where Lord Collins stated that this was 'the normal commercial intention'.

7 Barlow Lyde & Gilbert LLP, *Reinsurance Practice and the Law* (Informa Law from Routledge 2009) para 16.10; Colin Edelman and Andrew Burns, *The Law of Reinsurance* (2nd edn, OUP 2013) para 3.12; Merkin, Hodgson and Tyldesley (n 2) para 18–050.

8 *Groupama Navigation et Transports v Catatumbo CA Seguros* (n 6); *Forsikringsaktieselskapet Vesta v Butcher* [1989] AC 852 (HL) 911 (Lord Lowry); *Wasa International Insurance Co Ltd v Lexington Insurance Co* (n 6), where it was held that the reinsurance contract could not reasonably be construed to be back-to-back with the underlying primary insurance contract. See also Robert M Merkin, *A Guide to Reinsurance Law* (Informa Law from Routledge 2007) 195 ff.

9 *Forsikringsaktieselskapet Vesta v Butcher* (n 8) 911 (Lord Lowry); *Groupama Navigation et Transports v Catatumbo CA Seguros* (n 6); *HIH Casualty and General Insurance Ltd v New Hampshire Insurance Co* [2001] EWCA Civ 735, [2001] 2 All ER 39 [107] (Rix LJ); *Wasa International Insurance Co Ltd v Lexington Insurance Co* (n 6) [58] (Lord Collins); *Amlin Corporate Member Ltd v Oriental Assurance Corp* [2012] EWCA Civ 1341; [2013] 1 Lloyd's Rep IR 131 [21] (Longmore LJ).

10 *Wasa International Insurance Co Ltd v Lexington Insurance Co* (n 6) [60] (Lord Collins).

11 *Forsikringsaktieselskapet Vesta v Butcher* (n 8).

12 *Forsikringsaktieselskapet Vesta v Butcher* (n 8) 895 (Lord Griffiths).

13 *Youell v Bland Welch and Co Ltd (No 1)* [1992] 2 Lloyd's Rep 423 (CA), where Staughton LJ stated that 'one can (...) readily assume that a reinsurance contract was intended to cover the same risks on the same conditions as the original contract of insurance, in the absence of some indication to the contrary'. See also *Groupama Navigation et Transports v Catatumbo CA Seguros* (n 6); *Wasa International Insurance Co Ltd v Lexington Insurance Co* (n 6) [60] (Lord Collins).

Forsikringsaktieselskapet Vesta v Butcher[14] and *Groupama Navigation et Transports v Catatumbo CA Seguros.*[15]

7.9 These were both cases where the inward contract and the outward contract were governed by different laws. However, the inward and outward contracts contained similar or identical language in both cases. More specifically, the inward and the outward contracts contained the same or a similar warranty in both cases. The reinsurers argued that the contract of reinsurance was governed by English law and that a warranty in the contract of reinsurance was to be interpreted in line with section 33(3) of the Marine Insurance Act 1906, which provided that:

[a] warranty (…) is a condition which must be exactly complied with, whether it be material to the risk or not. If it be not so complied with, then subject to any express provision in the policy, the insurer is discharged from liability as from the date of the breach of warranty (…).[16]

7.10 By contrast, the inward contracts were subject to Norwegian and Venezuelan law, respectively. Under these laws, insurers and reinsurers cannot avoid liability for the insured's or reinsured's breach of a warranty if such breach of warranty did not cause the loss.[17] In both cases, the courts dealt with the question whether the effect of similar or identical clauses in the inward and outward contracts was co-extensive where they are governed by different laws.

7.11 The courts held that 'in the absence of any express declaration to the contrary in the reinsurance policy, a warranty [should] produce the same effect in each policy. The effect of a warranty in the reinsurance policy [was] governed by the effect of the warranty in the insurance policy because the reinsurance policy [was] a contract by the underwriters to indemnify [the reinsured] against liability under the insurance policy'.[18] In other words, although the contracts of reinsurance were governed by English law, the warranty clauses in the reinsurance contracts 'took [their] effect from the particular original insurance, being shaped in [their] application by the provision[s] of' the Norwegian and Venezuelan law, respectively.[19]

2 Rebutting the presumption of back-to-back cover

7.12 The presumption that the underlying contract and the contract of reinsurance are co-extensive is merely a rule of contract construction.[20] The presumption that a

---

14 *Forsikringsaktieselskapet Vesta v Butcher* (n 8).

15 *Groupama Navigation et Transports v Catatumbo CA Seguros* (n 6).

16 Marine Insurance Act 1907, s 33(3), partially amended by the Insurance Act 2015. It is, hence, to be noted that English law has changed in this point. Under the Insurance Act 2015, the insurer is now only entitled to avoid the contract for breach of warranty if there was some causative link between the loss and that breach.

17 *Forsikringsaktieselskapet Vesta v Butcher* (n 8) 907 f (Lord Lowry); *Groupama Navigation et Transports v Catatumbo CA Seguros* (n 6).

18 *Forsikringsaktieselskapet Vesta v Butcher* (n 8) 892 (Lord Templeman). See also *Groupama Navigation et Transports v Catatumbo CA Seguros* (n 6).

19 *Groupama Navigation et Transports v Catatumbo CA Seguros* (n 6).

20 *Forsikringsaktieselskapet Vesta v Butcher* (n 8) 911 (Lord Lowry); *Groupama Navigation et Transports v Catatumbo CA Seguros* (n 6); Gürses (n 5) para 2.95.

proportional facultative reinsurance contract is back-to-back with its underlying contract is rebuttable.[21] In fact, if either party can demonstrate that when concluding the contract, the parties cannot reasonably be taken to have intended to design the reinsurance contract back-to-back with the underlying contract, the presumption will be rebutted.[22]

7.13 The presumption can be rebutted by showing that the terms of the underlying contract and those of the reinsurance contract are quite different.[23] In *Gan Insurance Co Ltd v Tai Ping Insurance Co Ltd*, the Court of Appeal held that 'where by its express terms, the risk presented to underwriters is materially different from that assumed by the reinsured, it cannot reasonably be presumed that underwriters intended to afford back-to-back cover'.[24]

7.14 Moreover, even in cases where the inward and the outward contracts contained similar language, it was held to be possible to rebut the presumption.[25] In *Wasa International Insurance Co Ltd v Lexington Insurance Co*,[26] the underlying cover and the cover of the reinsurance were both taken out for a period of three years. The issue before the court was, 'whether [the] same period of cover should receive the same interpretation in both the original insurance and the reinsurance'.[27]

7.15 A US court held that the underlying primary insurance contract was governed by the law of Pennsylvania.[28] Under the law of Pennsylvania, the reinsured was obliged to indemnify the primary insured for losses that occurred before, during and after the three-year policy period of the underlying insurance contract.[29] The reinsurer argued that the contract of reinsurance was subject to English law under which a reinsurer could not be bound to provide cover for losses occurring before and after the actual period of reinsurance.[30]

7.16 The House of Lords noted that at the time when the underlying insurance contract and the reinsurance contract were concluded, it was by no means foreseeable what 'system of law' would be applicable to the primary insurance contract. Hence, it was uncertain how the cover period in the primary insurance contract would be construed. In this respect, the case before the House of Lords differed from the cases in *Forsikringsaktieselskapet Vesta v Butcher* and *Groupama Navigation et Transports v Catatumbo CA Seguros* where the reinsurers were able to ascertain the proper law of the

---

21 Gürses (n 5) para 2.95; Birds, Lynch and Paul (n 2) para 35–067.

22 Gürses (n 5) para 2.95.

23 *Groupama Navigation et Transports v Catatumbo CA Seguros* (n 6); Merkin (n 8) 198; Gürses (n 5) para 2.95; Edelman and Burns (n 7) para 3.21.

24 *Gan Insurance Co Ltd v Tai Ping Insurance Co Ltd* [1999] EWCA Civ 1524.

25 Birds, Lynch and Paul (n 2) para 35–065.

26 *Wasa International Insurance Co Ltd v Lexington Insurance Co* (n 6).

27 *Wasa International Insurance Co Ltd v Lexington Insurance Co* (n 6) [106] (Lord Collins).

28 *Wasa International Insurance Co Ltd v Lexington Insurance Co* (n 6) [3] (Lord Phillips).

29 *Wasa International Insurance Co Ltd v Lexington Insurance Co* (n 6) [58] (Lord Collins).

30 Cf *Wasa International Insurance Co Ltd v Lexington Insurance Co* (n 6) [13] (Lord Brown).

underlying contracts.[31] For this reason, the law according to which the contract of re-insurance would–in line with the presumption–have to be construed[32] was unpredictable.[33] The House of Lords ruled that it seemed 'wholly uncommercial and outside any reasonable commercial expectation of either party' to consider the reinsurer bound to indemnify the reinsured for losses occurring before and after the reinsurance period.[34]

7.17 The House of Lords' judgment in *Wasa International Insurance Co Ltd v Lexington Insurance Co* demonstrates that the presumption of back-to-back cover is 'no inflexible rule of law that the cover of insurance and reinsurance always matched'. The presumption 'may be ousted by (…) relevant circumstances'.[35] The House of Lords applied the law of contract construction according to which the meaning of a contract is to be ascertained at the time when it is concluded, having regard to 'all the background knowledge which would reasonably have been available to the parties' at that time.[36]

3 Back-to-back cover and non-proportional reinsurance contracts

7.18 The presumption that the inward and the outward contracts are co-extensive does not extend to non-proportional reinsurance.[37] In this regard, Lord Mustill emphasised in *Axa Reinsurance (UK) Ltd v Field* that:

> *[the] assumption that where a direct insurer takes out reinsurance, and where both policies contain provisions enabling the amount of losses to be added together, the parties are likely to have intended their effect to be much the same (…) may very well be correct where the reinsurance is of the proportionate kind, under which the reinsurer is sharing the risk assumed by the direct insurer. (…) But where a reinsurer writes an excess of loss treaty for a layer of the whole account (…) of the reinsured I see no reason to assume that aggregation clauses in one are intended to have the same effect as aggregation clauses in the other. The insurances are not in any real sense back-to-back.*[38]

7.19 In excess of loss reinsurance, ie non-proportional reinsurance, the reinsurers' and the reinsureds' interest are not necessarily fully aligned. The bases on which the reinsurance premiums are assessed in proportional and non-proportional re-

---

31 *Wasa International Insurance Co Ltd v Lexington Insurance Co* (n 6) [108] (Lord Collins).

32 *Forsikringsaktieselskapet Vesta v Butcher* (n 8) 911 (Lord Lowry); *Groupama Navigation et Transports v Catatumbo CA Seguros* (n 6), where the courts held that even though the contracts of reinsurance were governed by a different law than the underlying contracts, they were to be construed to the effect that they mirrored the clauses of the underlying contract under the latter's proper law.

33 *Wasa International Insurance Co Ltd v Lexington Insurance Co* (n 6) [108] (Lord Collins).

34 *Wasa International Insurance Co Ltd v Lexington Insurance Co* (n 6) [111] (Lord Collins).

35 Merkin, Hodgson and Tyldesley (n 2) para 18–059.

36 *Investors Compensation Scheme Ltd v West Bromwich Building Society* [1997] 1 WLR 896 (HL) 912; Edelman and Burns (n 7) paras 3.04 ff.

37 *Axa Reinsurance (UK) Ltd v Field* (n 1) 1033 f (Lord Mustill); *Tokio Marine Europe Insurance Ltd v Novae Corporate Underwriting Ltd* [2013] EWHC 3362 (Comm), [2014] Lloyd's Rep IR 490 [35] (Hamblen J); Birds, Lynch and Paul (n 2) para 35–067; Merkin, Hodgson and Tyldesley (n 2) para 18–060.

38 *Axa Reinsurance (UK) Ltd v Field* (n 1) 1033 f (Lord Mustill).

insurance differ substantially.[39] As the parties do not each share a percentage of the same risk,[40] there is no reason why the terms of the underlying contract should be identical with the terms of the contract of reinsurance.[41]

7.20 This does, however, not mean that a non-proportional reinsurance contract cannot be designed to be back-to-back with the underlying contract. On the contrary, Lord Mustill suggests, the parties may write the two contracts on identical terms in order to ensure that the contracts are construed as having the same meaning.[42]

II Aggregation and the concept of back-to-back cover

7.21 If a reinsurance contract is designed to be back-to-back with its underlying policy, the aggregation clause in the reinsurance contract is to be construed as having the same meaning as the aggregation clause in the underlying policy.[43] By contrast, if the two contracts are not co-extensive, it may be that they contain different aggregation language and consequently provide for different aggregation mechanisms.[44]

7.22 Aggregation mechanisms are primarily used in excess of loss, ie non-proportional, reinsurance.[45] Yet, in quota share and surplus reinsurance treaties in particular, which are generally of the proportional type, the parties often provide for cover limits per event if they are taken out against natural catastrophes.[46] By so doing, they introduce a non-proportional element into an otherwise proportional reinsurance treaty. Whenever there is a limit or deductible per event, it appears apposite to not treat the aggregation mechanisms in the inward contract and the outward contract as being co-extensive.[47]

7.23 Consequently, there is no presumption that the aggregation mechanisms in the inward and the outward contracts are co-extensive.[48] This may be illustrated by *Axa Reinsurance (UK) Ltd v Field*.

---

39 For more detail as to the pricing of the different types of reinsurance, see Merkin (n 8) 197; Peter Liebwein, *Klassische und moderne Formen der Rückversicherung* (3rd edn, VVW 2018) 91 ff, 223 ff.

40 See paras 1.34 f.

41 Merkin, Hodgson and Tyldesley (n 2) para 18–060.

42 *Axa Reinsurance (UK) Ltd v Field* (n 1) 1034 (Lord Mustill); Edelman and Burns (n 7) para 3.28; Merkin, Hodgson and Tyldesley (n 2) para 18–060. Whether this holds true where the two contracts are governed by different laws will be discussed below, see para 7.45 ff.

43 *Axa Reinsurance (UK) Ltd v Field* (n 1) 1034.

44 *Axa Reinsurance (UK) Ltd v Field* (n 1) 1033 f (Lord Mustill). Cf also Robert W Hammesfahr and Scott W Wright, *The Law of Reinsurance Claims* (Reactions 1994) 153, where it is noted that excess of loss reinsurance contracts 'often contain an occurrence definition different from the occurrence definition in the original insurance policies reinsured'.

45 See paras 1.38, 1.42, 1.43 ff, 1.58.

46 See paras 1.28, 1.33.

47 This is because introducing a deductible or a limit into the reinsurance treaty is the equivalent of breaking up the proportional basis of the reinsurance. Consequently, the parties' interests may diverge with regard to the deductible and the cover limit. Therefore, there is no reason to assume that the aggregation mechanism in the underlying contract is intended to operate on the same terms as the aggregation mechanism in the reinsurance.

48 *Axa Reinsurance (UK) Ltd v Field* (n 1) 1033 f (Lord Mustill). See also Edelman and Burns (n 7) para 3.28; O'Neill, Woloniecki and Arnold-Dwyer (n 4) para 4–079.

1 *Axa Reinsurance v Field*

7.24 In *Axa Reinsurance (UK) Ltd v Field*[49] the issue arose as to whether the aggregation mechanisms in the inward and the outward contracts were co-extensive. In this case, three insurance underwriters negligently underwrote insurance policies. They were insured under professional liability insurance contracts containing the following aggregation language:

> *(...) the insurer's total liability under this policy in respect of any claim or claims **arising from one originating cause, or series of events or occurrences attributable to one originating cause** [or related causes] shall in no event exceed the sum stated in 3(a) of the schedule.*[50]

7.25 The errors and omissions insurer was covered under an excess of loss reinsurance treaty which was taken out on an 'each and every loss basis' and provided for a deductible as well as a cover limit. The contract further contained a definition of the term 'each and every loss' which read: 'For the purpose of this reinsurance the term "each and every loss" shall be understood to mean each and every loss (...) **arising out of one event**'.[51]

7.26 Dealing with the very same primary errors and omissions insurance policy, the Commercial Court in *Cox v Bankside Members Agency Ltd* held that the losses arose from three originating causes as three separate underwriters caused the individual losses.[52] Each of the three had failed to take adequate underwriting decisions.[53] The reinsured settled claims under the inward contract on this basis. Thereafter, it sought to recover from its reinsurer on the same basis under the reinsurance treaty.[54]

7.27 In this regard, the Court of Appeal, in *Axa Reinsurance (UK) Ltd v Field*, considered whether 'the meaning of the [aggregation] clause in the reinsurance contract [was] the same as that in the [underlying] insurance contracts'.[55] As the losses were attributable to three originating causes, the court determined whether they correspondingly arose from three events within the meaning of the aggregation clause in the reinsurance treaty.

7.28 The Court of Appeal concluded 'that there [was] no relevant difference between the two clauses' and 'that there were three events out of which (...) all the [losses] arose'.[56] In the House of Lords, Lord Mustill argued that the Court of Appeal had reached this conclusion because it had assumed that the aggregation

49 *Axa Reinsurance (UK) Ltd v Field* [1995] CLC 1504 (CA); *Axa Reinsurance (UK) Ltd v Field* (n 1).
50 *Axa Reinsurance (UK) Ltd v Field* (n 1) 1032 (Lord Mustill; emphasis added).
51 *Axa Reinsurance (UK) Ltd v Field* (n 1) 1031 f (Lord Mustill; emphasis added).
52 *Cox v Bankside Members Agency Ltd* [1995] CLC 180 (Comm) 205 (Phillips J).
53 *Cox v Bankside Members Agency Ltd* (n 52) 205 (Phillips J); *Axa Reinsurance (UK) Ltd v Field* (n 49) 1512 (Staughton LJ).
54 *Axa Reinsurance (UK) Ltd v Field* (n 49).
55 *Axa Reinsurance (UK) Ltd v Field* (n 49) 1514 f (Staughton LJ).
56 *Axa Reinsurance (UK) Ltd v Field* (n 49) 1515 (Staughton LJ).

clauses under the inward and the outward contracts were designed to be back-to-back.[57]

7.29 Lord Mustill clarified, however, that in the case of non-proportional reinsurance, there was no presumption that the terms of the inward contract had been intended to have the same effect as those in the outward contract. More specifically, he deliberated, that he could not see any reason 'to assume that aggregation clauses in one are intended to have the same effect as aggregation clauses in the other [as] [t]he insurances [were] not in any real sense back-to-back'.[58]

7.30 For procedural reasons, the House of Lords did not have a chance to pronounce its opinion about how many events the underwriters' negligent acts constituted. However, Lord Mustill stated that he believed that when interpreting the aggregation clauses in the inward and the outward contracts, 'the only safe course [was] to fall back on the words actually used'.[59] He further defined the terms 'event' and 'originating cause' and concluded that the aggregation mechanism contained in the underlying contract had 'a much wider connotation than' the one provided for in the reinsurance treaty.[60]

7.31 *Axa Reinsurance (UK) Ltd v Field* shows that there is no presumption that the aggregation mechanisms provided for in the inward and the outward contracts are intended to be back-to-back.[61] Consequently, where the aggregation clauses in the two contracts differ, the parties are taken to have intended that different aggregation mechanisms apply.[62] In such cases, an 'aggregation gap'–as Merkin calls it–opens up.[63]

2 Aggregation gap

2.1 Problem of an aggregation gap

7.32 It may be that both the underlying contract and the contract of reinsurance contain a deductible and a cover limit. In such a case, both provide for a mode of calculating the relevant loss to be tested against the deductible and the cover limit. Aggregation clauses define a mechanism for adding together individual losses to one single loss which is then presented to the insurer or the reinsurer and tested against the deductible and the cover limit in the respective contracts.[64]

---

57 *Axa Reinsurance (UK) Ltd v Field* (n 1) 1033 f (Lord Mustill). See the Court of Appeal's judgment in *Axa Reinsurance (UK) Ltd v Field* (n 49) 1511, where Phillips J stated that were a different test of causation to be applied in the inward and the outward contracts, the consequence would be a confusion which the Court of Appeal tried to avoid in *Hill v Mercantile and General Reinsurance Co Plc* [1996] 1 WLR 1239. See also *Denby v English and Scottish Maritime Insurance Co Ltd; Yasuda Fire and Marine Co of Europe Ltd v Lloyd's Underwriting Syndicates no 209, 356* [1998] Lloyd's Rep IR 343 (CA), [1998] CLC 870, 882 f (Hobhouse LJ).

58 *Axa Reinsurance (UK) Ltd v Field* (n 1) 1034 (Lord Mustill).

59 *Axa Reinsurance (UK) Ltd v Field* (n 1) 1036 (Lord Mustill).

60 *Axa Reinsurance (UK) Ltd v Field* (n 1) 1035 (Lord Mustill).

61 Rob Merkin, 'Reinsurance Aggregation' (1998) 114 LQR 390, 390.

62 Cf *Axa Reinsurance (UK) Ltd v Field* (n 1) 1034 (Lord Mustill).

63 Merkin, 'Reinsurance Aggregation' (n 61) 390.

64 See paras 3.16 ff.

7.33 The mode of calculation of the relevant loss, ie the aggregation mechanism, ultimately determines the reinsured's liability under the inward contract and the reinsurer's liability under the outward contract. Furthermore, the part of the loss that is ultimately covered by the reinsured depends on the part of the loss that is covered by the reinsurer under the outward contract. Correspondingly, the re-insurance premium is determined with regard to the relation of the reinsured's potential liability under the inward contract and the reinsurer's potential liability under the outward contract.

7.34 Consequently, the parties to a reinsurance contract must be able to pre-estimate the effects of the respective aggregation mechanisms and to compare them. In order to do so, it appears sensible to coordinate the modes of calculation of the relevant losses and, thus, the aggregation mechanisms. According to Merkin '[i]n an ideal world the bases of aggregation in the direct insurance and the reinsurance would match'.[65]

7.35 As has been set out, however, there is no presumption that the aggregation mechanism in the underlying contract is co-extensive with the aggregation mechanism in the outward contract. Where the aggregation mechanism in the underlying contract differs from the aggregation mechanism in the reinsurance contract, an aggregation gap arises[66] and complicates the assessment as to which parts of a potential loss are to be covered by the reinsured and the reinsurer respectively.

2.2 Exemplification of the effects of an aggregation gap

7.36 As mentioned previously, the House of Lords concluded in *Axa Reinsurance (UK) Ltd v Field*[67] that there is no presumption that aggregation clauses in the inward and the outward contracts are back-to-back where non-proportional re-insurance contracts are concerned.[68] This case was decided on the facts that three insurance underwriters negligently wrote insurance policies and thereby triggered liability towards Names at Lloyd's.

7.37 The extent of the loss and the structure of the inward cover are not fully known. Let us assume that the inward contract provided for a deductible of £200,000.00 and a cover limit of £1,000,000.00 per originating cause and that each of the three underwriters negligently wrote 10 policies causing a loss of £100,000.00 per written policy, so that the losses amounted to £3,000,000.00 in total. The losses were settled on the basis that they originated from three different causes. Consequently, the primary insured had to bear three deductibles. The reinsured was bound to pay three times £800,000.00,[69] ie £2,400,000.00, under the inward contract.

---

65 Merkin, 'Reinsurance Aggregation' (n 61) 390.

66 Merkin, 'Reinsurance Aggregation' (n 61) 390; O'Neill, Woloniecki and Arnold-Dwyer (n 4) para 7–018.

67 *Axa Reinsurance (UK) Ltd v Field* (n 1).

68 See paras 7.29 ff.

69 In other words, the difference between the losses stemming from one cause (10 times £100,000.00) and one deductible (£200,000.00).

7.38 By contrast, the outward contract provided for an aggregation per event. As noted above, the House of Lords did not have a chance to decide how many events the underwriters' negligent acts constituted due to procedural reasons.[70] Yet, in *Caudle v Sharp*,[71] the Court of Appeal dealt with a similar fact pattern as well as an aggregation clause similar to the one contained in the outward contract in the case at hand.[72] The Court of Appeal held that each act of negligent underwriting was to be considered a separate event.[73] Applying the Court of Appeal's reasoning to the case in *Axa Reinsurance (UK) Ltd v Field* where the three underwriters negligently underwrote 10 policies each, this amounts to 30 events in total.

7.39 Consequently, the reinsured was required to bear the deductible under the outward contract 30 times. The outward contract provided for a deductible of £500,000.00 per event.[74] As the individual losses associated with the negligent underwriting of each policy only amounted to £100,000.00, the deductible was not exhausted in any of the 30 events, so that the reinsurer's liability was not triggered.

7.40 The different definitions of what a 'loss' means under the inward and the outward contracts has led to an aggregation gap. As a consequence of the different modes of aggregating losses under the two contracts, the reinsured was bound to pay out insurance money totalling £2,400,000.00 and was unable to recover any of it from its reinsurer. Had the outward contract provided for the same aggregation mechanism as the inward contract, the losses under the outward contract would equally have been settled on the basis that three separate causes provoked the individual losses. Under this hypothesis, the reinsured would have been able to recover £500,000.00 from its reinsurer three times, ie £1,500,000.00 in total. Hence, had there not been an aggregation gap, the reinsured and the reinsurer would have both participated in covering the original loss.

3 Strategies to avoid or overcome an aggregation gap

7.41 As an aggregation gap can have adverse effects on either party, the parties may wish to avoid the effects of such a gap. They may either avoid the emergence of an aggregation gap by explicitly providing that the same aggregation mechanism applies in the outward contract as in the inward contract. Alternatively, they may provide for an aggregate extension clause in the reinsurance contract that is said to deal with the adverse effects of an aggregation gap.[75] Whether an aggregate extension clause is, in fact, a suitable means to reach that goal will be discussed.

7.42 Yet, it is to be borne in mind that, in setting the deductible and the cover limit in a contract of reinsurance, the parties will generally have regard to the applicable

---

70 See para 7.30.

71 *Caudle v Sharp* [1995] CLC 642 (CA).

72 The aggregation clause in this case read: 'For the purpose of this reinsurance the term "each and every loss" shall be understood to mean each and every loss (...) arising out of one event'.

73 In *Caudle v Sharp* (n 71) 648, Evans LJ stated that the underwriting of each policy was a separate occurrence.

74 *Axa Reinsurance (UK) Ltd v Field* (n 1) 1031 f (Lord Mustill).

75 Edelman and Burns (n 7) para 4.76.

aggregation mechanism.[76] In fact, the broader the aggregation mechanism, the easier it is for both the deductible and the cover limit to be exceeded. Thus, where the aggregation mechanism is broad, the parties might want to provide for both a higher deductible and a higher cover limit. By contrast, where the aggregation mechanism is narrow, the parties might want to provide for a lower deductible as well as a lower cover limit.

7.43 Thus, it is important to note that simply aligning the aggregation mechanism in the reinsurance agreement with the one in the underlying contract may not be enough. It is essential that the deductible and the cover limit in the reinsurance policy be chosen in relation to the aggregation mechanism to be imported from the underlying policy.

3.1 Back-to-back formulation of the aggregation clauses

7.44 When the House of Lords gave recognition to the 'aggregation gap', it acknowledged that it might have adverse effects on either party.[77] Lord Mustill emphasised that it was up to the parties to avoid an aggregation gap. 'The natural way to achieve that result is to make sure that the aggregation clauses are the same'.[78]

7.45 Yet, since there is no presumption that non-proportional reinsurance contracts are intended to be back-to-back, it is doubtful whether the parties can avoid an aggregation gap simply by using the same aggregation language in the inward and the outward contracts. As Lord Mustill stated in *Axa Reinsurance (UK) Ltd v Field*, there was 'no good reason why the meaning of a clause in (...) the direct polic[y], should necessarily fix the outer limits of the aggregation under the reinsurance'.[79] In fact, where the inward and the outward contracts are not governed by the same law, it may well be that the same aggregation language is construed differently under the respective contracts.

7.46 For example, where an inward contract is subject to New York law and provides for the aggregation of all individual losses that arise from any one event, such an event would be determined in accordance with the 'unfortunate event test'.[80] By contrast, where a reinsurance contract governed by English law contains the same aggregation language, an event would be determined having regard to the 'unities test'.[81] Clearly, the New York unfortunate event test and the English unities test are different,[82] so that an aggregation gap may potentially arise.

---

76 Cf paras 2.73 ff, 2.90.

77 *Axa Reinsurance (UK) Ltd v Field* (n 1) 1034 (Lord Mustill).

78 *Axa Reinsurance (UK) Ltd v Field* (n 1) 1034 (Lord Mustill). See also O'Neill, Woloniecki and Arnold-Dwyer (n 4) para 7–018.

79 *Axa Reinsurance (UK) Ltd v Field* (n 1) 1035 (Lord Mustill).

80 See for instance *The Arthur A Johnson Corp v Indemnity Insurance Co of North America* (1958) 6 AD2d 97 (Supreme Court, Appellate Division, First Department, New York); *Hartford Accident and Indemnity Co v Edward Wesolowski* (1973) 33 NY2d 169 (Court of Appeals of New York); *National Liability and Fire Insurance Co v Itzkowitz* (2015) 624 FedAppx 758 (United States Court of Appeals for the Second Circuit). It is to be noted that the unfortunate event test only applies in cases of third-party liability insurance.

81 For more details as to the unities test, see paras 4.14 ff.

82 Cf Graydon Shaw Staring and Dean Hansell, *Law of Reinsurance* (Thomson Reuters Westlaw 2018) s 15:4.

7.47 As there is no presumption that non-proportional reinsurance contracts are intended to be back-to-back with their underlying contracts, the reasoning of the House of Lords in *Forsikringsaktieselskapet Vesta v Butcher*[83] and the Court of Appeal in *Groupama Navigation et Transports v Catatumbo CA Seguros*[84] does not apply.[85] More specifically, if the inward and the outward contracts are not presumed to be back-to-back, the construction of the aggregation clause in the reinsurance contract does not necessarily follow the construction of the aggregation clause in the underlying contract. Indeed, there is no reason to assume that the parties intended the aggregation mechanisms in the respective contracts to produce the same effects in each policy even if they used similar or identical language.

7.48 Thus, when construing the aggregation clause in the reinsurance contract, the general English rules of contract construction apply.[86] In *Investors Compensation Scheme Ltd v West Bromwhich Building Society,* Lord Hoffmann held that '[i]nterpretation is the ascertainment of the meaning which the document would convey to a reasonable person having all the background knowledge which would reasonably have been available to the parties in the situation in which they were at the time of the contract' conclusion.[87] Consequently, when construing the aggregation clause in the reinsurance contract in light of the parties' background knowledge, it is to be determined whether they intended the aggregation mechanism contained in the reinsurance contract to produce the same effect as the one contained in the underlying policy. There is no legal presumption that the parties intended the aggregation clauses in the two contracts to be back-to-back, nor that they did not.

7.49 In summary, where the parties ensure that the aggregation clauses in the inward and the outward contracts are the same–as Lord Mustill suggested–they will also have to ensure that the two contracts are governed by the same law in order to avoid an aggregation gap. Otherwise, it may be that the aggregation clauses in the inward and the outward contracts are construed differently, each according to its governing law.

7.50 In order to avoid an aggregation gap, the parties should, therefore, expressly provide in the reinsurance contract that the aggregation mechanism in the re-insurance policy is intended to produce the same effect as the one in the underlying contract, irrespective of the law applicable to the reinsurance contract. A clause to this extent might be termed 'follow the aggregation clause'. If the parties choose to provide for a follow the aggregation clause, they should bear two things in mind. First, they should abstain from explicitly providing for an aggregation clause in the reinsurance contract that deviates from the one in the underlying policy. In including a follow the aggregation clause, the parties should agree to incorporate the aggregation mechanism contained in the underlying contract into the reinsurance

---

83 *Forsikringsaktieselskapet Vesta v Butcher* (n 8).

84 *Groupama Navigation et Transports v Catatumbo CA Seguros* (n 6).

85 In respect of this reasoning, see paras 7.21 ff.

86 *Tokio Marine Europe Insurance Ltd v Novae Corporate Underwriting Ltd* (n 37) [28] (Hamblen J).

87 *Investors Compensation Scheme Ltd v West Bromwhich Building Society* (n 36) 912 (Lord Hoffmann).

agreement. Secondly, the parties should ensure that the deductible and cover limit in the reinsurance policy is set by having regard to the aggregation mechanism to be imported from the underlying contract.

3.2 Aggregate extension clauses

7.51 Aggregate extension clauses are said to adjust the aggregation mechanism in the outward contract to the aggregation mechanism in the inward contract, provided that the inward contract is taken out on an aggregate basis.[88] Before discussing whether an aggregate extension clause can be a means to overcome the adverse effects of an aggregation gap, the basic concept of an aggregate extension clause will be laid out. Furthermore, the significance of aggregate extension clauses in treaty reinsurance will be discussed.

a Basic concept of aggregate extension clauses

7.52 Aggregate extension clauses have existed for more than 80 years.[89] Barlow, Lyde and Gilbert point out that it was 'misleading to talk about "the" aggregate extension clause (...), because there is a large number of such clauses and not one standard clause'.[90] It has been acknowledged by the Court of Appeal that there are 'varying forms' of aggregate extension clauses. In one relevant case, however, it opined that, in particular, the opening paragraph of most aggregate extension clauses appeared 'to follow a standard wording':[91]

> As regards liability incurred by the reinsured for losses on risks covering on an aggregate basis, this agreement shall protect the reinsured excess of the amounts as provided for herein in the aggregate any one such aggregate loss up to the limit of indemnity as provided for herein in all any one such aggregate loss.[92]

7.53 Consequently, the Court of Appeal emphasised that the standard wording should have an effect which does not vary from one contract to another unless the parties' intention suggested otherwise.[93] The court pointed out that aggregate extension clauses fulfil two purposes.

7.54 First, an aggregate extension clause is designed to ensure that reinsurance cover is in place where the reinsured is covering 'aggregated losses exceeding certain limits'.

---

88 Edelman and Burns (n 7) para 4.75.

89 *Denby v English and Scottish Maritime Insurance Co Ltd; Yasuda Fire and Marine Co of Europe Ltd v Lloyd's Underwriting Syndicates no 209, 356* (n 57) 879 (Hobhouse LJ). The Court of Appeal said in 1998 that aggregate extension clauses had existed for more than 60 years, ergo such clauses have now (2020) existed for more than 80 years. For a history of aggregate extension clauses, see John Butler and Robert Merkin, *Butler and Merkin's Reinsurance Law*, vol 2 (Looseleaf, Sweet & Maxwell) paras C–0314 ff.

90 Barlow Lyde & Gilbert LLP (n 7) para 28.58.

91 *Denby v English and Scottish Maritime Insurance Co Ltd; Yasuda Fire and Marine Co of Europe Ltd v Lloyd's Underwriting Syndicates no 209, 356* (n 57) 879 (Hobhouse LJ).

92 *Denby v English and Scottish Maritime Insurance Co Ltd; Yasuda Fire and Marine Co of Europe Ltd v Lloyd's Underwriting Syndicates no 209, 356* (n 57) 873 (Hobhouse LJ).

93 *Denby v English and Scottish Maritime Insurance Co Ltd; Yasuda Fire and Marine Co of Europe Ltd v Lloyd's Underwriting Syndicates no 209, 356* (n 57) 879 (Hobhouse LJ).

This is particularly important in cases of product liability.[94] In such cases, large numbers of sold products may each involve a relatively small product liability risk. Consequently, none of the individual losses exceeds the deductible, so that the insurance cover is not triggered.[95] In such a case, a producer may want to take out product liability cover which protects him against the risk of having to pay a very large number of such small claims. Where the original insurance is taken out on an 'aggregate basis', the producer is protected against 'the risk of having to pay out more than a certain sum in the aggregate in respect of such claims'.[96] Under this type of cover, the original insurer becomes liable to indemnify the original insured for every loss that the latter sustains once the aggregate of such losses has exceeded the relevant deductible. For such small losses to be aggregated they do not have to arise from the same event or cause, ie they do not have to be related, but they must accrue within the same period of insurance.[97]

7.55 An aggregate extension clause entitles the primary insurer to pass on the losses covered under the primary insurance contract in the aggregate.[98] In other words, an aggregate extension clause extends the underlying policy's 'aggregate basis' into the reinsurance contract.[99]

7.56 Secondly, providing for different mechanisms of aggregation in the underlying contract and in the contract of reinsurance results in an aggregation gap with potentially adverse effects for either party.[100] Aggregate extension clauses are said to be means to overcome such adverse effects.[101]

b Aggregate extension clause as a means to overcome the adverse effects of an aggregation gap

7.57 It has been suggested that one purpose of an aggregate extension clause is to avoid the problems associated with an aggregation gap.[102] More specifically, where the underlying cover provides for a broader aggregation mechanism than the one in the

---

94 Klaus Gerathewohl, *Rückversicherung, Grundlagen und Praxis*, vol 2 (Verlag Versicherungswirtschaft eV 1979) 325; Barlow Lyde & Gilbert LLP (n 7) paras 28.59 ff; Edelman and Burns (n 7) para 4.75; Birds, Lynch and Paul (n 2) para 35–073; O'Neill, Woloniecki and Arnold-Dwyer (n 4) para 7–017.

95 Merkin, 'Reinsurance Aggregation' (n 61) 391.

96 *Denby v English and Scottish Maritime Insurance Co Ltd; Yasuda Fire and Marine Co of Europe Ltd v Lloyd's Underwriting Syndicates no 209, 356* (n 57) 879 f (Hobhouse LJ). See also Birds, Lynch and Paul (n 2) para 35–073.

97 *Denby v English and Scottish Maritime Insurance Co Ltd; Yasuda Fire and Marine Co of Europe Ltd v Lloyd's Underwriting Syndicates no 209, 356* (n 57) 882, where Hobhouse LJ stated that the issue was to be assessed in the two cases concerned 'unrelated claims' rather than 'claims' or losses which have some causal relationship; Gerathewohl (n 94) 325; Merkin, 'Reinsurance Aggregation' (n 61) 391. Cf also Barlow Lyde & Gilbert LLP (n 7) paras 28.57, 28.62.

98 *Denby v English and Scottish Maritime Insurance Co Ltd; Yasuda Fire and Marine Co of Europe Ltd v Lloyd's Underwriting Syndicates no 209, 356* (n 57) 880 (Hobhouse LJ).

99 *Denby v English and Scottish Maritime Insurance Co Ltd; Yasuda Fire and Marine Co of Europe Ltd v Lloyd's Underwriting Syndicates no 209, 356* (n 57) 880 (Hobhouse LJ).

100 See paras 7.32 ff.

101 *Denby v English and Scottish Maritime Insurance Co Ltd; Yasuda Fire and Marine Co of Europe Ltd v Lloyd's Underwriting Syndicates no 209, 356* (n 57) 880 (Hobhouse LJ).

102 *Denby v English and Scottish Maritime Insurance Co Ltd; Yasuda Fire and Marine Co of Europe Ltd v Lloyd's Underwriting Syndicates no 209, 356* (n 57) 880, 882 (Hobhouse LJ).

reinsurance contract, an aggregate extension clause is said to entitle the reinsured to treat the losses that were aggregated in line with the aggregation mechanism in the underlying contract as an aggregated loss for the purpose of the reinsurance contract.[103]

7.58 In *Denby v English and Scottish Maritime Insurance Co Ltd*, it was held that a typical aggregate extension clause only applied where the underlying contract was taken out on an aggregate basis.[104] Generally, a contract is considered to have been taken out on an aggregate basis if the individual losses are aggregated not because they are related, ie have some causal connection, but because they occurred during the same policy period.[105] Where 'each and every loss' must be tested against the deductible and the cover limit individually, there is no aggregation whatsoever. This, the Court of Appeal stated, was the 'antithesis of providing cover on an aggregate basis'.[106]

7.59 In *Denby v English and Scottish Maritime Insurance Co Ltd*, the Court of Appeal considered whether the underlying contract had been taken out on an aggregate basis. Hobhouse LJ clarified that the contract under consideration did not provide for an aggregation of related claims, ie for an aggregation based on a common causal connection.[107] In other words, *Denby v English and Scottish Maritime Insurance Co Ltd* was not a case where the aggregate extension clause had been used to avoid the adverse effects of an aggregation gap. Rather, the issue before the court was whether unrelated claims were to be aggregated because they had been paid under the original policies during the same policy year.[108] In this regard, the Court of Appeal concluded that the underlying contract had been taken out on an 'each and every loss' rather than on an aggregate basis, meaning that the contract of reinsurance was triggered only if a single claim exceeded the deductible.[109]

7.60 Accordingly, the Court of Appeal's decision is not pertinent to the issue under scrutiny here. This is because the Court of Appeal did not examine whether a contract taken out on a per event or per cause basis, ie a contract that provides for an aggregation of related claims, can also be considered to have been taken out on an aggregate basis enabling the application of the aggregate extension clause. Yet, Hobhouse LJ noted, *obiter*, that:

---

103 *Denby v English and Scottish Maritime Insurance Co Ltd; Yasuda Fire and Marine Co of Europe Ltd v Lloyd's Underwriting Syndicates no 209, 356* (n 57) 882 (Hobhouse LJ).

104 *Denby v English and Scottish Maritime Insurance Co Ltd; Yasuda Fire and Marine Co of Europe Ltd v Lloyd's Underwriting Syndicates no 209, 356* (n 57) 874, 879 f (Hobhouse LJ); Merkin, 'Reinsurance Aggregation' (n 61) 392.

105 Deborah Tompkinson, 'Jabberwocky: Recent Decisions on the Meaning of "Event" and "Occurrence" in the English Courts' (1995) 3 International Insurance Law Review 82, 84. See also Gerathewohl (n 94) 325; Stefan Pohl and Joseph Iranya, *The ABC of Reinsurance* (VVW 2018) 36.

106 *Denby v English and Scottish Maritime Insurance Co Ltd; Yasuda Fire and Marine Co of Europe Ltd v Lloyd's Underwriting Syndicates no 209, 356* (n 57) 884 (Hobhouse LJ).

107 *Denby v English and Scottish Maritime Insurance Co Ltd; Yasuda Fire and Marine Co of Europe Ltd v Lloyd's Underwriting Syndicates no 209, 356* (n 57) 884 f (Hobhouse LJ).

108 Cf *Denby v English and Scottish Maritime Insurance Co Ltd; Yasuda Fire and Marine Co of Europe Ltd v Lloyd's Underwriting Syndicates no 209, 356* (n 57) 882 (Hobhouse LJ).

109 *Denby v English and Scottish Maritime Insurance Co Ltd; Yasuda Fire and Marine Co of Europe Ltd v Lloyd's Underwriting Syndicates no 209, 356* (n 57) 886 (Hobhouse LJ).

[w]here there is no each and every claim provision, or where there is some other provision which expressly provides for the aggregation of claims in one respect or another or in one situation or another, then such further enquiry will probably rapidly lead to the conclusion that the cover has been provided on an aggregate basis.[110]

7.61 In Edelman and Burns' view, an aggregation based on any one event or cause would be such a case.[111] In the context of aggregate extension clauses, contracts providing for an aggregation of causally related claims are, under this view, considered to have been taken out on an aggregate basis. Hobhouse LJ stated, *obiter*, that it was undisputed among the parties in the case before the court that an aggregate extension clause was applicable to overcome the problems of an aggregation gap,[112] in that the aggregation mechanism provided for in the underlying contract was carried through into the reinsurance policy.[113]

7.62 This appears remarkable for two reasons. First, the notion of 'aggregate basis' generally refers to an aggregation mechanism that is not based on the unifying factors of 'event' or 'cause'.[114] Thus, it seems odd to apply the aggregate extension clause despite the fact that the underlying contracts have not, strictly speaking, been taken out on an aggregate basis. Secondly, if the aggregation mechanism imported from the underlying contract governs the aggregation of individual losses in the reinsurance contract, this means that the imported aggregation mechanism prevails over the aggregation mechanism expressly stated in the reinsurance agreement. It is doubtful that this can be said to be in line with the parties' intention. In general, where a clause expressly contradicts an express provision in the reinsurance contract, it cannot be incorporated into the reinsurance contract.[115]

7.63 In summary, the statement in *Denby v English and Scottish Maritime Insurance Co Ltd* that an aggregate extension clause was capable of overcoming the adverse effects of an aggregation gap must be taken to be *obiter dictum*.[116] It appears doubtful that a typical aggregate extension clause will be applied where the contract provides for an event- or cause-based aggregation mechanism. Furthermore, it seems questionable whether the aggregation mechanism incorporated from the underlying contract into the contract of reinsurance will prevail over the aggregation mechanism expressly provided for in the reinsurance contract. In this regard, O'Neill and Woloniecki opine that using an aggregate extension clause to overcome an aggregation gap was 'surely something of a verbal sledgehammer being used to crack a

---

110 *Denby v English and Scottish Maritime Insurance Co Ltd; Yasuda Fire and Marine Co of Europe Ltd v Lloyd's Underwriting Syndicates no 209, 356* (n 57) 885 (Hobhouse LJ).

111 Edelman and Burns (n 7) para 4.79.

112 *Denby v English and Scottish Maritime Insurance Co Ltd; Yasuda Fire and Marine Co of Europe Ltd v Lloyd's Underwriting Syndicates no 209, 356* (n 57) 884 f (Hobhouse LJ).

113 Cf *Denby v English and Scottish Maritime Insurance Co Ltd; Yasuda Fire and Marine Co of Europe Ltd v Lloyd's Underwriting Syndicates no 209, 356* (n 57) 880 (Hobhouse LJ).

114 Tompkinson (n 105) 84. See also Gerathewohl (n 94) 325; Pohl and Iranya (n 105) 36.

115 Edelman and Burns (n 7) para 3.44. There is no indication that this is different where a reinsurance contract contains an aggregate extension clause.

116 *Denby v English and Scottish Maritime Insurance Co Ltd; Yasuda Fire and Marine Co of Europe Ltd v Lloyd's Underwriting Syndicates no 209, 356* (n 57) 882, 884 f (Hobhouse LJ).

semantic nut'.[117] Consequently, there remains substantial legal uncertainty as to whether the parties can avoid the adverse effects of an aggregation gap by providing for an aggregate extension clause of the type discussed above.[118]

7.64 If they want to avoid such effects, they are well advised to expressly state in their reinsurance agreement that the aggregation mechanism in the reinsurance contract is intended to produce the same effect as the one in the underlying contract, irrespective of the law applicable to the reinsurance contract. Such a clause might be termed 'follow the aggregation clause'. When including such language into the re-insurance contract, the parties will incorporate the aggregation mechanism contained in the underlying contract into the contract of reinsurance. Consequently, they should avoid providing for an aggregation mechanism in the reinsurance agreement that deviates from the one to be incorporated into it. Further, the parties are well advised to set the reinsurance agreement's deductible and cover limit by having re-gard to the aggregation mechanism to be imported.[119]

c Aggregate extension clauses in treaty reinsurance

7.65 In treaty reinsurance, multiple underlying insurance policies may be re-insured under one contract.[120] Generally, under a reinsurance treaty the reinsured takes out reinsurance for a whole book of business,[121] for example for all motor insurance policies underwritten by the reinsured during a specified period of time. Consequently, the risks of multiple different original insureds may be covered in a reinsurance treaty.

7.66 The fourth paragraph of the aggregate extension clause transcribed and addressed in *Denby v English and Scottish Maritime Insurance Co Ltd*[122] and also discussed in Barlow, Lyde & Gilbert LLP[123] deals with the situation where one event or originating cause affects more than one underlying policy:

Furthermore, in circumstances in which one event or occurrence or series of events or occurrences, originating from one cause, affects more than one policy or contract issued to different assured[s] or reinsureds, then in such circumstances a series of polices or contracts so issued shall be deemed to constitute one aggregate risk for the purposes of this agreement, provided that each original policy or contract has incepted during the period of this agreement (...).[124]

---

117 O'Neill, Woloniecki and Arnold-Dwyer (n 4) para 7–018.

118 For the wording of the clause, see para 7.52.

119 See also para 7.50.

120 For more details, see paras 1.11 ff.

121 Gerathewohl (n 94) 2; Andreas Schwepcke and Alexandra Vetter, *Praxishandbuch: Rückversicherung* (VVW 2017) para 641.

122 *Denby v English and Scottish Maritime Insurance Co Ltd; Yasuda Fire and Marine Co of Europe Ltd v Lloyd's Underwriting Syndicates no 209, 356* (n 57) 889 f, where the aggregate extension clause is transcribed and addressed.

123 Barlow Lyde & Gilbert LLP (n 7) para 28.65.

124 *Denby v English and Scottish Maritime Insurance Co Ltd; Yasuda Fire and Marine Co of Europe Ltd v Lloyd's Underwriting Syndicates no 209, 356* (n 57) 889 f, where the different paragraphs of the aggregate extension clause are transcribed.

7.67 This paragraph appears to have the effect that individual losses sustained by different original insureds are to be aggregated if they all arose from one unifying event or cause.[125] It suggests that where a reinsurance treaty does not contain this or a similar paragraph, losses sustained under different underlying policies cannot be aggregated even if they arose out of the same event or cause.

7.68 It is uncontroversial that aggregate extension clauses were developed in order to extend aggregation mechanisms in third-party liability insurance contracts to the respective contracts of reinsurance.[126] In such cases, it appears less likely that losses covered under different underlying policies will be aggregated under the reinsurance treaty.[127] However, aggregation gaps may arise where first-party insurance policies are reinsured under a reinsurance treaty. In catastrophe excess of loss reinsurance treaties, in particular, the risks of multiple different original insureds are reinsured under one contract. In such cases, it appears self-evident that the losses suffered by multiple different primary insureds may be aggregated under one treaty if they result from the same event or catastrophe.[128] To this extent, Merkin affords the example of the Christchurch earthquakes. In his paper, he opines that a plurality of losses that was reinsured under an excess of loss catastrophe treaty may be aggregated where the losses arise out of the same event or cause.[129]

7.69 Thus, it is submitted that individual losses incurred by different original insureds under different primary insurance policies may be aggregated under an excess of loss reinsurance treaty if they are connected by the unifying factor designated in the treaty. This is so, regardless of whether the excess of loss reinsurance treaty contains the fourth paragraph of the aggregate extension clause as mentioned above.[130]

d *American Centennial Insurance Co v INSCO Ltd*

7.70 The fourth paragraph of the model aggregate extension clause[131] was discussed in *American Centennial Insurance Co v INSCO Ltd.*[132] This case was about a D&O policy covering 14 directors and officers as well as a third-party liability policy covering the company's auditors. INSCO was reinsuring the D&O insurers and, at the

---

125 Barlow Lyde & Gilbert LLP (n 7) para 28.65.

126 Cf Barlow Lyde & Gilbert LLP (n 7) paras 28.56 ff; *Denby v English and Scottish Maritime Insurance Co Ltd; Yasuda Fire and Marine Co of Europe Ltd v Lloyd's Underwriting Syndicates no 209, 356* (n 57) 879 f (Hobhouse LJ).

127 This appears to be the case at least if an event-based aggregation mechanism is contained in the reinsurance treaty. This is because, as held in *Caudle v Sharp* (n 71), the liability triggering act or omission is to be considered the relevant event. Hence, losses resulting from different wrongful acts or omissions each covered under a different underlying policy are not to be aggregated.

128 Jacques Bourthoumieux, 'La notion d'événement dans les traités de réassurance en excédent de sinistres' (1969) 40 Revue générale des assurances terrestres 457, 459; Rob Merkin, 'The Christchurch Earthquakes Insurance and Reinsurance Issues' (2012) 18 Canterbury Law Review 119, 144.

129 Merkin, 'The Christchurch Earthquakes Insurance and Reinsurance Issues' (n 128) 144 ff.

130 For the wording of the fourth paragraph of the aggregate extension clause, see para 7.66.

131 For the wording of the fourth paragraph of the aggregate extension clause, see para 7.66.

132 *American Centennial Insurance Co v INSCO Ltd* [1996] 1 LRLR 407 (Comm).

same time, issued a direct policy to the company's auditors. INSCO then retroceded or reinsured these two policies respectively with American Centennial Insurance Co under two excess of loss reinsurance contracts.[133]

7.71 The Commercial Court mainly dealt with the interpretation of the notion of 'event'. It concluded that an event consisted of an act or omission that triggered the directors', officers' and auditors' liabilities.[134] As the fourth paragraph of the aggregate extension clause contains the words 'one event or occurrence (…) originating from one cause', the court briefly discussed whether multiple events might have ensued from one originating cause on the basis of which multiple individual losses were to be aggregated.[135]

7.72 The Commercial Court held that, in the arbitral award, there were 'no findings (…) about the nature of the acts or omissions of [the] directors and officers which gave rise to the claims against them, and nothing to indicate that those acts or omissions' resulted from one originating cause.[136] Consequently, the court did not have a chance to decide whether the 14 individual losses were to be aggregated under the contract of reinsurance on the basis that they all originated in the same cause.

7.73 It is, in fact, remarkable that the Commercial Court even considered an aggregation based on the fourth paragraph of the aggregate extension clause. The wording of this paragraph suggests that it only applies 'in circumstances in which one event (…) affects **more than one policy or contract** issued to different insureds or reinsureds'.[137] However, the question before the court was whether the 14 individual losses that occurred to 14 different directors who were insured under **one single** underlying policy were to be aggregated.[138]

7.74 Thus, *American Centennial Insurance Co v INSCO Ltd* was not a case where the operation of the fourth paragraph of the above discussed aggregate extension clause[139] could be tested. The Commercial Court could not give any guidance on the effect that such a clause has in cases where multiple individual losses are covered under more than one underlying contract issued to different insureds or reinsureds. Further, there is no indication that the Commercial Court considered aggregating the losses caused by the 14 directors with the loss caused by the auditors across two excess of loss reinsurance contracts. Indeed, there is no reason to aggregate losses across multiple reinsurance contracts.

4 Aggregation and the principle of back-to-back cover under the PRICL

7.75 The PRICL follow the English position on this point. Under the PRICL '[t]here is no presumption that aggregation clauses in reinsurance contracts are to be

---

133 *American Centennial Insurance Co v INSCO Ltd* (n 132) 408 (Moore-Bick J).

134 *American Centennial Insurance Co v INSCO Ltd* (n 132) 413 (Moore-Bick J).

135 *American Centennial Insurance Co v INSCO Ltd* (n 132) 413 f (Moore-Bick J).

136 *American Centennial Insurance Co v INSCO Ltd* (n 132) 414 (Moore-Bick J).

137 *American Centennial Insurance Co v INSCO Ltd* (n 132) 409 (Moore-Bick J; emphasis added).

138 See *American Centennial Insurance Co v INSCO Ltd* (n 132) 409 (Moore-Bick J).

139 For the wording of the fourth paragraph of the aggregate extension clause, see para 7.66.

interpreted in compliance with the primary insurance policies' aggregation clauses'.[140] Consequently, where the aggregation language in the underlying contract differs from the wording in the contract of reinsurance, each aggregation clause merits an autonomous construction under the PRICL.[141]

III Summary of the chapter

7.76 The underlying contract and the contract of reinsurance are back-to-back if the scope and the nature of the covers afforded by the two contracts are the same.[142] In fact, there is a presumption that a proportional reinsurance contract is to be construed back-to-back with its underlying contract. This presumption does not, however, extend to non-proportional reinsurance contracts.

7.77 As the subject matter of the aggregation of losses is primarily relevant in excess of loss reinsurance, ie in non-proportional reinsurance, there is no presumption that the aggregation clause set out in the reinsurance contract is to be construed in line with the aggregation clause contained in the underlying contract.[143]

7.78 If the aggregation mechanisms in the two contracts are not co-extensive, an aggregation gap arises. Such a gap can have adverse effects on either party. Therefore, the parties may seek to avoid the emergence of an aggregation gap or to overcome the adverse effects of an existing aggregation gap.

7.79 Lord Mustill suggested that an aggregation gap could be avoided by using the same aggregation language in the inward and the outward contracts. If the two contracts are governed by the same law, the parties may well avoid an aggregation gap by using the same language in both contracts. However, where the underlying contract and the contract of reinsurance are governed by different laws, it may be argued that the aggregation clauses under the inward and the outward contracts should be construed in accordance with the respective governing law. If this happens and the clauses are not construed identically under the two laws, an aggregation gap will arise.

7.80 It is said that an aggregation gap may be overcome by means of an aggregate extension clause contained in the contract of reinsurance. This would entail the aggregation mechanism contained in the underlying contract being extended to apply in the outward contract even if the outward contract expressly provides for a different aggregation mechanism. It appears questionable whether an aggregate extension clause in the reinsurance contract has the power to incorporate or integrate the underlying contract's aggregation mechanism into the reinsurance policy in cases where the reinsurance contract expressly provides for a different aggregation mechanism. Moreover, it appears to be uncertain whether an aggregate extension clause applies

---

140 Comment 36 to Article 5.1 PRICL.

141 Comment 36 to Article 5.1 PRICL.

142 *Groupama Navigation et Transports v Catatumbo CA Seguros* (n 6); *Wasa International Insurance Co Ltd v Lexington Insurance Co* (n 6) [58], [60] (Lord Collins) where the House of Lords held that this was 'the normal commercial intention'.

143 *Axa Reinsurance (UK) Ltd v Field* (n 1) 1033 f (Lord Mustill).

where the underlying contract is taken out on a per event or per cause basis rather than an aggregate basis.

7.81 Therefore, if the parties wish to avoid the adverse effects of an aggregation gap, they are well advised to expressly provide in the reinsurance contract that the aggregation mechanism in the reinsurance policy is intended to produce the same effects as the one in the underlying contract, irrespective of the law governing the reinsurance contract. Such a clause could be termed 'follow the aggregation clause'.

7.82 In line with the English position, it is not presumed under the PRICL that the aggregation mechanism in the reinsurance contract is the same as the one in the underlying contract.

CHAPTER 8

Aggregation and the principle of follow the settlements

8.1 In this chapter, the relation between the principle of follow the settlements and the aggregation of losses will be discussed. As a starting point, the need for follow the settlements clauses will be set out. Thereafter, two different well-used follow the settlements clauses will be presented and examined.

8.2 The next step will be to put the different follow the settlements clauses into context with the concept of the aggregation of losses. In so doing, the fact that aggregation clauses may be encountered in underlying contracts[1] as well as in re-insurance contracts[2] will be considered. Before closing the chapter with a summary, the relation between the subject matter of aggregation and the concept of follow the settlements in more complicated settings will be presented.

I The concept of follow the settlements

1 Starting point

8.3 As a general rule, in order to recover from its reinsurers, the reinsured 'must prove the loss in the same manner as the original assured must have proved it against [it], and the reinsurers can raise all defences which were open to the [reinsured] against the original assured'.[3] In *Hill v Mercantile and General Reinsurance Co Plc*, Lord Mustill noted that:

> *[t]here are only two rules, both obvious. First, that the reinsurer cannot be held liable unless the loss falls within the cover of the policy reinsured and within the cover created by the reinsurer. Second, that the parties are free to agree on ways of proving whether these requirements are satisfied.*[4]

8.4 However, the first rule, in particular, may prove to be very burdensome and to some extent inefficient.[5] It can be very difficult for the reinsured to prove its legal liability towards the original insured as well as the quantum of the original claim.[6]

---

1 In this chapter, the reinsured contract is either termed 'underlying contract' or 'inward contract'.

2 Having regard to the fact that risks are sometimes covered by multiple levels of reinsurance and ret-rocession agreements, the relevant contract of reinsurance is sometimes termed 'outward contract'.

3 *Re London County Commercial Reinsurance Office Ltd* [1922] 2 Ch 67 (Ch) 80 (Lawrence J); *Wasa International Insurance Co Ltd v Lexington Insurance Co* [2009] UKHL 40, [2009] 4 All ER 909 [35] (Lord Mance). See also *Equitas Ltd v R and Q Reinsurance Co (UK) Ltd* [2009] EWHC 2787 (Comm), [2009] 2 CLC 706 [46] (Gross J).

4 *Hill v Mercantile and General Reinsurance Co Plc* [1996] 1 WLR 1239 (HL) 1251 (Lord Mustill).

5 Cf Robert M Merkin, *A Guide to Reinsurance Law* (Informa Law from Routledge 2007) 237; Özlem Gürses, *Reinsuring Clauses* (Informa Law from Routledge 2010) para 6.04.

6 Robert M Merkin, Laura Hodgson and Peter J Tyldesley, *Colinvaux's Law of Insurance* (12th edn, Sweet & Maxwell 2019) para 18–070.

DOI: 10.4324/9781003080480-8   181

In treaty reinsurance, this can 'be virtually impossible'.[7] Furthermore, due to the first rule, the costly investigations of certain issues may have to be conducted twice, ie under the underlying policy and under the reinsurance policy.[8]

8.5 Yet, as Lord Mustill remarked, the reinsurer has an interest in ensuring 'that the integrity of [its] bargain is not eroded'.[9] In fact, it is in the reinsurer's interest that the reinsured only indemnifies the original insured for losses that are covered by the original policy and that it pays only the amount contracted for under the policy.[10] In certain cases, however, the reinsured has no incentive to bear the costs of examining or contesting a loss because, for example, the loss will go to an excess layer anyway.[11] Consequently, there may be good reasons for why the reinsurer does not want to be obliged to reimburse the reinsured simply on the basis that the latter has accepted liability to pay towards the original insured.[12]

8.6 'These tensions have [existed] for a century'.[13] The reinsurance market has tried to ease them by following the second rule stated by Lord Mustill.[14] It has formulated clauses defining the way in which a reinsured must prove that a loss is covered by both the underlying cover and the reinsurance contract.[15] This is precisely the aim behind so-called 'follow the settlements' clauses.

2 Follow the settlements in treaty reinsurance

8.7 The question of whether a reinsured that has paid losses pursuant to a settlement under an inward contract may recover from its reinsurer under the outward contract is pertinent to treaty reinsurance, just as it is to facultative reinsurance.[16] However, it seems to be controversial whether the concept of follow the settlements is used in treaty reinsurance.

8.8 O'Neil and Woloniecki opine that '"follow the settlements" is a concept that comes into play in facultative reinsurance' only.[17] By contrast, they argue in relation to treaty reinsurance that this question was answered by reference to the 'scope of coverage and [in the performance of which] obligations the reinsured ha[d] to exercise

---

7 Barlow Lyde & Gilbert LLP, *Reinsurance Practice and the Law* (Informa Law from Routledge 2009) para 29.2.

8 *Hill v Mercantile and General Reinsurance Co Plc* (n 4) 1251 (Lord Mustill); Merkin (n 5) 237; Gürses (n 5) para 6.02.

9 *Hill v Mercantile and General Reinsurance Co Plc* (n 4) 1251 (Lord Mustill).

10 Terry O'Neill, Jan Woloniecki and Franziska Arnold-Dwyer, *The Law of Reinsurance in England and Bermuda* (5th edn, Sweet & Maxwell/Thomson Reuters 2019) para 5–001.

11 O'Neill, Woloniecki and Arnold-Dwyer (n 10) para 5–001. For further examples, see *Hill v Mercantile and General Reinsurance Co Plc* (n 4) 1252 (Lord Mustill).

12 Merkin (n 5) 237; O'Neill, Woloniecki and Arnold-Dwyer (n 10) para 5–001.

13 *Hill v Mercantile and General Reinsurance Co Plc* (n 4) 1252 (Lord Mustill).

14 *Assicurazioni Generali SpA v CGU International Insurance Plc* [2003] EWHC 1073 (Comm), [2003] 2 All ER 425 [29]–[30] (Gavin Kealey QC); Barlow Lyde & Gilbert LLP (n 7) para 29.3; Gürses (n 5) para 6.38.

15 *Hill v Mercantile and General Reinsurance Co Plc* (n 4) 1251 (Lord Mustill).

16 O'Neill, Woloniecki and Arnold-Dwyer (n 10) para 5–004.

17 O'Neill, Woloniecki and Arnold-Dwyer (n 10) para 5–004.

care and skill in [its] management of the portfolio risks that [were] being reinsured'.[18] Gürses points out that in *Hill v Mercantile and General Reinsurance Co Plc*, Lord Mustill had said that 'a follow the settlements clause operate[d] in facultative reinsurance contracts'.[19]

8.9 Barlow, Lyde & Gilbert disagree. They acknowledge that the 'formula "follow the settlements" is largely confined to facultative reinsurances'. However, they see no reason 'why the Court of Appeal's decision [in *The Insurance Co of Africa v Scor*] on the effect of a follow the settlements clause should not be applied in a case concerning a treaty rather than a facultative contract'.[20]

8.10 The Commercial Court dealt with an excess of loss reinsurance treaty in *Hiscox v Outhwaite (No 3)*. The treaty provided that it was 'being understood that all loss settlements made by the Reassured whether by way of compromise, ex gratia or otherwise [should] in every respect be unconditionally binding upon the Reinsurers'.[21] In this context, Evans J specifically stated that '[t]he leading English authority [was] the Court of Appeal's judgment in *The Insurance Co of Africa v Scor (UK) Reinsurance Ltd*'.[22]

8.11 In *Baker v Black Sea and Baltic General Insurance Co Ltd*, the Commercial Court was likewise concerned with a reinsurance treaty which provided that '[b]eing a reinsurance subject to all terms, clauses and conditions as the original and to follow the settlements and agreements of [the reinsured] in all respects'.[23] Potter J essentially found that the principles developed in *The Insurance Co of Africa v Scor (UK) Reinsurance Co Ltd* were applicable where a reinsurance treaty contained a follow the settlements clause.[24]

8.12 In *IRB Brasil Resseguros SA v CX Reinsurance Co Ltd*, the Commercial Court dealt with an excess of loss reinsurance treaty. The treaty contained a double proviso follow the settlements clause of the type described in *Hill v Mercantile and General Reinsurance Co Plc*.[25] Burton J held that in the case of a double proviso follow the settlements clause, the reinsured was required to prove on a balance of probabilities that the losses fell within the inward and the outward covers as a matter of law.[26]

---

18 O'Neill, Woloniecki and Arnold-Dwyer (n 10) para 5–004.

19 Gürses (n 5) para 6.39. This does not, however, mean that follow the settlements clauses cannot be found in treaty reinsurance. In fact, Lord Mustill mentioned facultative reinsurance just as an example, see *Hill v Mercantile and General Reinsurance Co Plc* (n 4) 1251 f.

20 Barlow Lyde & Gilbert LLP (n 7) para 29.36.

21 *Hiscox v Outhwaite (No 3)* [1991] 2 Lloyd's Rep 524 (Comm).

22 *Hiscox v Outhwaite (No 3)* (n 21) (partly italicised by the author).

23 *Baker v Black Sea and Baltic General Insurance Co Ltd* [1995] LRLR 261 (Comm) 266 (Potter J). The case subsequently went to the Court of Appeal and the House of Lords. Neither of the courts discussed Potter J's comments on the follow the settlements clause.

24 *Baker v Black Sea and Baltic General Insurance Co Ltd* (n 23) 283 ff (Potter J).

25 *IRB Brasil Resseguros SA v CX Reinsurance Co Ltd* [2010] EWHC 974 (Comm), [2010] Lloyd's Rep IR 560 [9] (Burton J). For the double proviso follow the settlements clause, see *Hill v Mercantile and General Reinsurance Co Plc* (n 4) 1242 (Lord Mustill).

26 *IRB Brasil Resseguros SA v CX Reinsurance Co Ltd* (n 25) [41] (Burton J).

However, where treaty reinsurance is concerned in particular, it is often impossible for a reinsured to prove the validity of every individual claim comprised in a settlement.[27]

8.13 Consequently, it is to be assumed that the concept of follow the settlements is used in treaty reinsurance and that it is subject to the same rules that apply under a facultative reinsurance contract. Yet, if multiple primary insurance policies are re-insured under one reinsurance treaty, it appears even more difficult to determine legal liability for each and every loss on an individual basis.[28] This may, in fact, imply a complication with regard to the subject matter of aggregation.[29]

3 Construction of follow the settlements clauses in English law

8.14 In reinsurance contracts, a variety of different loss settlement clauses may be encountered.[30] Each different loss settlement clause merits its own construction. Lord Mustill argued that he could not see how the decision in *The Insurance Co of Africa v Scor (UK) Reinsurance Co Ltd*[31] could have any decisive bearing on the issues before him in *Hill v Mercantile and General Reinsurance Co Plc* as the loss settlement clauses were not identical in the two cases.[32]

8.15 In the following section, two different well-used follow the settlements clauses will be discussed.

3.1 Follow the settlements clause as in *ICA v Scor*

8.16 In *The Insurance Co of Africa v Scor (UK) Reinsurance Co Ltd*, the Court of Appeal dealt with the construction of the so-called 'full reinsurance clause', which read: 'Being a Reinsurance of and warranted same…terms and conditions as and to follow the settlements of the [reinsured]'.[33]

8.17 With this clause, the parties tried to ease the tension between the reinsured's need to efficiently and commercially settle inward claims and the reinsurer's need to 'ensure that the integrity of the reinsurer's bargain' is not eroded by [a settlement] over which [it] has had no control'.[34]

8.18 In the Court of Appeal's judgment, Goff LJ held that

> [i]n [his] judgment, the effect of a clause binding reinsurers to follow settlements of the insurers, [was] that the reinsurers agree[d] to indemnify insurers in the event that they settle[d] a claim by their assured, i.e. when they dispose[d], or [bound] themselves to dispose, of a claim, whether by reason of admission or compromise, provided that the claim so recognised by them [fell]

---

27 Cf *IRB Brasil Resseguros SA v CX Reinsurance Co Ltd* (n 25) [30] (Burton J); Merkin, Hodgson and Tyldesley (n 6) para 18–078. See also *Equitas Ltd v R and Q Reinsurance Co (UK) Ltd* (n 3) [62]–[72] (Gross J). For more details on this, see para 8.4.

28 Barlow Lyde & Gilbert LLP (n 7) para 29.2; Merkin, Hodgson and Tyldesley (n 6) para 18–078.

29 See paras 8.29 ff.

30 Barlow Lyde & Gilbert LLP (n 7) para 29.3.

31 *The Insurance Co of Africa v Scor (UK) Reinsurance Co Ltd* [1985] 1 Lloyd's Rep 312 (CA).

32 *Hill v Mercantile and General Reinsurance Co Plc* (n 4) 1252 (Lord Mustill).

33 *The Insurance Co of Africa v Scor (UK) Reinsurance Co Ltd* (n 31).

34 Barlow Lyde & Gilbert LLP (n 7) para 29.5. For the quote, see *Hill v Mercantile and General Reinsurance Co Plc* (n 4) 1251 (Lord Mustill).

within the risks covered by the policy of reinsurance as a matter of law, and provided also that in settling the claim the insurers [had] acted honestly and ha[d] taken all proper and businesslike steps in making the settlement.[35]

8.19 Hence, Goff LJ argued that, by the use of their follow the settlements clause, the parties to the reinsurance contract had agreed upon a way to ease the re-insured's duty to prove that a loss fell within the cover of both the underlying policy and the reinsurance contract. Under the relevant follow the settlements clause, Goff LJ noted, the reinsured's proof was built on two provisos, outlined below.[36]

8.20 First, even under the follow the settlements clause, the reinsured is required to prove that the claim as recognised and settled by the reinsured under the inward contract falls within the reinsurance cover as a matter of law.[37] It is important to note that the reinsured is not required to prove that the original loss falls within the outward contract, but only that the underlying loss *as recognised* by the reinsured falls within the outward cover as a matter of law.[38]

8.21 Secondly, applying the follow the settlement clause, the reinsured is relieved from proving that the actual loss is covered under the inward contract. Rather, the reinsured merely has to show that it has 'acted honestly and (...) taken all proper and businesslike steps in making a settlement' regarding the inward claims.[39] According to Merkin, there are two aspects to an honest and businesslike settlement:[40]

- the reinsured must reasonably interpret the underlying insurance contract and determine the chances that the original insured's claim is within the underlying policy and that there are no defences available to it, and
- the reinsured must investigate the facts in order to determine whether the inward claim is justified. If necessary, the reinsured is required to obtain expert advice on the matter.

8.22 As a consequence, the reinsurer is bound by the reinsured's honest and businesslike settlement even if it is later able to prove that there was in fact no cover under the inward contract.[41] Therefore, the reinsurer may not re-litigate the question of whether or not the reinsured was in fact liable under the underlying insurance contract.[42] The reinsurer is released from its obligation to follow the reinsured's

---

35 *The Insurance Co of Africa v Scor (UK) Reinsurance Co Ltd* (n 31).

36 Cf Gürses (n 5) paras 6.38 ff.

37 *The Insurance Co of Africa v Scor (UK) Reinsurance Co Ltd* (n 31); Gürses (n 5) para 6.38.

38 *The Insurance Co of Africa v Scor (UK) Reinsurance Co Ltd* (n 31); *Assicurazioni Generali SpA v CGU International Insurance Plc* [2004] EWCA Civ 429, [2005] Lloyd's Rep IR 457 [8] (Tuckey LJ); Gürses (n 5) para 6.38.

39 *The Insurance Co of Africa v Scor (UK) Reinsurance Co Ltd* (n 31).

40 Merkin, Hodgson and Tyldesley (n 6) para 18–071.

41 *The Insurance Co of Africa v Scor (UK) Reinsurance Co Ltd* (n 31); Barlow Lyde & Gilbert LLP (n 7) para 29.16.

42 *Assicurazioni Generali SpA v CGU International Insurance Plc* (n 38) [18] (Tuckey LJ); O'Neill, Woloniecki and Arnold-Dwyer (n 10) para 5–019.

settlement only if it[43] can demonstrate that the reinsured acted in bad faith or in an unbusinesslike manner and that but for this conduct there would have been a different outcome.[44]

8.23 In summary, where a contract of reinsurance, which is subject to English law, contains a follow the settlements clause of the type discussed in *The Insurance Co of Africa v Scor (UK) Reinsurance Co Ltd*,[45] the reinsured may recover from the reinsurer where it has recognised an inward claim, has deemed it capable of cover under the inward policy, has compromised it properly and then has proved that the claim so recognised falls within the outward cover.

3.2 Follow the settlements clause as in *Hill v Mercantile*

8.24 In *Hill v Mercantile and General Reinsurance Co Plc*, the House of Lords dealt with the construction of a so-called 'double proviso follow the settlements clause',[46] which read:

> All loss settlements by the reassured including compromise settlements and the establishment of funds for the settlements of losses shall be binding upon the reinsurers, providing such settlements are within the terms and conditions of the original policies and/or contracts ... and within the terms and conditions of this reinsurance.[47]

8.25 Lord Mustill divided this clause into two provisos, the first being that 'such settlements are within the terms and conditions of the original policies and/or contracts', the second being that the settlements are also 'within the terms and conditions of [the] reinsurance'.[48] Pursuant to this follow the settlements clause, the reinsured is under the burden to prove that it satisfies both provisos to a standard of a balance of probabilities.[49]

8.26 By contrast to the follow the settlements clause in *The Insurance Co of Africa v Scor (UK) Reinsurance Co Ltd*, the follow the settlements clause used in *Hill v Mercantile and General Reinsurance Co Plc* requires stricter proof. Under Lord Mustill's first proviso, it does not suffice that the reinsured proves that it had acted honestly and had taken all proper and businesslike steps in making the settlement under the inward contract. Rather, the reinsured is required to prove that the settlement is within the cover of the underlying contract as a matter of law.[50]

---

43 In fact, the burden is on the reinsurer to prove that the reinsured did not act in good faith and in a businesslike fashion when settling the underlying claim, see *Charman v Guardian Royal Exchange Assurance Plc* [1992] 2 Lloyd's Rep 607 (Comm) 613 (Webster J).

44 Merkin, Hodgson and Tyldesley (n 6) para 18–072. See also Colin Edelman and Andrew Burns, *The Law of Reinsurance* (2nd edn, OUP 2013) para 4.20.

45 *The Insurance Co of Africa v Scor (UK) Reinsurance Co Ltd* (n 31).

46 Edelman and Burns (n 44) para 4.15.

47 *Hill v Mercantile and General Reinsurance Co Plc* (n 4) 1242 (Lord Mustill).

48 *Hill v Mercantile and General Reinsurance Co Plc* (n 4) 1247 (Lord Mustill).

49 *Equitas Ltd v R and Q Reinsurance Co (UK) Ltd* (n 3) [65] (Gross J).

50 *Equitas Ltd v R and Q Reinsurance Co (UK) Ltd* (n 3) [66] (Gross J). Gürses (n 5) para 8.34. See, however, *IRB Brasil Resseguros SA v CX Reinsurance Co Ltd* (n 25) [13], where Burton J stated that '[g]uidance in respect of satisfaction of the first proviso can and should be drawn from the "single proviso" cases, particularly where (...) the settlements by the insurer were pursuant to a compromise

8.27 Two further aspects of the judgment in *Hill v Mercantile and General Reinsurance Co Plc* are to be noted. First, the follow the settlements clause was held to have 'draw[n] a distinction between the facts which generate claims under [the inward and outward] contract(...) [respectively], and the legal extent of the respective covers'.[51] Lord Mustill noted that the purpose of this distinction was 'to ensure that the reinsurer's original assessment and rating of the risks assumed are not falsified by a settlement which, even if soundly based on the fact, transfers into the inward or outward policies, or both, risks which properly lie outside them'.[52]

8.28 Secondly, Lord Mustill emphasised that the follow the settlements clause in the outward contract[53] dealt with settlements under the inward contract and not any other contract.[54] Consequently, if the follow the settlements clause is contained in a retrocession agreement, the relevant settlement is the one undertaken in the reinsured reinsurance contract and not a settlement in the primary insurance policy.[55]

II Aggregation and the concept of follow the settlements

8.29 Both follow the settlements clauses, ie the one dealt with in *The Insurance Co of Africa v Scor (UK) Reinsurance Co Ltd*[56] and the one interpreted in *Hill v Mercantile and General Reinsurance Co Plc*, embrace Lord Mustill's first rule that a reinsurer cannot be held liable unless the reinsured can prove that the loss falls within the cover of the policy reinsured and within the cover created by the reinsurance.[57] Yet, the clauses differ in the proof required of the reinsured.[58]

8.30 Aggregation clauses characterise the quantitative scope of the insurance and reinsurance cover.[59] Under both types of follow the settlements clauses, the questions of whether a loss is within the quantitative scope of the underlying

---

agreement'. Burton J then quoted *Hiscox v Outhwaite (No 3)* (n 21). 'Evans J concluded that "the reinsurer may well be bound to follow the insurer's settlement of the claim which arguably, as a matter of law, is within the scope of the original insurance, regardless of whether the court might hold, if the issue were fully argued before it, that as a matter of law the claim would fail." The common ground between the parties (...) was that assistance could be drawn in this case (notwithstanding that it is a "double proviso" case) from the first instance and Court of Appeal decisions in *Assicurazioni Generali SpA v CGU International Insurance Plc*'.

51 *Hill v Mercantile and General Reinsurance Co Plc* (n 4) 1252 f (Lord Mustill).

52 *Hill v Mercantile and General Reinsurance Co Plc* (n 4) 1253 f (Lord Mustill).

53 He thereby refers to the retrocession agreement.

54 *Hill v Mercantile and General Reinsurance Co Plc* (n 4) 1246 f, 1253 f (Lord Mustill). See also *Equitas Ltd v R and Q Reinsurance Co (UK) Ltd* (n 3) [67] (Gross J).

55 *Hill v Mercantile and General Reinsurance Co Plc* (n 4) 1246 f, 1253 f (Lord Mustill); *Equitas Ltd v R and Q Reinsurance Co (UK) Ltd* (n 3) [67] (Gross J).

56 *The Insurance Co of Africa v Scor (UK) Reinsurance Co Ltd* (n 31).

57 *Hill v Mercantile and General Reinsurance Co Plc* (n 4) 1251 (Lord Mustill).

58 See para 8.26.

59 Cf Klaus Gerathewohl, *Rückversicherung, Grundlagen und Praxis*, vol 1 (Verlag Versicherungswirtschaft eV 1976) 187; Andreas Schwepcke and Alexandra Vetter, *Praxishandbuch: Rückversicherung* (VVW 2017) para 858; Peter Liebwein, *Klassische und moderne Formen der Rückversicherung* (3rd edn, VVW 2018) 184, 191.

cover and within the cover of the reinsurance may depend on aggregation clauses.

8.31 Furthermore, it is to be noted that the concept of the aggregation of losses refers to the losses that are incurred by the primary insured and not to losses sustained by any insurance or reinsurance company due to their duty to pay insurance money,[60] whereas the concept of follow the settlements only deals with settlements under the inward contract and not necessarily a settlement between the primary insured and the primary insurer.[61] Bearing this in mind, different follow the settlements clauses may have different implications on the aggregation of losses. These implications will be discussed in the next section.

1 Follow the settlements clause as in *ICA v Scor*

8.32 Under a follow the settlements clause of the type discussed in *The Insurance Co of Africa v Scor (UK) Reinsurance Co Ltd*, the reinsured is required to prove that it had acted honestly and had taken all proper and businesslike steps in making a settlement under the inward contract (second proviso).[62] Furthermore, the reinsured has to prove that its settlement *as recognised* under the inward contract falls within the risks covered by the outward contract as a matter of law (first proviso).[63]

1.1 Settlement in good faith and a businesslike manner (second proviso)

8.33 A contract of reinsurance is triggered where a loss falls both within the inward and the outward cover.[64] An analysis of the relation between the second proviso of the follow the settlements clause as discussed in *The Insurance Co of Africa v Scor (UK) Reinsurance Co Ltd* and aggregation clauses must be undertaken against this background.

a Aggregation under the inward contract is relevant for determining whether the inward contract is triggered

8.34 As has been mentioned, a reinsurer is required to indemnify its reinsured only where a loss is covered under the inward contract.[65] Under the second proviso of the follow the settlements clause as discussed in *The Insurance Co of Africa v Scor (UK) Reinsurance Co Ltd*, the reinsured must, therefore, act in good faith and in a

---

60 For more detail, see paras 2.19 ff.

61 *Hill v Mercantile and General Reinsurance Co Plc* (n 4) 1246 f, 1253 f (Lord Mustill); *Equitas Ltd v R and Q Reinsurance Co (UK) Ltd* (n 3) [67] (Gross J). See, however, *Tokio Marine Europe Insurance Ltd v Novae Corporate Underwriting Ltd* [2014] EWHC 2105 (Comm), [2014] Lloyd's Rep IR 638 [23]–[32], where in respect of a retrocession agreement, Field J discussed whether a settlement between the primary insured and the primary insurer had been made in good faith and in a businesslike fashion.

62 *The Insurance Co of Africa v Scor (UK) Reinsurance Co Ltd* (n 31).

63 *The Insurance Co of Africa v Scor (UK) Reinsurance Co Ltd* (n 31).

64 *Hill v Mercantile and General Reinsurance Co Plc* (n 4) 1251 (Lord Mustill); Edelman and Burns (n 44) para 4.01.

65 *Hill v Mercantile and General Reinsurance Co Plc* (n 4) 1251 (Lord Mustill); Edelman and Burns (n 44) para 4.01.

businesslike fashion in determining whether a loss falls within the cover of the inward contract.[66]

8.35 This comprises two aspects. First, the reinsured is obliged to determine the inward contract's scope of cover by interpreting the policy.[67] This, for example, entails determining the inward contract's quantitative scope of cover as well as the operation of an aggregation mechanism which may be contained in the inward contract.

8.36 Secondly, the reinsured is required to ascertain the facts of the case and determine whether the inward policy has been triggered and the amount claimed is justified in a specific case.[68] The aggregation mechanism contained in the inward contract is to be applied to the facts at hand. The resulting (aggregated) loss is then to be tested against the inward contract's deductible and its cover limit. Under the inward contract, a loss is only covered if the (aggregated) loss exceeds its deductible.

8.37 Where the reinsurer can prove that the reinsured has acted in bad faith or in an unbusinesslike manner in determining whether the inward claims were within the inward contract's quantitative scope of cover, the latter loses its prerogatives flowing from the follow the settlements clause.[69]

b Reinsurer bound to follow the reinsured's good faith identification of individual losses

8.38 As mentioned previously, the concept of aggregation of losses refers to the losses that are incurred by the primary insured and not to losses sustained by any insurance or reinsurance company due to its duty to pay insurance or reinsurance money.[70] Consequently, the aggregation mechanisms of both the inward and the outward contracts are based on the primary insured's original losses. Hence, the identification of these individual losses is of crucial importance.

8.39 This begs the question of whether, under the second proviso of the follow the settlements clause as discussed in *The Insurance Co of Africa v Scor (UK) Reinsurance Co Ltd*, the reinsurer is bound by the identification of the individual losses *as recognised* in the settlement of the inward contract. There appears to be no case law dealing with this question. Yet, the nature and the quantum of the individual losses sustained by the primary insured are factual matters and it is likely that a reinsurer will not be allowed to second-guess a settlement of relating issues under the inward contract.

---

66 Cf *Equitas Ltd v R and Q Reinsurance Co (UK) Ltd* (n 3) [29], where Gross J stated that 'the question arises whether but for the erroneous aggregation (...), the underlying layers would have been properly exhausted'. It may be noted, however, that the court was not faced with a follow the settlements clause of the type discussed in *The Insurance Co of Africa v Scor (UK) Reinsurance Co Ltd* (n 31). The issue exists irrespective of the type of the follow the settlements clause.

67 Merkin, Hodgson and Tyldesley (n 6) para 18–071.

68 Merkin, Hodgson and Tyldesley (n 6) para 18–071.

69 Cf *Charman v Guardian Royal Exchange Assurance Plc* (n 43) 613 (Webster J); Edelman and Burns (n 44) para 4.20.

70 For more detail, see paras 2.19 ff.

8.40 Therefore, it is likely that, under a follow the settlements clause of the type as discussed in *The Insurance Co of Africa v Scor (UK) Reinsurance Co Ltd*, the reinsured must act in good faith and take all businesslike steps in identifying the individual losses incurred by the primary insured and covered under the inward contract.[71] In fact, the reinsured is required to act in good faith and in a businesslike manner in classifying an individual loss, in determining its quantum as well as in identifying where and when it occurred. The individual losses identified and recognised in good faith and in a businesslike manner under the inward contract will then form the basis for applying the outward contract's aggregation mechanism (first proviso).

8.41 In order to be able to examine whether the reinsured acted in good faith and in a businesslike fashion, the reinsurer has a right to be provided with information and documents evidencing how a claim was settled.[72] The reinsurer may claim and prove that the reinsured acted in bad faith or in an unbusinesslike fashion in recognising the individual losses covered under the inward contract. For instance, the reinsurer may prove that an individual loss recognised by the reinsured as a fire loss was an excluded flood loss rather than a fire loss and that the reinsured was aware of this. If the reinsurer succeeds in so proving, it will not be bound to follow the reinsured's settlement on this point.[73] This is to say that the reinsured will lose its prerogatives flowing from the follow the settlements clause, so that it is required to prove the existence and the quantum of each individual loss under the inward contract as a matter of law.[74]

8.42 Yet, where the reinsured has acted in good faith and taken all businesslike steps to identify the individual losses suffered by the primary insured and covered under the inward contract, the reinsurer has no right to second-guess whether the individual losses recognised by the reinsured in its settlement under the inward contract were truly within the cover of the inward contract as a matter of law.[75] Rather, the reinsurer is obliged to accept that the recognised individual losses incurred by the primary insured fall within the cover of the inward contract. On this basis, the reinsured is then required to prove that the individual losses *as recognised* are within the cover of the reinsurance as a matter of law (first proviso).[76]

8.43 For example, where a reinsured acting in good faith and in a businesslike manner recognises an individual loss as a fire loss in the amount of £10,000 that occurred in London on 1 January 2020, the reinsurer may not second-guess this

---

71 Cf *Assicurazioni Generali SpA v CGU International Insurance Plc* (n 14) [36]–[40] (Gavin Kealey QC); Edelman and Burns (n 44) para 4.23. Both sources deal with the first proviso rather than the second.

72 *Charman v Guardian Royal Exchange Assurance Plc* (n 43) 614 (Webster J); Edelman and Burns (n 44) para 4.20.

73 Cf Merkin, Hodgson and Tyldesley (n 6) para 18–071.

74 Cf Edelman and Burns (n 44) para 4.12.

75 This is precisely the prerogative provided to the reinsured under the follow the settlements clause of the type discussed in *The Insurance Co of Africa v Scor (UK) Reinsurance Co Ltd* (n 31). Cf also *Assicurazioni Generali SpA v CGU International Insurance Plc* (n 38) [8], [18] (Tuckey LJ).

76 Cf *The Insurance Co of Africa v Scor (UK) Reinsurance Co Ltd* (n 31); *Assicurazioni Generali SpA v CGU International Insurance Plc* (n 38) [18] (Tuckey LJ).

settlement. Rather, the reinsurer must accept that the presented loss is a fire loss in the said amount that occurred in London on 1 January 2020. Under the first proviso of the follow the settlements clause, the aggregation clause in the outward contract will then be applied to this loss *as recognised*.[77]

8.44 In summary, it is likely that a reinsurer will be bound to follow a reinsured's good faith and businesslike identification of individual losses under the inward contract. The aggregation mechanism provided for in the outward contract will be applied to the individual losses *as recognised* under the inward contract.

c Aggregation under the inward contract is no basis for aggregation under the outward contract

8.45 As has been mentioned, it is the individual losses suffered by the primary insured that are the subject of aggregation under both the inward and the outward contracts.[78] Therefore, the aggregation mechanism under the outward contract is not based on an aggregated loss that was added together in compliance with the aggregation mechanism provided for in the inward contract. Rather, the aggregation mechanism under the outward contract is applied directly to the individual losses suffered by the primary insured.[79]

8.46 Where the question of how a loss is calculated under the outward contract is concerned, the mode of operation of an aggregation mechanism under the inward contract, thus, appears wholly irrelevant. Therefore, the reinsured's conduct in settling a point of aggregation under the inward contract should not have any bearing on the operation of an aggregation clause under the outward contract.

8.47 This may be illustrated by *Axa Reinsurance (UK) Ltd v Field*.[80] In this case, the relation between a follow the settlements clause in an excess of loss treaty and the concept of aggregation was discussed. Three insurance underwriters were held liable for the negligent underwriting of insurance policies. The underwriters were insured under errors and omissions professional indemnity insurance contracts. In *Cox v Bankside Members Agency Ltd*,[81] where the same clause and the same facts were under scrutiny, it was held that the underwriters' liability arose from three originating causes. In *Axa Reinsurance (UK) Ltd v Field*, the reinsured settled claims under the inward contract on this basis and sought to recover from its reinsurers under the outward contract.[82]

8.48 At first instance, Phillips J dealt with the question of whether, by reason of the follow the settlements clause in the outward contract, the reasoning of *Cox v Bankside Members Agency Ltd*, based as it was on the aggregation clause in the

---

77 This is, of course, provided that the individual loss is within the outward contract's geographical and temporal scopes of cover and is not otherwise excluded.

78 See paras 2.19 ff.

79 See paras 2.19 ff.

80 *Axa Reinsurance (UK) Ltd v Field* [1995] CLC 1504 (CA).

81 *Cox v Bankside Members Agency Ltd* [1995] CLC 671 (CA).

82 *Axa Reinsurance (UK) Ltd v Field* (n 80).

inward contract, applied to the aggregation clause contained in the outward contract.[83] The parties and Phillips J agreed that where the aggregation clause under the inward contract and the one in the outward contract were not back-to-back, the reinsured could not rely on the follow the settlements clause.[84] In other words, a follow the settlements clause does not affect the relation between the mode of operation of an aggregation mechanism under the inward contract and the operation of the aggregation mechanism under the outward contract where the aggregation clauses are not co-extensive.

8.49 However, even in cases where the aggregation mechanisms under the inward and the outward contracts are back-to-back, the settlement of an issue of aggregation under the inward contract does not dictate the operation of an aggregation mechanism under the outward contract by reason of a follow the settlements clause.

8.50 In *Assicurazioni Generali SpA v CGU International Insurance Plc,* it was held that 'where the contracts are back to back any proper businesslike settlement by the [re]insured' did not dictate that it was entitled to an indemnity from its reinsurer. Rather, where the claim *as recognised* by the reinsured did not fall within the risks covered by the reinsurance as a matter of law, it would follow that the reinsured was not required to follow the reinsured's settlement.[85]

8.51 Where aggregation clauses are concerned, the claims *as recognised* do not refer to the aggregated loss under the inward contract. They refer to the individual losses sustained by the primary insured.[86] Accordingly, testing whether the claim recognised under the inward contract is within the cover of the outward contract means applying the aggregation clause contained in the outward contract to the individual losses suffered by the primary insured *as recognised* under the inward contract.[87]

8.52 In summary, as the aggregation mechanism provided for in the outward contract is not based on the aggregation undertaken in the inward contract, the

---

83 See *Axa Reinsurance (UK) Ltd v Field* (1996) 1 WLR 1026 (HL) 1032, where Lord Mustill presented the case's procedural history.

84 *Axa Reinsurance (UK) Ltd v Field* [1995] CLC 1504 (Comm) 1505 ff (Phillips J; transcribed in the Court of Appeal's decision). The case went on to the Court of Appeal which approved this conclusion. It further held that the aggregation mechanism in the inward contract and the one in the outward contract were back-to-back which was why the reinsurer was bound to follow the settlement of the aggregation point in the inward contract, *Axa Reinsurance (UK) Ltd v Field* (n 80). The House of Lords disagreed on the latter point, holding that the aggregation mechanisms in the inward and outward contract were not back-to-back and, thus, merited an autonomous interpretation, *Axa Reinsurance (UK) Ltd v Field* (n 83) 1034 ff (Lord Mustill).

85 *Assicurazioni Generali SpA v CGU International Insurance Plc* (n 38) [9] (Tuckey LJ). See also *Hiscox v Outhwaite (No 3)* (n 21) 530 (Evans J).

86 See paras 8.38 ff. See also paras 2.19 ff.

87 See, however, *IRB Brasil Resseguros SA v CX Reinsurance Co Ltd* (n 25) [46], where Burton J agreed with the arbitrators that 'in any event (...) there was a finding of fact that "in the context of the excess of loss (...) reinsurance written by IRB the claim was settled by CX Re as a single loss"'. It seems that the Commercial Court thereby expressed that IRB was bound to follow CX Re's settlement with regard to the number of losses as the aggregation clauses under the inward and the outward contract were back-to-back.

settlement of an aggregation issue under the inward contract does not affect the operation of an aggregation mechanism under the outward contract by reason of a follow the settlements clause.

1.2 Within the terms of the outward contract as a matter of law (first proviso)

8.53 Under the first proviso discussed in *The Insurance Co of Africa v Scor (UK) Reinsurance Co Ltd*, the reinsured is not required to prove that the original loss falls within the risks covered by the reinsurance agreement, 'but rather that the [loss] *so recognised* by [the reinsured] falls within the risks covered by the policy of re-insurance as a matter of law'.[88]

8.54 This is to say that the reinsured does not have to prove that the original loss was in fact covered under the outward contract. It is solely required to show that the basis on which it settled the inward claim was one which fell within the terms of the reinsurance as a matter of law.[89]

8.55 It has been submitted that the individual losses suffered by the primary insured and recognised by the reinsured under the inward contract are crucial for applying the aggregation mechanism under the outward contract.[90] They are, consequently, 'the basis on which [the reinsured] settle[s]' an issue of aggregation under the inward contract.[91] Under the first proviso, the individual losses *as recognised* under the inward contract must, therefore, fall within the cover of the reinsurance as a matter of law. Where the individual losses *as recognised* by the reinsured in the settlement of the inward contract are generally[92] within the cover of the outward contract, the latter's aggregation mechanism will be applied to them. The product of this aggregation is then to be tested against the outward contract's deductible and cover limit, by virtue of which it is determined whether the aggregated loss is within the outward contract's quantitative scope of cover.

2 Follow the settlements clause as in *Hill v Mercantile*

8.56 Under a follow the settlements clause of the type interpreted in *Hill v Mercantile and General Reinsurance Co Plc*, the reinsured is required to establish two things. First, it has to show that a settlement under the inward contract actually falls within the cover of the inward contract as a matter of law.[93] Secondly, the reinsured

---

88 *The Insurance Co of Africa v Scor (UK) Reinsurance Co Ltd* (n 31) (emphasis added); *Assicurazioni Generali SpA v CGU International Insurance Plc* (n 38) [8] (Tuckey LJ).

89 *Assicurazioni Generali SpA v CGU International Insurance Plc* (n 38) [18] (Tuckey LJ).

90 See paras 8.38 ff, 8.45 ff. See also paras 2.19 ff.

91 For the quote, see *Assicurazioni Generali SpA v CGU International Insurance Plc* (n 38) [18] (Tuckey LJ). By contrast, the mode of operation of the aggregation mechanism under the inward contract or its product of aggregation is irrelevant for testing whether a loss is within the quantitative scope of cover provided by the outward contract.

92 This concerns the outward contract's geographical and temporal scopes of cover and also its exclusions.

93 Expressly dealing with the follow the settlements clause discussed in *Hill v Mercantile and General Reinsurance Co Plc* (n 4), see *Equitas Ltd v R and Q Reinsurance Co (UK) Ltd* (n 3) [66] (Gross J).

also has to prove that the settlement falls within the cover of the outward contract as a matter of law.[94]

8.57 In fact, the reinsured is required to separately determine the scopes of cover of the inward and the outward contracts. This includes determining the quantitative scope of cover of each contract. In so doing, the reinsured is required to identify possible aggregation clauses in the inward and the outward contracts and to assess their modes of operation. Further, it must ascertain the facts of the case at hand and separately determine whether the inward contract and the outward contract have been triggered. As the concept of aggregation of losses deals with losses incurred by the primary insured,[95] this latter task entails the determination of the individual losses sustained by the primary insured.

8.58 In determining whether a loss is within the quantitative scope of cover of the inward contract, the reinsured has to determine the individual losses sustained by the primary insured and apply the aggregation mechanism contained in the inward contract to these losses. The aggregated loss must then be tested against the inward contract's deductible and cover limit.

8.59 The situation is similar in respect of determining whether a loss is within the outward contract's quantitative scope of cover. The reinsured, first, has to determine each individual loss suffered by the primary insured that is covered under the inward contract. Secondly, it must be examined whether the individual losses suffered by the primary insured are generally within the cover of the outward contract.[96] Thirdly, the aggregation mechanism provided for in the outward contract is to be applied to these individual losses. In order to determine whether the reinsured's claim is within the outward contract's quantitative scope of cover, the aggregated loss must then be tested against the outward contract's deductible and cover limit.

3 Aggregation and follow the settlements clauses in more complicated settings

8.60 In particular, where there is a chain of direct insurance, reinsurance and retrocession agreements, it is more difficult to cope with the relation between aggregation clauses and follow the settlements clauses. Moreover, challenges may also arise where a global settlement has been reached under insurance or reinsurance contracts down the chain. In the following section, these situations shall be discussed.

3.1 Multiple levels of reinsurance and retrocession

8.61 With particular regard to multiple levels of reinsurance and retrocessions, it may prove difficult to determine whether the underlying layers have been properly exhausted.[97] Where an aggregation mechanism is applied erroneously at an underlying layer, this layer may faultily be perceived to have been exhausted when it has in

---

94 Expressly dealing with the follow the settlements clause as interpreted in *Hill v Mercantile and General Reinsurance Co Plc* (n 4), see *Equitas Ltd v R and Q Reinsurance Co (UK) Ltd* (n 3) [65] (Gross J).

95 For more detail, see paras 2.19 ff.

96 This is to say that it is to be examined whether the individual losses are within the outward contract's geographical and temporal scopes of cover and are not otherwise excluded.

97 *Equitas Ltd v R and Q Reinsurance Co (UK) Ltd* (n 3) [1] (Gross J).

fact not been. Where an underlying layer has not been exhausted, all the layers above that layer will not have been triggered. Hence, whether aggregation mechanisms have been applied correctly may be crucial at every level of the chain of contracts, as this may have an impact on whether any particular contact of reinsurance in the chain has been triggered.

8.62 In *Equitas Ltd v R and Q Reinsurance Co (UK) Ltd*, the Commercial Court dealt with various retrocessional excess of loss contracts.[98] The facts of the case were as follows: in August 1990, Iraq invaded Kuwait and seized 15 aircraft and spares owned by Kuwait Airways Corp (KAC) at Kuwait International Airport. At this time, a British Airways (BA) aircraft was also at that airport,[99] which was un-planned. Subsequently, the KAC aircraft and spare parts were flown to Iraq, while the BA aircraft was left at Kuwait International Airport. In February 1991, the BA aircraft was eventually destroyed by allied forces during 'operation "Desert Storm"'.[100]

8.63 The KAC fleet, together with the BA aircraft, had been reinsured. In the London Market excess of loss spiral, these risks had been retroceded multiple times.[101] Equitas was a retrocedent and R and Q was a retrocessionaire at a higher level within the spiral.[102] The reinsurance contracts contained an aggregation clause of the following type: '"Loss" under this contract means loss, damage, liability or expense arising from any one event (...)'.[103]

8.64 In the London Market excess of loss spiral, the KAC losses and the BA loss were all considered to have arisen from the invasion of Kuwait by Iraq, ie from one single event. Consequently, the individual losses were presented and paid as one single loss under the applicable aggregation clauses.[104] In fact, 'the market operated on that basis in relation to inwards and outwards claims for a period of about five years'.[105]

8.65 However, in *Scott v The Copenhagen Reinsurance Co (UK) Ltd*, the aggregation of KAC losses with the BA loss was questioned. In this case, the Court of Appeal held that the BA loss had not resulted from the invasion of Kuwait by Iraqi forces. Consequently, the KAC losses and the BA loss had not arisen from the same event and ought not to have been aggregated with the KAC losses.[106] After the

---

98 *Equitas Ltd v R and Q Reinsurance Co (UK) Ltd* (n 3) [1] (Gross J).

99 '[F]or simplicity', this was not explicitly dealt with in *Hill v Mercantile and General Reinsurance Co Plc* (n 4) 1241 (Lord Mustill).

100 *Equitas Ltd v R and Q Reinsurance Co (UK) Ltd* (n 3) [9] (Lord Mustill).

101 For more details regarding the London Market excess of loss spiral, see *Deeny v Gooda Walker Ltd* [1994] CLC 1224 (Comm) 1231 f (Phillips J).

102 *Equitas Ltd v R and Q Reinsurance Co (UK) Ltd* (n 3) [1] (Gross J).

103 *Scott v The Copenhagen Reinsurance Co (UK) Ltd* [2003] EWCA Civ 688, [2003] 2 All ER 190 [6] (Rix LJ).

104 *Equitas Ltd v R and Q Reinsurance Co (UK) Ltd* (n 3) [11] (Gross J).

105 *Equitas Ltd v R and Q Reinsurance Co (UK) Ltd* (n 3) [11] (Gross J).

106 *Scott v The Copenhagen Reinsurance Co (UK) Ltd* (n 103) [83] (Rix LJ).

judgment in *Scott v The Copenhagen Reinsurance Co (UK) Ltd*, it was clear that the individual losses had wrongly been aggregated under the reinsurance and retrocession agreements further down the spiral. Thus, the question arose as to whether Equitas as retrocedent further up the spiral was required to present to R and Q as retrocessionaire correctly aggregated losses upwards through the entire spiral.[107]

8.66 As the retrocession agreement between Equitas and R and Q contained a follow the settlements provision of the type discussed in *Hill v Mercantile and General Reinsurance Co Plc*,[108] Equitas was required to prove that the losses settled under the inward contract were covered by the inward contract and the outward contract as a matter of law.[109]

8.67 As Equitas was required to prove that the losses fall within the cover of the inward policy as a matter of law, R and Q argued that Equitas 'need[ed] to re-present correctly aggregated losses upwards through the spiral',[110] ie that the losses were covered under every underlying contract throughout the London Market excess of loss spiral.[111] The root of this reasoning was arguably that a loss cannot possibly be covered by the inward contract if it was not covered by the chain of contracts in the spiral leading up to the inward contract.[112]

8.68 Yet, the Commercial Court held that '[a]s a matter of logic it [did] not follow that because at some much lower level in the spiral a claim may have been paid out with the cover furnished at that level', a retrocedent at a higher level cannot satisfy its burden to prove that a settlement was within the inward contract as a matter of law.[113] Gross J argued that 'regardless of the errors at the lower level/s of the spiral, nonetheless the attachment points at higher levels may be reached by properly re-coverable losses'.[114]

8.69 Gross J does not seem to have suggested that an individual loss that had been wrongly aggregated at a lower level of the spiral and would not have been covered by a reinsurance contract at that level could be regarded as covered under a reinsurance contract at a higher level of the spiral.[115] Rather, he appears to have stated that those losses that were not affected by the wrongful aggregation and that are, hence,

---

107 Cf *Equitas Ltd v R and Q Reinsurance Co (UK) Ltd* (n 3) [44] (Gross J).

108 See *Hill v Mercantile and General Reinsurance Co Plc* (n 4) 1242 (Lord Mustill).

109 *Equitas Ltd v R and Q Reinsurance Co (UK) Ltd* (n 3) [65]–[66] (Gross J).

110 *Equitas Ltd v R and Q Reinsurance Co (UK) Ltd* (n 3) [44] (Gross J).

111 *Equitas Ltd v R and Q Reinsurance Co (UK) Ltd* (n 3) [65] (Gross J).

112 Cf *Hiscox v Outhwaite (No 3)* (n 21); Barlow Lyde & Gilbert LLP (n 7) para 1.102; Merkin, Hodgson and Tyldesley (n 6) paras 18–062 f; O'Neill, Woloniecki and Arnold-Dwyer (n 10) para 8–002.

113 *Equitas Ltd v R and Q Reinsurance Co (UK) Ltd* (n 3) [67] (Gross J).

114 *Equitas Ltd v R and Q Reinsurance Co (UK) Ltd* (n 3) [67] (Gross J).

115 This was, in fact, contrary to the principle that 'if the reinsured is not legally liable to pay a claim, such a claim would not be binding and would not fall within the reinsurance agreement'. See Barlow Lyde & Gilbert LLP (n 7) para 1.102. Cf also *Hiscox v Outhwaite (No 3)* (n 21).

properly recoverable, flowed through the spiral and may reach the attachment points at higher levels.[116]

8.70 In a manner compatible with this understanding of Gross J's reasoning, the follow the settlements clause of the type discussed in *Hill v Mercantile and General Reinsurance Co Plc* provided that Equitas was required to prove that its settlements of aggregation issues under the inward contracts were within the cover of the inward contracts upwards through the spiral as a matter of law. However, the clause did not set out the manner in which a loss should be proven on a properly aggregated basis.[117] More specifically, 'Equitas [was] entitled to seek to discharge the legal burden resting upon it (...) by the use of the best evidence it [had] available; should such evidence *prima facie* suffice to discharge that legal burden, Equitas [did] not need to undertake a process of regression'.[118]

8.71 In conclusion, it appears that the Commercial Court found that only individual losses that were covered under all of the insurance and reinsurance contracts throughout the spiral could be covered under the inward contract. Therefore, the reinsured was required to prove that the losses were properly aggregated throughout the spiral and that each layer of the chain of contracts was properly exhausted. Under the standard or proof of a balance of probabilities, however, it was not necessary to strictly prove that the aggregation of losses was properly undertaken at each level of the spiral. Rather, applying an actuarial model was considered as sufficient to discharge the burden of proof resting upon Equitas.[119]

3.2 Global settlements and treaty reinsurance

8.72 Under an excess of loss reinsurance treaty, the reinsured cannot recover from its reinsurer unless the aggregated loss reaches an excess point specified in the treaty.[120] As *IRB Brasil Resseguros SA v CX Reinsurance Co Ltd* shows, it may be very difficult, in respect of treaty reinsurance in particular, to determine the individual losses suffered by the primary insureds.[121] The Commercial Court, therefore, held that the reinsured was able to discharge its burden of proof by showing that a global settlement had been reached and that on the balance of probabilities 'the arguable claims which were settled by the compromise agreement fell within the terms of the insurance agreement and that the claims so compromised fell within the terms of the reinsurance agreement'.[122]

8.73 Yet, how can an aggregation clause in the outward contract be applied if the individual losses suffered by the primary insured are unknown? Where the individual

---

116 *Equitas Ltd v R and Q Reinsurance Co (UK) Ltd* (n 3) [67] (Gross J).

117 *Equitas Ltd v R and Q Reinsurance Co (UK) Ltd* (n 3) [69] (Gross J).

118 *Equitas Ltd v R and Q Reinsurance Co (UK) Ltd* (n 3) [70] (Gross J).

119 *Equitas Ltd v R and Q Reinsurance Co (UK) Ltd* (n 3) [208] (Gross J).

120 Cf Merkin, Hodgson and Tyldesley (n 6) paras 18–076 ff.

121 Merkin, Hodgson and Tyldesley (n 6) para 18–078.

122 *IRB Brasil Resseguros SA v CX Reinsurance Co Ltd* (n 25) [41] (Burton J). Also see Merkin, Hodgson and Tyldesley (n 6) para 18–078.

losses cannot be determined, the aggregation clause–just like the follow the settlements clause–must be applied on the basis of an approximation of the individual losses.

8.74 In *IRB Brasil Resseguros SA v CX Reinsurance Co Ltd*, the Commercial Court dealt with an appeal from an arbitral award in a case where the primary insured manufactured and produced products containing asbestos. By 1998, the manufacturer was faced with approximately 318,000 claims as a result of its operations. The primary insurers who provided insurance cover to the manufacturer had taken out reinsurance cover. The reinsurers were, in turn, protected under retrocession agreements.

8.75 The claims under the outward contract were subject to an aggregation as per 'any one event' clause.[123] It was argued that the 'single event [was] the determination of the company to engage in the insulation business and to install (...) insulation products (...)' containing asbestos.[124] The arbitral tribunal found that 'the loss each year stemmed from a single [event], being [the manufacturer's] liability arising from [its] installation activities'.[125] The Commercial Court held that the arbitral tribunal was entitled to so conclude.[126]

8.76 As mentioned previously, this case involved approximately 318,000 individual losses. Tracing back each individual loss and determining whether it aggregated with other losses appears highly impracticable. It is perhaps for this reason that the Commercial Court stated that the arbitrators' findings regarding the aggregation of losses was compliant with the decision in *Axa Reinsurance (UK) Ltd v Field* and met the unities test as cited in *Kuwait Airways Corp v Kuwait Insurance Co SAK*.[127]

8.77 It is not entirely clear, however, how a company's determination to engage in the insulation business and to install products containing asbestos or a company's overall insulation activities could be considered a single event. In fact, in *Caudle v Sharp*, the Court of Appeal held in respect of third-party liability that the relevant event was the triggering of the primary insured's liability.[128] In *IRB Brasil Resseguros SA v CX Reinsurance Co Ltd*, the primary insured's liability was not triggered by its determination to engage in the insulation business or by its insulation activities as such, but rather by each instance of installing its contaminated products.[129] It is, furthermore, unlikely that all the 318,000 losses occurred in spatial and temporal proximity. Therefore, both the arbitrators' and the

---

123 *IRB Brasil Resseguros SA v CX Reinsurance Co Ltd* (n 25) [26] (Burton J).

124 *IRB Brasil Resseguros SA v CX Reinsurance Co Ltd* (n 25) [26], Burton J quoting the arbitral award.

125 The arbitral tribunal's findings are quoted by Burton J in *IRB Brasil Resseguros SA v CX Reinsurance Co Ltd* (n 25) [46].

126 *IRB Brasil Resseguros SA v CX Reinsurance Co Ltd* (n 25) [46] (Burton J).

127 For more information as to the unities test, see paras 4.14 ff.

128 *Caudle v Sharp* [1995] CLC 642 (CA) 649 (Evans LJ).

129 For decisions to that effect, cf *Caudle v Sharp* (n 128) 649 (Evans LJ); *Seele Austria GmbH Co v Tokio Marine Europe Insurance Ltd* [2008] EWCA Civ 441, [2009] 1 All ER 171 [57] (Moore-Bick LJ).

Commercial Court's decision were arguably influenced by the difficulty and impracticability of determining the 318,000 individual losses.

8.78 Consequently, it may be concluded that it is difficult to determine the individual losses incurred by the primary insureds in cases of global settlements where a substantial number of losses are settled together. This translates into a challenge in applying an aggregation clause.

III Summary of the chapter

8.79 In reinsurance contracts, a variety of different follow the settlements clauses may be encountered.[130] It is not sensible to lay down general principles with regard to the operation of follow the settlements clauses.[131] Hence, the interaction between a follow the settlements clause and an aggregation clause depends on the specific language used by the parties.

8.80 In this chapter, the two well-used follow the settlements clauses of the types discussed in *The Insurance Co of Africa v Scor (UK) Reinsurance Co Ltd* and in *Hill v Mercantile and General Reinsurance Co Plc* were presented. Furthermore, the interaction between such follow the settlements clauses and aggregation clauses was examined.

8.81 It has been established that under the second proviso of a follow the settlements clause of the type discussed in *The Insurance Co of Africa v Scor (UK) Reinsurance Co Ltd*, the reinsured must in good faith and in a businesslike manner determine the inward contract's quantitative scope of cover. This includes studying the operation of an aggregation mechanism, if included. The reinsured is further under the duty to act in good faith and in a businesslike fashion when identifying the individual losses to be aggregated. The reinsurer is prevented from second-guessing such a good faith settlement. Under the second proviso of the follow the settlements clause, the reinsurer is bound by the reinsured's identification of the individual losses as far as they are within the outward contract's scope of cover.

8.82 Under a follow the settlements clause of the type interpreted in *Hill v Mercantile and General Reinsurance Co Plc*, the reinsured is required to prove that the loss is within the underlying contract's quantitative scope of cover as well as within the quantitative scope of the reinsurance agreement. Under such a clause, the reinsurer is not bound by a good faith settlement of the claims under the inward contract. Rather, the reinsured must prove that the inward and the outward contracts have been triggered. This includes identifying the individual losses to be aggregated and applying the inward and the outward contracts' aggregation mechanisms to them respectively. The reinsured is required to show that the loss aggregated in accordance with the inward contract is within the inward contract's quantitative scope of cover. Similarly, it must demonstrate that the loss aggregated in compliance with the aggregation mechanism under

---

130 Barlow Lyde & Gilbert LLP (n 7) para 1.101.
131 Barlow Lyde & Gilbert LLP (n 7) para 1.101.

the outward contract is within the outward contract's quantitative scope of cover.

8.83 Furthermore, in case of a chain of reinsurance and retrocession agreements or in case of global settlements where it is difficult to determine the individual losses sustained by the primary insured(s), the requirements of proof may be eased for the reinsured.

Bibliography

Alt DK, Hull N and Killelea JT, 'A Reinsurance Perspective: The Aggregation of Losses Following the Tohoku Earthquake and Tsunami' (2011) *22 Mealey's Litigation Report* 1.

Barlow, Lyde & Gilbert LLP, *Reinsurance Practice and the Law* (Informa Law from Routledge 2009).

Baumunk JA, 'New York's "Unfortunate Event" Test: Its Application Prior to the Events of 9/11' (2003) *39 California Western Law Review* 323.

Birds J, Lynch B and Paul S, *MacGillivray on Insurance Law* (14th edn, Sweet & Maxwell 2018).

Bourthoumieux J, 'La notion d'événement dans les traités de réassurance en excédent de sinistres' (1969) *40 Revue générale des assurances terrestres* 457.

Butler J and Merkin R, *Butler and Merkin's Reinsurance Law*, vol 2 (Looseleaf, Sweet & Maxwell).

Cannawurf S and Schwepcke A, '§ 8 Das Vertragsrecht der Rückversicherung' in Lüer DW and Schwepcke A (eds), *Rückversicherungsrecht* (CH Beck 2013).

Cannon M, 'When Two Become One: Aggregation of Claims in Professional Indemnity Insurance' (IMC Insurance Market Conferences 2012) <http://www.imc-seminars.com/uploads/papers/Mark%20Cannon%20QC%20Paper.pdf> accessed 29 January 2019.

Castle J, 'Reinsurance: Net Loss Clause' (1996) *4 International Insurance Law Review* 133.

Clarke MA, *The Law of Insurance Contracts* (6th edn, Informa Law from Routledge 2009).

Clyde & Co, 'Aggregation Words' (*The Insurance Hub*, 26 April 2016) <https://www.clydeco.com/uploads/Blogs/employment/Aggregation_Words_-_Clyde__Co.pdf> accessed 30 January 2019.

Dickinson A, 'Hours Clause: Definition of Loss Occurrence' (2009) IUA Circular 116/09 <http://www.iuaclauses.co.uk/site/cms/contentDocumentDownload.asp?filename=200.doc&id=200&windowed=1&r=4499> accessed 1 March 2019.

Edelman C and Burns A, *The Law of Reinsurance* (2nd edn, OUP 2013).

Gerathewohl K, *Rückversicherung, Grundlagen und Praxis*, vol 1 (Verlag Versicherungswirtschaft eV 1976).

Gerathewohl K, *Rückversicherung, Grundlagen und Praxis*, vol 2 (Verlag Versicherungswirtschaft eV 1979).

Grossmann M, *Rückversicherung – Eine Einführung* (2nd edn, Institut für Versicherungswirtschaft an der Hochschule St Gallen 1982).

Gürses Ö, *Reinsuring Clauses* (Informa Law from Routledge 2010).

Hammesfahr RW and Wright SW, *The Law of Reinsurance Claims* (Reactions 1994).

Heiss H, *'From Contract Certainty to Legal Certainty for Reinsurance Transactions: The Principle of Reinsurance Contract Law (PRICL)'* (2018) *64 Scandinavian Studies of Law* 92.

Hoffman W, 'Facultative Reinsurance Contract Formation, Documentation, and Integration' (2003) *38 Tort Trial & Insurance Practice Law Journal* 763.

Kiln R, *Reinsurance in Practice* (Witherby 1981).

Kiln R, *Reinsurance in Practice* (4th edn, Witherby 1991).

Lewis S, '"Pay as Paid" and the Ultimate Net Loss Clause' (1995) *3 International Insurance Law Review* 308.

Liebwein P, *Klassische und moderne Formen der Rückversicherung* (3rd edn, VVW 2018).

Looschelders D, 'Das IPR der Rückversicherung' in DW Lüer and A Schwepcke (eds), *Rückversicherungsrecht* (CH Beck 2013).

Lord Hoffmann, 'Causation' in Richard Goldberg (ed), *Perspectives on Causation* (Hart Pub 2011).

Louw K and Tompkinson D, 'Curiouser and Curiouser: The Meaning of "Event"' (1996) *4 International Insurance Law Review* 6.

Maloney III FJ, 'The Application of "per-Occurrence" Deductible Provisions in First-Party Property Claims' (2002) *37 Tort and Insurance Law Journal* 921.

Merkin R, 'Reinsurance Aggregation' (1998) *114 Law Quarterly Review* 390.

Merkin R, *A Guide to Reinsurance Law* (Informa Law from Routledge 2007).

Merkin R, 'The Christchurch Earthquakes Insurance and Reinsurance Issues' (2012) *18 Canterbury Law Review* 119.

Merkin R, Hodgson L and Tyldesley P, *Colinvaux's Law on Insurance* (12th edn, Sweet&Maxwell/Thompson Reuters 2019).

Munich Reinsurance America Inc, *Re-in-sur-ance: A Basic Guide to Facultative and Treaty Reinsurance* (2010) <https://cefor.no/globalassets/documents/education/one-year-part-time/2018---2019-programme/munich-re---basic-guide-to-reinsurance.pdf> accessed 1 March 2019.

O'Neill PT, Woloniecki JW and Arnold-Dwyer F, *The Law of Reinsurance in England and Bermuda* (5th edn, Sweet & Maxwell/Thomson Reuters 2019).

Oxford English Dictionary (100th edn, 2020), 'Claim' <https://www.oed.com/view/Entry/33645?rskey=SKgr6b&result=1&isAdvanced=false#eid> accessed 1 July 2020.

Pohl S and Iranya J, *The ABC of Reinsurance* (VVW 2018).

Roberts J, 'Aggregation Triggers: The Wait Continues' (*The Insurance Hub*, 20 April 2016) <https://www.clydeco.com/blog/insurance-hub/article/aggregation-triggers-the-wait-continues> accessed 30 January 2019.

Schwepcke A, Arndt D and Deutsche Versicherungsakademie (eds), *Rückversicherung: produktorientierte Qualifikationen* (2nd edn, VVW 2004).

Schwepcke A and Vetter A (eds), *Praxishandbuch: Rückversicherung* (VVW 2017).

Soar K, *'Interpretation of Wordings Key to Settling Aggregation Claims'* (2010) *Lloyd's List Insurance Day*, published 19 February 2010, 7.

Staring GS and Hansell D, *Law of Reinsurance* (Thomson Reuters Westlaw 2020).

Suga Heres K and St. Peter P, 'The "Number of Occurrences" Dispute of the Century' (2016) *46Fall Brief* 15–19.

Tompkinson D, 'Jabberwocky: Recent Decisions on the Meaning of "Event" and "Occurrence" in the English Courts' (1995) *3 International Insurance Law Review* 82.

Tompkinson D, 'Reinsurance: "Originating Cause" and "Event"' (1995) *3 International Insurance Law Review* 231.

Viney R and Sneed WM, 'Aggregation of Reinsurance Claims in the U.K. and the U.S.: Court Decisions' (2000) *4 Nr. 16 Andrews International Reinsurance Dispute Reporter* 5.

Witthoff E, '§ 15 Schadenbearbeitung in der Rückversicherung' in DW Lüer and A. Schwepcke (eds), *Rückversicherungsrecht* (CH Beck 2013).

Wright J, 'Defining the Word "Event" in a Reinsurance Policy' (1997) *5 International Insurance Law Review* 361.

INDEX

INDEX

failure of putting in place adequate system to protection 3.32, 3.49, 6.28
faulty installation 3.31, 4.45, 4.50, 8.75
fire 2.37, 2.91, 2.95, 2.96, 2.97, 3.8, 4.101, 4.157, 8.41, 8.43
follow the settlements
  double proviso 8.12, 8.24–28
  full reinsurance clause 8.16–23
  global settlements 8.72–78
  identification of individual losses 8.38–44
  treaty reinsurance 8.7–13, 8.47, 8.72–78

happening 2.62, 2.64, 4.6, 4.74, 4.90, 4.153, 4.156, 4.157
hijacking of an aircraft 2.27, 3.31, 4.27, 4.32, 4.41, 4.42, 4.53, 4.61, 4.62, 4.67, 4.70, 4.85
hours clauses
  catastrophe 4.88, 4.89, 4.90, 4.92, 4.94, 4.95, 4.96, 4.97, 4.100, 4.101, 4.103, 4.105
  causal link 4.101, 4.102
  named peril 4.93, 4.94
  problems 4.98–104
  purpose 4.88–91
  relation to cause-based aggregation mechanism 4.105–110
  unnamed peril 4.93
hurricane 3.31, 3.78, 4.90, 6.40

impartial feature 3.2–4
implication of aggregation clause 3.5–10
in connection with 3.122–125
individual loss
  allocation 6.22, 6.23, 6.30, 6.41, 6.51, 6.53
  delimiting 2.26–42
  follow the settlements 8.38–44, 8.45, 8.51, 8.55, 8.57, 8.58, 8.59, 8.64, 8.65, 8.69, 8.71, 8.72, 8.73, 8.76, 8.77, 8.78
  insured unit 2.27–31
  peoples' action 2.32–42
  primary insured 2.19–25, 8.57, 8.58, 8.59
installation of insulation material 3.31, 4.45, 4.50, 8.75
invasion of a country 3.31, 4.54, 8.64, 8.65
inward contract 7.3, 7.9, 7.10, 7.14, 7.18, 7.22, 7.23, 7.24, 7.26, 7.28, 7.29, 7.30, 7.31, 7.33, 7.36, 7.37, 7.40, 7.41, 7.45, 7.46, 7.46, 7.49, 7.51, 8.7, 8.12, 8.17, 8.20, 8.21, 8.22, 8.23, 8.26, 8.27, 8.28, 8.31, 8.32, 8.34–37, 8.37, 8.39, 8.40, 8.41, 8.42, 8.44, 8.45–52, 8.54, 8.55, 8.56, 8.57, 8.58, 8.59, 8.64, 8.66, 8.67, 8.68, 8.70, 8.71

issuance of speed restrictions 4.44, 4.49, 4.63, 4.68

lack of legal certainty 3.1, 3.44, 3.56, 3.80, 3.86, 4.2, 4.8–13, 4.38, 4.47, 4.56, 4.64, 4.76, 5.6–10
lack of proper training 3.32, 3.48, 3.52, 3.87, 4.83
legal certainty, lack 3.1, 3.44, 3.56, 3.80, 3.86, 4.2, 4.8–13, 4.38, 4.47, 4.56, 4.64, 4.76, 5.6–10
limit, *see cover limit* 2.86–99
linking phrase
  arising out of/arising from 3.114–118
  consequent upon or attributable to 3.119–121
  in connection with 3.122–125
  shall result from 3.126–129
loss
  deprivation of insured subject matter 2.9
  financial detriment 2.6, 2.8, 2.9, 2.12, 2.31, 2.39
  individual loss 2.18–42
  total or partial loss 2.7, 2.8
  ultimate net loss 2.11–17
loss occurrence 3.58, 4.90, 4.92, 4.94, 4.97, 4.105, 4.140
losses' circumstances 4.15, 4.29, 4.46, 4.48

materialisation of a peril 2.6, 2.44, 4.132, 4.139, 4.140, 4.141, 4.142, 4.144, 4.153, 4.156, 4.157, 4.158, 5.16, 5.17, 5.18, 5.23, 5.24, 5.25, 5.26, 5.27, 5.28, 5.30, 5.35
misselling of products 3.48, 3.87, 3.91, 3.96, 3.99, 5.7
misunderstanding as to the result of a discussion 3.32, 3.50, 5.7
monitoring of employees 3.87

natural disaster 1.28, 1.33, 1.56, 3.31, 4.88, 4.90, 4.142, 5.6, 7.22
negligent underwriting 3.31, 4.117, 7.38, 7.39, 8.47
non-proportional reinsurance
  definition 1.34–36
  no presumption of back-to-back cover 7.18–20
  per event excess of loss treaty 1.36, 1.38, 1.43–46, 1.57
  per risk excess of loss treaty 1.36, 1.40–42, 1.57
  premium calculation 1.35, 1.37, 2.68, 2.99, 6.29, 7.19, 7.33
  stop loss treaty 1.36, 1.47–53, 1.57

INDEX